Enhancing Evidence Preservation With Blockchain

Dorottya Edina Kozma
https://orcid.org/0000-0002-4948-8815
University of Pannonia, Hungary

Swarnima Gorani
https://orcid.org/0009-0004-2052-6891
Sharda University, India

Otilia Manta
https://orcid.org/0000-0002-9411-7925
Romanian Academy, Romania

IGI Global
Scientific Publishing
Publishing Tomorrow's Research Today

Vice President of Editorial	Melissa Wagner
Director of Acquisitions	Mikaela Felty
Director of Book Development	Jocelynn Hessler
Production Manager	Mike Brehm
Cover Design	Jose Rosado

Published in the United States of America by
IGI Global Scientific Publishing
701 East Chocolate Avenue
Hershey, PA, 17033, USA
Tel: 717-533-8845 | Fax: 717-533-7115
Website: https://www.igi-global.com E-mail: cust@igi-global.com

Library of Congress Cataloging-in-Publication Data

LCCN: 2026013787 (CIP Data Pending)
ISBN13: 9798337397306
Isbn13Softcover: 9798337397313
EISBN13: 9798337397320
British Cataloguing in Publication Data
A Cataloguing in Publication record for this book is available from the British Library.

Table of Contents

Preface xiv

Chapter 1
Addressing Online Cyber Fraud Through Blockchain: Challenges and Opportunities in Legal Evidence Preservation 1
Priya Nigam, Amity University, Gwalior, India
Hemant Singh, Amity University, Gwalior, India
Jitendra Kumar Gautam, Department of Law, SRM University, Delhi-NCR, India

Chapter 2
Adulteration in Milk and Dairy Products: A Study of Evidentiary Frameworks and Blockchain Intervention 19
Yashika Jain, Amity University, Gwalior, India
Hemant Singh, Amity University, Gwalior, India
Govind Singh Rajpal, School of Law, MIT Art, Design, and Technology University, Pune, India

Chapter 3
AI-Driven Digital Forensics for Police Investigations: Strengthening Cybercrime Detection and Response in Modern India 37
Kiranbhai R. Dodiya, Gujarat University, India
Bhagirath Gohil, DySP Chikhli Division, Gujarat Police, India

Chapter 4
Blockchain in Criminal Investigations: Preserving Digital Forensics and Cybercrime Evidence 69
Sonia Pandey, Lloyd Law College, Greater Noida, India

Chapter 5
Criminal Investigations With Blockchain Technology: Stabilizing Digital Forensics and Cybercrime Evidence for Admission 87
Divya S. Khurana, School of Legal Studies, CGC University, Mohali, India
Bhrigu Raj Mourya, MATS Law School, MATS University, Raipur, India
Om Prakash Kannaujia, MATS Law School, MATS University, Raipur, India

Chapter 6
Cross-Border Evidence Sharing: Blockchain for International Legal Cooperation 107
Pooja, Reliable Institute of Law, Ghaziabad, India
Saurabh Chandra, Symbiosis International (Deemed to be) University, India

Chapter 7
Data Security and Vulnerabilities: Hacking Brains, Unauthorized Access, and Cloud Storage Risks 123
Mohd Faiz Khan, School of Legal Studies, CGC University, Mohali, India
Saurabh Chandra, Symbiosis International (Deemed to be) University, India

Chapter 8
Ensuring Transparency and Accountability in Right to Information Regimes: The Role of Blockchain in Legal Evidence Justification 139
Malvika Pandey, Amity University, Gwalior, India
Vijay Srivastava, Amity University, Gwalior, India
Priyansh Samadhiya, Amity University, Gwalior, India

Chapter 9
Exploring Blockchain in Criminal Investigations for Protecting Evidence and Digital Forensics 155
Vinod Kumar, Amity University, Jaipur, India
Abhijay Chakraborty, Amity University, Jaipur, India
Sanjiv Bhadauria, Amity University, Gwalior, India

Chapter 10
Exploring Privacy-Preserving Techniques in Blockchain: Zero-Knowledge Proofs and Confidential Evidence Handling 173
Arunima Shastri, Christ University, Bangalore, India

Chapter 11
Harnessing Blockchain for Legal Evidence Preservation: A Cyber Law Perspective 189
Vedullapalli Leelakrishna Sai Prasad, Amity University, Gwalior, India
Vijay Srivastava, Amity University, Gwalior, India
Priyansh Samadhiya, Amity University, Gwalior, India

Chapter 12
Intellectual Property and Contractual Disputes: Blockchain as a Notarization. 209
Arunima Shastri, Christ University, Bangalore, India

Chapter 13
Mediation in the Digital Age: Ensuring Justice Through Blockchain Technology 225
Vijaishree Tiwari, RKDF University, Bhopal, India
Nilesh Verma, RKDF University, Bhopal, India
Sheersha Saxena, Vivekananda Global University, Jaipur, India

Chapter 14
Regulatory and Admissibility Challenges: Blockchain Evidence in Courts...... 243
Pradip Kumar Kashyap, School of Legal Studies, CGC University, Mohali, India
Nirbhay Kumar Sharma, Mohammad Ali Jauhar University, Rampur, India

Chapter 15
Regulatory and Admissibility Challenges in Male Victimization in Domestic Violence: Blockchain Evidence in Courts 261
Sakshi Bhatnagar, Amity University, Gwalior, India
Vijay Srivastava, Amity University, Gwalior, India
Govind Singh Rajpal, MIT Art, Design, and Technology University, Pune, India

Chapter 16
The Use of Blockchain Technology in the Provision of Public Health Service: A Study on the Estonian Health System 277
Emre Akcagunduz, Trakya University, Turkey

Compilation of References 299

About the Contributors 327

Index 333

Detailed Table of Contents

Preface.. xiv

Chapter 1
Addressing Online Cyber Fraud Through Blockchain: Challenges and Opportunities in Legal Evidence Preservation 1
Priya Nigam, Amity University, Gwalior, India
Hemant Singh, Amity University, Gwalior, India
Jitendra Kumar Gautam, Department of Law, SRM University, Delhi-NCR, India

Online cyber fraud has grown at an explosive pace, leading to huge financial losses, and diminishing trust in digital environments. Traditional centralized systems are prone to evidence tampering and lack transparency, which can pose a problem when it comes to proving the case in court. These centralized systems can be susceptible to evidence tampering and lack transparency, a problem when seeking to prove the case in court. A promising solution could come from the blockchain's transparent and immutable ledger system, which is decentralized. This chapter addresses potential methods for enhancing legal evidence preservation in cyber fraud by providing blockchain with integrity, an unbreakable chain of custody and verifiable timestamping. It deep dives into the prospects, technical possibilities, and the legal hurdles that arise when it comes to integrating blockchain in fraud prevention and judicial activities.

Chapter 2
Adulteration in Milk and Dairy Products: A Study of Evidentiary Frameworks and Blockchain Intervention 19
Yashika Jain, Amity University, Gwalior, India
Hemant Singh, Amity University, Gwalior, India
Govind Singh Rajpal, School of Law, MIT Art, Design, and Technology University, Pune, India

The Milk Adulteration is one of the most common and hazardous forms of food fraud and can be extremely harmful to public health, the economy and consumer confidence. Although traditional evidentiary frameworks have been governed by strict procedures, they have a number of weaknesses that impact their use and success, such as sample tampering, compromised chain of custody, delay in sample submission for laboratory analysis and low conviction rates. The present study critically analyzes the challenges in milk and dairy product related adulteration cases from the point of view of evidence. It also elaborates on the concept of blockchain technology as a strong tradeable tool to foster transparency, traceability, and immutability along the entire dairy supply chain. The chapter explores the legal and technical architectures, implementation challenges, and policy suggestions. The results suggest that implementing blockchain could greatly improve the quality of the dairy industry's forensics, regulatory compliance, and consumer trust.

Chapter 3
AI-Driven Digital Forensics for Police Investigations: Strengthening Cybercrime Detection and Response in Modern India 37
Kiranbhai R. Dodiya, Gujarat University, India
Bhagirath Gohil, DySP Chikhli Division, Gujarat Police, India

This chapter examines the role of Artificial Intelligence (AI) in enhancing digital forensic investigations for cybercrime detection and response in modern India. Rapid digitalisation has increased the scale and sophistication of cyber offences, challenging conventional investigative methods. This chapter per the authors explores how AI technologies—including machine learning, natural language processing, computer vision, and predictive analytics—support intelligent evidence triage, behavioural analysis, fraud detection, and synthetic media authentication. It also addresses implementation challenges such as skill gaps, infrastructure limitations, legal admissibility, and algorithmic bias. The chapter highlights the need for governance frameworks, explainable AI, and capacity building to ensure responsible adoption. AI-driven digital forensics is presented as a strategic pathway toward more efficient, scalable, and intelligence-led cybercrime investigations in India.

Chapter 4
Blockchain in Criminal Investigations: Preserving Digital Forensics and Cybercrime Evidence 69
Sonia Pandey, Lloyd Law College, Greater Noida, India

Blockchain technology is a groundbreaking decentralized electronic registry that captures transactions and data on a network of computers in an insecure, transparent and tamper-proof context. At its most fundamental level, blockchain systematizes the information framed into blocks and each block includes a list of transactions or documents, a timestamp and a cryptographical hash connecting it to the last block creating an immutable chronological chain. In contrast with the conventional and centralized databases, which are managed by one party, blockchain runs on a distributed system of nodes where each one of them keeps an identical copy of the registry. This architecture ensures elimination of single points of failure and improves on the use of intermediaries. Consensus mechanisms, like Proof-of-Work or Proof-of-Stake, are used to authenticate transactions and provide agreement among participants prior to the addition of new blocks. This chapter explores the use of blockchain technologies in scientific criminal investigations.

Chapter 5
Criminal Investigations With Blockchain Technology: Stabilizing Digital Forensics and Cybercrime Evidence for Admission 87
Divya S. Khurana, School of Legal Studies, CGC University, Mohali, India
Bhrigu Raj Mourya, MATS Law School, MATS University, Raipur, India
Om Prakash Kannaujia, MATS Law School, MATS University, Raipur, India

The chapter investigates how blockchain technology can be implemented to solve some major challenges in criminal investigation, particularly with respect to identifying some of the serious vulnerabilities found in a digital forensics investigation and the evidence handling procedure of cybercrime. Volatile, easily tampered nature of traditional digital evidence often means that traditional digital evidence is susceptible to tampering, is difficult to formulate, and may not be admissible in court without problems with the chain of custody. The key characteristics of blockchain immutability, decentralization, cryptographic hashing, and audit trails provide a secure and efficient way to capture physical evidence at time of collection to when it enters the courtroom. It focuses on that the multi-agency partnership as well as privacy-preserving methods and case studies should be examined, together with technical architectures and legal compliance, including admissibility criteria.

Chapter 6
Cross-Border Evidence Sharing: Blockchain for International Legal Cooperation 107
Pooja, Reliable Institute of Law, Ghaziabad, India
Saurabh Chandra, Symbiosis International (Deemed to be) University, India

Cybercrime has gone global, making the exchange of evidence a critical component in the fight against it in criminal investigations. Typical processes like Mutual Legal Assistance Treaties (MLATs) are time-consuming, cumbersome and frequently insufficient for time sensitive digital evidence. In this chapter, the author illustrates how blockchain technology could help transform the way the world enters into international collaboration by answering some of the key questions, including how can blockchain technology enable the secure and immutable exchange of evidence in international legal processes and execute it without compromising the principles of national sovereignty. The use of blockchain can provide a plausible chain of custody, interestingly, requests and requests can be automated using smart contracts, and privacy preserving architectures are also possible, establishing trust between countries.

Chapter 7
Data Security and Vulnerabilities: Hacking Brains, Unauthorized Access, and Cloud Storage Risks 123
Mohd Faiz Khan, School of Legal Studies, CGC University, Mohali, India
Saurabh Chandra, Symbiosis International (Deemed to be) University, India

This chapter discusses the most important issues related to data security and vulnerabilities in blockchain assisted criminal investigations, particularly in relation to "hacking brains", unauthorized access vectors, and potential risks of cloud storage in a hybrid setup. Blockchain is a solution that is unalterable & transparent but has allowed incorporation of humans, instructions/executable smart contracts and cloud solutions, creating enormous attack surfaces. A thorough analysis of social engineering attacks, insider threats, authentication vulnerabilities, smart contracts exploits and the unique vulnerabilities within the cloud computing environment that may impact the integrity and chain of custody of digital evidence. This chapter analyzed and a focus is laid on the importance of using comprehensive security measures, including those centered on humans, policies and technologies, to safeguard sensitive forensic data in the current threatening cyber landscape.

Chapter 8
Ensuring Transparency and Accountability in Right to Information Regimes: The Role of Blockchain in Legal Evidence Justification 139
Malvika Pandey, Amity University, Gwalior, India
Vijay Srivastava, Amity University, Gwalior, India
Priyansh Samadhiya, Amity University, Gwalior, India

The Right to Information (RTI) is a fundamental pillar of democratic governance, providing citizens with access to public information and helps them hold public authorities accountable. Conventional models of RTI typically have a variety of problems, however: evidence is stripped or embellished, documents are tampered with, there is bureaucratic opacity, and they don't really hold up in court. The Blockchain technology has unique characteristics, such as immutability, decentralization, and cryptographic security, which make it a revolutionary solution. Blockchain can offer end-to-end transparency with legal evidence for requests, answers, as well as all supporting documents, to ensure all stakeholders are transparent and to produce strong legal records. This chapter examines the possibilities of applying blockchain to RTI systems, arguing that the distributed ledger can help to reduce corruption risks, boost public trust and improve the admissibility of judgments.

Chapter 9
Exploring Blockchain in Criminal Investigations for Protecting Evidence and Digital Forensics 155
Vinod Kumar, Amity University, Jaipur, India
Abhijay Chakraborty, Amity University, Jaipur, India
Sanjiv Bhadauria, Amity University, Gwalior, India

As cybercrime continues to grow in size and scope, the problem of receiving and maintaining the integrity and admissibility of digital evidence is growing larger in criminal matters, with greater complexity. The traditional approach to digital forensics can face problems like data volatility, weak chain of custody, cross jurisdiction sharing, and tampering. The key characteristics of blockchain technology immutability, decentralization, transparency and cryptographic time stamping are key attributes that make it a transformative solution. The Blockchain's hashes, evidence metadata and custody transfers are stored in a decentralized way, creating a way to improve the trustworthiness of records and maximize chances of their being usable in court. It sheds light on the potential of blockchain to fortify evidence preservation, tackle privacy and scalability issues, and pave the way for more sound and dependable cybercrime investigations in the digital age.

Chapter 10
Exploring Privacy-Preserving Techniques in Blockchain: Zero-Knowledge Proofs and Confidential Evidence Handling 173
Arunima Shastri, Christ University, Bangalore, India

The transparency of the blockchain technology makes privacy issues acutely challenging in certain highly sensitive applications such as IP protection and contractual arguments. This chapter is an overview of privacy preserving methods and in particular Zero-Knowledge Proofs (ZKPs) and confidential evidence handling mechanisms. ZKPs are set to transform notarization by allowing parties to prove that information or statements are true without disclosing the information that they have associated with them. The study covers the concept of use of blockchain and how they can be used to combine with smart contracts for privacy-preserving IP access rights governance and dispute resolution. It also covers confidential computing, homomorphic encryption, and secure multi-party computation for processing privacy sensitive evidence on the blockchain. In regulated industries, these technologies hold the promise of increasing prevalence, but encounter challenges relating to regulations and trusted setup, as well as computational overhead issues.

Chapter 11
Harnessing Blockchain for Legal Evidence Preservation: A Cyber Law Perspective 189
Vedullapalli Leelakrishna Sai Prasad, Amity University, Gwalior, India
Vijay Srivastava, Amity University, Gwalior, India
Priyansh Samadhiya, Amity University, Gwalior, India

The use of blockchain in legal evidence preservation is a paradigm shift in the domain of cyber law, and it is a solution to a long-standing vulnerability in the field of digital forensics that includes tampering, chain of custody breaches, and admissibility challenges. The essence attributes of blockchain such as the impossibility of being tampered with due to the cryptographic hashing, the decentralization of record keeping to allow transparent audit trails, and the time stamping allow recording evidence handling, including its collection, and its presentation in the courtroom in an impeccable manner. This chapter examines the transformative effect of blockchain as an enhancement of the reliability of evidence, the reduction of risks of manipulation, and the establishment of trust in the judicial system, offers models of hybridization and policy changes that can lead such practices to be smoothly integrated into legal systems across the globe.

Chapter 12
Intellectual Property and Contractual Disputes: Blockchain as a Notarization. 209
Arunima Shastri, Christ University, Bangalore, India

Blockchain's decentralized ledger is a game-changer for processing and documenting contracts, while also offering a solution to the long-standing problems in intellectual property (IP) protection. It ensures consistent and secure proof of creation and ownership using cryptographic hashes, minimizing risks of infringement, forgery, and dispute over ownership, without needing non-dependant archives or centralized trust. Minimal human intervention and intervention conflicts, thanks to the automation of smart contracts involved with the licensing, royalty payment and enforcement process. This chapter dives into various technical, legal and practical issues surrounding the application of blockchain in IP management and identifies how it can boost transparency, security, and efficiency in managing IP assets and agreements.

Chapter 13
Mediation in the Digital Age: Ensuring Justice Through Blockchain Technology 225
Vijaishree Tiwari, RKDF University, Bhopal, India
Nilesh Verma, RKDF University, Bhopal, India
Sheersha Saxena, Vivekananda Global University, Jaipur, India

The Blockchain technology offers a truly revolutionary framework for Online Dispute Resolution (ODR), lends transparency, security and enforceability to the process. This paper examines the advantages and disadvantages of these different blockchain platforms, as measured by their technical features, and their potential for mediation and arbitration. The capability to execute smart contracts, manage evidence and handle settlements automatically is considered on public blockchains like Ethereum, permissioned networks like Hyperledger Fabric as well as specialized solutions like Kleros and Aragon. The research is informative on how these platforms help to overcome a number of problems that hinder the application of the digital mediation process such as the problem of trust, the problem of enforcement, and the problem of confidentiality, among others, and investigates the problem of the legal recognition of these platforms and the issue of its practical application.

Chapter 14
Regulatory and Admissibility Challenges: Blockchain Evidence in Courts...... 243
Pradip Kumar Kashyap, School of Legal Studies, CGC University, Mohali, India
Nirbhay Kumar Sharma, Mohammad Ali Jauhar University, Rampur, India

The chapter critically analyzes regulatory and admissibility issues arising from the use of blockchain evidentiary in court. However, as blockchain is increasingly being adopted in the field of digital forensics and criminal investigation, law enforcement and judicial authorities around the globe are encountering considerable challenges in assessing blockchain technology's reliability, authenticity and compliance with current evidentiary rules and procedures. The chapter discusses how the nature of digital evidence has changed over time, the new legal issues that blockchain immutability and decentralized structure creates, and its significant impact on cybercrime prosecutions. It covers a range of admissibility considerations, regulatory deficiencies, authentication issues, privacy concerns and precedent. The main objective of this study is to fill the gap between technological innovation and judicial acceptance, so evidence collected via blockchain can be withstand in strict court procedures, and enhance the global combat against cybercrime.

Chapter 15
Regulatory and Admissibility Challenges in Male Victimization in Domestic Violence: Blockchain Evidence in Courts 261
Sakshi Bhatnagar, Amity University, Gwalior, India
Vijay Srivastava, Amity University, Gwalior, India
Govind Singh Rajpal, MIT Art, Design, and Technology University, Pune, India

The social stigma, gender stereotypes, and systems biases experienced by men who have been victims of domestic violence (DV) extend underreporting to their cases, limiting access to justice. Threatening messages, contacts, financial documents, and videos are important pieces of evidence, but easily tampered with, or questioned as to authenticity, in these cases. The Blockchain technology is a potentially helpful solution as blockchain technology ensures immutability, no tampering, chain of custody and verifiable integrity of digital evidence. It aims to discuss the regulatory frameworks and the admissibility of the blockchain evidence in court, specifically in the context of a typical male victimisation case. It studies legal rules (Daubert/Frye tests), privacy issues related to data protection laws, that judges don't consider, and that additional male bias adds to the difficult hurdle of evidence.

Chapter 16
The Use of Blockchain Technology in the Provision of Public Health Service: A Study on the Estonian Health System 277
Emre Akcagunduz, Trakya University, Turkey

Simply explained, blockchain is a distributed system in which all transactions are recorded and documented by the system's users (also known as the blockchain network). Blockchain is a form of data-storing mechanism. It is a system in which the data to be saved is laid out into structures known as "blocks," with each block connected to the next by stamping/sealing. The present study investigates how blockchain technology is being used in the provision of healthcare services in Estonia, what benefits it offers, and how it improves the delivery of public services. The study concluded that blockchain-based medical applications offer considerable time, space, and financial benefits in the delivery of healthcare services in Estonia. This particular situation suggests that blockchain-based medical applications will be adopted in many different countries in the future.

Compilation of References 299

About the Contributors 327

Index 333

Preface

Trust in evidence is the basis of justice, governance and accountability in an age where the physical and digital can be imperiled of keeping. The centralized evidence management approaches that have long been dependent on centralized databases, paper trails and human oversight are now susceptible to tampering, chain of evidence compromise, data manipulation and unauthorized access that can threaten the integrity of legal proceedings, forensic investigations and compliance with regulatory mandates. In the face of these challenges, this edited book namely "Enhancing Evidence Preservation With Blockchain" becomes a timely and transformative solution, offering a comprehensive dive into the potential of distributed ledger technology to transform how evidence is gathered, stored, verified, and shared in various fields.

CHAPTER OVERVIEW

The chapters provide insight into novel solutions that rely on smart contracts, cryptographic hashing and decentralized consensus techniques to guarantee provenance, auditability and long-term integrity in such fields as criminal investigations, corporate litigation, IP disputes and international human rights. The contributors also discuss the important issues of scalability, interoperability with other legal systems, privacy considerations in the light of such directives as the GDPR, and the ethics of implementing this kind of technology in situations of high stakes. This joint effort will be not only academically useful but will also be accessible for practitioners, policymakers and technologists fighting on the frontlines of the fight for increased trust in our processes of evidence. With the harnessing of blockchain, we are ushered into a time where truth is not just said, but instead can be verifiably preserved for posterity.

Chapter 1

Addressing Online Cyber Fraud Through Blockchain:

Challenges and Opportunities in Legal Evidence Preservation

Priya Nigam
Amity University, Gwalior, India

Hemant Singh
http://orcid.org/0000-0002-1258-5187
Amity University, Gwalior, India

Jitendra Kumar Gautam
http://orcid.org/0009-0009-9332-9326
Department of Law, SRM University, Delhi-NCR, India

ABSTRACT

Online cyber fraud has grown at an explosive pace, leading to huge financial losses, and diminishing trust in digital environments. Traditional centralized systems are prone to evidence tampering and lack transparency, which can pose a problem when it comes to proving the case in court. These centralized systems can be susceptible to evidence tampering and lack transparency, a problem when seeking to prove the case in court. A promising solution could come from the blockchain's transparent and immutable ledger system, which is decentralized. This chapter addresses potential methods for enhancing legal evidence preservation in cyber fraud by providing blockchain with integrity, an unbreakable chain of custody and

DOI: 10.4018/979-8-3373-9730-6.ch001

verifiable timestamping. It deep dives into the prospects, technical possibilities, and the legal hurdles that arise when it comes to integrating blockchain in fraud prevention and judicial activities.

1. INTRODUCTION

The digital revolution has taken over much of commerce, communication and governance all over the world, but also given the opportunity for advanced cyber-fraud. With a wealth of DNS knowledge, hackers are targeting vulnerabilities within the systems, weaknesses in users and gaps in regulations to defraud to an alarming degree, as more and more financial transactions, identity verification, and other services are moving online. Fraud prevention and the need to ensure legality admissible evidence is maintained has been overcome by the power of blockchain technology. It has unique qualities of immutability, transparency, decentralization, and cryptographic security, which have new applications in creating trust in digital interactions (Apsimet et al., 2026).

This research explores the consequences of the use of blockchain for fighting cybercrime in the online environment and improving the reliability and admissibility of digital evidence in court. It explores the evolving threat landscape, the emerging technical abilities of blockchain, the potential for being able to preserve evidence, and the legal/regulatory issues. The Indian legal framework, specifically the Information Technology Act, 2000, the Bharatiya Nyaya Sanhita and the Digital Personal Data Protection Act, 2023, will receive special attention (Joseph & Pandey, 2026).

The adoption of blockchain in anti-fraud solutions can be seen will to change the security paradigm from reactive to proactive, from centralized to decentralized. But these implementation challenges need to be mitigated, including technical, privacy, jurisdictional and judicial issues, along with successful implementation. It begins with an overview of the problem of cyber fraud, the role of blockchain in cyber fraud prevention, and how blockchain has the potential to evolve legal evidence capture. The study further identifies the regulatory gaps, especially in India, suggests some changes to the regulatory framework, and poses recommendations for implementations for cyber fraud prevention and for credible management of digital evidence for officials in the Government, law enforcement and judicial establishments to better utilise the blockchain for such purposes (Smith & Tiwari, 2024).

1.1 The Growing Threat of Online Cyber Fraud

Online cyber fraud is among the pressing issues of the digital economy. The latest report on the worldwide impact of financial cyber-crime was cited as a loss of more than $10 trillion a year by 2025, with the most prevalent techniques being phishing attacks, investment frauds, identity theft, business email compromise and frauds using deep fakes. Indian Cyber Crime Coordination Centre (I4C) received more than 1.50 lakh complaints of cyber fraud in India during 2024-25 resulting in thousands of crores of rupees in losses. The increase in the sophistication of the attacks and the use of new technologies like deepfakes (falsified videos and images), ransomware, and mule accounts make it easier for fraudsters to carry out their attacks.

Because of their anonymity and low level of verification and the ease with which they are international in character and can operate outside the countries of their registration, detection and prosecution are created significant problems. Traditional centralized databases can be hacked and manipulated, and they can also suffer from the presence of internal threats; investigators may end up with compromised or lacking evidence. Victims often hear and wait for justice, and because transactions are difficult to prove, intent is hard and can be obscured, and because of difficult chain of custody (electronic records) maintenance, it can never be achieved in time.

The dangers are even higher due to the swift pace of getting digital payments systems (UPI, mobile banking) adopted and the increase in cryptocurrency related scams. Police organisations need to tackle a number of extremely challenging issues around technical capacity, jurisdictional challenges, as well as the velocity of fraudsters. This is a constantly expanding threat, which has a direct monetary cost, and also impacts the trust of digital systems (Prashad et al., 2026).

1.2 Overview of Blockchain Technology in Fraud Prevention

The blockchain technology is an open ledger system which is distributed among many computers that securely, transparently and permanently records transactions. It is decentralized design, which means it is free of SPOF that is found in most traditional systems.

There are a number of uses of blockchain technology in fraud prevention. It allows for identity verification in a secure manner using Self-Sovereign Identity (SSI) systems which decreases identity theft. Smart contracts can be used to trigger a chain of transactions based on conditions without releasing funds until specific pre-established conditions are met and help reduce advance-fee fraud and escrow scams. With these blockchain-based Know Your Customer (KYC) solutions, it is possible to prove that a customer's identity has been verified once and for all and to verify it without exposing the data again in the process (Kumar, 2022).

The chain-tracking on a block chain can help minimize the risk of products becoming counterfeit or documentation fraud. The Blockchain-based systems, in the financial sector, offer real-time transaction surveillance and detection of anomalies. It guarantees the verifiability of data while maintaining the confidentiality of the data by implementing cryptographic techniques. The Private blockchains are ideal for regulated industries due to their controlled accessibility while maintaining transparency (Yeoh, 2017).

India is looking into blockchain, for instance, in its regulatory sandbox as launched by the Reserve Bank of India and in states' land record projects. Examples of successful implementation of blockchain in the fraud prone industries are the Global platforms such as IBM Food Trust and Everledger.

1.3 Role of Blockchain in Legal Evidence Preservation

The Blockchain is reshaping the landscape of legal evidence creation by tackling the major issues blockchain in evidence management faces, such as manipulation, missing chain of custody, and the challenges of authenticity. It can be embedded at once; it is not changeable if you want to make something change into your data that is known in advance you are not going to be able to change the data. The time-stamping feature helps to establish a date for the event because cryptographic timestamps offer a time-bounded guarantee that an event actually took place, which enhances the probative worth of evidence in court (Liu & Zheng., 2024).

The Blockchain can provide cyber fraud applications with an immutable record of transactions, communications, KYC documents, and audit trails. All accesses and changes are recorded permanently making the records clear and unalterable. This is especially important for proving counterfeit transactions, intent and tracing money trails in money laundering situations. Smart contracts have the ability to create court-proof evidence as soon as there is a "trigger event".

For the law enforcement community, blockchain-based evidence management can ensure that evidence is collected and kept safe from the field to the investigation and into the courtroom. Blockchain has been deployed in several countries to design digital evidence management platforms. In India, Section 65B of the Indian Evidence Act has introduced the concept of electronic evidence to the courts, which are still accepting such evidence; however, there are issues relating to the authenticity of electronic evidence. To comply with the requirements of the judiciary for reliable operations, blockchain can be used to deliver the required technological infrastructure. The legal recognition of the blockchain evidence does, however, need to be established by clear guidelines, frameworks of expert testimony, as well as training and education of judges and lawyers. Hybrid solutions of traditional forensic tools and blockchain are the most viable solution (Krishna & Kumar, 2026).

2. BLOCKCHAIN TECHNOLOGY FOR COMBATING CYBER FRAUD: KEY FEATURES OF BLOCKCHAIN RELEVANT TO FRAUD MITIGATION

The Blockchain Technology is now proving to be an effective Crusader in the fight against the online army of cyber fraudsters. This decentralized, transparent and tamper proof nature helps mitigate a myriad of vulnerabilities seen in conventional centralised financial or data systems. Typical weakness of cyber fraudsters are single points of failure, manipulations of data and absence of the audit trail. The core architecture of blockchain makes it difficult to tamper with or misuse the data, helping to prevent these risks.

The Blockchain Technology provides the ability to track transactions in real-time, verify identities with security and automate compliance measures in the battle against cyber fraud. Being distributed, it's very hard for the attacker to break its whole network. The consensus-based blockchain technology is being embraced by financial institutions, governments, and businesses to curb digital payments fraud, trade finance, insurance losses, and cross border transactions. In India, companies are increasingly aware of the potential of blockchain, with major initiatives such as the Reserve Bank of India's projects and state government pilots making strides in this area.

The Blockchain Technology, however, is not a stand-alone solution. This has to be supported through integration with systems in place and regulatory backing, and other technologies like artificial intelligence and machine learning have to be used alongside. The Public blockchains ensure high transparency but public-private blockchain is preferred in regulated industries where balancing privacy and security is an important factor. The Blockchain's capacity to store immutable data and provide a verifiable data provenance will have a huge part to play in the evolution of modern fraud prevention tools, and bolster their effectiveness in a growing landscape of increasingly sophisticated cyber fraud tactics. The strategic implementation can have a huge impact on minimizing financial damages, build trust of digital platforms, and improve legal enforcement mechanisms (Hossain, 2026).

The blockchain technology is especially beneficial for combating fraud due to a number of its critical attributes. The first one is immutability, which means that after a transaction, it can't be modified or deleted. The document cannot be forged or manipulated, which reduces the chances of a forgery and document manipulation, and creates a permanent, tamper-proofing audit trail. Second, decentralisation is done without having to rely on a single central authority, which is often the target of fraudsters.

Thirdly, transparency can help authorized participants monitor the transaction history there and then, which can assist them to detect any irregular activity early.

The Cryptographic security guarantees that by using hashing and digital signatures, only legitimate parties are allowed to start and/or approve transactions (Popal et al., 2025). Each user of the blockchain has to agree on which new block to add to the chain after each valid block, this is called the consensus mechanism and even the entry where fraud might happen would take a tremendously long time.

Further, if a transaction took place, there is a verifiable document of when it happened and this is important when finding timelines for fraud investigations. By using the smart contract functionality, the predefined rules can be automatically executed which significantly minimizes the need for human interaction and therefore the scope for any manipulation. Such characteristics well match the needs of the Information Technology Act alongside, the recent regulations on digital payment in India.

These capabilities together with AI-powered anomaly behaviour detection add a comprehensive multi-layered protection against cyber fraud. But issues like scalability, energy usage in some consensus protocols, and regulatory uncertainty will have to be overcome to make these approaches more popular (Shami et al., 2025). Overall, these technical accomplishments put blockchain in a much better place to become a pillar technology for trustworthy digital financial ecosystems.

2.1 Blockchain-Based Tools and Platforms for Fraud Detection

The Fraud detection is undergoing a transformation across industries with a growing ecosystem of tools and platforms that use blockchain technology to detect fraud. However, specialized platforms such as Chainalysis and Elliptic specialize in providing blockchain analytics, which enables law enforcement officials and financial institutions to track and find money laundering and patterns and map wallet addresses connected to cyber fraud. Some of these instruments are effective in ransomware and investment fraud investigations in the big leagues worldwide (Saputra & Kusumah, 2025).

The Solutions like the Signzy, Khatabook were being used by platforms in India for real-time KYC verification and transaction monitoring. The Platforms like Signzy, Khatabook were able to use blockchain solutions in India, provided by the government for real-time KYC verification and transaction monitoring. The Banks widely employ some blockchain technologies like Hyperledger Fabric and Corda in the inter-bank reconciliation and trade finance fraud prevention processes.

Other interesting products include digital identity solutions on the blockchain and decentralized finance (DeFi) surveillance systems designed to detect rug pulls, phishing scams and Ponzi schemes (Adewumi & Afe, 2025). Several of these offer machine-learning algorithms combined with blockchain information to detect abnormal trends with great precision. Investigators' ability to react fast is greatly enhanced by real-time alerts, automated risk scoring and graphical display of transactions in real-time.

Such tools also help people better collect evidence with cryptographic evidence to create court admissible reports. But there are still data privacy compliance issues, undid-edged banking system integrations, and higher implementation cost issues for smaller entities. With the constant transformation of cyber fraud, creating indigenous solutions especially cyber fraud detection tools that align with local fraud trends in India and the regulatory framework will be vital to fostering a secure digital economy (Yadav et al., 2026).

2.2 Smart Contracts and Decentralized Identity Systems

The Smart Contracts and Decentralized Identities are two major and impactful innovations of the blockchain that can help in the fight against cyber fraud. Smart contracts are blockchain programming that automatically execute the terms of a contract if certain conditions are met. In fraud prevention, their ability to program to make funds available after multiple points of verification, escrow and/or KYC checks could be used to ensure the right person controls the money (Igonor et al., 2025). This can help to minimize risks in instances of advance-fee fraud, as well as fake escrow and invoice frauds.

The Decentralized Identity systems or Self-Sovereign Identity (SSI) grant a control to individuals over their own digital identities in a blockchain way. It enables the users to store verifiable credentials in a distributed ledger and only the information they need to be shared using zero-knowledge proof. This is an enormous step towards decreasing identity theft and synthetic identity fraud - two leading enablers of online financial crime.

The synergy of smart contracts with blockchain-based KYC with the Aadhaar identity in India provides for tremendous possibilities. The Smart contracts and blockchain based KYC with Aadhaar in India with privacy is a rich combination of possibilities. Examples of blockchain based use cases in land records, education and supply chain verification illustrate possibilities. Furthermore, smart contracts can streamline the insurance and government schemes at the same time, minimising the chances of fraudulent claims as per the new regulations (Kulkarni et al., 2025).

While these benefits exist, they are accompanied by certain drawbacks such as code vulnerabilities (smart contract bugs), scalability concerns and legal enforceability of the smart contracts under Indian legislation. Smart contracts and decentralized identities need to be made legally binding under the Information Technology Act, and the forthcoming Digital India guidelines should include specific provisions for this. Design and auditing can make these technologies fraud-proof, and at the same time give users increased control over their data and identity (Elijah, 2025).

3. OPPORTUNITIES IN LEGAL EVIDENCE PRESERVATION USING BLOCKCHAIN

The Blockchain technology offers transformative possibilities in preserving legal evidence, even in cases of cyber fraud involving the Internet where there is often an issue of digital evidence. The Conventional digital records are easy to tamper with from discontinuity to uncertainty, and are often called into question in court and rejected. The immutability, verifiability and transparency of blockchain technology can effectively enhance the trust in digital evidence to address these limitations (Harris, 2023).

In the context of financial transactions, blockchain can securely record the data of these transactions, communication logs, login records and audit trail from the initial stage. In financial transactions, cases of identity theft or phishing, blockchain can securely record data of all transactions, as well as communication logs, login records, audit trails and everything from the initial point (Park & Jeong, 2026). This ensures the import of the investigation and trial process is kept "trusted" and is not harmed by the records or witness testimony. The technology provides cryptographic proof of authenticity, accurate time-stamps and clear access logs that are extremely important for establishing facts in front of judicial authorities.

Indian law enforcement agencies and judiciary can leverage systems based on Blockchain technology for additional technological protection towards electronic records under Section 65B of Indian Evidence Act, 1872. The use of subjectively derived opinions on data integrity can be eliminated in Court. Furthermore, blockchain allows for the secure exchange of evidence among police, public prosecutors and courts, while tracking any access to it on the blockchain.

Beyond fraud, it appears there are much bigger opportunities for the civil justice field to be enhanced with new techniques to the processing of digital evidence in cybercrime, economic, and IP cases. With its adequate implementation, blockchain can boost the rates of conviction, ease the pace of trials, as well as boost the public trusts in the justice delivery system. But it is vital that these opportunities be recognized legally, trained at the bench and have the technical infrastructure in place for each. This part delves into the various aspects of blockchain that can have a transformative effect on how legal evidence is kept when combating online cyber fraud.

3.1 Immutability, Time-stamping, and Chain of Custody

Three core properties of the blockchain system such as immutability, time-stamping and chain of custody are great assets for preserving legal evidence. The data that is written on the blockchain once cannot be changed or deleted without being detected to ensure its immutability. Such change of any record would involve changing all of the blocks of the network, which is impractical if the system was well structured. This provides transparency over transactions and events that play a key role in cyber fraud investigations, and cannot be altered or removed. Time-stamping gives an exact time, chronologically, that a transaction or event has taken place, which is cryptographically verifiable. Important for lay-back times, establishing the sequences of actions and to refute false alibis in fraud cases. The ability to mark on the day helps then to connect the dots between devices, and build a case story in court.

A critical weakness in computer evidence is chain of custody, which is taken to a new level of security through blockchain. Digital Signatures and Timestamps are generated on all accesses, transfers and modifications of evidence. This allows a seamless and clear trail of who accessed the evidence, when and for what purpose. This is a powerful tool to show proponents in cyber fraud cases, that important transaction records or communication logs were not altered from the time of collection to presentation at trial (Abdullah et al., 2025).

The characteristics can facilitate the establishment of reliability in the Indian legal setting required by the Bharatiya Sakshya Adhiniyam 2023.The features can assist in establishing reliability, which is required by the Bharatiya Sakshya Adhiniyam, within the Indian law setting. They lessen manipulation difficulties and offer increased judge's trust in the e records. The change brought about by blockchain makes digital evidence not only a failable line of evidence, but also one of the most reliable in today's litigations.

3.2 Enhanced Admissibility and Authenticity of Digital Evidence

For cyber fraud cases, blockchain has a tremendous impact on the admissibility and authenticity of digital evidence. Authenticity and integrity of electronic records has been one of the biggest challenges to entering electronic records. Blockchain does this by integrating cryptographic hashing, digital signatures, and distributed consensus which give blockchain mathematical evidence of authenticity (Khan & Ahmed, 2025). By storing or referencing evidence on a blockchain, the courts can check for integrity of that evidence since hash values can be compared and create a lot less uncertainty moving forward with traditional digital forensics. This technolqical assurance could help to meet the requirement of getting the certification under Section 65B of the Indian Evidence Act. An added layer of authenticity is built into blockchain-based evidence, which may help to minimize the need for the extensive expert witness examinations related to system security and potential tampering.

In addition, that blockchain is decentralized makes it more difficult to successfully sue a party for fabrication of evidence. Each record has several "authenticating" nodes, thereby establishing multi-negative and multi-positive authentication for each record, possibly much stronger than traditional server logs. This could help the likelihood of digital evidence being accepted in trials for law enforcement agencies. Additionally, blockchain technology can help generate “evidence tokens” or digital certificates to be not only created securely and shared with courts, but held as evidence of their origin. This skill is particularly important in cases of complex cyber fraud, across jurisdiction and where there is a lot of transactional data.

3.3 Real-Time Auditability and Transparency Benefits

Having a shared real-time auditability and transparency is one of the key benefits of blockchain for the preservation of legal evidence. Spending time with a traditional system, audit logs can be altered or deleted by an administrator, while a blockchain based system generates an immutable log, tracking each transaction with the information. The entire history of evidence (from creation through presentation) is available for investigation, prosecution and judicial review at any time.

In cases of cyber fraud, this real-time auditability speeds up investigations by enabling quick verification of transactions, communication logs and access logs. Each of the transparency features allows designated signatories to access a specific part of the record without releasing of sensitive data on the basis of innovative privacy methods like Zero-knowledge proofs.

Transparency of and accountability on evidence in the judicial process diminishes the dispute on authenticity and enhances mutual trust between the parties. Prosecutors can assert that they have some sort of digital records, but defense counsel can review those documents independently, which can speed up a settlement negotiation or narrow via trial a defense. Real-time monitoring systems are valuable tools for regulatory agencies and law enforcement authorities, enabling them to proactively identify and prevent fraud and one possibility of preserving the evidence for the prosecution in the future. Transparency, in the context of India aligns with principles of natural justice and can go a long way towards mitigating concerns over evidence planting or manipulation that can arise with high-profile cases. Together with its auditability attributes and with suitable access to the blockchain and protection of privacy, this balance between accountability and sensitivity of information makes a system which can be used.

4. CHALLENGES AND LEGAL BARRIERS

The Blockchain has huge promise at eliminating online cyber fraud and at helping preserve the legal evidence, but there are some challenges and legal obstacles to its implementation. Noticeably, India faces significant challenges in the seamless integration of blockchain technology into the financial and legal landscape, ranging from technical intricacies and regulatory hurdles to privacy considerations and judicial reluctance. Owning its technical capabilities and knowledge, many police departments and courts still do not have the ability to fully leverage the provided evidence from blockchain.

That there is no specific legislation that acknowledges existence of the blockchain records as main evidence adds to the difficulty. Challenges like scalability of blockchain networks, high implementation costs and legacy systems integration are inhibiting progress (Badkul et al., 2025). Furthermore, cross-border cybercrime incidents also pose significant challenges from jurisdictional conflicts, given that blockchain transactions can occur across various countries and jurisdictions. The transparency of blockchain also presents a problem in the context of the Digital Personal Data Protection Act, 2023 (DPDP) because there is an inherent conflict between the transparency of blockchain and privacy concerns.

The barriers need to be tackled in a balanced manner that fosters innovation and safeguards the integrity of the judiciary, as well as the provision of law and data protection. These issues cannot be addressed without first finding a solution. The high-level technical, regulatory, privacy and evidentiary challenges to address are discussed.

4.1 Technical and Scalability Limitations

However, blockchain technology has significant technical and scalability challenges that can hinder its ability to be useful for large-scale cyber fraud prevention and evidence preservation. The public blockchains, such as Bitcoin and Ethereum, offer limited transaction volume, generally around a few transactions per second, but not enough for financial networks like UPI or banks in India.

The Permissioned blockchain are faster and more private, but depend on trusted validators, thus reinstating the risks of the centralization. How energy intensive Proof-of-Work consensus systems are is still considered a major issue, but newer systems, such as Proof-of-Stake, are more efficient. The amount of storage space required for storage of complete ledgers also increases significantly over time, being a challenge for smaller organisations or law enforcement agencies with limited infrastructure.

An Interoperability between different blockchain networks and legacy systems remains problematic, leading to integration difficulties. Future risks are related to the preservation of the old blockchain records in evidence preservation, as it requires making them accessible over time and migrating them. Naturally in permissioned systems these technical vulnerabilities are hard to occur, but they are possible, such as smart contract bugs and 51% attacks.

4.2 Regulatory and Jurisdictional Issues

The Regulatory and jurisdictional challenges are huge hurdles to effectively utilize blockchain to combat cyber fraud. There is still no single law across India focused on the blockchain and its inclusion as evidence in law. The Information Technology Act, 2000, and the Bharatiya Sakshya Adhiniyam include electronic records but fail to specifically take into account the unique attributes of blockchain technology.

The Jurisdictional issues especially come into play in the instances of cyber fraud cross borders, where transactions a part of a blockchain based on many countries might have different legislations. Issues of which laws would apply, which court would have jurisdiction and what would happen to judgments if they were not recognised or enforced are unanswered. The Reserve Bank of India (RBI) and other authorities have maintained a rosy stance, leaving businesses and law enforcement agencies uncertain.

Moreover, the current legal landscape around smart contracts is not clearly defined and does not have a clear resolution, therefore impacting their acceptability in Indian courts. While there are regulatory sandboxes, they can only be used in a limited way. It is imperative to have clarity as to admissibility of blockchain evidence in court, localization provisions and ways of cooperating internationally. Balancing the regulatory landscape with global best practices, while keeping into mind India's national security and sovereignty needs, will be essential in unlocking the potential of blockchain technology in combating online fraud.

4.3 Privacy Concerns and Data Protection Conflicts

With the transparency that is one of the core attributes of blockchain, there is significant tension and transgression of laws regarding data protection and privacy. According to the Digital Personal Data Protection Act, 2023, the financial information (like any personal information) is categorized as sensitive, which requires it to be collected only on the basis of consent and with limited purposes, and in adherence with data minimization principles. But public blocks are by nature transparent – compliance is difficult.

With permissioned blockchains, concerns related to unauthorized access and the "right to be forgotten" arise for personal or transaction data purchased. Even in the case of permissioned blockchains, concerns may exist regarding unauthorized access and the "right to be forgotten", which is challenging to implement because of the immutability of the blockchain. When it comes to cyber fraud incidents, capturing evidence and protecting the privacy of victim and third parties complicates matters.

Some technologies like ZK proof, off-chain data storage, and data hashing provide partial solutions, increase complexity, and can potentially diminish the weight of evidence. Ensuring security is paramount when it comes to law enforcement access to blockchain data, so it is necessary to have clear safeguards in place to prevent the misuse of data. India should have clear and specific policies that conciliate transparency in order to fight fraud and protect privacy.India should have specific policies that strike a balance between transparency for fraud prevention and privacy concerns.

4.4 Evidentiary Challenges in Courts and Enforcement

However, one of the challenges that make the use of blockchain for legal proceedings difficult is the difficulty of challenges in court. Indian courts are more accepting of electronic evidence, however they are hesitant of new technologies (Chamim et al., 2025). The lack of technical understanding about blockchain mechanics among judges and lawyers has made it complex and cumbersome to evaluate blockchain proof of authenticity and reliability.

Ensuring records in the blockchain are accurate can be costly and time-consuming, and may require expert testimony that is required before a court of law for most records. Questions of what kind of blockchain records can be used, how much should be weighted on different consensus systems and forensic guidelines are yet unclear. Poor technical expertise is also a challenge among law enforcement bodies in securing and introducing blockchain evidence. Chain evidence is often used as an argument for prosecution and defense. Chain evidence is often used as an argument against prosecution and/or defense.

5. CONCLUSION AND FUTURE DIRECTIONS: BALANCING INNOVATION WITH LEGAL SAFEGUARDS

The Blockchain technology has huge potential to combat cyber frauds in online platforms and improve the legal policing of evidence in India. From its features of immutability, transparency and cryptographic security, this can greatly improve the level of trust in digital transactions and create more conviction in the investigation of cybercrime cases. To realize this potential, however, technological innovation needs to be carefully balanced with judicious protection, privacy and law.

The approach will be to enact specific legislation to acknowledge the value of blockchain records as evidence, create national codes of practice for blockchain forensics and establish specialized cyber courts with technical expertise. There is a need to strengthen Indian law enforcement, judiciary and legal sectors with capacity building and encourage the development and usage of the indigenous blockchain solutions suitable to the local needs in India. The best practice is to use a hybrid combination that includes blockchain, AI, cloud computing and traditional forensics.

An equitable system that strikes the right balance between promoting responsible innovation and ensuring adequate privacy and security, and resolving jurisdictional issues is necessary.

REFERENCES

Abdullah, H. O., Maqsood, M., & Nadeem, A. (2025). Digital Evidence in Criminal Proceedings: Legal Standards, Chain of Custody, and Evidentiary Reliability in the Digital Era. *Research Journal for Social Affairs*, *3*(5), 795–805. DOI: 10.71317/RJSA.003.05.0375

. Adewumi, I. O., & Afe, O. F. (2025). Integrating Artificial Intelligence and Blockchain for Secure Digital Evidence Management: Advances in Cyber Forensics and Data Privacy.

Apsimet, N., Alimkulov, Y., Konysbay, B., Zhanibekov, A., & Muratova, A. (2026). Challenges of using digital evidence in pretrial investigations of online fraud: Lessons for Kazakhstan from international practice. *IDP. Revista de Internet. Derecho y Política*, (44), 1–17. DOI: 10.7238/idp.v0i44.433072

Badkul, S., Kishor, A., Juchnevicius, E., & Madvariya, S. (2025). Blockchain and the Future of Digital Evidence: Opportunities and Challenges for Law Enforcement. *Rethinking the Police for a Better Future: Navigating Policing Challenges with Accountability and Trust*, 287-297.

Chamim, M., Widodo, K., Riyadi, S., Achyarsyah, P., & Faisal, F. (2025). The role of digital evidence in criminal law enforcement: Challenges of authentication and admissibility in court. *Research Horizon*, *5*(6), 2987–2998. DOI: 10.54518/rh.5.6.2025.950

Elijah, J. (2025). *Navigating the Legal Challenges of Cybersecurity and Forensic Evidence in the Digital Era*. Law Nectar.

Harris, M. (2023). Blockchain-Based Evidence in Courts: Standards, Reliability, and Admissibility Challenges. *Legal Studies in Digital Age*, *2*(3), 49–63.

Hossain, M. Z. (2026). Emerging trends in forensic accounting: Data analytics, cyber forensic accounting, cryptocurrencies, and blockchain technology for fraud investigation and prevention. *Journal of Artificial Intelligence and Technological Development*, *2*(2), 183–208. DOI: 10.59324/jaitd.2026.2(2).14

Igonor, O. S., Amin, M. B., & Garg, S. (2025). The application of blockchain technology in the field of digital forensics: A literature review. *Blockchains*, *3*(1), 5. DOI: 10.3390/blockchains3010005

Joseph, J., & Pandey, A. (2026). Cybercrimes in Bharatiya Nyaya Sanhita: A Critical Study on Indian Legal Scenario. In Reshaping Criminology with AI (pp. 155-174). IGI Global Scientific Publishing.

Khan, M. N. I., & Ahmed, I. (2025). A systematic review of judicial reforms and legal access strategies in the age of cybercrime and digital evidence. *International Journal of Scientific Interdisciplinary Research, 5*(2), 01-29.

Krishna, A. Y. V., & Kumar Chaudhary, N. (2026). Enhancing Evidence Integrity and Trust in the Criminal Justice System: A Design and Evaluation of the Blockchain Enabled Evidence Securing and Tracking (BEST) Application. *Journal of the Institution of Electronics and Telecommunication Engineers*, •••, 1–10. DOI: 10.1080/03772063.2026.2617871

Kulkarni, A. V., Mondal, T., & Modi, D. (2025). Enhancing privacy in banking systems: A blockchain-based access management and KYC solution. *Cogent Business & Management*, *12*(1), 2570063. DOI: 10.1080/23311975.2025.2570063

Kumar, Y. (2022). AI techniques in blockchain technology for fraud detection and prevention. In *Security engineering for embedded and cyber-physical systems* (pp. 207–224). CRC Press. DOI: 10.1201/9781003278207-14

Park, Y., & Jeong, D. (2026). A blockchain-based digital evidence management system: Integrating forensic procedures and multi-party authorization. *Information Processing & Management*, *63*(5), 104654. DOI: 10.1016/j.ipm.2026.104654

Popal, M., Ahmad, A., & Arshad, M. (2025). The Significance of Blockchain Technology in Preserving Digital Evidence Integrity in Forensic Investigations. *Journal of Computing & Biomedical Informatics*, *9*(02).

Saputra, D. H., & Kusumah, F. (2025). Blockchain Forensics and the Evidentiary Challenges of Crypto-Based Corruption in Developing Countries. *Indonesian Journal of Criminal Law Studies*, *10*(2), 615–658.

Shami, A. Z. A., Saleem, M., & Ashraf, J. (2025). Cybercrime and Digital Evidence: Investigating the Challenges and Opportunities in Prosecuting Cybercrime and Handling Digital Evidence. *Research Consortium Archive*, *3*(2), 401–411.

Smith, M., & Tiwari, M. (2024). The implications of national blockchain infrastructure for financial crime. *Journal of Financial Crime*, *31*(2), 236–248. DOI: 10.1108/JFC-01-2023-0006

Yadav, A., Srivastava, V., & Singh, H. (2026). Enhancing Green Investment Through AI and Automation: A Critical Legal Study of Regulatory Frameworks Effectiveness in Tackling Cybersquatting in India. In AI Governance, Law, Policy and Ethics in Green Finance and ESG (pp. 149-166). IGI Global Scientific Publishing. DOI: 10.4018/979-8-2600-1308-3.ch009

Yeoh, P. (2017). Regulatory issues in blockchain technology. *Journal of Financial Regulation and Compliance*, *25*(2), 196–208. DOI: 10.1108/JFRC-08-2016-0068

Chapter 2
Adulteration in Milk and Dairy Products:
A Study of Evidentiary Frameworks and Blockchain Intervention

Yashika Jain
Amity University, Gwalior, India

Hemant Singh
http://orcid.org/0000-0002-1258-5187
Amity University, Gwalior, India

Govind Singh Rajpal
http://orcid.org/0000-0002-3078-311X
School of Law, MIT Art, Design, and Technology University, Pune, India

ABSTRACT

The Milk Adulteration is one of the most common and hazardous forms of food fraud and can be extremely harmful to public health, the economy and consumer confidence. Although traditional evidentiary frameworks have been governed by strict procedures, they have a number of weaknesses that impact their use and success, such as sample tampering, compromised chain of custody, delay in sample submission for laboratory analysis and low conviction rates. The present study critically analyzes the challenges in milk and dairy product related adulteration cases from the point of view of evidence. It also elaborates on the concept of blockchain technology as a strong tradeable tool to foster transparency, traceability, and immutability along the entire dairy supply chain. The chapter explores the legal and technical architec-

DOI: 10.4018/979-8-3373-9730-6.ch002

tures, implementation challenges, and policy suggestions. The results suggest that implementing blockchain could greatly improve the quality of the dairy industry's forensics, regulatory compliance, and consumer trust.

1. INTRODUCTION

The Milk adulteration is one of the essential nations' food safety problems, especially in India which is the biggest milk producer in the world. Various agents like water, urea, formalin, detergents, veg oil, starch, synthetic milk (from harmful chemicals) make up for the volume, fat content, and prolong the shelf life. It not only misleads consumers, but creates many health problems such as gastrointestinal disorders, kidney disease, risks of cancer, and developmental problems in children. The root of the issue is the disjointed supply chain, with millions of small dairy farmers, middlemen, processors and retailers, and it is difficult to trace the origin and who is accountable for the problem (Trivedi et al, 2026). A more credible evidentiary ecosystem can be created by combining blockchain and linking it to the IoT sensors, fast testing devices and smart contracts.

The line of circumstantial evidence that traditionally has been used in milk adulteration cases mainly involves physical sampling, the analysis of such samples in a chemical laboratory and documentary evidence submitted in accordance with the Food Safety and Standards Authority of India (FSSAI), 2006. These systems are plagued, however, with several flaws that do not exist in other systems. The Samples obtained from raids can be easily substituted or tampered with between the time of collection and when they reach the laboratory. Fragile chain of custody, based on the manual register of chain of custody which can be easily manipulated. Sample collection often occurs sometime after the sample comes into the laboratory and changes may occur during this time interval that can lead to the loss of important information. In addition, laboratories are backlogged and this delays crime-solving as offenders are able to operate, or destroy records, in the meantime (Vajpayee et al, 2025).

The burden of proof of establishing adulteration 'beyond reasonable doubt' becomes more difficult when samples are doubted and/or test reports are doubted in court. The cross-examination of expert food testing witnesses is extensive and brings to the surface any inaccuracies in their evidence: defence lawyers make their mark on the scene by exploiting any procedural weaknesses, thus successfully acquitting their clients. The success rate of milk adulteration cases is still low as incidents of high-profile milk cases seldom lead to a conviction. As a weak evidentiary system, it does not provide sufficient incentive for poorly enforced "clean up the dairy value chain" which ensures that there is widespread adulteration (Polu et al., 2026).

The sheer inefficiencies in the evidence are stark contrasts to what is possible in blockchain technology. Blockchains can keep a verifiable record of all the actors in the entire milk chain, from the collection of milk on the farm to the processing, packaging and distribution. Every milk lot can be given a distinctive code. At the collection centre, thanks to the IoT technology, sensors can automatically measure critical parameters, including fat content, the SNF (Solids-Not-Fat), the temperature, the pH stage and the urea content of milk products in real time. These reading are immediately captured on the blockchain forming an immutable digital "audit trail" of the reading.

Additionally, rapid test kits are integrated with blockchain, allowing for even more authenticity of data. As the tests are done on the spot, the result is automatically hashed while simultaneously sharing this information with the distributed ledger, such as GPS coordinates, the time of the test and the inspector's identity. If experimental data is modified at any time in the future, this can be identified immediately. Smart contracts can be used to set alerts for suspicious variations in the quality parameters and alert authorities.

The chain of custody is gain cryptographically secure in a blockchain-based system. Each vendor-farmer milk transaction is individualised and captured.All milk delivered by farmer to the vendor is traced as a transaction. Easily accessing the complete history of a suspect batch is a huge time and resource saver for regulatory officers – and by scanning a QR code, they can do it in seconds. It can provide high-confidence evidence forensically— much harder to be contested in court than would conventional paper-based evidence.

There are a number of examples of pilot projects that have been carried out around the world. The cooperative movement such as Amul and several state governments have started to have their own grafts by leveraging blockchain technology for tracking a single cow in India. Some nations such as New Zealand and the Netherlands have established such a blockchain-based system for high-quality dairy products to export, protecting the origin and quality (Khan et al., 2025). Such systems can also help to ensure the integrity of milk production, allow for the sale of premium traceable, high-quality milk, and thereby provide economic motivation for ethical production practices.

However, there are some key. Although blockchain technology has its potential in the Indian dairy industry, there are some significant challenges. The sector has a very high fragmentation ratio, millions of smallholder farmers who are less digitally savvy, and who have limited access to smartphones. Issues of data privacy standards, nonstandard implementation and high costs are some of them that should be addressed. The other significant challenge is to ensure that different cooperatives, private dairies and regulatory systems are interoperable. To make blockchain records legally admissible, legal clarity needs to be provided and judicial training needs to be given.

A combination of blockchain seems to be the most viable solution for India. Permissioned Consortium Blockchain with FSSAI, state food departments, dairy co-operatives and accredited labs can store critical quality and transaction data. For less sensitive bulk data there are cryptographic anchors on the main ledger which can keep data off-chain. Publicly available product dashboards can be used by consumers to check the authenticity of products, thus boosting market pressure on the deceleration of product adulteration.

2. TYPES, METHODS AND DETECTION OF ADULTERATION IN DAIRY PRODUCTS: COMMON ADULTERANTS IN MILK AND DAIRY PRODUCTS

The Milk and dairy products are known to be amongst the most commonly adulterated foods in the majority of countries around the world, mainly because of economical motives. Adulterators add cheap substances to increase the volume, make it look better, make it last longer or make it look like higher quality in order to maximize any profits. This malpractice is particularly prevalent in developing nations, such as India, where milk supply chains are very disorganized, and there is a lack of capacities to rigorously monitor these activities.

The most frequent milk adulterant is only water. Added to bulk up, simply diluting nutrition. Water dilution may seem benign, but it means a reduction in the nutrients that are needed and much worse, provides a transport vehicle for other harmful adulterants. Various chemicals are added back to compensate for the dilution and to restore thickness/fat content. The most common and most harmful of the adulterants is urea. It is compounded and added to increase protein values in the quality test, since its value is based on nitrogen which is used in the standards and appears in urea, artificially inflating the value. Milk that has been mixed with urea may result in serious kidney injury, gastrointestinal issues and acidity (Azad & Ahmed, 2016).

Another serious adulterant that is used to kill bacteria and lengthen the shelf life of milk is formalin which is actually a solution of formaldehyde. Is a known carcinogen, causes respiratory problems, skin irritation, and also chronic organ damage. Another chemical used as preservative, like hydrogen peroxide, changes the composition of milk, which leads to the elimination of beneficial enzymes.

The Skewed increased whiteness and thickness in milk is often achieved by the additional of detergents and soaps. They include toxic ingredients such as sodium lauryl sulphate which can irritate the bowel and lead to food poisoning. Fat is usually added back to milk in the form of a mixture of vegetable oils (including palm oil or soybean oil) and refined fats; this often happens in toned or double toned milk. To create a thicker look, starch from maize or wheat is incorporated.

Some of the most harmful kind of adulteration is the making of synthetic milks prepared with a combination of urea, detergent, vegetable oil, caustic soda and water. This 'milk' is shaped and tastes just like regular milk and even froths and acts just like regular milk in many respects, but it isn't made from any milk products. Inhaling one can carry serious health hazards, such as cancer and neurological damage.

However, adulterations in other dairy products vary. Vegetable fats, palm oil and animal fats (from pigs and not cattle intended for human consumption) are often combined in ghee and butter. To aid in volume sometimes paraffin wax is added. To increase the yield as well as shelf life of the product starch, vegetable proteins and chemical preservatives have been added in paneer and cheese products. Often yogurt or curd should be diluted with water and thickened by starch or gelatin. The most common adulterant added to skim milk powder is maltodextrin or other fillers.

The Melamine came into the limelight during the 2008 China milk scandal. It's added to make the protein density seem higher. Melamine may lead to acute kidney failure and is particularly toxic to infants. Some other nitrogenous compounds, as well as ammonium sulphate and melamine-formaldehyde resin, are also used for the same purpose. The Other significant forms of adulteration are from antibiotics and veterinary drug residue. A small number of farmers and/or processors may use antibiotics in milk in order to extend its useful life or disguise mastitis in the animal. This is a factor of the rapidly emerging challenge of antibiotic resistance on the planet (Malik et al., 2026).

The Physical adulterants are any dirt, dust, dung or extraneous matter, more likely to be found in loosely collected raw milk. Biological contamination refers to pathogens or contaminated water, and can result in outbreaks of foodborne illnesses. The techniques used to adulterate the products have become more advanced. Standard test equipment measures specific gravity, fat percentage, and SNF (Solids-Not-Fat) of the product, while adhering to the specific gravity, fat percentage and SNF level blend requirements established by the adulterators. Others use multi-stage adulteration where other components are added as the process gets closer to the end of the supply chain (farm, collection centre, processing unit, and retail location).

It's driven by a business purpose. The price of milk depends on the amount of fat and SNF. The Suppliers can make a lot more money changing these parameters by using cheap chemicals. An Adulteration of Milk is common in India where majority of milk is produced by small and marginal farmers, which are subjected to pressure from middle men to incorporate adulterants into their milk or the middlemen do the same themselves.

The Health injuries have broad and extensive consequences. The per capita milk and milk products consumption has become a hidden community health problem due to being adulterated. The high consumption of milk by children is linked to stunted growth and malnutrition, even with sufficient milk consumption, as well as organ damage in the long term. In adults, digestive disorders, allergies, hormonal imbalances, and risk of cancer are among the consequences. There's also the economic cost, which comes in the form of higher health care and lost productivity.

Testing is still difficult as a large number of common adulterants are deliberately formulated to evade simple-quality assurance methods. Most adulterants can be detected by using advanced laboratory techniques, such as High-Performance Liquid Chromatography (HPLC), Gas Chromatography-Mass Spectrometry (GC-MS) and Nuclear magnetic resonance (NMR) spectroscopy, however these are prohibitively expensive and are time consuming and cannot be scaled up for routine use in the field.

These are a few of the many reasons why there is an urgent need to effect systemic change in the adulteration of milk and milk products related laws. Reactive tests are inadequate. The technology-driven solutions of blockchain-based supply chain monitoring systems, IoT enabled real-time quality sensors and lightning-fast testing devices at the point of sale, can definitely produce tamper-proof evidence documentation. Unless the underlying causes are eliminated and new eloquent testing is implemented, honey will remain susceptible to adulteration and consumers' confidence in it as one of humanity's fundamental food products will be lost.

3. EVIDENTIARY FRAMEWORKS FOR MILK ADULTERATION CASES

The regulatory enforcement and prosecution of dairy milk fraud cases are largely supported by fraud evidentiary frameworks. These are frameworks for the systematic gathering, preserving, analyzing, and presenting evidence to prove the adduction for conclusive evidence. They are regulated mainly by the Food Safety and Standards Act, 2006 and the Bharatiya Nyaya Sanhita and the Bharatiya Sakshya Adhiniyam, 2023 in India. Any system of evidence should be scientifically reliable, be fairly conducted and be legally admissible. Milk adulteration, however, is a special case because of the freshness of the product, complicated supply chains and sophisticated milk adulteration methods (Khanna et al., 2022). The Evidence needs to connect the adulterated sample to specified players in the value chain, ranging from farmers, collection points, processors to the retailers. Although the dorying has been so prevalent, weak evidentiary frameworks lead to low level of conviction. The key factors to effective coordination within a robust framework are: food safety officers, forensic laboratories and judiciary. As technology becomes more prevalent, modern evidentiary systems are trending towards traceability, real-time testing and tamper-proof documentation of evidence. These systems are important for consumer safety and to restore confidence in the dairy industry; strengthening them is vital.

3.1 Principles of Food Forensics and Evidence Collection

The Food forensics is the science used to investigate food crime, and food fraud, one of the food crimes, is adulteration of milk. Meets internationally recognised standards including those of ISO 17025 and Codex Alimentarius guidelines. The core principles include integrity, reliability, repeatability, and defensibility of evidence. For Milk Adulteration case, evidence collection starts with correct collection of samples as per guidelines of FSSAI. The Food Safety Officers are required to take "representative samples" in clean containers and seal the containers with witnesses present and logged a record. The Factors that are important involve prompt collection to ensure that degradation is not occurring, use of a calibrated piece of equipment, and following the chain of custody protocol. There are several samples, including the original, duplicate and referee samples, for re-testing. Appropriate labelling must be used, including date, time, place and batch information. More and more it is recommended to use digital photography and GPS tagging of sampling sites. Impartiality and avoiding contamination is also a point highlighted by the principles. If these principles are violated, the whole case may be a weak case. The Food forensics- dairy adulteration requires both chemical and microbiological analysis and is a training need issue for officers (Noor et al., 2024).

3.2 Chain of Custody in Dairy Product Investigations

In order to establish a chain of custody is a key part of the evidence in milk adulteration proceedings. Chronological recording of a seizure, custody and controlling of samples, transfer and analysis of such samples. A continuous chain of custody is especially difficult to maintain in dairy investigations because milk is a perishable product and the various individuals that come into contact with dairy products. Signatures, times of transfers and reasons for transfers should be documented for all transfers, from sampling point to the laboratory (Padma et al., 2023). Manual systems involve the use of paper forms that can be fragile to manipulation, loss, and tampering. A poor chain of custody can be the most common basis for a defense attorney challenging a prosecution in court. Best practices today suggest the use of a digital chain of custody on blockchain or an app connected to mobile devices that logs each movement with a time-stamp and GPS data. All samples are to be hermetically sealed and kept under conditions of the temperature of storage. The evidence may be discredited if the chain of custody is broken or compromised at any time.

3.3 Scientific and Documentary Evidence in Adulteration Cases

The Milk adulteration prosecution is based on scientific and documentary evidence. The Laboratory test reports which show presence of such additives as urea, formalin, melamine, starch, vegetable oils or detergents are examples of scientific evidence. HPLC, GC-MS, and FTIR spectroscopy are advanced methods that are used to yield definite results regarding certain adulterants. But, the testimony is dependent on the reliability and speed of the tests. The Documentary evidence covers the licence, the invoice, the transport log, the quality testing report at the collection centres and the CCTV surveillance records at processing centres. In many instances, deviation from a declared quality parameter and laboratory testing results are significant corroborative evidence (Anagwa et al,. 2024). By examining the records of bank transactions or cash memos, suppliers and adulterators can be linked. Digital evidence like WhatsApp messages, GPS data of milk tankers, ERP system logs are all increasing being used. The issue is to make sure that there is a connection between the adulterated sample and the accused person.

3.4 Role of Laboratories and Expert Witnesses

The Laboratories and expert witness are pivotal in a milk adulteration (procurement) case. Accredited food analysis laboratories that are FSSAI-notified or NABL accredited, are tasked with giving reports with evidentiary significance itself towards the analyzed samples. Often times experts from these laboratories serve as witnesses to help explain the methodology and results of tests, as well as the scientific implications thereof. Their testimony aids the court in finding out complicated technical matters such as the action of urea on the reading of the proteins, or the presence of formalin in milk. Judicial decisions are greatly affected by the reputation of the lab and the credentials of the expert. In most government laboratories, however, there is delapidated equipment, over load and time lag for reporting. This diminishes the scope of prosecution cases. An expert witness should be unbiased and able to stand the pressure of inquiries at cross examination. They will be expected to justify the scientific reliability of their methods as will now be required by the Indian courts under Daubert-like standards. It is crucial to train food crime professionals and assist with capacity development of forensic food labs.

3.5 Admissibility Challenges in Courts

The issue of admissibility of evidence still continues to be a significant hurdle in milk adulteration prosecutions. Judicial assessments given to ensure that samples were properly handled, sealed, transported, and analyzed. Many cases slip through the cracks because there were minor procedure gaps: None of the signatures were printed, it wasn't securely sealed, or perhaps samples were not submitted in a timely fashion to laboratories. Section 63 of Bharatiya Sakshya Adhiniyam, 2023, stipulates that electronic records and reports from laboratories must be appropriately certified. Samples will often be contested by defence lawyers; an individual who may be questioning for possible tampering. Another major factor relates to the time between sample collection and sample testing and may influence the trustworthiness of the results obtained for perishable food such as milk (Polu et al., 2026). The courts also requires evidence that the sample analyzed was representative of the full batch. Absence of uniform national procedures for the admissibility of digital evidence adds to the factors complicating admissibility. In a number of its High Court judgments, cases have been dropped because the chain of custody or FSSAI sampling were broken or not followed.

4. LEGAL AND REGULATORY FRAMEWORK GOVERNING DAIRY ADULTERATION

The Legal and regulatory provisions for adulteration of dairies in India have been established to help guarantee food safety, preserve consumer health and integrity of the dairy supply chain. India is the largest milk producer country in the world with a large, unorganized and fragmented milk sector, presenting its own share of problems. The main legislation that covers adulteration is the Food Safety and Standards Act, 2006 (Food Safety Act) which is an amalgamation of various older provisions. It does this by means of preventive, punitive and compensatory measures. It gives the Food Safety and Standards Authority of India (FSSAI), as the top food safety government authority, powers to create standards, oversee and take steps to ensure compliance. Various legislation provides support such as Indian Penal Code (oday Bangladesh Nyaya Sanhita), and Consumer Protection Act, 2019, and a few state-specific legislations on medical device devices (Acharya et al., 2026). The structure highlights the principles of traceability and licensing, quality surveillance, and the tough penalties. In spite of having a solid legislative framework, however, implementation is poor, because of inadequate infrastructure, lack of manpower and low conviction rates. The idea of regulation is to move away from a punishment approach to a scientific-based or preventing approach. As consumer awareness expands and technologies improve, it is more and more being pushed to be reinforced with the integration of digitisation and it is becoming more stringent than ever. Thus, regulation of the adulteration of dairy products plays a key role not just in terms of its importance to public health, but also its significance for India's dairy exports and the economic growth of the dairy sector.

4.1 Indian Legal Framework: FSSAI Act, 2006 and Related Laws

The Food Safety and Standards Act, 2006 stands as the main legislation in the battle against milk or milk products adulteration in India. The law was enacted to bring together the different "scattered" legislations into one, creating a single-point contact for all food related issues, the Food Safety and Standards Authority of India (FSSAI). The milk and milk products under the cover of the Act would be regulated by certain standards prescribed under the Food Safety and Standards (Food Products Standards and Food Additives) Regulations, 2011. The regulations include the requirements established for the quality parameters of fat, Solids-Not-Fat (SNF) and the prohibition of the addition of any foreign substances (Gandhi et al., 2020).

Some important sections concerning adulteration are part of Section 3(1) (zx) substandard food, Section 59 Unsafe food and Section 272 of Bharatiya Nyaya Sanhita 2023, where under adulteration of food is a criminal offence to be punished. The Act provides powers for Food Safety Officers to take samples, make inspections and even to instigate prosecution. The FSSAI has also given the notification of packaging and labelling, surveillance guidelines and accreditation of laboratories (Malik et al., 2024). The Consumer Protection Act, 2019 provides scope to approach the court against adulterated dairy products and the Essential Commodities Act, 1955 can be invoked in case of large scale hoarding or adulterated milk being sold adulteration black marketing.

The Bharatiya Sakshya Adhiniyam, 2023 has updated the definition of admissibility of electronic records thereby extending to laboratory reports, which is becoming more and more pertinent in the digital era of enforcement. The current legal regime is, however, still much dependent on traditional sampling methods and laboratory testing, resulting in substantial delays. The tough law is well drafted but limited enforcement due to inadequate central and state coordination and lack of modern technology monitoring and evidence gathering.

4.2 Penalties, Prosecution and Enforcement Mechanisms in Adulteration of Milk and Dairy Products

The FSSAI Act, 2006 has stringent penalties for milk adulteration based on the level of offence committed. If the adulteration does not cause any injury, then penalties are 5 lakh, imprisonment upto 6 months. Those who adulterate the food and make it injurious to the health can be punished with up to 7 years imprisonment and up to 10 Lakhs fine. The level of punishment may be life imprisonment if the result of that was death.

It can be started mostly by the Food Safety Officers by giving a complaint to the Adjudicating Officer or Magi. The Act sets up a three-level adjudication system

(Adjudicating Officers, Food Safety Appellate Tribunals and High Courts) for processing cases. Enforcement actions include food safety audits, food sampling, and recurrent inspections & food product recall. FSSAI carries out nationwide drives, like Operation Amul and has rolled out State-level drives against milk adulteration (Rohilla & Ghoshal, 2026).

According to the government, there are several practical challenges for enforcement, despite the fact that there is robust legislation. Food Safety Officers are being urgently sought and coverage of inspections is low. In most prosecutions the idea of a long delay is caused by long laboratory analysis and the courts are backlogged. Lacking strong evidence collection and procedural gaps, conviction rates remain low (in many states estimated to be less than 30%). It does not deter behavior as many cases doesn't result in full prosecution; instead they are compounded (settled with fine). There is a low level of proactive enforcement. The fact of digitization of the licensing (FoSCoS) as well as integration with state enforcement portals and online sampling represents potential solutions with however hardly or not being done to a large extent. Greater collaboration between FSSAI, food departments in the state, police and judiciary is critical for effective deterrence.

4.3 Gaps in Current Regulatory and Evidentiary Systems

Although India has a convenient legal framework, there are very few omissions regarding the regulations of the dairy product and the proof that can be created. India has a convenient legal framework but still, there are some gaps in the evidence and regulations for the adulteration of the dairy product. The most significant gap to address is that the supply chain is disorganized and difficult to follow, making tracing of the chain very challenging. There are more than a million small farmers and informal vendors to monitor.

This is especially, the case for evidentiary gaps. The manual sampling methods are time consuming, cumbersome and subject to manipulation. No real time and foolproof system to ensure the chain of custody. The Lab facilities are limited and not fully equipped; there are not sufficient fully-equipped, accredited labs in many states which delays test reports for several weeks. The Results do not arrive until there's a lot of evidence disposed of and/or the operation continues.

The Low levels of conviction, the result of procedural weaknesses, inadequate staffing and agency coordination, is another significant limitation. The existing system relies significantly on physical samples and involves several risks: these are perishable, easily challenged in court. Limited usage of advanced forensic tools, digital evidence and pattern detection using data analytics. Some regulatory deficiencies are poor penal measures for those that repeat crimes, a lack of attention to middlemen and big processors, and poor consumer awareness measures. Still, there's not a lot of prevention in the system. There is no integration between the various databases: (licensing testing, surveillance and prosecution).

5. CHALLENGES IN TRADITIONAL EVIDENTIARY SYSTEMS

The existing standard systems for detecting milk/dairy products adulteration have inherent structural, procedural and technical flaws that make them inefficient. Physical samples are among other things easily lost. The Milk is sensitive to heat, light and air and may quickly change its composition if stored under different temperatures. The Transportation times for samples to laboratories can lead to degradation, which can give inconclusive or unreliability test results. Frequently, a defence lawyer has been able to prove that a sample analysed was not a typical sample made from the original batch as a result of poor sample storage or transit delays (Nabi et al., 2026) .

There is another significant deficiency weak chain of custody. In traditional systems, all such data is recorded on paper and is susceptible to tampering, loss, and forgery. So there are several crossovers between people in the field and other members of the food safety team to be involved in: analyse and present results at court. If any of the signatures are missing, the seal is broken, or if the evidence was not documented, the entire evidence can be deemed admissible (Malik et al., 2025). Even if only minor steps in chain of custody fail, accused individuals have been released time and time again.

Further adds to the problem resource constraints. The Acute shortage of trained Food Safety Officers in most of the states leading to low frequency of inspection. The government laboratory is overextended, inadequately equipment, and without sophisticated analytical equipment like HPLC, GC-MS or NMR spectroscopy. This results in huge queues and the dispatch of test reports may take 15–45 days. At the time of receiving the results, the accused may have destroyed documents and/or ongoing adulteration activity. The cost of the advanced testing is another disincentive for regular sampling. The Supplier corruption and collusion at different tiers in the supply chain and other enforcement agencies is very serious. It has been documented that "food safety officers collude with dairy operators, give clean dairy records in exchange for bribes and/or deliberately mishandle the samples provided". There are serious impacts on the rule of law are detrimental to the capabilities of the regulatory system to bring trust to the public.

The Lack of traceability is another significant problem. Milk is sourced from thousands of small farmers, all within a very fragmented dairy industry, in India and it is virtually impossible to trace a single batch back to the farm if there is any adulteration. Past solutions do not have the end-to-end capabilities needed to ensure that a third party or large processor is held responsible (Poonia et al., 2017).

The Judicial battles are also important. The duration of cases is years because of the backlogs in court. The Defence experts are equally adept at discrediting scientific evidence and judges often with little or no technical knowledge are more likely to believe the defence than the prosecution when technical procedure issues come into play. Across most States there is still a dismal rate of convictions of perpetrators of milk adulteration.

In addition, the existent practice is largely 'after the fact' (reactive) as opposed to 'before the fact' (preventive). Data analytics, risk profiling or real-time monitoring is only used to a limited extent. As the methods of adducing more and more sophisticated tricks become available to eliminate the simple tests, it is difficult for the evidentiary system to keep up (El-tahlawy & Alahmad, 2025).

These systemic problems have led to poor deterrent effect, ongoing problems for consumers' health and large economic losses. It is obvious that the traditional evidentiary system, which was applicable before the modern era and in a small-scale production system, is not suitable for dealing with today's complex, large-scale production system complaint with food fraud issues. This has made the case for technology based interventions, notably blockchain, to advance evidence collection, preservation and evidence presentation, stronger than ever.

6. BLOCKCHAIN INTERVENTION IN COMBATING DAIRY ADULTERATION: APPLICATION OF BLOCKCHAIN FOR SUPPLY CHAIN TRACEABILITY

The solution to the dairy frauds is a revolutionary technology called Blockchain which is facilitating effective trace-ability in the supply chain. Blockchain can provide a record of all transactions and all quality parameters from the farm to the consumer, making it hard to adulterate any data in between, leaving a strong sense in place that the records are immutable, decentralized and transparent (Nukapeyi et al., 2024).

At the farm level, each batch of milk can be given a unique digital identifier, such as a QR code or an RFID tag, to assemble into a blockchain-enabled dairy supply chain.Each batch of milk can be given a unique digital identifier at the farm level, such as a QR code or an RFID tag, to be used in a blockchain-enabled dairy supply chain. Using IoT sensors at the village-level collection centres the critical data points such as actual farmer name, date of sampling, temperature, fat content, SNF content, urea content and pH are automatically recorded (Abid et al., 2025). This information is instantly uploaded to a permissioned blockchain network, generating a record that is unalterable and can't be changed after it is put on the platform. Any changes to data are immediately visible throughout the network.

The technology allows for the end to end traceability. By scanning a QR code, regulators, dairy processors, retailers and even consumers can trace a milk packet back to its source farmer in seconds. At this stage, adulteration by any member of the chain becomes highly visible and it acts as a great deterrent. Should the adulteration be detected, he or she will be able to swiftly discover the time and person responsible and thus, prosecute the act speedily, effectively and efficiently.

The Smart contracts could be created to automatically manage the quality compliance process. For example, in case of the quality parameters going off the recommended values, the smart contract could automatically stop offloading money to the supplier or alert the FSSAI officials etc. This results in a "self-tending" system which, in turn, decreases the need for manual inspection. A blockchain is also a significant reinforcement of the framework of evidence. Lab tests, inspection reports and sampling information could be. Hash coded and placed on the blockchain, with date on the blockchain and digital signature on the data. This gives strong evidence which cannot be disputed in court and is extremely easy to generate cryptographically. The chain of custody is automated and transparent, not leaving room for manual documentation mistakes.

This method has been tried in a few pilot projects and is proving successful. There are some Indian companies such as Amul, Nandini, Nestlé and Danone that have dabbled with blockchain traceability for high value dairy goods. Globally, the dairy sector in Ireland and New Zealand have seen example based implementation of blocks – with enhanced trust and quality control.

A consortium blockchain setup where FSSAI, State dairy federations, cooperatives and large processors collaborate would be best suited for India. This results in subsidiary access which is controlled and transparent. Connectivity with the existing platforms, such as that of the National Dairy Development Board (NDDB), with the FoSCs Board portal of FSSAI, can speed up the adoption process. The blockchain traceability supports with premium pricing of verified pure milk, improves farmers' motivation for quality control, and enhances exports by attaining international quality standards. It also gives a informed consumer with accurate information on its milk powders (Kisku et al., 2025). Despite this, there are some major obstacles that need to be tackled and digital literacy amongst the small farmers, the lack of infrastructure in rural areas and the initial investment costs being major ones. A stepped strategy of "organized dairy clusters" and 'scale up' later is feasible.

7. CONCLUSION, RECOMMENDATIONS AND FUTURE DIRECTIONS

The use of AI by a blockchain can improve the detection capabilities even more. The semench periodi can be used to calculate risks from one or multiple suppliers, areas of risk or risk suppliers by machine learning algorithms. This proactive approach would change methodology and the current paradigm of punishment to prevention of punishment.

The traditional evidential framework has not been proven to significantly prevent adulteration of milk products due to the several vulnerabilities, however Blockchain technology offers an effective, transparent and efficient solution. It enhances all aspects of the process of gathering, preserving and presenting evidence. The adoption of packaging technologies and packaging dyes is crucial for garlic to prevent drugs from being mixed into packs and promote India's national grafted garlic program. Electronic surveillance and facilitation of packaging technologies and packaging dyes are critical to defeating the mixing of drugs into packages and to the potential success of the national grafted garlic program in India. Smartly leveraging blockchain intervention can revolutionize the dairy sector and enhance food safety, regaining consumer trust, and set up a more responsible and transparent supply chain.

REFERENCES

Abid, H. M. R., Aslam, S., Alwan, N., & Khalid, N. (2025). Current readiness on food fraud risk mitigation in developing countries: A review. *Agriculture & Food Security*, *14*(1), 9. DOI: 10.1186/s40066-025-00528-1

Acharya, B. S., Nair, S., & Abdul Salam, A. A. (2026). Quality Analysis and Detection of Adulterants and Contaminations in Milk/Milk Powder by Raman Spectroscopy. *Comprehensive Reviews in Food Science and Food Safety*, *25*(1), e70403. DOI: 10.1111/1541-4337.70403 PMID: 41578976

Azad, T., & Ahmed, S. (2016). Common milk adulteration and their detection techniques. *International Journal of Food Contamination*, *3*(1), 22. DOI: 10.1186/s40550-016-0045-3

El-tahlawy, A. S., & Alahmad, W. (2025). Next-Generation Solutions to Combat Food Adulteration: Integrating Advanced Detection Technologies and Risk Mitigation Strategies. In *Advanced Techniques against Food Adulteration* (pp. 123–158). Springer Nature Switzerland. DOI: 10.1007/978-3-031-99454-8_5

Gandhi, K., Sharma, R., Gautam, P. B., & Mann, B. (2020). Safety and regulatory aspects of dairy industry. In *Chemical quality assurance of milk and milk products* (pp. 273–312). Springer Singapore. DOI: 10.1007/978-981-15-4167-4_10

Khan, M. U., Zhen, L., Tian, J., Farid, A., Chen, Z., & Liu, H. (2025). From detection to prevention: A cyber-secure AI ecosystem for mitigating milk adulteration and dairy fraud. *Trends in Food Science & Technology*, •••, 105503.

Khanna, A., Jain, S., Burgio, A., Bolshev, V., & Panchenko, V. (2022). Blockchain-enabled supply chain platform for Indian dairy industry: Safety and traceability. *Foods*, *11*(17), 2716. DOI: 10.3390/foods11172716 PMID: 36076901

Kisku, U., Singh, A. K., Barman, B., Mohammad, A., Bhakat, C., Pola, A., & Meenia, P. (2025). Blockchain technology for Indian dairy industry: A sustainable food safety model. *Indian Journal of Animal Health*, *64*(1), 27–36. DOI: 10.36062/ijah.2025.06524

. Malik, M., Dalal, M., Mor, A., Toor, K., Yadav, D. K., & Gahlawat, V. K. (2025). Dairy Traceability: Pathways to a Sustainable and Resilient Supply Chain. *Trends in Animal-Based Foods*, 137-148.

Malik, M., Gahlawat, V. K., Mor, R. S., & Singh, M. K. (2024). Unlocking dairy traceability: Current trends, applications, and future opportunities. *Future Foods : a Dedicated Journal for Sustainability in Food Science*, *10*, 100426. DOI: 10.1016/j.fufo.2024.100426

Malik, M., Mor, R. S., Gahlawat, V. K., & Kumar, V. (2026). Unlocking the potential: Hybrid blockchain and AI-enabled traceability model development and implementation in the dairy industry–proof-of-concept. *Transportation Research Part E, Logistics and Transportation Review*, *205*, 104552. DOI: 10.1016/j.tre.2025.104552

Nabi, M., Saghir, K., Ullah, F., Hussain, A., & Safeer, A. (2026). Challenges in botanical extract standardization: Adulteration, misidentification, and supply chain variability. In *Botanical extracts* (pp. 180–190). CRC Press. DOI: 10.1201/9781003662785-17

Noor, A., Raza, A., & Rehman, F. U. (2024). Recent advances in forensic science for evidence collection and preservation: Innovations in sample handling techniques to enhance analytical accuracy and case-specific investigations. *Forensic Insights and Health Sciences Bulletin*, *2*(2), 60–66.

Nukapeyi, S., Bommala, R., Kondreddy, D. S., Amalakanti, C., Ravi, C., & Konuri, T. A. (2024, April). Milk chain with ML & blockchain: Revolutionizing transparency for ensuring milk purity in dairy industry. In 2024 10th International Conference on Communication and Signal Processing (ICCSP) (pp. 970-975). IEEE.

Padma, T., Aruna, S., Sujipriya, J., & Zainab, M. (2023). Blockchain based solutions for milk procurement management and adulteration detection. In *ITM Web of Conferences* (Vol. 56, p. 02008). EDP Sciences. DOI: 10.1051/itmconf/20235602008

Polu, P. R., Vyas, M., & Ravindra Babu, M. (2026). State-of-the-art analytical technologies for detection of food adulteration: Advances, validation, and future horizons. *Critical Reviews in Analytical Chemistry*, •••, 1–27. DOI: 10.1080/10408347.2026.2625392 PMID: 41686425

Polu, P. R., Vyas, M., & Ravindra Babu, M. (2026). State-of-the-art analytical technologies for detection of food adulteration: Advances, validation, and future horizons. *Critical Reviews in Analytical Chemistry*, •••, 1–27. DOI: 10.1080/10408347.2026.2625392 PMID: 41686425

Poonia, A., Jha, A., Sharma, R., Singh, H. B., Rai, A. K., & Sharma, N. (2017). Detection of adulteration in milk: A review. *International Journal of Dairy Technology*, *70*(1), 23–42. DOI: 10.1111/1471-0307.12274

Rohilla, P., & Ghoshal, G. (2026). Food adulteration be preservatives, colors etc.—Control strategies. In *Public and Environmental Health* (pp. 483–513). Academic Press. DOI: 10.1016/B978-0-443-43986-5.00001-1

Trivedi, M., Singh, H., & Intaratat, K. (2026). *Role of artificial intelligence in water and energy efficiency for food sustainability. AI and machine learning for clean water and sustainability: Liquid gold.* Cambridge Scholars Publishing Inc.

Vajpayee, K., Parekh, P. B., Dash, H. R., & Shukla, R. K. (2025). Food forensics: Fundamentals and technical advancements. In *Advances in forensic science: Emerging technologies and techniques* (pp. 37–84). Springer Nature Singapore. DOI: 10.1007/978-981-96-8971-2_3

Chapter 3
AI-Driven Digital Forensics for Police Investigations:
Strengthening Cybercrime Detection and Response in Modern India

Kiranbhai R. Dodiya
http://orcid.org/0009-0001-9409-7303
Gujarat University, India

Bhagirath Gohil
DySP Chikhli Division, Gujarat Police, India

ABSTRACT

This chapter examines the role of Artificial Intelligence (AI) in enhancing digital forensic investigations for cybercrime detection and response in modern India. Rapid digitalisation has increased the scale and sophistication of cyber offences, challenging conventional investigative methods. This chapter per the authors explores how AI technologies—including machine learning, natural language processing, computer vision, and predictive analytics—support intelligent evidence triage, behavioural analysis, fraud detection, and synthetic media authentication. It also addresses implementation challenges such as skill gaps, infrastructure limitations, legal admissibility, and algorithmic bias. The chapter highlights the need for governance frameworks, explainable AI, and capacity building to ensure responsible adoption. AI-driven digital forensics is presented as a strategic pathway toward more efficient, scalable, and intelligence-led cybercrime investigations in India.

DOI: 10.4018/979-8-3373-9730-6.ch003

1. INTRODUCTION

1.1. Rise of Cybercrime in India

The last ten years have seen India undergo rapid digitalisation, which has had effects on almost all areas of society: social interaction, government functioning, and economic behaviour. The government has built services that provide users with access to digital transactions via smartphones. Consequently, the Indian populace has convenient digital access to everything government. However, the convenient, digital access to government services increases reliance on the Internet and, with it, increases the risk of cybercrime. Reliance on devices increases the digital interconnections among individuals, companies, and the government, and therefore increases the opportunities for cybercriminals. The uninterrupted potential use of cyberspace has led to an overwhelming perception of the digital environment as the primary source of crime.(Tripathy, 2025).

India has seen the evolution of cybercrime from individual instances of hacking or website defacement to organised and sophisticated criminal activities. There has been an increase in the prevalence of cybercrime that incorporates it with financial fraud (i.e., online banking fraud, UPI fraud, phishing fraud, identity theft, online stalking, ransomware, social engineering, and phishing schemes). Cybercriminals use social media, cloud computing, encrypted communication, and other new technologies to think of innovative ways to conceal and increase the scale of their criminal activities. The emergence of cryptocurrency has created new challenges to financial investigations, as individuals can now engage in monetary transactions that are extremely difficult to trace(*(PDF) CYBERCRIME IN INDIA: LEGAL FRAMEWORKS, EMERGING THREATS, AND THE ROLE OF AI IN DETECTION AND DEFENCE*, n.d.-a).

The increasing amount of cybercrime directly impacts the public's trust in various digital systems. The public's trust in digital systems such as online banking, digital governance, and electronic communication processing systems can be eroded by the occurrence of additional data breaches and fraudulent acts. The increasing amount and degree of complexity of cybercrime cases have placed a high level of stress on conventional policing systems. Digital cyber divisions are frequently confronted with significant case overloads, and the investigations are of a highly technical nature that goes beyond ordinary police functions. While the I4C and CERT-In operated and managed the case from the top down, there was still a great deal of responsibility from the bottom up, particularly at the state and district levels. The situation above exemplifies the increasing need for greater productivity, adaptability, and smart systems in police investigations. (Raj & Nagpal, 2025).

Figure 1. Evolution of Cybercrime in India and Investigate Pressure

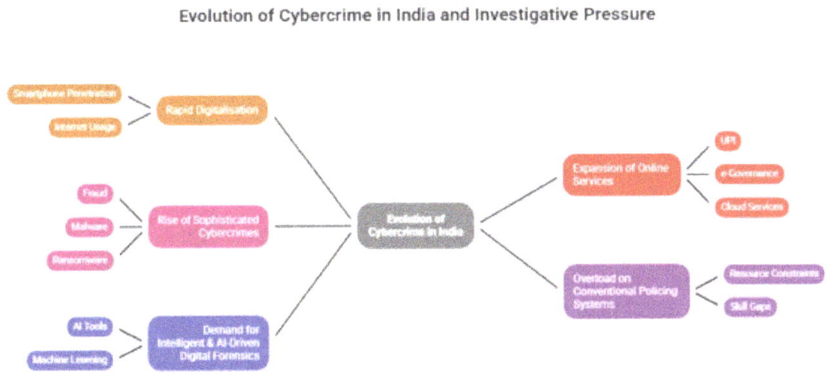

illustrates the progression of cybercrime in India alongside increasing digital dependence, highlighting how investigative pressure on law enforcement has necessitated the adoption of AI-enabled digital forensic approaches

1.2 Shortcomings of Conventional Investigative Methods

In law enforcement, traditional digital forensics is largely manual, tool-oriented, and reliant on the individual cop's experience. The elementary stages of evidence gathering, examination and interpreting the evidence are definitely stages that are time-consuming, such as manual imaging of the evidence, keyword searches, log reviews, and visual evidence review. The methods that law enforcement has employed are the ones that have not changed, and are the ones that are failing, as cybercrime continues to grow in volume and diversity. Cyber police divisions continue to experience significant administrative backlogs, which ultimately result in longer periods to complete investigations and increasing periods of time in which victims are exposed to the consequences of the crime.(Fakhouri et al., 2024).

Traditional investigative strategies face challenges due to their inability to scale. Mobile data, cloud data, social media data, financial records, audio-visual files, and network data are examples of different data types that need to be analysed for contemporary cybercrime investigations. Oversights, or total failures, in analysing a data set, especially larger and more complex data sets, tend to be the result of slower, partially automated analysis techniques. When they are working with incomplete data across different tools, and with a linear method of examining data, investigators are particularly inefficient and more likely to miss correlations among data across different tools and different time periods. (Yin et al., 2025).

1.3 Need for AI-Enhanced Digital Forensics

The human component of the investigative process can explain these challenges. When data sets are particularly complex, investigators tend to get fatigued; they can each define the data set in varying ways, and they may miss data segments because of personal bias. The results of a data set will differ based on the expertise of the individual analysing the data. This individual variability can lower the quality of the digital evidence that is presented in court, and the evidence presented may be inconsistent with the other data segments. Cybercrime techniques are also changing more rapidly than most investigators can adapt. These different factors show how traditional investigative processes need to be improved to combat newer cybercrime techniques. effectively(Toprak, 2009).

The role of artificial intelligence in the digital forensics of cybercrime in India can only grow as the digital forensics of cybercrime in India becomes more advanced and as more highly sophisticated technologies become more widely available.

The forensics of AI Digital forensics in India requires a more sophisticated application. Technologies and AI can assist in digital forensics in a variety of ways—the rapid development of computer technologies and the increased sophistication of technological cybercrime in India. With unmanageable and overwhelming amounts of data being created, more intelligent, automated, and sophisticated systems, such as intelligent systems, are required. Systems should possess the capability to examine data linked to cybercrime, determine unneeded data, and eliminate it.

The integration of AI in the field of cybercrime and its associated technology in India has been positively impacted and propelled further through the integration of AI tools. Given the large spectrum of AI tools and technologies, it is safe to assume that there is an evolution in India's cybercrime digital forensics.(*(PDF) CYBERCRIME IN INDIA: LEGAL FRAMEWORKS, EMERGING THREATS, AND THE ROLE OF AI IN DETECTION AND DEFENCE*, n.d.-b).

2. AI FOUNDATIONS IN DIGITAL FORENSICS

2.1 An Introduction to AI, ML, DL, and NLP.

Artificial Intelligence (AI) is a term that pertains to computer systems that can complete tasks that would necessitate a human's reasoning, learning, and perception. The field of digital forensics is concerned with the automation of processes and the generation of intelligence from large quantities of digital information. By automating complicated processes in digital forensics, AI is streamlining investigative processes. Digital forensics is becoming more automated because of AI.

Forensic investigations benefit from Machine Learning (ML) methods, particularly in the domain of cybercrimes, where the complexity exceeds the rules that can be established. (Manasi Pritam Zirpe et al., 2024).

Figure 2. AI Applications in Digital Forensics

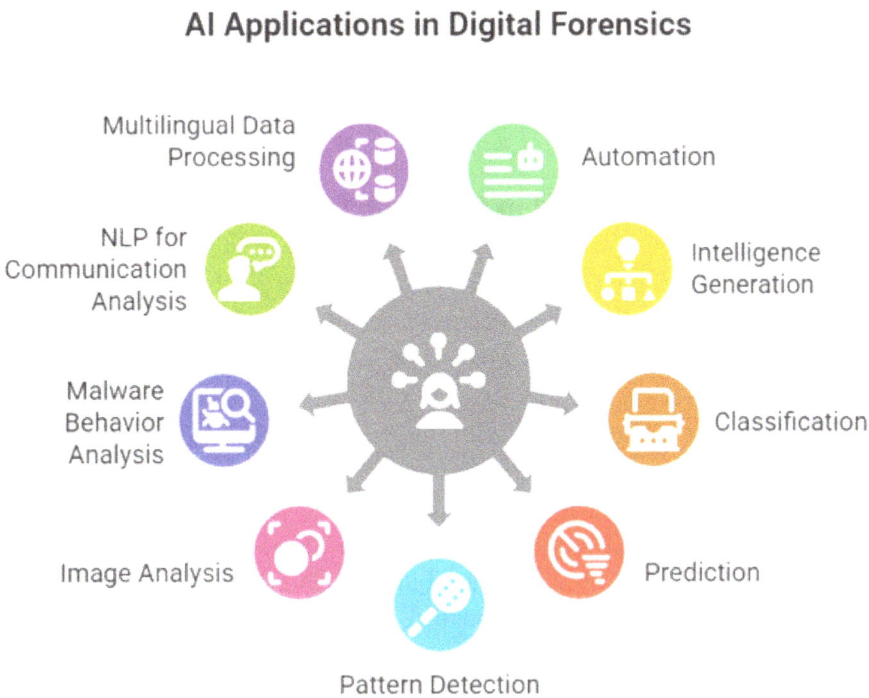

presents the hierarchical foundation of Artificial Intelligence technologies—AI, Machine Learning, Deep Learning, and Natural Language Processing—that collectively support advanced digital forensic investigations.

ML is being supplemented with Deep Learning (DL), which is one branch of ML involving layered neural networks and additional data to discern intricate patterns and associations that less advanced systems cannot capture. In digital forensics, DL is especially pertinent and has the capability to perform tasks such as image and speech recognition as well as behavioural patterning. AI subfield, Natural Language Processing (NLP), can be utilised in the forensics analysis of relevant digital communications, such as emails, chat transcripts, texts, social media, and digital relics. One useful way of classifying AI applications is the distinction between supervised and unsupervised learning. In supervised learning, there are annotated data sets, as in classification tasks, for example, the identification of malware families or the classification of transactions as fraudulent.

On the other hand, unsupervised learning, which operates on unlabelled data, is particularly effective for anomaly detection or the identification of other hidden structures or clusters in large volumes of forensic data. This kind of distinction is particularly relevant for the forensic analysis of the digitally and structurally (logs, databases, transaction records) as well as the unstructured (free text, images, video, audio) evidentiary materials. AI renders a uniform and holistic response to such problems and improves how forensic practitioners undertake examination of evidentiary data streams, which, for other, more conventional digital forensics, would be out of reach.(Bau et al., 2010).

2.2 AI Algorithms Utilised in Forensics

A wide array of AI algorithms has been deployed across the spectrum of digital forensic applications to serve specific purposes at different phases of the digital forensics process. One of the most common is classification algorithms, which help in the sorting of digital artefacts into different categories. These categories include benign and malware files, relevant and irrelevant data, or legitimate and fraudulent transactions. Such techniques are especially important for filtering and prioritising evidence, particularly in the case of large volumes of data following a seizure.(Dunsin et al., 2024).

The absence of any prior information about the underlying data structure provides investigators with the opportunity to analyse the underlying data structure through exploratory forensic analyses using clustering algorithms. Clustering, by grouping artefacts of similar behaviour or statistical features, analyses the structure and potential relationships among entities, which could lead to the detection of potential coordinated actions or previously unknown patterns of criminal behaviour. The analysis of evidence related to cybercrimes, in particular, benefits from anomaly detection methods, as they identify deviations from normal users and from normal system-related actions, which could lead to the abnormal actions that could comprise peripheral threats to a system, internal attacks, or targeted attacks that deviate from the ordinary and thus remain undetected by systems that are structured to identify threats by signature. (Liao & Vemuri, 2002).

Deep neural networks, and neural networks in particular, are foundational to the analysis of patterns in digital forensics, as they serve in the analysis of a diverse set of complex data types, including video, images, and even data from networks such as network traffic. For instance, neural networks can assist in the detection of faces in videos from closed-circuit televisions, the detection of altered or edited multimedia content, or the identification of malware through the tracking of behaviour during malware execution. Likewise, the analysis of evidence that is heavily textual in nature relies more and more on natural language. (Buczak & Guven, 2016)language processing (NLP) technologies. These technologies are used in the automated processing of data that is in multiple languages, and that consists of a large volume of text by employing techniques such as tokenisation, feature generation, and language modelling and semantic analysis, particularly in the Indian context, where forensic evidence is often multilingual, containing several regional languages, dialects, and combinations of languages. (Nayerifard et al., n.d.).

Table 1. Artificial Intelligence Techniques and Their Applications Across Digital Forensic Tasks

AI Technique	Core Function	Digital Forensic Application	Typical Evidence Type
Supervised Machine Learning	Classification	Malware detection, fraud transaction identification	Executables, financial logs
Unsupervised Learning	Clustering & anomaly detection	Identifying suspicious user behaviour, unknown attack patterns	Network logs, access records
Deep Learning (CNN, RNN)	Pattern recognition	Image/video enhancement, malware behaviour modelling	CCTV footage, binaries
Natural Language Processing (NLP)	Semantic and sentiment analysis	Chat analysis, threat detection, hate speech identification	Emails, chats, social media
Graph Analytics	Relationship discovery	Network and entity linkage analysis	OSINT, call records, wallets

Table 1 summarises the major AI techniques employed in digital forensics and maps them to specific investigative functions relevant to cybercrime investigations.

2.3 Advantages Versus Conventional Forensic Approaches

Undoubtedly, the most clear-cut advantages when comparing digital forensics with AI and traditional digital forensics lie in the area of speed, scalability, and consistency/objectivity. AI systems provide these clear advantages when applied to any investigative criminal case, especially ones in which time is of the essence, such as in the case of a felon who is actively committing additional cyber or financial crimes, as a delay can prove harmful. AI systems in digital forensics, in contrast to traditional digital forensics, can be applied to a larger variety of cases. In digital forensics, the data is AI systems can provide faster results and can be applied to a larger variety of cases. The time and human resource investments, which typically could be downsized, do not need to be scaled for data. The additional divisions of human resources create additional divisions of data synthesis and results reporting, traditionally, resource input, which could downsize additional divisions human systems create additional divisions of human resources data synthesis and results reporting.(Sharma, 2025).

Another way in which AI is advantageous is the mitigation of the lack of consistency and the variability of the results in traditional forensics systems. While traditional systems relied on human users and skill sets to create the baselines, AI, through uniform training and validation, improves these metrics for each individual case and for each individual user. For the courts and the legal system, the chain of evidence improves through hybrid systems, and AI improves the more traditional systems through the lack of human intervention. AI replaces the more traditional systems through the lack of human intervention.

Improved evidentiary linkage and insight building are two of AI's biggest advantages. AI can build records of a crime by connecting disparate data points from different data sets, periods, and formats. Beyond predicting future patterns, AI fosters evidentiary insight by discovering relationships that were previously unrecognised and drawing from records. With all the mentioned benefits, AI can be seen more positively than just an enhanced technological tool. For digital forensic investigations, AI represents a radical change. It allows law enforcement to adapt to the shifting landscape of cybercrime. (Yadav, n.d.).

3. AI-FACILITATED FORENSIC WORKFLOWS IN INVESTIGATIVE WORK OF THE POLICE

Table 2. AI-Enabled Digital Forensic Workflow for Police Cybercrime Investigations

Conventional Approach	Forensic Phase	AI-Enhanced Approach	Operational Benefit
Full device imaging	Evidence Acquisition	Intelligent triage & selective capture	Time and storage efficiency
Manual keyword searches	Evidence Examination	Automated relevance scoring	Faster prioritisation
Tool-centric linear analysis	Data Analysis	Multimodal AI correlation	Hidden linkage discovery
Investigator-dependent	Interpretation	Model-assisted insight	Reduced cognitive bias
Manual reconstruction	Reporting	AI-supported timelines & summaries	Court-ready clarity

The integration of AI across the forensic lifecycle transforms traditional investigative workflows, as outlined in Table 2.

3.1 Evidence Acquisition and Triage Automation

From the beginning of AI-enabled workflows in forensics, both the triage and the gathering of evidence occur simultaneously. Digitally collecting evidence in the past was done by taking images of the data from storage devices and mobile phones, and then analysing an absurdly large amount of data. Given the sheer amount of data these devices hold, it is an extremely inefficient and often impractical method. AI-assisted triage tools help eliminate this obstacle by assisting an investigator in making an intelligent assessment of a digital device at the crime scene or in the initial stages of the device's custody.(Zamil & Khan, 2025).

AI problem devices research tools will analyse metadata, device file structures, user behaviour, and other primitive aspects of digital device identification and classification. For instance, communication attempts with a missing file, a blocked communication tool, a possibly logged-in document, a cut-off agent, or some other strangely disorganised data. Such data analysis allows investigators to concentrate more on data that has legal value and spend less on data and information that has no value. In India, mobile crimes are commonplace; analytical evidence helps investigators understand and select data that is problematic in mobile communications, monetary transfers, and related documents that were compromised or tampered with(Barbone et al., 2026).

Figure 3. Ai-Enabled Digital Forensic Workflow

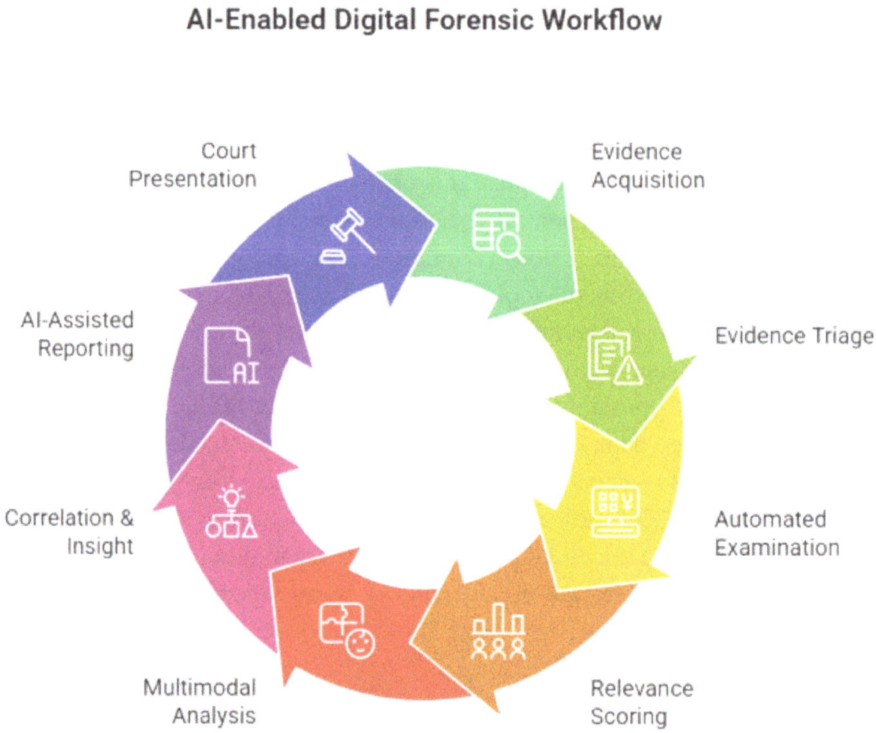

depicts an AI-enabled digital forensic workflow, demonstrating how intelligent automation enhances evidence acquisition, analysis, correlation, and reporting in cybercrime investigations.

Police cyber cells expedite evidence analysis with an evidence hierarchy. Instead of analysing a dataset linearly, AI evaluates evidence on multiple parameters and assigns scores based on relevance, nearness to the incident, and user involvement. This maximises operational effectiveness, enabling quick execution of judicial processes, such as charge sheet construction. Absence of the principles of forensic soundness, AI augmented evidence acquisition still applies, but does improve decision quality based on the principles of custody, chain of custody, and operational judicial parameters of the evidence court competency. (Prasad et al., 2025).

3.2 Analysis of Face, Video, and Image Computer Vision

Visual information relies mostly on different digital means. These digital means include various social media sites, body-worn cameras, and smartphones. Innovations in AI and computer vision have enabled police to obtain transformative digital evidence for visual analysis. One such piece of evidence is CCTV footage analysis. AI can help analysts to remove background noise, enhance resolution, and stabilise various scenes in CCTV footage to help make features like faces, vehicle registration numbers, and other objects more visible. With object recognition and effective face recognition, analysts can quickly find and monitor a large number of suspects in a large video dataset. Instead of reviewing the footage, AI analysts can replace investigators and save them a lot of time. AI analysts can help investigators by identifying and tagging vehicles, faces, objects, and weapons of interest. The value of AI in policing is especially evident in the analysis of large videos of crowded places, public transport, and demonstrations. AI indexing helps investigators to rapidly analyse large datasets in order to value and retrieve a small portion of data. (Alazab et al., 2024a).

Identifying people is just one component of computer vision; it can also be used to analyse crowd behaviour and reconstruct crowd movement. AI systems analyse the spatio-temporal data to reconstruct the trajectories of movements and crowd behaviours in order to determine what happened and in what order. This is particularly useful in the analysis of riots, stampedes, and other synchronised movements, such as people colluding to commit crimes. When combined with temporal and spatial data, computer vision can provide intricate reconstructions of crime scenes. This can be used as corroborating evidence for use in court.(Alazab et al., 2024a).

3.3 Examination of the Text, Chat Logs, and Social Media via Natural Language Processing

The text is one of the primary forms of digital evidence that is collected during a cybercrime investigation. This evidence encompasses emails, instant messages, social media posts, online forum messages, and telephone call transcripts. Since the volume of the data is so overwhelming for a human to analyse, the Natural Language Processing (NLP) method is particularly useful for analysing copious amounts of text. AI systems that employ NLP techniques are able to understand the intent of a speaker and analyse the sentiment of a speaker in the context of a given conversation. This helps the investigators discern the conversations that are plotting a crime as opposed to those that are innocent.(Bokolo & Liu, 2024).

In India, the complexities of multilingualism present unique challenges. Embedded code-mixing in case files can be seen in English, Hindi, Gujarati, and several other Indian languages within the same document and sometimes the same sentence. This requires the creation of advanced NLP models tailored to code-mixing and multilingual datasets. Such systems can identify and mitigate threats and abusive language, online child sexual exploitation, and coordinated hate and disinformation campaigns across disparate socio-technical systems.

Forensic NLP tools assist in the analysis and resolution of challenges like cyberbullying, online harassment, and radicalisation. NLP's assistance in the analysis and resolution of hate speech, coercive speech, and fraud also aids in the implementation and operationalisation of countermeasures, remote victim support, and protective advocacy. NLP aids in analytical thinking by simplifying the investigative process, providing them with a streamlined cognitive load, and producing summaries of large data sets. This increases the analytical accuracy, rigour, and consistency of investigative efforts and draws attention to critical communications.(*(PDF) Better Understanding of Code-Mixed Social Media Data via Information Extraction*, n.d.).

3.4 AI systems that detect malware and analyse the behaviour of systems

Financial crimes, data breaches, and ransomware attacks are the types of cybercrimes that employ the use of malware. Previous approaches to malware analysis and detection relied on recognised signatures. AI has developed behavioural approaches to malware analysis and detection.

AI models can identify certain behavioural patterns, evasion techniques, and similarities with other malware using static analyses, which involve examining, and not executing, malware code. However, static methods tend to struggle with highly obfuscated or polymorphic malware.

Dynamic analysis is the process of examining the behaviours of a piece of malware while it is executing in a safe environment. Artificial intelligence (AI) attempts to understand behavioural models created from system calls, network activity, file changes, and communications between processes. These analyses help an investigator understand the purpose, potential, and scale of the threat that malware poses. Such analysis is especially useful in the case of zero-day exploits, or those that have not previously left a detectable signature. (Jada & Mayayise, 2024).

AI can help attribution efforts beyond simple detection by analysing and correlating behavioural patterns of different malware samples and campaigns. Analyses of these behaviours can identify relationships between otherwise unrelated attacks, which can aid law enforcement in identifying a cyber criminal enterprise. This is particularly beneficial in aid of sophisticated investigations and in offering a definitive technical explanation in court, where it may be difficult to describe malware behaviours in layman's terms.

3.5 Predictive Forensic Intelligence and Threat Anticipation

The use of AI in digital forensics that enables predictive forensic intelligence may be the most cutting-edge example to date. AI is used to assess past criminal activity, incident reports, network logs, and behavioural analysis to identify patterns and emerging threats in cybercrime and to issue alerts.

This provides law enforcement the opportunity for proactive action instead of reactive control.

Knowing potential future threats requires a selection of historical data along a certain time continuum to help build predictive models about patterns, susceptible targets, and time frames, and therefore, reasonable, actionable predictions. AI, for example, may identify and analyse certain seasonal patterns relating to certain types of offence or may predict the likelihood of certain phishing attacks or other forms of collusive offence. This type of intelligence can support operational and strategic business decisions.(*(PDF) The Use of Artificial Intelligence in Digital Forensics and Incident Response (DFIR) in a Constrained Environment*, n.d.).

In the Indian case, the combination of predictive forensic intelligence and policing satisfies the objectives of the preventive theory of policing. The understanding of AI, for the most part, helps the prevention of crime and the improvement of the safety of the public through targeted awareness, proactive surveillance, and the efficient deployment of the means. Predictive systems, however, may provide abuse or unintended consequences in policing and, therefore, need to be framed within the adequate boundaries of governance. The capacity of AI to predict and potentially offensive data sets is the most advanced form of predictive policing and is, within certain boundaries, highly developed and sophisticated, and provides the ability to construct an adaptive, intelligence-based response to cybercrime.(Rajeev et al., n.d.).

4. APPLICATION AREAS FOR LAW ENFORCEMENT IN INDIA

Table 3. Key AI-Driven Digital Forensic Application Areas in Indian Policing

Application Area	AI Capability Used	Investigative Objective	Indian Context Relevance
Mobile & Cloud Forensics	Behaviour modelling, timeline reconstruction	Recover deleted and remote data	Multi-device, cloud-heavy usage
OSINT Intelligence	Entity resolution, network analysis	Criminal network identification	Social media–centric crimes
Financial Cybercrime	Transaction anomaly detection	Fraud and mule account tracing	UPI and digital payment dominance
Synthetic Media Forensics	Deepfake detection models	Evidence authentication	Political & social misuse
Online Abuse Investigation	NLP-based sentiment & intent analysis	Victim protection & attribution	Multilingual digital abuse

Table 3 outlines major application domains where AI-driven digital forensics is actively strengthening cybercrime investigation capabilities in India.

4.1 Mobile and Cloud Forensics

With the rise of smartphones in India, there is now an increasing reliance on mobile devices for investigations related to cyber crimes. Financial fraud, online harassment, and organised crimes are some examples where smartphones are used as repositories of communication, transactions, multimedia files, and data related to various applications. For mobile forensics, user behaviour and timelines of events can be reconstructed. Investigators are assisted by tools that apply artificial intelligence, as they can examine applications and recognise peculiar usage to identify evidence that is of greater importance, such as deleted conversations, concealed media, or suspicious activity on apps.

More challenges are added by cloud forensics. Users now store data on social media, cloud services, and outside third-party vendors and service providers, causing data to be outside of national borders. These factors contribute to challenges that are legal, procedural, and related to data access, preservation, and the creating of admissibility. AI is used in cloud forensics by using automation to identify data correlations that exist across devices and cloud storage, helping investigators build timelines that are comprehensive and contain both local and remote data.

In India, where cases often involve many devices, accounts, and platforms, AI-assisted timeline reconstruction is useful. AI timelines reduce manual work and improve the presentation of evidence. AI timelines improve evidence presentation in court by reducing the manual work involved in reconstructions.(*Cyber Crime Cases: Issues, Challenges & Solutions Reading Material*, 2025).

4.2 OSINT and AI-Driven Intelligence Gathering

Social media, forums, and messaging applications provide channels for users to engage in unlawful activities. Law enforcement, especially in the prosecution of cybercrimes, has found value in using OSINT. With the aid of AI, OSINT offers the ability to gather, process, and analyse massive quantities of publicly available information to create cohesive and valuable silos of intelligence. A growing and valuable feature of social media networks is the ability for machine learning to analyse networks and identify dangerous users, social media users, and other types of violence.

OSINT has focused applications in monitoring the dark web. Cybercriminals utilise the dark web to buy and sell stolen and proprietary information, malware, and other illicit services. AI systems assist investigators by scanning dark web marketplaces, classifying materials, and analysing them for patterns associated with threats. This type of intelligence collection is critical for understanding and combating cybercrime.

The automation of entity and network mapping has great potential for expanding OSINT capabilities. Algorithms can process and relate social media profiles, email accounts, crypto wallets, and social connections across multiple social media platforms. This tool for intelligence-led policing aids Indian law enforcement agencies in the identification of early-stage cybercriminals, their organised structures, and operational networks.(Szymoniak & Foks, 2024).

4.3 The Examination of Financial Fraud and Cryptocurrencies

Financial cybercrime in India comprises UPI fraud, phishing attacks, fake customer support frauds, mule account fraud networks, and a multitude of other diverse frauds, which are growing with the myriad financial services available. The rapid and widespread adoption of digital payment systems has not only eased payment transactions but has also increased the speed and volume of fraudulent transactions. Although fraud is quick and prevalent, fraudulent transactions are detectable, and the tracing of fraudulent payments can be done with the appropriate use of Artificial Intelligence (AI) and Machine Learning (ML).

AI/ML can be trained to detect and learn certain patterns of behaviour for rapid fraudulent transactions, such as exceedingly large sums of payments, strange patterns of payment cycles (e.g., bursts of payments for a short period of time), or batches of rapid transactions for the same amount across multiple accounts. This ability improves the tracking of payment flows and the identification of mule accounts. Within the scope of cryptocurrencies and blockchain technology, Artificial Intelligence that analyses blockchains improves the ability to de-anonymise transactions by clustering wallet addresses and combining on-chain with off-chain data.

These capabilities are important for law enforcement to intervene and recover assets quickly. AI can help with more detailed fraud investigations because financial data can be cross-referenced with telecommunication data and other records derived from Open Source Intelligence (OSINT). This effort resulted in an increased success rate for prosecution and conviction, as well as a reduction in repeat offences for cybercrime and financially motivated crime.(*(PDF) AI-Powered Fraud Detection in Digital Payment Systems: Leveraging Machine Learning for Real-Time Risk Assessment*, n.d.).

4.4. The Detection of Deep Fakes and the Forensics of Synthetic Media

The other problem for enforcement is the omnipresence of new, AI-generated products in the more complex and evolving market in India. More and more, AI-generated media, including deep-fakes, is being used for political misinformation, as well as extortion and harassment. The hyper-realism of such media products makes traditional media forensics not only near-impossible but raises other concerns, including the credibility of the evidence.

In order to detect deep-fakes and other AI-generated media, one technique analyses the media for signs of inconsistency, such as odd movements, lighting, or other sounds. If trained properly, AI can detect such inconsistencies and analyse the media, even if the alterations are minuscule. The verification of synthetic audio and video recordings is essential for the protection of the potential victims of such recordings, as well as to prevent false accusations and other forms of manipulative coercion.

There are also legal issues created by the forensics of deepfakes, which are complicated. Courts face digital evidence that needs to be authenticated. The most rational way to approach this problem is through AI. AI can provide evidence that is more certain than other evidence and may even provide a rationale for its evidence. This may elevate the value of digital evidence in court and aid experts in testifying with greater clarity and credibility.(Amerini et al., 2024).

4.5 Cases of Online Abuse, Harassment, and Cyber Bullying

In India, online hate speech, cyberbullying, and tech-facilitated violence and abuse are disproportionate to other violence and include women, children, and other vulnerable groups. There is evidence of repeated abuse across different and multiple social media platforms, and the legal evidentiary frameworks do not cover these social media platforms to enable the capturing of evidence. Forensic AI will help legal professionals combine disparate evidence from social media, messaging, and other online platforms.

A clear victim-focus is one of the positive aspects of the AI-driven methods. The Natural Language Processing (NLP) algorithms detect abusive, threatening, and coercive language, and the analyses loss of time and other Opportunity Costs to reconstruct timelines. This provides the totality of the evidence, which will facilitate legal action, and abuse may be adequately described in the evidence. AI fosters swifter victim assistance by minimising delays in investigations. The automation of evidence processing leads to faster offender detection and supports prompt actions such as takedowns and restraining orders. With greater efficiency and sensitivity, these facets of AI digital forensics strengthen the response of law enforcement to online abuse while respecting the rights and dignity of victims.(Alazab et al., 2024b).

5. CASE STUDIES AND REAL-WORLD EXAMPLES

5.1 AI Tools Emerging in Global Police Forces

As the complexity and scale of cyber crimes increase, police all over the world are adopting AI technology in digital forensics and investigations. Best practice guidelines globally recommend machine learning for automating the triage of digital evidence, computer vision for the analysis of large-scale CCTV, and predictive analytics for pattern recognition in crime. Some law enforcement agencies in some parts of the world use AI to review digital evidence from confiscated digital devices, prioritise relevant digital evidence, and cross-reference digital evidence with emails, logs, digital evidence, and Internet usage. This practice improves the quality of evidence and reduces investigation time.

More and more agencies are applying AI to the analysis of open source intelligence and identifying networks of organised crime, as well as predicting cyber threats. In the analysis of behavioural patterns and monitoring of transactions to fight against malware and financial crime, AI has helped in the identification of networks of fraud and transnational cybercrime, which manual processes could not detect.

For India, the main global practices takeaway should not lie in the adoption of new technologies, but in the successful integration of new technologies. Successful implementations have illustrated the capture of legal frameworks, ongoing assessment, and the importance of explainable and transparent AI. Legal explainability will require institutions to have a good allocation of competencies, infrastructure, governance, and readiness. This assists the framework within which the employing of AI in the policing ecosystem in India will be designed.(*(PDF) AI-BASED FORENSIC ANALYSIS OF DIGITAL IMAGES: TECHNIQUES AND APPLICATIONS IN CYBERSECURITY*, n.d.).

5.2 India-Specific Scenarios and Practical Challenges

The use of AI in digital forensics in India is developing amidst a complex and varied law enforcement ecosystem. There is a three-tiered structure of cybercrime cells at the district and state levels, as well as specialised State Police units and Central Agencies, each of whom have different levels of technological proficiency in the investigation of cybercrime. While the metropolitan areas may have higher levels of technology, personnel training, and higher levels of technology, resource, and personnel shortages across levels of skilled investigators, forensics, and analysis are present in a significant number of districts.

Resource limitations are still one of the most challenging hurdles to adopting AI-enabled forensic solutions. AI Forensic solutions have been proven to assist with budget limitations, heavy workloads, and reliance on outdated systems. Added to this, differences in regions, web access, and digital skills impact the equal use of advanced technologies. Investigators often have to wait for outsourced services. The use of external experts or centralised services creates lags, and coordination may be lost.

The intertwining of legal, digital, and socio-cultural complexities largely determines the uniqueness of the Indian context. The Indian context combines digital, legal, and socio-cultural challenges. The Indian context is, therefore, a strong example of how complex a field AI is. The Indian case illustrates intricacy in the field of AI. The Indian case illustrates how complex the AI field is. The regional heterogeneity further adds to the complexity of the training and validation of AI models. Evidence of this is the failure of international models of AI in India. The diverse cultural backgrounds and languages of the region are the key components to the difficulty in the training and validation of AI models. These challenges lend valuable lessons about the need for context-based aspects in the design of international models being adopted for AI. (Sood et al., 2024).

5.3 Lessons Learned from AI-Assisted Investigations

Investigations involving AI around the world, especially in India, have shown us what to do and what not to do. AI models should switch from being autonomous systems to being decision support systems. In investigations, AI is most effective when processing information, while human investigators exercise legal, judgmental, and interpretive reasoning. This way, the system is designed for accountability and also for improving efficiency.

In AI-system use, the challenges that an AI system lacks control and benchmarks are evident, and the use of AI systems is the same. An example of the system's difficulty is in the law, and it breeds bias, misunderstanding, unsupported evidence, and so on. The best systems put emphasis on the most operational, explainable, auditable, and customizable systems at the time. Similarly, in systems with AI, investigators need to be trained in what to do and what not to do with the system.

The concepts of governance and oversight come into play. Responsible AI in policing means steering the purpose of AI in policing, the AI in policing standard operating procedures, and the AI in policing ethical frameworks. Responsible AI in policing encompasses all the purposes of governance, as it looks to maintain public confidence, protect fundamental rights, and balance the pace of technological advancement with the normative order of rights and laws. The above lessons indicate that, in the realm of digital forensics, it is not the level of sophistication of the AI technologies that matters; it is the level of thought, clarity, and governance accompanying the use of the technologies.(Miedema et al., 2026).

6. CHALLENGES IN IMPLEMENTING AI FOR DIGITAL FORENSICS

6.1 Skill Gaps and Capacity Limitations

One of the biggest obstacles when applying AI to digital forensic science is the integration of policing and forensic science, coupled with sophisticated AI technology. Digital forensic investigators can be proficient in handling evidence with the related legal and investigative context. However, the digital forensic investigation using AI is in need of advanced skill integration, such as in the realms of data analytics, machine learning, and systems thinking. The absence of such training frameworks in AI-forensics diminishes the optimal use of sophisticated digital forensic tools and mechanisms in law enforcement agencies, particularly when in need of advanced digital forensic tools.

The situation is made particularly worse by the variation in levels of development around the different regions of India, particularly when comparing the urban and rural divide. The more advanced police departments in the metropolitan areas, along with the specialised cyber units, tend to be more developed systems, have greater access to external consultants, and have more advanced training systems. Rural and semi-urban areas, on the other hand, tend to have low levels of system and technological advancement. This unequal distribution of advanced technology severely limits the investigative systems and tools within the boundaries of different regions and subsequently limits the effectiveness of the justice system.

The lack of time and resource investment is a crucial barrier to the implementation of AI and the development of new tools. Continuity of skill development is crucial. AI tools need to be continually improved. Otherwise, they will be misapplied or become disused, severely undermining their purpose.(Bajpai & Panda, 2024).

6.2 Ethical, Legal, and Privacy Issues

The use of AI technologies in digital forensics raises important ethical questions, especially in regard to surveillance and the possible infringement of rights. Although the surveillance of large data sets is beneficial to AI technologies in digital forensics, it is important to exercise caution to avoid breaches of civil liberties and unregulated monitoring. Maintaining a balance of power in the use of AI for digital forensic investigations is essential in order to maintain public trust.

There are additional problems related to consent and the protection of personal data. Digital investigation files contain sensitive data about victims, offenders, and other relevant parties. If there are no protective measures available, the application of AI for automated data processing is even more likely to collect more data and increase the risk of data being abused. Ignoring data protection requirements and the expectations from the courts continues to become more unreasonable in relation to the use of AI.

Another consideration is the evidentiary value of AI in court. Digital information/evidence generated or analysed using Artificial Intelligence (AI) tools must be reliable, transparent, and reproducible. The defence can dispute the validity of the outputs generated by the algorithm, especially when the underlying model is not available. During the proceedings, the police must be able to explain the scientific basis, reasoning, and proof of AI-generated evidence. (Rodrigues, 2020).

6.3. The Requirements for Infrastructure and Technical Tools.

Technical and infrastructural challenges can complicate the extent to which AI-driven forensic tools can be used. Most law enforcement agencies use outdated technology that cannot support advanced analytics or the processing of large data sets. Incompatible forensic tools, databases, and various cross-platforms contribute to the challenges of using AI to its full potential.

One more issue of concern relates to the quality of data sets. For AI systems to perform optimally, the data must be of high quality, well-structured, and representative. Models may suffer accuracy issues due to incomplete records, and their reliability may suffer when records are poorly structured. Available computational and data storage infrastructures pose challenges to the more advanced technologies and standardised systems, especially for organisations with limited resources. Modernisation, which often incurs high costs, is required to apply more advanced technologies and more standardised systems.(Anand & Thakur, 2025).

6.4 Potential Dangers of AI Bias and Misinterpretation

The biases or limitations of an AI system (including assumptions and specific datasets used during the training of AI systems) can also impact the AI systems. The way predictive policing biases and misinterpretation work can target the same individuals. Bias and misinterpretation occur due to a lack of data or a system designed to learn from and filter out specific historical or structural datasets.

Developers and users alike have pointed to the tendency of over-reliance on AI to provide answers that rely solely on the processed and compiled data. Confidence in AI systems is a huge factor, and at a drastic scale, the misinterpretation of predictive police systems can have catastrophic consequences. AI systems can provide benefits to police and the systems around them. The value of AI is in its systems directed to improve policing. AI systems that remove bias or predict the systems to improve for equitable policing are advanced. Moreover, AI systems that provide equitable decision-making within a system and remove bias are advanced systems for policing.(Murikah et al., 2024).

Table 4. Challenges in Implementing AI-Based Digital Forensics in India and Recommended Mitigation Measures

Challenge Category	Identified Issue	Impact on Investigation	Recommended Mitigation
Skills & Training	Lack of AI literacy	Underutilisation of tools	Structured AI-forensics training
Infrastructure	Legacy systems	Limited analytical capacity	Cloud-enabled forensic labs
Legal & Ethics	Explainability concerns	Court admissibility issues	Auditable & transparent AI
Bias & Fairness	Skewed datasets	Discriminatory outcomes	Contextual dataset validation
Governance	Lack of SOPs	Inconsistent practices	National AI forensic standards

The principal challenges associated with AI adoption in digital forensics and corresponding mitigation strategies are summarised in Table 4.

7. REFORM PATHWAYS AND POLICY RECOMMENDATIONS

7.1. Integration of Artificial Intelligence into Policing: Areas of Improvement

In order for AI to be integrated into India's policing and digital forensics employed, a more structured and phased approach is necessary. The integration of AI into policing is also better suited for a phased approach over a short period of time, as opposed to extensive and rapid integration. Specialised cyber units should be equipped to assess the potential benefits, operational, and legal concerns of the new technologies being employed in a confined environment. This will be critical for informing subsequent initiatives of a broader scope at the state and district levels.

The integration of artificial intelligence into policing must also establish the requisite governance and accountability frameworks to guide the structures. The role of AI in a policing framework is to pseudonymize some data sets and to provide automation for processes and data-driven decisions. Legal, ethical, and operational boundaries must be integrated through the collaboration of disparate disciplines: legal and forensic sciences, technology, law enforcement, and police command.

To establish accountability and foster trust within the community, the frameworks used, the AI systems employed, and the evaluations documented from an outcomes-based perspective must be transparent.

AI systems should never be construed as systems for making any determinations. AI should only be viewed as a system to assist human decisions. Investigations with legal claims and evidence should always be human-centric. This is a novel principle, leaving the most critical part to be human, and it is a principle that honours the very tenets of the Constitution.(Pei, 2025).

7.2 Developing Capacity and Providing Training

In order for AI to be incorporated into digital forensics in a manner that is effective and sustainable, the development of capacity is essential. Training in AI and digital forensics should be integrated into basic and advanced training curricula in law enforcement training institutions. These curricula should include fundamentals of data analytics, machine learning, AI outputs, the law and algorithms as evidence, and other relevant areas. Real case-based training can be used to instruct investigators on the use of AI technologies.

Aside from training, the rapid advancement of technology and the quickly evolving nature of cybercrime require that additional learning be undertaken. Gaps in knowledge can be filled through refresher training, certification programs, and workshops. Improvements in technical skills and competencies can be facilitated through collaboration with educational and research institutions.

The creation of new positions in law enforcement agencies, such as AI-forensics analysts and digital intelligence officers, is equally critical. The institutionalisation of such roles, along with clearly defined career trajectories, could improve retention and bolster the agency's memory. If new positions remain unfilled, the most advanced AI systems will have little appreciable effect on operational improvements. (Guia et al., 2025).

7.3 Evidence Management Standardisation

Standardisation produces the reliability, admissibility, and reproducibility of digitally rendered, AI-supported evidence. The AI-assisted chain of custody, including acquisition, analysis, storage, and evidence presentation in court, should be governed by a set of standard operating procedures. These procedures should ensure that at each step of the forensics process, the AI's actions are documented, verified, and validated.

Normalisation of auditability is an improvement that can be made to aid in the acceptance of the judiciary. There should be logs of data input, data analysis, model version, and output instructions for AI systems used in the investigations. This is to ensure that these logs and supplementary info can be analysed and authenticated by forensics and members of the judiciary. Furthermore, the results of the investigation are reproducible. This can be done by having different individuals conduct the same investigation under the same conditions. With the same conditions, investigators are more likely to obtain and replicate the evidence in the different jurisdictions and investigative teams.(*Indian Journal of Integrated Research in Law AI-GENERATED EVIDENCE IN INDIAN COURTS: ADMISSIBILITY, RELIABILITY AND THE CHAIN OF CUSTODY CHALLENGE*, n.d.).

7.4 Partnerships Between the Public and Private Sectors for the Advancement of AI

Combining the private and public sectors can be effective in the advancement of AI for digital forensics. Partnerships can be made with academic institutions, research and development organisations, and technology companies to aid in the development, refinement, and modification of tools for digital forensics. Public law enforcement agencies may obtain more sophisticated and advanced technology, while such partnerships may be more responsive to the unique legal, linguistic, and operational needs of India.

To enhance native data ownership and lessen reliance on foreign proprietary tools, the development of local tools should be prioritised. India should create more innovation.

Figure 4. Roadmap for Ai-Based Digital Forensics in India

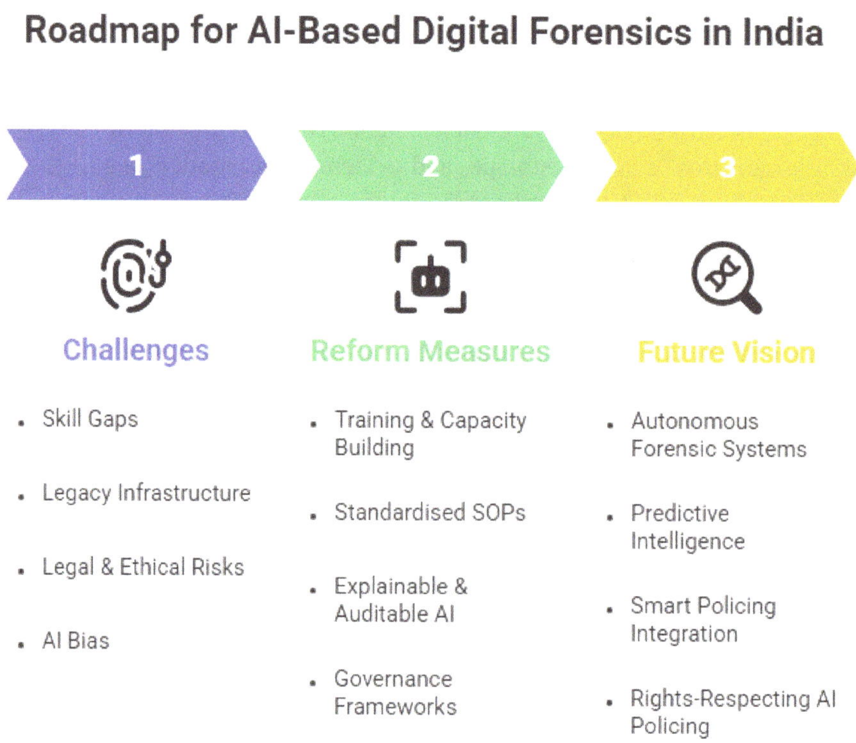

outlines a strategic roadmap linking existing challenges in AI-based digital forensics with reform measures and future-oriented policing visions in the Indian context.

8. FUTURE DIRECTIONS

8.1 Autonomous Forensic Systems

ecosystems with police agencies, academic institutions, and private sector organisations to design more contextual, safe, and sustainable AI solutions for digital forensics.

Fully autonomous forensic systems implementing advanced analytical capabilities are among the most promising prospects in digital forensics. Such systems would require minimal or no human involvement. For example, fully autonomous systems could employ various machine learning approaches to improve their effectiveness as new data, crime patterns, and investigative outcomes are made available. Given their adaptable design, autonomous systems will most likely outperform traditional, rigid, and rule-based systems when combating emerging and dynamic cybercrime.

Systems of self-learning digital forensics will be capable of automating complete work processes, from evidence triage and artefact classification to behavioural pattern analysis and preliminary reporting. By freeing systems of thinking from analytical tasks, data-intensive, and repetitive tasks, they will be able to shift the role of the investigator to that of an analyst. This is especially pertinent to high-volume environments where cybercrime is prevalent, and there are backlogs in investigations.

The more we increase the level of autonomy, the more the supervision of such systems will be of human origin. This means that in order to ensure legal compliance, ethics, and oversight, fully autonomous systems will need to rely on audit and control systems that are designed to be transparent and explainable.(*(PDF) The Future of Artificial Intelligence in Forensics: Advancements, Challenges, and Ethical Considerations*, n.d.).

8.2 AI for Crime Forecasting and Decision Support

The forecasting of crimes using Artificial Intelligence (AI) is an essential area of innovation within the field of digital forensics, as it enables the transition of digital forensics from a reactive area to an area of proactive strategy. AI models, which learn from historical crime data along with forensic records and various social-technical indicator data sets, provide actionable insights for anticipating and forecasting potential crimes and their related threats. With the help of AI, law enforcement agencies may deploy and/or implement crime control strategies to prevent the occurrence/service of cyber crimes before they reach a certain level of critical mass.

AI decision support systems may assist law enforcement executive officers, also called chiefs, policymakers, and resource strategists, with community police executives, operational resource planners, and/or operational resource strategists helps cybercrime optimizing o—operational planners. AI decision support systems may assist law enforcement executive officers, also called chiefs, policymakers, and resource strategists, with community police executives, operational resource planners, and/or operational resource strategists helps cybercrime optimizing o. operational planners. AI's operational planners. AI's AI may assist law enforcement executive officers, also called chiefs, policymakers, and resource strategists, with community police executives, operational resource planners, and/or operational resource strategists helps cybercrime optimizing o—operational planners. AI may assist law enforcement executive officers, also called chiefs, policymakers, and resource strategists, with community police executives, operational resource planners, and/or operational resource strategists helps cybercrime optimizing o. operational planners. AI's operational planners.

In the realm of policymaking, AI also generates insights that can improve evidence-based policymaking; as a result of identifying various systemic weaknesses, gaps, and longer periods of time. An adaptive approach to policymaking, integrating forensic intelligence within the decision-making process, strengthens institutional resilience. (*(PDF) Artificial Intelligence and Crime Detection: A Critical Review*, n.d.).

8.3 Integration with Smart Policing Architectures

AI-driven digital forensics combined with smart policing architectures is a key future path for Indian law enforcement. Smart policing is reliant on a web of connected systems that combine data from surveillance systems, communication systems, emergency response systems, and intelligence systems. Smart systems that integrate forensic AI can provide rapid data exchange and orchestrated response systems across law enforcement agencies.

AI command and control systems that are fused with other technologies can provide situational awareness and actionable intelligence when cyber incidents occur. Increased inter-agency data fusion creates greater collaboration for peripheral police (local), state, and central police units by facilitating the seamless exchange of digital forensics and threat intelligence. This collaboration is more cohesive and less fragmented.

For the successful integration of systems, law enforcement agencies need to create systems of governance that include frameworks for standards and interoperability. Smart policing will provide the greatest benefit by continuously monitoring and legally balancing the selection of parameters of secure data transfer, role-based access, and accountability with the privacy of individuals' data.(Fontes et al., 2022).

9. CONCLUSION

9.1 Summary of Insights and Vision for AI-Based Investigative Transformation

The chapter demonstrated how rapid technological advancement of cybercrime in India has revealed the inadequacies of current investigations and the need for digital forensic approaches. Here in this chapter have demonstrated how AI is more than a new technology—we can think of AI as a groundbreaking way to re-imagine how digital evidence is collected, processed, and understood in relation to the legal systems and/or policing structures. Leveraging AI within digital forensics allows law enforcement to effectively address the magnitude, rapidity, and intricacy of contemporary cybercrime in a way that other manual and tool-centred approaches simply cannot.

The chapter also contextualised all of the instances of how AI is viewed as enhancing law enforcement and how it transcends each of the stages of the forensic process: from evidence collection to automated evidence acquisition and intelligent case triage, to advanced analytics, AI analysis modules over text, audio, and video, AI analysis over transactional data, and AI analysis over malicious software (malware) behavioural analysis. These capabilities facilitate the transition of law enforcement from simply reactive case management to proactive, intelligence-led policing. AI fosters consistency and scalability, assisting investigators to gain new insights into evidence and, in the process, reducing the risk of human bias and the exhaustion that often accompanies analysis.

Ethical and legal issues and frameworks should guide the use of AI in digital forensics. The right to privacy and the potential for biased algorithms and a lack of transparency in AI technologies are issues that must be taken seriously. Robust oversight, validated procedures, and frameworks for AI system monitoring must be developed and implemented. Technology should be an aid, and not an authority.

The chapter provides a vision for India's cybercrime investigation system that is integrated, flexible and resilient. The vision includes incremental AI integration, continuous training, standardisation of evidence collection and innovation through PPPs. India can realise the potential of AI in digital forensics by regulating the integration of technology with institutional preparedness and constitutional principles. Such an approach will bolster India's digital trust, public safety, and the efficacy and legitimacy of the criminal justice system against cybercrime.

REFERENCES

Alazab, M., Ouda, A., George Bokolo, B., & Liu, Q. (2024a). Artificial Intelligence in Social Media Forensics: A Comprehensive Survey and Analysis. *Electronics 2024, Vol. 13, Page 1671, 13*(9), 1671. DOI: 10.3390/electronics13091671

Alazab, M., Ouda, A., George Bokolo, B., & Liu, Q. (2024b). Artificial Intelligence in Social Media Forensics: A Comprehensive Survey and Analysis. *Electronics 2024, Vol. 13, Page 1671, 13*(9), 1671. DOI: 10.3390/electronics13091671

Amerini, I., Barni, M., Battiato, S., Bestagini, P., Boato, G., Bonaventura, T. S., Bruni, V., Caldelli, R., De Natale, F., De Nicola, R., Guarnera, L., Mandelli, S., Marcialis, G. L., Micheletto, M., Montibeller, A., Orru', G., Ortis, A., Perazzo, P., Puglisi, G., … Vitulano, D. (2024). *Deepfake Media Forensics: State of the Art and Challenges Ahead.* 33–48. DOI: 10.1007/978-3-031-85386-9_3

Anand, K. S., & Thakur, D. S. (2025). Challenges and Limitations of AI in Forensic Science: A Critical Review. *International Journal of Research Publication and Reviews*, *6*(6), 5621–5632. DOI: 10.55248/gengpi.6.0125.0672

Bajpai, N., & Panda, V. (2024). INTERNATIONAL JOURNAL OF LEGAL SCIENCE AND INNOVATION Role of Artificial Intelligence in the Detection of Crime & Administration of Justice. *International Journal of Legal Science and Innovation*, *6*. Advance online publication. DOI: 10.10000/IJLSI.111872

Barbone, A., Bicocchi, N., Martinelli, M., Morandi, R., & Picone, M. (2026). On-device AI and digital twins: A synergistic approach to intelligent cyber-physical systems. *Future Generation Computer Systems*, *175*, 108068. DOI: 10.1016/j.future.2025.108068

Bau, J., Bursztein, E., Gupta, D., & Mitchell, J. (2010). State of the art: Automated black-box web application vulnerability testing. *Proceedings - IEEE Symposium on Security and Privacy*, 332–345. DOI: 10.1109/SP.2010.27

Bokolo, B. G., & Liu, Q. (2024). Artificial Intelligence in Social Media Forensics: A Comprehensive Survey and Analysis. *Electronics (Basel)*, *13*(9), 1671. Advance online publication. DOI: 10.3390/electronics13091671

Buczak, A. L., & Guven, E. (2016). A Survey of Data Mining and Machine Learning Methods for Cyber Security Intrusion Detection. *IEEE Communications Surveys and Tutorials*, *18*(2), 1153–1176. DOI: 10.1109/COMST.2015.2494502

Cyber Crime Cases: Issues, Challenges & Solutions Reading Material. (2025). www.jajharkhand.in

Dunsin, D., Ghanem, M. C., Ouazzane, K., & Vassilev, V. (2024). A comprehensive analysis of the role of artificial intelligence and machine learning in modern digital forensics and incident response. *Forensic Science International Digital Investigation*, *48*, 301675. DOI: 10.1016/j.fsidi.2023.301675

Fakhouri, H. N., Alsharaiah, M. A., Al Hwaitat, A. K., Alkalaileh, M., & Dweikat, F. F. (2024). Overview of Challenges Faced by Digital Forensic. *2nd International Conference on Cyber Resilience, ICCR 2024*. DOI: 10.1109/ICCR61006.2024.10532850

Fontes, C., Hohma, E., Corrigan, C. C., & Lütge, C. (2022). AI-powered public surveillance systems: Why we (might) need them and how we want them. *Technology in Society*, *71*, 102137. DOI: 10.1016/j.techsoc.2022.102137

Guia, M. J., Mihai, I.-C., & Kordaczuk-Was, M. (2025). Artificial Intelligence Innovations in Law Enforcement Training: CEPOL Strategy 23-27. *Belügyi Szemle*, *73*(9), 1897–1912. DOI: 10.38146/bsz-ajia.2025.v73.i9.pp1897-1912

Indian Journal of Integrated Research in Law AI-GENERATED EVIDENCE IN INDIAN COURTS: ADMISSIBILITY, RELIABILITY AND THE CHAIN OF CUSTODY CHALLENGE. (n.d.).

Jada, I., & Mayayise, T. O. (2024). The impact of artificial intelligence on organisational cyber security: An outcome of a systematic literature review. *Data and Information Management*, *8*(2), 100063. DOI: 10.1016/j.dim.2023.100063

Liao, Y., & Vemuri, V. R. (2002). Use of the K-Nearest Neighbor classifier for intrusion detection. *Computers & Security*, *21*(5), 439–448. DOI: 10.1016/S0167-4048(02)00514-X

Miedema, E., Waschull, S., & Emmanouilidis, C. (2026). Towards trustworthy artificial intelligence for decision-making: A lifecycle perspective on knowledge- and data-driven artificial intelligence systems. *Computers in Industry*, *174*, 104409. DOI: 10.1016/j.compind.2025.104409

Murikah, W., Nthenge, J. K., & Musyoka, F. M. (2024). Bias and ethics of AI systems applied in auditing - A systematic review. *Scientific African*, *25*, e02281. DOI: 10.1016/j.sciaf.2024.e02281

Nayerifard, T., Amintoosi, H., Ghaemi Bafghi, A., & Dehghantanha, A. (n.d.). *Machine Learning in Digital Forensics: A Systematic Literature Review. (PDF) AI-BASED FORENSIC ANALYSIS OF DIGITAL IMAGES: TECHNIQUES AND APPLICATIONS IN CYBERSECURITY.* (n.d.). Retrieved January 23, 2026, from https://www.researchgate.net/publication/389279515_AI-BASED_FORENSIC_ANALYSIS_OF_DIGITAL_IMAGES_TECHNIQUES_AND_APPLICATIONS_IN_CYBERSECURITY

(PDF) AI-Powered Fraud Detection in Digital Payment Systems: Leveraging Machine Learning for Real-Time Risk Assessment. (n.d.). Retrieved January 23, 2026, from https://www.researchgate.net/publication/388675296_AI-Powered_Fraud_Detection_in_Digital_Payment_Systems_Leveraging_Machine_Learning_for_Real-Time_Risk_Assessment

(PDF) Artificial Intelligence and Crime Detection: A Critical Review. (n.d.). Retrieved January 23, 2026, from https://www.researchgate.net/publication/395788481_Artificial_Intelligence_and_Crime_Detection_A_Critical_Review

(PDF) Better Understanding of Code-Mixed Social Media Data via Information Extraction. (n.d.). Retrieved January 22, 2026, from https://www.researchgate.net/publication/377336560_Better_Understanding_of_Code-Mixed_Social_Media_Data_via_Information_Extraction

(PDF) CYBERCRIME IN INDIA: LEGAL FRAMEWORKS, EMERGING THREATS, AND THE ROLE OF AI IN DETECTION AND DEFENCE. (n.d.-a). Retrieved January 22, 2026, from https://www.researchgate.net/publication/392367232_CYBERCRIME_IN_INDIA_LEGAL_FRAMEWORKS_EMERGING_THREATS_AND_THE_ROLE_OF_AI_IN_DETECTION_AND_DEFENCE?utm_source=chatgpt.com

(PDF) CYBERCRIME IN INDIA: LEGAL FRAMEWORKS, EMERGING THREATS, AND THE ROLE OF AI IN DETECTION AND DEFENCE. (n.d.-b). Retrieved January 22, 2026, from https://www.researchgate.net/publication/392367232_CYBERCRIME_IN_INDIA_LEGAL_FRAMEWORKS_EMERGING_THREATS_AND_THE_ROLE_OF_AI_IN_DETECTION_AND_DEFENCE

(PDF) The Future of Artificial Intelligence in Forensics: Advancements, Challenges, and Ethical Considerations. (n.d.). Retrieved January 23, 2026, from https://www.researchgate.net/publication/390976605_The_Future_of_Artificial_Intelligence_in_Forensics_Advancements_Challenges_and_Ethical_Considerations

(PDF) The Use of Artificial Intelligence in Digital Forensics and Incident Response (DFIR) in a Constrained Environment. (n.d.). Retrieved January 23, 2026, from https://www.researchgate.net/publication/361241108_The_Use_of_Artificial_Intelligence_in_Digital_Forensics_and_Incident_Response_DFIR_in_a_Constrained_Environment

Pei, Y. (2025). The Integration of Artificial Intelligence into Smart Policing Systems: Applications and Risk Governance. *Advances in Management and Intelligent Technologies*, *1*(4). Advance online publication. DOI: 10.62177/amit.v1i4.486

Prasad, N., Diro, A., Warren, M., & Fernando, M. (2025). A survey of cyber threat attribution: Challenges, techniques, and future directions. *Computers & Security*, *157*, 104606. DOI: 10.1016/j.cose.2025.104606

Raj, Y., & Nagpal, K. (2025). *Cybercrime, Data Breaches & Cybersecurity In India.* www.tijer.org

Rajeev, S., Sharma, K., Dg, I., Ravi, S., Lokku, J., & Adg, I. (n.d.). Editorial Board Chief Patron Editor-in-Chief. *The Indian Police Journal, 72*(1).

Rodrigues, R. (2020). Legal and human rights issues of AI: Gaps, challenges and vulnerabilities. *Journal of Responsible Technology*, *4*, 100005. DOI: 10.1016/j.jrt.2020.100005

Sharma, R. (2025). The Role of Artificial Intelligence in Digital Forensics: Balancing Efficiency and Privacy. *International Journal of Research Publication and Reviews Journal*, *6*(11), 4482–4486. Www.Ijrpr.Com. DOI: 10.55248/gengpi.06.1125.38159

Sood, A., Aggarwal, S., & Singh, S. (2024). *ANALYSIS OF DIGITAL FORENSIC PRACTICES IN INDIA*. https://jcsdf.nfsu.ac.in/

Szymoniak, S., & Foks, K. (2024). Open Source Intelligence Opportunities and Challenges – A Review. *Advances in Science and Technology Research Journal*, *18*(3), 123–139. DOI: 10.12913/22998624/186036

Toprak, S. (2009). The new face of terrorism in Turkey: Actor unknown political murders. *Journal of Forensic Sciences*, *54*(6), 1388–1392. DOI: 10.1111/j.1556-4029.2009.01154.x PMID: 19737338

Tripathy, S. S.Sudhanshu Sekhar Tripathy. (2025). A comprehensive survey of cybercrimes in India over the last decade. *International Journal of Science and Research Archive*, *13*(1), 2360–2374. DOI: 10.30574/ijsra.2024.13.1.1919

Yadav, R. T. (n.d.). AI-Driven Digital Forensics. *International Journal of Scientific Research & Engineering Trends*, *10*, 2395–2566.

Yin, Z., Wang, Z., Xu, W., Zhuang, J., Mozumder, P., Smith, A., & Zhang, W. (2025). *Digital Forensics in the Age of Large Language Models*. https://arxiv.org/pdf/2504.02963v1

Zamil, M. Z. H., & Khan, T. M. (2025). AI-Driven Digital Evidence Triage in Digital Forensics: A Comprehensive Review. *ISDFS 2025 - 13th International Symposium on Digital Forensics and Security*. DOI: 10.1109/ISDFS65363.2025.11011908

Manasi Pritam Zirpe, Shravani Santosh Potdar, & Harshali Rohit Kadaskar. (2024). AI IN DIGITAL FORENSICS. *International Journal of Scientific Research in Modern Science and Technology, 3*(5), 01–06. DOI: 10.59828/ijsrmst.v3i5.208

Chapter 4
Blockchain in Criminal Investigations:
Preserving Digital Forensics and Cybercrime Evidence

Sonia Pandey
http://orcid.org/0009-0000-5674-4066
Lloyd Law College, Greater Noida, India

ABSTRACT

Blockchain technology is a groundbreaking decentralized electronic registry that captures transactions and data on a network of computers in an insecure, transparent and tamper-proof context. At its most fundamental level, blockchain systematizes the information framed into blocks and each block includes a list of transactions or documents, a timestamp and a cryptographical hash connecting it to the last block creating an immutable chronological chain. In contrast with the conventional and centralized databases, which are managed by one party, blockchain runs on a distributed system of nodes where each one of them keeps an identical copy of the registry. This architecture ensures elimination of single points of failure and improves on the use of intermediaries. Consensus mechanisms, like Proof-of-Work or Proof-of-Stake, are used to authenticate transactions and provide agreement among participants prior to the addition of new blocks. This chapter explores the use of blockchain technologies in scientific criminal investigations.

1. INTRODUCTION

When data is stored, it is effectively unchangeable due to cryptographic connections and hashing of each element- it would demand rewriting all the following blocks in

DOI: 10.4018/979-8-3373-9730-6.ch004

the entire system, which metacognitively even is unfeasible. Blockchain also offers information wall, allowing decentralized information exchange because blockchain is sourced with the truth, and privacy is ensured by the means of such techniques as the cryptography of the keys of the public and the private one. The technology was first popularized in 2008 by Bitcoin but has gone far beyond the cryptocurrency sphere, being used in supply chain monitoring, health records, voting and currently in digital forensics (Ratul et al., 2024). It is especially useful in high-stakes settings in which trust and integrity hold importance owing to its intrinsic security, auditing and efficiency capabilities. Blockchain in criminal justice provides a strong platform of dealing with sensitive data without undermining the authenticity.

1.1 Evolution of Blockchain from Cryptocurrencies to Forensic Applications

In 2008, the whitepaper of Bitcoin, a peer-to-peer electronic cash system, became the infrastructure of a blockchain-based system that introduced a solution to the issue of the double-spending problem created by Satoshi Nakamoto aiming to eliminate trusted third parties. The initial adoption concerned majorly cryptocurrencies, which allowed safe, cross-border financial transactions to be remembered on a written, immutable registry. In the next ten years, the software developed at a fast pace as applications such as Ethereum added smart contracts, or automated code that automatically executes an agreement, to blockchain, such as decentralized finance (DeFi), non-fungible tokens (NFTs), and supply chain management. By the mid-2010s, it became apparent to researchers and practitioners that the fundamental advantages of blockchain, namely, immutability, transparency, and cryptographic protection, can be tubing to overcome long-standing issues in other fields, especially in digital forensics and evidence management. This trend accelerated as the number of cybercrimes such as ransomware, cryptocurrency fraud, and dark Web grew, and investigators had to have sponsorable instruments to follow the transactions and maintain integrity.

1.2 Key Characteristics: Decentralization, Immutability, Transparency, and Cryptographic Security

In this paper, I will explain the revolutionary nature of blockchain by examining four key features: cryptographic security, transparency, decentralization and impeccability. The ledger is distributed to a network of independent nodes and increasingly this is enforced through decentralization to ensure that a single authority has no control over the system (Popal et al., 2025).

The rapid increase in cybercrime has brought forth a pressing demand of blockchain in the current criminal investigations to address the issue of constraints in the preservation and presentation of digital evidence. Leveraging ransomware, hacks, and Internet fraud, and offenses made possible by cryptocurrency, investigators are now daily working with large volumes of unstable digital evidence that traditional approaches have not been able to protect reliably. The blockchain fills these holes, giving an immutable, decentralized registry in which evidence acquisition, hashing, and timestamping and transfers are registered, and complements the chain of custody between collection and courtroom presentation. It is tamper proof, so that any effort to manipulate records is noticed at once, and disagreements over evidence is implied and disputes over wrongful dismissal are minimized. Multi-jurisdictional cases define a time in which law enforcement agencies share data despite all being secure and transparent without loss of control, which is made possible by blockchain (Sakshi & Sharma, 2024).

2. DIGITAL FORENSICS AND CYBERCRIME EVIDENCE: CORE CONCEPTS AND CHALLENGES

Cyber forensics or digital forensics is a field of forensic science that focuses on how to identify, acquire, preserve, examine, and present digital evidence in a way that upholds its integrity and makes it admissible in a court of law. Digital forensics fundamentally succeeds through recovering and processing electronic data on computers, mobile phones, a network, and cloud services on the internet of things, and so on, to reconstruct events, assign actions to participants, and either assist in criminal investigations or civil litigation. In contrast to the conventional forensic that involved the physical evidence, the digital evidence is in binary representation; bits and bytes that are volatile by nature, can be easily edited or altered, and subject to easy destruction or loss. The discipline came into the limelight during the late 1990s and early 2000s as personal computers and the internet started taking off and has evolved since then to deal with more complex cyber threats.

There are a vast range of data types included in digital evidence, which are important in cybercrime investigations. These sources are often files and documents on hard drives or USB drives, emails, chat logs, browser histories, metadata (timestamps, geolocation, device data), files deleted or fragmented but recognized through carving techniques, system logs, network captures, data in mobile apps, social media posts and direct messages, records stored in cloud storage systems, and even data captured by IoT devices such as smart cameras or wearables. In cybercrime situations, user activities, communication, transaction logs or the malicious code execution will be indicated in the evidence. As an example, with hacks, logs and memory dumps can be searched to track the routes of intrusions; online fraud exchange records of bank accounts, IP addresses, cryptocurrency wallets are investigative leads. Ransomware incidents often include ransom notes and encryption evidence and additional tracks of payment, whereas cases of child exploitation or human trafficking utilize image, video, and thread of communication left behind on devices or dark web forums (Akhtar & Feng, 2022). Blockchain-based assets have a pseudonymous but traceable properties that have put a further layer on the issue, where specialized tools are necessary to track illicit flows. Digital evidence is volatile: turn on a computer or open a file and timestamps or metadata can get changed, which is where the idea of evidence handled with write-blockers and forensic imaging to produce bit-identical copies without having to alter the original is accepted.

Cybercrimes have become rampant and have resulted in the need to have powerful digital forensics. Examples are ransomware attacks, which encrypt systems and require a fee, network and unauthorized access, financial exploitation through phishing, business email compromise, identity theft, distribution of child exploitation materials over the internet, and activities of the dark web, such as drug trafficking, weapons sales, and stolen data. Each of them creates different digital footprints: ransomware activities leave encryption keys and communications with command-and-control servers; phishing frauds leave spoofed emails and credentials-gathering logs; dark web cases leave Tor browser records and cryptocurrency transactions. International statistics put the size of the issue into perspective (Kamal et al., 2022). The Internet Crime Complaint Center (IC3) of the FBI in 2025 showed more than 1 million complaints and loss of about 21 billion dollars in the United States alone, surpassing the preceding years, with cyber-enabled fraud, investment scams and ransomware being the main drivers behind the growth. The cybercrime costs worldwide are projected to be over 10.5 trillion by 2025/2026, which is expected to be higher than the GDP of certain economies, and is even more than some conventional areas of crime. It is predicted to keep expanding through 20262027 due to AI-enabled attacks, the use of clouds, and geopolitical conflicts. This explosion is to say that nowadays digital evidence is included in about 90 percent of criminal cases, reshaping the process of work of law enforcement, but overloading under-funded forensic laboratories.

The conventional digital forensics workflow adheres to a strict and cyclical but linear workflow that has been developed to maintain evidentiary rigor. It starts with identification, and investigators determine possible sources, which could be the devices seized, cloud accounts, or network traffic logs, depending on the particularities of the case. Preservation immediately comes next: isolating devices (e.g. keeping phones in Faraday bags to fight-off signals) and generating forensic images to protect the originals (Kreso, 2025).

Cloud forensics presents some special jurisdictional and technical challenges. The data that is scattered on the world servers can be subject to the laws of other countries which will make them hard to acquire but will present sovereignty and privacy issues under laws such as GDPR. Cloud platform multi-tenancy endangers the commingling of innocent user data, the retention policy of different providers may hold permanent evidence unlike other users, which may be lost forever. These problems are exacerbated by new risks: AI-generated deep fakes are capable of creating videos or audio, requiring the multimedia evidence to be highly reliable, adversarial machine learning poisons machine learning used by forensics, and quantum computing jeopardizes existing cryptography. All of this is made worse by resource limitations, with too many law enforcers being undertrained, or lack access to advanced tools or budget to deal with advanced cases, especially in under-developed regions. Anti-forensic is more rapid than defensive, and the technologies change rapidly (new OS versions, updates to apps, new devices) making the tools become outdated very often (Balmiki, 2023).

Digital evidence is also problematic when it comes to legal and admissibility issues. Courts require evidence that documents that it is genuine (the evidence is what it claims to be), that it is not changed in some way it is not supposed to be, that it is relevant and that it is reliable. In standards such as the Federal Rules of Evidence of the United States (FRE 901902), the party should provide the authenticity of documents through witness testimony, system/process authentication, or through self-authenticating certification.

3. BLOCKCHAIN AS A SOLUTION FOR EVIDENCE PRESERVATION AND CHAIN OF CUSTODY

The blockchain technology offers a solid platform to evidence preservation as the technology is based on immutability that can be used to form records that are impractically impossible to modify without being noticed. Generally, blockchain is essentially a distributed registry in which data is sequentially packaged into blocks. Every block is a cryptographic hash of its own contents usually calculated with the help of such algorithms as SHA-256, the hash of the previous block, the time-stamp, and the details of the transaction. Such a chaining mechanism forms a cryptographic dependency, so any single-bit change in an individual block of data alters its hash, thereby invalidating all the following blocks in the chain. Since the ledger is copied into a large number of independent nodes in a decentralized network, it would be computationally impractical to change a record without the concurrent agreement of the majority of nodes in a consensus mechanism (such as Proof-of-Work or Proof-of-Authority).

The vulnerability of traditional evidence is directly covered by this property in digital forensics when files, images or logs can be modified over time, but in a way that is difficult to detect. To be included in the blockchain, a cryptographic hash of a digital piece of evidence, like an image of a confiscated hard drive or a record of an email folder or an IoT sensor device, is calculated and stored with some metadata such as the date of acquisition and the person or entity who acquired it. Any further effort to violate the original file would result in an incompatible hash, alerting to the violation (Igonor et al., 2025).

3.1 How Blockchain Ensures Immutability and Tamper-Proof Records: Blockchain-Based Chain of Custody (CoC) Mechanisms

Chain of Custody (CoC) systems built upon blockchain technology have been able to transform the management of evidence by automating and cryptographically securing a record of all handling events, between their initial seizure and trial in a courtroom, in a manner that is transparent and verifiable. Classical CoC uses manual logs, spreadsheets or paper reports, which can be easily misplaced by humans, missing or intentionally falsified, usually omitting evidence. In contrast, blockchain creates a decentralized, append-only ledger where each custody transfer is recorded as an immutable transaction (Chakraborty, 2026). An exclusive digital token or a record is created on the blockchain when evidence is gathered, which is associated with the hashed evidence file.

A digital signature or public-private key pair is used to initiate a transaction, where information like timestamp, identity of the person handling the transaction, the location, intended purpose of the access, and other activities performed are recorded (e.g., imaging or analysis). Smart contracts would be able to execute pre-defined procedures and check them autonomously, allowing permissions to be automatically validated and transferring to be announced to the interested groups, minimizing human input and mistakes.

The decentralized aspects of blockchain ensure secure sharing in multi-agency or cross-jurisdictional investigations (where sharing data to centralized intermediaries is not allowed) as well as permissioned ledgers where only the relevant parties are permitted to see the data. Such frameworks as B-CoC (Blockchain-based Chain of Custody) or systems based on Hyperledger Fabric and Ethereum are showing practical implementation, in which each custody event is a signed block entry. This offers non-repudiation-handlers have no deniability- and complete auditability, such that courts can check the unbroken history by just comparing hashes. In cases with cybercrime and volatile data, such as ransomware artifacts or cloud logs, blockchain ensures that logs are done in real-time and eliminates the possibility of disputes post-acquisition. In general, CoC built upon blockchain is turning evidence management as a weak paper trail into a cryptographically secured, collaboration-driven interaction that maximizes legal admissibility, collaboration across agencies, and reduces chances of miscarriage of justice in more and more digital criminal environment (Sonawane et al., 2024).

3.2 Timestamping and Hashing Techniques for Digital Evidence Integrity

Blockchain demystified techniques are based on timestamping and hashing, which are essential in guaranteeing the correct temporal information and verifiable integrity of evidence during its lifecycle in digital forensic use. Hashing starts with cryptographic functions, usually a variant of SHA-256 which transforms any digital file, such as a document, image, video, memory dump or network log, into an identical-sized, fixed-length, unique fingerprint. Such a one-way function generates a deterministic value: when the input is the same, the result is always the same hash, but a bit-flip in the input can result in a completely different value. The original evidence in forensic use is hashed right after the acquisition, with write blockers, to generate a reference value that is stored off-chain or on a secure media (AlKhanafseh & Surakhi, 2024).

This hash is then included in a blockchain transaction and it is usually Warped together with Merkle tree as an efficiency measure when dealing with a large quantity of files. Timestamping builds on hashing, but adds a document on the time when the hash was rolled into the blockchain, capitalizing on the time of consensus built by the network when appending a block to it, or a trusted timestamp authority (e.g., by RFC 3161 compliant services). After being written, the hash + timestamp provides unchangeable evidence of being and condition at a particular moment. The truth of any future check is to re-hash the evidence presented and make it compare against the blockchain record, whereby, a match not only confirms integrity (no alterations), but also chronology (was present at the time of the record). This is vital in investigating cybercrime when volatile evidence like RAM contents, browser caches, or encrypted communications may otherwise become out of date over time. Blockchain uses an improved version of hashing through distributing the timestamp over a decentralized network, thus making it computationally infeasible to backdate or forge without a majority of the nodes themselves. Practical systems combine these approaches to IoT multimedia evidences, cloud VM research, or judicial preservation methods, with smart connections utilizing smart contracts to do logging and validation.

4. BLOCKCHAIN WITH DIGITAL FORENSICS TOOLS AND FRAMEWORKS: BLOCKCHAIN-ENABLED DIGITAL FORENSICS PLATFORMS

On-chain digital forensics platforms are yet another major breakthrough as they both combine the non-modifiable nature of distributed registers with evidence preservation, analysis, and reproducibility solutions, as well as crime investigation involving cryptocurrencies. Conventional digital forensic tools, such as Autopsy, Encase, and FTK, are primarily aimed at device imaging, file carving, timeline reconstruction and metadata extraction. These capabilities are augmented with blockchain integration which ensures tamper-proof logging of evidence handling and allows on-chain analysis. Major tools like Chainalysis Reactor, Elliptic Investigator, TRM Labs Forensics, and Crystal provide color-coded visualization of transaction flows, address clusters, and risk scores on various blockchains, enabling searches of illicit funds by scammers involved in ransomware, money laundering, or fraud cases. These tools typically include graph analysis and behavioral intelligence to de-anonymize wallet activities, and assure evidentiary integrity with cryptographic hashing and timestamping.

Hybrid systems suggest middleware layers that bridge classical forensics tools with blockchain registers- such as automatic hashing of forensic pictures in EnCase or Autopsy and adding them to a permissioned blockchain to verify a chain of custody. Approaches to research, such as models of blockchain-based IoT forensics and evidence management systems based on smart contracts, attempt to automate the recording of the acquisition, transfer, and analysis steps, eliminating the chance of a human error and increasing the admissibility to the court. An open-source open-source project such as BlockSci or GraphSense can be used with commercial blockchain data to provide customizations to the querying of blockchain data (Bashir, 2024).

Practically, the law enforcement agencies cross these platforms to put devices evidence off-chain evidence matched with on-chain transactions, and produce a coherent investigative workflow. Scalability and interoperability of tools and training are still problematic, though blockchain-based solutions are also changing the fact that digital forensics currently isolates analysis of each device, turning it into a fully verifiable ecosystem that can deal with the pseudonymous and distributed characteristics of current cyber-crimes. With adoption, these platforms hold potential to increase conviction rates, as they will generate evidence that can be defended and audited, and stands up to legal examination.

4.1 Standards and Protocols for Blockchain-Forensics Interoperability

Blockchain-forensics interoperability standards and protocols are necessary to guarantee a smooth integration of the various blockchain networks, conventional forensics tools and systems across jurisdictional boundaries and into the systems, to tackle the current problem of fragmentation, which significantly affects efficient sharing of evidence and in-depth analysis. In the absence of shared models, virtual investigators struggle to share data on different platforms, such as Chainalytics, Elliptic, or Autopsy/EnCase integrations, resulting in inconsistent formats, semantic incompatibilities, and inability to demonstrate the reliability of evidence in court. Emerging initiatives address the harmonized needs of attribution tag data schema, common terminologies, shared investigation documentation to allow sharing of transaction graphs while securing proprietary intelligence. Externalities [protocols] follow forensic quality evidentiary standards such as chain-of-custody logs, cryptographic authentication mechanisms such as SHA-256 hash with blockchain time (or timestamping), and API compatibility to integrate blockchain modules into existing software. Programs, such as the proposed API standards suggested by NIST (SP 500-345), are meant to assist in supporting plug-and-play compatibility, and the cross-chain protocols that are used to transfer values and data safely between the permissioned and the public ledgers.

Formatting of evidence and metadata Standardization of evidence formatting and metadata (e.g., common JSON schemas of forensic artifacts) facilitate collaboration without revealing sensitive information. Streams of legal and governance deal with admissibility through establishing provenance documentation and compliance standards, which are both in line with international standards, such as GDPR. Studies indicate that interoperable frameworks in IoT and cloud forensics are necessary, in which blockchain solutions need to interface with tools such as FTK or Volatility. Lack of global standards poses a danger of customized solutions that create new vulnerabilities or problems of trust. Stakeholders can promote effective cross-border collaboration, minimize the rates of evidence exclusion, and gain confidence in blockchain-verified records by creating open blockchain intelligent standards (ex: standardized APIs and format of investigations). Strong standards of interoperability will finally be able to bridge the divide between decentralized ledger technology and traditional digital forensics to establish a coherent ecosystem that enables scalable and legally sound investigations in the increasingly complex cyber threat environment.

4.2 Role of Distributed Ledger Technology (DLT) in Multi-Agency Collaboration

The wider field of Distributed Ledger Technology (DLT), which includes blockchain, offers a potentially game-changing solution to the multi-agency cooperation process as it offers a secure and decentralized platform to share forensic evidence and intelligence without using fragile centralized systems. Another problem arises in criminal investigations related to cross-jurisdiction cybercrimes, like ransomware or cryptocurrency frauds: agencies frequently encounter issues with their data silos, bureaucracy, and lack of trust. DLT has solutions to these by allowing permissioned ledgers in which approved individuals (police forces, forensic laboratories, prosecutors, and international collaborators) keep synchronized, tamper-evident records of evidence acquisition, transfers and analysis (Chougule et al., 2022).

Every action is recorded as a read-only transaction with cryptographic hashes, time stamps, and digital signatures, making them non-repudiable and fully auditable, and keep any secrets confidential with access controls and zero-knowledge schemes. Applications to the real world, such as Beacon Network of real-time flagging of illegal wallets across exchanges and police force, or suggested frameworks of providing criminal case information in real time to expedite the process of serving justice. In cross-border functions, DLT enables the transfer of evidence securely without employing the sluggish mutual legal assistance agreements and minimizes the chances of information being interfered with along the way. Collaborative systems enable agencies to add to a common ledger- by publishing hashed forensic images using tools such as EnCase or interpreting patterns on-chain using tools like Chainalysis, and using smart contracts to deliver notifications and compliance checks.

This promotes efficiency in operations, such as in collaborative crypto war rooms where various forces train and exchange knowledge. Governance agreements, the differing laws of different countries on privacy, as well as the technical integration with old systems are some of the challenges, yet the transparency and resilience provided by DLT might make more participants trust it. Through verifiable, real-time cooperation, DLT enhances collective efforts in countering transnational cyber threats, enhances evidence integrity in collective prosecution, and ultimately makes cyber global law enforcement efforts more efficient in the digital age.

5. APPLICATIONS OF BLOCKCHAIN IN SPECIFIC CYBERCRIME INVESTIGATIONS

The blockchain technology has emerged as an invaluable asset in the process of investigating criminal activities surrounding cryptocurrencies because it alters the pseudonymous quality of digital assets into an imprinted, unalterable record that can be used by law enforcement services to break down illegal financial trophies. Criminals find cryptocurrencies like Bitcoin, Ethereum, and privacy coins useful in transferring funds internationally in crimes such as money laundering, investment scams, evading sanctions, and transactions in the dark web, which are perceived to be anonymous. Nevertheless, due to the open and fixed nature of public blockchains, forensic scientists can trace any payment through the source to destination with the help of advanced analytics tools. Chainalysis, Elliptic and TRM Labs tools use address clustering and graph-based mixing services and behavioral heuristics to cluster related wallets, identify mixing services, and trace cross-chain transactions across bridges and decentralized exchanges (Sanjalawe et al., 2024). By 2025, illicit crypto transactions were at highest levels in known history, and reports by Chainalysis and TRM Labs show that illicit transactions of $154 and 158 billion to illicit addresses in 2025 were fuelled by nation-state actors, massive hacks and organized laundering services. In the same year, a single group of North Korean hackers had stolen more than $2 billion in cyber, which in large part was tracked using on-chain patterns despite their advanced obfuscation methods. Combining on-chain and off-chain intelligence (exchange KYC records, IP logs, or confiscated devices) allows blockchain forensics to connect on-chain data with the real-world. As an example, major cases have involved law enforcement using Reactor (Chainalysis) or other such tools to map the transaction graphs, identify the presence of peel chains, and identify high-risk counterparties, which has resulted in asset seizures and prosecutions.

5.1 Blockchain in Cryptocurrency-Related Crimes (Tracing Illicit Transactions)

The Beacon Network developed by TRM Labs is the intelligence sharing community among law enforcement and the private sector in real-time, speeding up the process of attribution and cash freezing until cashed in. This functional capability has been vital in the sanctions-based flows as well as infrastructure provider networks that are used to launder scam and hack proceeds. As criminals can change with mixers, chain-hopping, or privacy enhancing features, blockchains are permanent so that past histories can be analyzed retrospectively. With AI-assisted improvements, tracing time has been reduced to disrupt criminal ecosystems at a much faster pace. Finally, blockchain makes what was previously a favorite tool of criminals an effective investigative resource and offers evidence of the flow of funds that, in court, will prove useful in cases involving cryptocurrency-based fraud, terrorist money laundering, and cross-border organized crime. With the increasing illicit volumes, ongoing cooperation between the two sectors (public and private) will increase the efficacy of blockchain tracing in serving justice and implementing restitution.

5.2 Ransomware Attacks and Ransom Payment Tracking

Ransomware attacks are one of the most disruptive types of cybercrimes, in which blockchain contributes in both aspects: extortion demands through cryptocurrency payments and the possibility of law enforcement to monitor and occasionally retrieve those payments because of the transparent ledger. With digital assets having high speed and being deemed impossible to track, attackers encrypt the victim systems and demand a payment, usually in Bitcoin or alternative cryptocurrencies to release the decryption keys. In 2025, the sum paid in ransomware hit about $820 million on-chain (this is projected to grow with attribution), despite the number of attacks growing and median demands skyrocketing.

The scale of the threat is emphasized by high-profile cases such as the $75 million reported as paid by a large distributor of pharmaceuticals to the Dark Angels group. When a payment is reported and address details are available, the tail of payment can be traced, and matched with a known malicious cluster using address attribution, behavioral analysis and cross-reference with off-chain information available in exchanges or confiscated infrastructure. Recent recoveries like the freezing of Colonial Pipeline funds partially in previous years or more recent multimillion dollar freezes show that blockchain can be used to establish an evidentiary trail to support asset forfeiture and prosecutions due to its immutability. Contemporary systems preserve tracking by providing smart contracts and automated notifications to signal suspicious location of outflows to ransom addresses.

Nevertheless, there are still problems to overcome: cross-chain bridges or privacy tools/ affiliate models allow criminals to obscure tracks, and not all victims report payments, making them less visible (Mahajan & Pandit, 2024). Nonetheless, global partnerships such as the Operation Cronos (against LockBit) and enhanced collaboration involving the government and the business community has stopped key operations by using blockchain data to map ransomware ecosystems, such as initial access brokers or money launderers. Blockchain helps create better arguments to deal with courts as well, since it offers events proof and connections to previous and later digital signatures that show the trail of stolen money. Blockchain analysis continues to be one of the pillars of attribution, disruption, and deterrence as the ransomware moves towards more decentralized and volatile forms. The increasing sophistication of law enforcement in integrating on-chain tracing with conventional investigative abilities has reversed the tide, transforming ransom payments into an untraceable bonanza, but providing victims with a chance to recover part of the devastating category of crime.

6. LEGAL, REGULATORY AND ETHICAL CONSIDERATIONS

The adoption of blockchain by digital forensics and crime investigations brings forth tricky legal, regulations, and ethical implications that should be well maneuvered to ensure the admissibility of evidence, safeguard human rights, and sustain the trust of society as a source of justice. The admissibility of evidence maintained using blockchain varies legally based on an already existing set of evidentiary provisions rather than totally new provisions. Courts in the United States use common standards pursuant to the Federal Rules of Evidence (FRE 901 authentication, FRE 803(6) business records, and Daubert standards expert testimony), the blockchain information is treated just like any other digital evidence in case of the support of an adequate chain-of-custody documentation, hash verification, and expert descriptions (Rani et al., 2025). Vermont and Illinois landmark cases and state laws have accepted blockchain records as potentially self-authenticating with qualified affidavits. The more recent legal rulings in the European Union, including the March 2025 Tribunal Judiciaire de Marseille decision, have found blockchain timestamps to be accepted as definitive in rebutting copyright anteriority, leading to increasingly judicial acceptance. Blockchain evidence in India comes under the Indian Evidence Act, 1872 and Section 65B of the Information Technology Act, 2000, and will necessitate electronic records to be certified, although issues of cross-border data and standardization are still prevalent. There is still little international harmonization, and there are different approaches to cases within frameworks such as the Budapest Convention on Cybercrime, which can lead to and cause jurisdictional conflicts in the context of multi-agency cases.

Regulatory issues revolve around adherence to data protection regulations. The GDPR of the EU brings tremendous conflict with the immutable nature and decentralization of blockchain especially with regard to the right to be forgotten (Article 17), the right to rectification (Article 16), and the principle of data minimization. Public blockchains are not responsive to erasure requests, and regulating agencies such as the CNIL in France have been asked to audit projects on whether they violate privacy laws, and permissioned ledgers have been proposed that store personal data off-chain and place the resultant hashes on-chain. Corresponding issues exist in the Digital Personal Data Protection Act, 2023 of India and other world regimes. Anti money laundering (AML) and know your customer (KYC) regulations further complicate forensic applications where there need to be a balance between transparency and the effectiveness of the investigation. The possibility of irrevocable stigmatization by dint of inefficient records (even of exonerated individuals), the use of biases in algorithm analysis, the invasion of privacy through extensive data gathering, and the necessity of unbiasedness in evidence management are all ethical concerns. Forensic practitioners should maintain confidentiality, integrity and non-overreach principles often guided by ISO sets of standards and ethics audit boards. Ensuring that the demands of law enforcement are balanced with human rights require continuous training, open methodologies, and good governance to avert abuse. It is suggested in policy recommendations to create hybrid models, form international collaboration as well as providing clear directions of what constitutes judicial acceptance to encourage responsible adoption and reduce the risk of evidence exclusion or violation of rights. Finally, dealing with these concerns will be key to making blockchain beneficial, not detrimental to the robes and bands of criminal justice.

7. CONCLUSION: FUTURE-PROOFING FORENSIC SYSTEMS AGAINST QUANTUM COMPUTING THREATS

Conclusively, blockchain has revolutionary potential in maintaining digital forensics and cyber-crime evidence, including immutability, a stronger chain-of-custody and the capacity to integrate effectively in multi agency cooperation, however, its sustainability in the long term depends on taking action to mitigate arising threats, especially quantum computing. With algorithms like the one proposed by Shor quantum computers promise to disrupt currently popular cryptographic primitives such as elliptic curve cryptography (ECC) and RSA, which most blockchain signature and key generation algorithms, and signature tools based on hash computations all use. An cryptographically relevant quantum computer would admit the vulnerability of exposed public keys embedded in a transaction, which would jeopardize historical and future forensic evidence, allow forgery of signatures, or weaken the integrity of timestamped evidence. It is estimated that although the large-scale threat might be realized between 2028 and more, the decrypt in the present and break in the future approach is already dangerous, and more recent developments (e.g., lower estimates of resources needed to break secp256k1) suggest the deadline could be sooner. Current blockchain implementations used as forensic systems are vulnerable to obsolescence without being future-proofed, possibly causing issue with evidence in court or flawed investigations in cryptocurrency tracing and ransomware cases.

A multi-layered approach is needed in future-proofing. To blockchain protocols, smart contracts, and forensic logging mechanisms, it will be important to transition to post-quantum cryptography (PQC) standards, and lattice-based algorithms, hash-based algorithms, and code-based algorithms are under standardization by NIST. Migration can be done through hybrid styles, using classical and quantum resistant algorithms and can ensure backward compatibility as well as system hardening. Law enforcement blockchains that are private and permissioned can more easily employ quantum-safe consensus mechanisms and cryptographic upgrades compared to a public network.

REFERENCES

Akhtar, M. S., & Feng, T. (2022). Using blockchain to ensure the integrity of digital forensic evidence in an iot environment. *EAI Endorsed Transactions on Creative Technologies*, *9*(31), e2. DOI: 10.4108/eai.3-6-2022.174089

AlKhanafseh, M., & Surakhi, O. (2024). Evidence preservation in digital forensics: An approach using blockchain and LSTM-based steganography. *Electronics (Basel)*, *13*(18), 3729. DOI: 10.3390/electronics13183729

Balmiki, V. (2023, October). An evidence collection using blockchain for cybercrime detection. In *2023 4th IEEE Global Conference for Advancement in Technology (GCAT)* (pp. 1-7). IEEE. DOI: 10.1109/GCAT59970.2023.10353259

Bashir, H.Dr. Hira Bashir. (2024). DIGITAL FORENSICS: TECHNIQUES FOR INVESTIGATING CYBERCRIMES. *Computer Science Bulletin*, *7*(01), 76–88. DOI: 10.71465/csb130

. Chakraborty, S. (2026). Next-Gen Digital Forensics: Investigating Cybercrime in the Era of AI, Blockchain, and the Dark Web. *The Science of Criminal Investigations*, 286.

Chougule, H., Dhadiwal, S., Lokhande, M., Naikade, R., & Patil, R. (2022). Digital evidence management system for cybercrime investigation using proxy re-encryption and blockchain. *Procedia Computer Science*, *215*, 71–77. DOI: 10.1016/j.procs.2022.12.008

Igonor, O. S., Amin, M. B., & Garg, S. (2025). The application of blockchain technology in the field of digital forensics: A literature review. *Blockchains*, *3*(1), 5. DOI: 10.3390/blockchains3010005

Kamal, R., Hemdan, E. E. D., & El-Fishway, N. (2022). Forensics chain for evidence preservation system: An evidence preservation forensics framework for internet of things-based smart city security using blockchain. *Concurrency and Computation*, *34*(21), e7062. DOI: 10.1002/cpe.7062

Kreso, I. (2025). Using blockchain technology for preserving digital evidence in digital forensics. *KNOWLEDGE-International Journal*, *68*(3), 331–336.

Mahajan, R., & Pandit, K. (2024, June). Cryptography and Computational Approaches in Ensuring Data Integrity for Digital Forensic Evidence. In *2024 16th International Conference on Electronics, Computers and Artificial Intelligence (ECAI)* (pp. 1-6). IEEE. DOI: 10.1109/ECAI61503.2024.10607526

Popal, M., Ahmad, A., & Arshad, M. (2025). The Significance of Blockchain Technology in Preserving Digital Evidence Integrity in Forensic Investigations. *Journal of Computing & Biomedical Informatics*, *9*(02).

Rani, D., Gill, N. S., Gulia, P., Yahya, M., Ahanger, T. A., Hassan, M. M., Abdallah, F. B., & Shukla, P. K. (2025). A secure digital evidence preservation system for an iot-enabled smart environment using ipfs, blockchain, and smart contracts. *Peer-to-Peer Networking and Applications*, *18*(2), 5. DOI: 10.1007/s12083-024-01855-z

Ratul, M. H. A., Mollajafari, S., & Wynn, M. (2024). Managing Digital Evidence in Cybercrime: Efforts Towards a Sustainable Blockchain-Based Solution. *Sustainability (Basel)*, *16*(24), 10885. DOI: 10.3390/su162410885

Sakshi, M., Malik, A., & Sharma, A. K. (2024). A survey on blockchain based IoT forensic evidence preservation: Research trends and current challenges. *Multimedia Tools and Applications*, *83*(14), 42413–42458. DOI: 10.1007/s11042-023-17104-z

Sanjalawe, Y., Makhadmeh, S., & Alqudah, H. (2024, February). Digital forensics meets blockchain: Enhancing evidence authenticity and traceability. In *2024 2nd International Conference on Cyber Resilience (ICCR)* (pp. 01-06). IEEE.

Sonawane, A., Lakade, N., Sarkar, S., & Dongre, N. (2024, August). Securing digital evidence in forensic investigation using blockchain. In *2024 4th Asian Conference on Innovation in Technology (ASIANCON)* (pp. 1-7). IEEE. DOI: 10.1109/ASIANCON62057.2024.10837800

Chapter 5
Criminal Investigations With Blockchain Technology:
Stabilizing Digital Forensics and Cybercrime Evidence for Admission

Divya S. Khurana
http://orcid.org/0009-0000-4367-1742
School of Legal Studies, CGC University, Mohali, India

Bhrigu Raj Mourya
http://orcid.org/0009-0000-6220-1295
MATS Law School, MATS University, Raipur, India

Om Prakash Kannaujia
http://orcid.org/0009-0008-4405-1682
MATS Law School, MATS University, Raipur, India

ABSTRACT

The chapter investigates how blockchain technology can be implemented to solve some major challenges in criminal investigation, particularly with respect to identifying some of the serious vulnerabilities found in a digital forensics investigation and the evidence handling procedure of cybercrime. Volatile, easily tampered nature of traditional digital evidence often means that traditional digital evidence is susceptible to tampering, is difficult to formulate, and may not be admissible in court without problems with the chain of custody. The key characteristics of blockchain immutability, decentralization, cryptographic hashing, and audit trails provide a

DOI: 10.4018/979-8-3373-9730-6.ch005

secure and efficient way to capture physical evidence at time of collection to when it enters the courtroom. It focuses on that the multi-agency partnership as well as privacy-preserving methods and case studies should be examined, together with technical architectures and legal compliance, including admissibility criteria.

1. INTRODUCTION

Digital transformation has changed the nature of the tools and methods law enforcement used in operations, moving them from manual to technology-dominated, data-based. Incorporating cutting-edge AI-driven analytics, predictive policing software, body-worn cameras, cloud storage, and real-time surveillance systems helps agencies work more efficiently and effectively for investigative purposes, reducing response times (Ratul et al., 2024). This change allows for optimal use of resources and better inter-agency cooperation, along with using the digital platforms and predictive threat detection through processing of large data sets. In the realm of cybercrime, digital forensics has been a crucial field enabling investigators to recover files that have been deleted, trace back IP addresses, and analyze metadata acquired from a variety of devices and networks.

Police departments around the world are spending substantial sums on the latest modern technology in an effort to tackle increasing online dangers. For example, the incorporation of encrypted data recovery tools and social media intelligence in the tools of digital forensic Tool used by federal agencies. But this shift comes with its own set of challenges like data overloading, risk of data security breaches in law enforcement systems and the requirement of special training. In places such as India, the Digital India initiative and cybercrime reporting portals demonstrate a concerted effort to ensure that police practices keep up with technological progress. The second development in India, for example, is the Digital India program and tools to report cybercrime; they show that they have taken adequate steps to make policing more technology friendly. Overall the digital transformation will enable higher transparency and accountability aspects by automated logging and evidence management system, however for securing higher integrity of processes, there is always a need of proper and robust security measures. If the underlying technologies are not secure, there is the danger of being undermined by evidence weaknesses. This background highlights the critical need to innovate the forensic practice with solutions, such as blockchain, that will counteract the pace of technology that is impacting the industry.

1.1 Overview of Digital Transformation in Law Enforcement

Cybercrime has come onto the scene rapidly and at a scale never before seen by law enforcement. The attacks are expected to be happening more often and with greater sophistication and causing damages of $10.5 trillion per year, which is as high as the value of many national economies. Actions involving ransomware, phishing, data breaches and dark web activity involve digital vulnerabilities and can create massive amounts of fragile digital evidence logs, transactions, images, devices and more.

Digital evidence is vulnerable as it may be altered, lost or destroyed without any obvious sign or impact and physical evidence cannot be altered. Cloud storage, IoT devices, and encryption add further layers of complexity in terms of collection and preservation, and are likely to be spread across a number of jurisdictions. While traditional chain of custody documentation can meet these challenges, it often fails to keep up at trial with challenges of authenticity and integrity (Akhtar & Feng, 2022). Prosecutions are hampered; many face or are thrown out because of allegations on tampering with evidence or procedural error.

Agencies struggling with a rising number of cases amid soaring caseloads due to the exponential increase in cyber incidents, especially during the pandemic, is facing yet another challenge. You need to deal with large sets of data and ensure it complies with forensic requirements (such as NIST, ISO). Different jurisdictions have different legal systems which can introduce cross-border cooperation complexities. The problems presented highlight the critical need of development of tamper-proof systems which can ensure the reliability of evidence.

1.2 The Growing Challenge of Cybercrime and Digital Evidence

Immutability and decentralization are the two key characteristics of blockchain technology that ensure digital forensics become stable. The decentralized and immutable (inconsistency-free) record of any action on the blockchain makes digital forensics stable. Because evidence files are being encrypted and stored on a blockchain, any tampered evidence file is easily noticeable as all the blocks affecting the file would fail to validate upon a change. Helps in maintaining the integrity of the evidence flow between the crime scene and courtroom.

Central to this are cryptographic timestamps for time stamping data with integrity, smart contracts for automating the transfer of custody and account, and permissioned (private/consortium) blockchains customised to law enforcement to ensure transparency and privacy. Features to mitigate risks of human error, tampering and facilitate multi-agency access, with audit trail and verifiable chain of custody.

Integration with the existing forensic tools is provided allowing real-time tracking and secure data sharing.

Blockchain supports the tracking of cryptocurrency transactions, in addition to being useful for gathering evidence from IoT sources in cybercrime investigations. It is append-only, which serves extremely well the purpose of forensic principles, thus improving auditability and non-repudiation. Even with the obstacles each one of these technologies brings, from the problems of scalability to legal recognition, blockchain is a valuable asset in helping to curb the fundamental weaknesses of conventional technologies and increase trust in digital evidence.

1.3 Role of Blockchain in Stabilizing Forensics

The central aim of the research is to examine the efficiency and ways to leverage the blockchain technology as an effective approach to ensure stability, integrity and admissibility of digital forensic and cybercrime evidence in the criminal investigation process. Specific objectives include: Study of technical architecture for evidence logging and chain of custody; Study of the legal and regulatory impacts of the evidence across various jurisdictions, focusing in on the legal aspects in India and how do they interact with the international aspects; identification of issues that may arise in the use of the evidence; and the suggestions of practical solutions for the law enforcement community.

Covering key blockchain applications in the field of digital evidence management such as hashing, time-stamping and privacy solutions such as zero-knowledge proofs, it explores how these can be integrated within forensic workflows and how they can be used for multi-stakeholder collaboration (Balmiki, 2023). It includes cybercrime typologies, the need for traditional forensic techniques such as cryptocurrency-specific forensics and the use of non-criminal applications, but does not cover in-depth cryptocurrency-specific forensics nor non-criminal applications. Variations on scalability and interoperability and ethical issues (such as data privacy) are mitigated. The study uses case studies from around the world, standards (NIST, ISO) and empirical literature to offer applicable suggestions for action.

1.4 Significance for Evidence Admissibility in Courts

The use of blockchain for evidence is extremely relevant and very powerful when it comes to the admissibility of evidence in court and offers the benefit of cryptographic proof of evidence integrity as well as transparency of evidence processing and a clear audit trail, which directly address some of the common bases of excluding evidence due to tampering and broken chain of custody. As more courts adopt the principles of Daubert reliability or the similar principles of other evidence acts (like India's Evidence Act), the requirement for a reliability the most courts impose on admissibility of digital materials is easy to meet.Increasingly, courts that use the principles of Daubert reliability or some similar evidence act (like the Evidence Act used by India) require proof of reliability from digital evidence, and blockchain's 'immutability' and timestamping play it is as reliable as it gets.

This technology adds strength to the evidence as it allows an independent examination of the evidence handling history by judges or juries, decreasing potential assertion conflicts and litigation length. It helps meet forensic best practice, and ensures acceptance in adversarial proceedings. Its capabilities include privacy preserving features which ensure sensitive information protection while keeping transparent for authorized parties (Igonor et al., 2025). The growing judicial openness has been indicated by the real world pilots and developments in policy (such as self-authenticating blockchain records in some jurisdictions).

2. BLOCKCHAIN TECHNOLOGY AND ITS CORE CONCEPTS: DECENTRALIZATION, IMMUTABILITY AND CRYPTOGRAPHY

The blockchain is a distributed, digital accounting book that keeps data and transactions on various nodes in the network, which helps in the transparency and security of transactions with no need for the help of a central authority. This originally inspired by Bitcoin in 2008 by Satoshi Nakamoto now has applications well beyond the scope of the cryptocurrency and is increasingly exploited in supply chain, healthcare etc. and, particularly, in digital forensics/criminal investigations. It has three key components decentralization, immutability and cryptography that make it a transformative tool in law enforcement.

Decentralisation means that there is no central one place to store data and control in a network, there is no central point. So in a decentralized system, each participant node is in possession of a full copy of the ledger. Such a system does not have a single point of failure, is harder to be manipulated through an internal source and provides better resistance to cyberattacks. When used in criminal investigations, decentralized systems enable various law enforcement agencies, forensic labs, and courts to access and inspect the evidence throughout without relying on a weak central repository system (sun, 2025). It encourages team-based investigations, without the ability for any party to make changes to the records without the other team.

The key features of immutability are that data cannot be changed or deleted without being noticed after it has been placed on the blockchain. This is done by cryptographic ties between blocks, each of which has a hash (digital fingerprint) of the next earlier block. A change to any of the transactions will alter the hash making the entire chain incorrect. Immutability is particularly challenging area of traditional evidence, digital forensics. Digital files and logs and metadata can be easily corrupted or deleted. Blockchain will also help produce a chain of custody that is trustworthy, as there is no way to tamper with it, and it will be admissible in court. Further proof of the provenance of evidence comes from timestamping mechanisms which can give a proof of when evidence is obtained or moved.

Many people say that the security of blockchain is guaranteed by cryptography. Many people say that block chain's security is based on cryptography. Uses hashing algorithms, like SHA-256, which are cryptographic functions that give outputs of fixed size from arbitrary inputs, which cannot be computed e.g. reverse engineered or devised to produce collisions. Public-key cryptography can be used for electronic signatures to assure that the evidence is genuine and from an expected source while not giving out private information. Advanced encryption and zero-knowledge proofs provide privacy levels, giving selected disclosure. Cryptographic proofs can establish the integrity of cryptocurrency transactions or network logs from devices recovered during a cybercrime investigation.

These concepts provide a solid foundation upon which digital evidence can be fixed. But there are still difficulties to overcome, such as the inability to be scalable to process large volumes of forensic data, energy requirements in some consensus algorithms, and the legal establishment of blockchain records. At its very core, blockchain technology directly counteracts the potential issues with contamination of evidence, improves audibility, and increases admissibility through mathematically guaranteed integrity all relevant to criminal justice. As law enforcement begins to employ this technology, it will help them catch up with the speed of innovation that has taken place in cybercrime and address the evidentiary requirements put forth by courts.

2.2 Types of Blockchain: Public, Private, Consortium and Hybrid

There are four main types of blockchain networks as Public, Private, Consortium, and Hybrid andthey each come with their pro's and cons, as far as accessibility and security, speed and governance. The choice of the right type is of paramount importance in law enforcement use cases for digital forensics and evidence management where having access to the correct information for the investigation while simultaneously maintaining data transparency, confidentiality, compliance, and operational efficiency is paramount.

Public blockchains are fully permissionless and open, e.g. Bitcoin, Ethereum. All can read the data, validate transaction, and be involved in the consensus. They are highly resistant to censure, provide maximum transparency and decentralize. However, they have the problem of transactions going slower, high cost and less privacy, which means they are not as well suited for the highly sensitive criminal investigations. Public blockchains work more well for public situations such as tracing the flow of public cryptocurrencies in money laundering cases and for evidence not sensitive in itself to public timestamps (times of your public elections).

Private chain is permissioned blockchains with single organization managing the chain. Access is restricted and only authorized participants can have access to read and modify data. They're fast, cheap and secure, and they're good for use in internal operations of a police department or forensic lab. However, because of centralization of controls, the emphasis on trustlessness is lost and it creates the possibility of internal control or compromise.

Consortium (or Federated) blockchains are managed by a group of predetermined groups, which fall somewhere in between the public and private chains. The network is coordinated by several trusted parties (polycentric governance), including various police forces, forensics, cybercrime teams, and the judiciary. An important example of Hyperledger is Hyperledger Fabric, which is employed in enterprise applications. This is a good model for such criminal investigations as involve several jurisdictions working together. It stays decentralized among trusted parties, sets up quicker consensus, and facilitates access and channels of privacy that assist to make sure that there is an unalterable audit trail suitable in a court of law.

Hybrid blockchain networks feature a mix of attributes from public and private systems. Sensitive data is kept on a private chain: hashes or non-sensitive verification data are anchored to a public blockchain, thus ensuring further immutability and public verifiability (Muragijimana et al., 2022). This is an architecture that is flexible - law enforcement can maintain the privacy of case information while evidence integrity is established via the properties of a public blockchain to be presented to defense counsel or judges. Adopting a hybrid approach for evidence management is becoming commonplace.

Consortium and hybrid blockchains are typically the preferred options for stabilizing digital forensics, as these blockchains are governed differently, have the potential for regulatory adherence, and can be compatible with current legal frameworks. They facilitate smart contracts to log and host evidence automatically and to transfer custody, while providing sophisticated cryptographic functions to tackle privacy issues. Careful design is required to implement and comply with standards such as NIST forensic guidelines along with local evidence law (e.g., Indian Evidence Act). Some of the challenges are interoperability among varying types of blockchains, and sustaining the architecture's legal standing for authenticity and reliability. The strategic choice of the type of blockchain can significantly contribute to increased confidence and admissibility of digital evidence in a cybercrime prosecution overall.

3. DIGITAL FORENSICS IN CRIMINAL INVESTIGATIONS

Digital forensics has become a very important aspect of criminal investigation, particularly in crime types that strongly involve the use of the Internet, as well as in crimes that leave "digital traces". It is the process of scientifically recovering, examining, analyzing and interrogating data on or passed via digital devices for court representation (Daoud, 2023). Today, the proliferation of smartphones, computers, cloud facilitation, internet of things (IoT) devices and networks is creating enormous amounts of data from which nearly every serious crime, ranging from murder to fraud, terrorism to human trafficking, leaves behind digital evidence that can identify suspects, victims and connections and give a sense of the time, place and events surrounding the crime.

The discipline brings together aspects of computer science, information technology and forensic science in order to ensure the preservation of evidence that is both forensically admissible and clear in court proceedings. Today practically every law enforcement agency has a department of digital forensics that utilizes technology and tools to work with volatile data, encrypted files, deleted information, and information in the cloud. This development reflects the weaknesses of the classic investigative process that can't usually deal with the intangible and-volatile characteristics of digital artifacts.

The challenges are numerous, ranging from the volume of data to be stored and processed to the fact that sophisticated criminals can implement anti-forensic tools, cross-jurisdictional issues in the cloud and the need for quick action in order to maintain the volatility of evidence like contents in RAM or current network sessions. BoP to ensure integrity, chain of custody, and reproducibly, based on standards of others such as NIST, ISO/IEC 27037, and SWGDE. In India, the Indian Evidence Act and Cybercrime wing in Information Technology Act, 2000 are benefiting with digital forensics.

Digital forensics also can augment the investigative process by reconstructing events, corroborating eyewitness reports and in prosecutions creating irrefutable connections. But requires ongoing skill training in response to changing technologies such as AI content creation, threats to quantum computers, and superior forms of encryption.

3.1 Principles and Processes of Digital Forensics

The concept and principles of Digital Forensics are that of integrity, reliability and repeatable evidence and legal admissibility. Some of the core concepts to output are dealing with the original evidence in the same way (forensic soundness), documenting all transactions for audition, using validated equipment and methods, etc., and confirming a clear chain of custody. They are consistent with good standards like ISO, NIST and ACPO (now widely used) which put great emphasis on not changing data that could be used in court. Identification involves identification of possible source of data, for example seized devices, network logs, cloud data. Preservation involves isolating and protecting evidence and preventing any alterations, which can be the use of a write blocker or rapid imaging.

Examination involves checking the data through professional software to help retrieve deleted data, analyse the meta data, and filter out the relevant information. Analysis involves using the information to make sense of it and creating timelines, cross-referencing messages or determining the origin of events.

Confidentiality, impartiality, and respect for the law are all very important standards of ethics. Investigators need to be mindful of the laws regarding privacy and only collect what's required. Within a criminal investigation, these processes have the effect of making sure evidence meets Daubert/Frye and similar standards of reliability.

3.2 Collection, Preservation, Analysis, and Presentation of Digital Evidence

The collection, preservation, analysis and presentation of digital evidence are a careful and precise process. Collection of evidence starts at the crime scene and/or upon proper, legal authority, during a raid. Scenes are documented with photos and notes and investigators identify and make a list of relevant devices and objects. While preserved data (files, registry) can be extracted from a live system, tools such as FTK Imager or Volatility are needed to preserve volatile data (running processes, network connections, RAM). Forensic imaging ensures that copies of the storage media are being manufactured exactly, based on the idea of using hardware that prevents the storage media from being modified (Patrick et al., 2025).

Preservation is key to preserve integrity and admissibility. This involves comparing original image files with duplicate image files to confirm their authenticity and leaving extensive chain-of-custody documentation of the opportunity, causes and holders of the images. In cases where the evidence is in the form of cloud evidence, there must be very particular legal procedures that must be implemented, such as a subpoena or MLATs related to cross-border access. Anti contamination methods such as Faraday bags for mobile devices will help stop remote wiping or interference signals from attacking devices.

Analysis involves intensive examination, using forensic software such as Autopsy, EnCase or Cellebrite. Experts reconstruct deleted files from unallocated space, extract metadata (date, geolocation etc.), view logs, emails, chat histories, and much, much more. Evidence is correlated across sources through timeline analysis, keyword searches and link analysis. Techniques for advanced topics include encryption and steganography.

Presentation makes technical findings accessible and understandable to juries, courts of law and legal counsel. Reports need to have a methodology, version numbers of tools used, details of limitations, and be objective and well-documented. Expert witnesses use simple terms, but teach in detail how they arrived at a conclusion. Support with visuals such as sanitized screenshots, charts and timelines enhance impact.

3.3 Cybercrime Typologies and Associated Digital Artifacts

There are two general basic types of cybercrime, namely, cyber-dependent crimes, those committed solely with a computer as the tool to commit the crime, and cyber-enabled crimes, those crimes which traditionally are committed using a computer to carry them out. These include phishing attacks, hacking, malware/ ransomware attacks, identity theft, online fraud, cyberstalking, child sexual exploitation, distributed denial of service (DDoS) attacks and cryptocurrency offences such as money laundering.

There are different digital artefacts that are created during each typology, which are all essential to investigations. These types of hacking logs, IP addresses, malware, registry 'entry' and command-line 'history' logs persist. Phishing attacks create spoofed e-mails, bogus Web sites, spoofed message metadata, and browser data logs. Ransomware victims provide you with encryption key, ransom notes, Bitcoins wallet addresses, or C2 (command and control) server communications (Haque et al., 2023).

Credential theft, transaction logs, evidence of fake account creation, and SIM-swapping evidence are examples of the contents that are often stolen in identity theft and financial fraud. Cyberstalking and harassment result in social media posts, messaging app chats (such as WhatsApp or Telegram), mobile device geolocation and call detail records (CDRs). CEM investigations involve analyzing image/video files, EXIF (extra information contained in the photo that provides information about the camera and location of the photograph), peer-to-peer sharing logs and dark web artifacts.

It is likely to generate device logs from smart cameras, wearables, or connected vehicles for the purposes of IoT-related crimes. A set of two artifacts for cloud-based crimes, namely Google Drive logs, AWS logs or Dropbox logs are needed. Network forensics can provide details on packet captures, firewall logs and VPN usage records.

These artifacts will tend to be volatile or easily changeable in nature and therefore will require timely collection. Often the metadata need not anticipate content of the document in order to be probative, for example, date of creation or modification can be an alibi or timeline, MAC addresses and browser fingerprints can help tie down authorship. Advanced carving and timeline normalization techniques are needed to recover data, because anti-forensic measures are used, such as secure deletion and time stamp manipulation.

4. CHALLENGES IN TRADITIONAL DIGITAL FORENSICS AND EVIDENCE ADMISSIBILITY

Conventional digital forensics is beset with a number of problems that lead to unreliable and unacceptable electronic evidence. In the face of technological progress, many law enforcement agencies have been forced to fall back on traditional methods that cannot seem to keep up with the quickly advancing cyber threats and complex cyber landscapes. Maintaining evidence integrity throughout its entire life cycle, demonstrating authenticity to a high standard and establishing an unbroken chain of custody in complex environments are key issues. These concerns often cause evidence to be discredited, weakened or excluded from trials, which obstructs investigations, leads to lack of confidence in the justice system, and results in unsuccessful prosecution.

Digital data is intangible and can be easily modified, compared to physical evidence, making it difficult to assure or maintain confidence about whether evidence has been tampered with, altered, or contaminated. Also, the technology is changing very quickly, including new file systems, encryption methods, and cloud-based computing, which has raised concerns about deficiencies in investigator training and capabilities (Kiressanth et al., 2025). The laws sometimes do not correspond with the actual state of things, thereby imposing a limitation on admissibility. The problems are even more prominent in States where forensic infrastructure is lacking depending on the State as in India, and also due to resource constraints under the IT Act when cybercrime cases have skyrocketed in India. Prior to the adoption of more sophisticated solutions, such as blockchain, to create more stable forensic practices, some changes in their characteristics are necessary to address these limitations.

4.1 Issues of Integrity, Authenticity and Chain of Custody

Traditional digital Forensics possesses the greatest vulnerabilities in integrity, authenticity, chain of custody. Integrity means that digital evidence will not be modified since it was collected. But a simple change in the hash code, whatever way, can cause error in the evidence. TO show authenticity, the evidence must be verified to be real and not invented or altered. Metadatas are in practice easily edit able and files can be created with forgery of metadata.

In digital environments, maintaining and holding a chain of custody comes with its own challenges ensuring it is followed, carelessly and, most importantly, flawlessly. When the evidence is digital, there is no easy way to identify someone who has made copies or transferred the evidence between networks or who has accessed evidence remotely without an easy audit trail. Having more than one handler on each drama of forensic, investigators and prosecutors enables the chance of gaps or clashing of meanings.

These are parts of which courts will give a searching look. The weaknesses that defense counsel see creates reasonable doubt, frequently resulting in evidence being suppressed. In high-profile cybercrime cases, acquittals have been reached even though there was strong evidence pointing to guilty verdicts if the case were to proceed had it not been that there were insufficient strong, automated tracking systems in place.

4.2 Tampering Risks and Data Volatility in Digital Environments

Digital evidence is highly volatile, can easily be altered or tampered with. Digital data can be altered, erased or changed instantly with no trace, and unlike physically recorded data can be altered in ways that degrade the signal very slowly. Anti-forensics refers to the different methods criminals use to obscure or destroy evidence, including the use of secure deletion tools (Shredders, Gutmann method), manipulation of timestamps, use of steganography, and encryption.

Another significant challenge is data volatility. Running applications (processes), encryption key files and open network connections, which are stored in volatile memory (RAM), are lost forever if the device is powered off. Service providers can automatically delete or modify network logs, cloud data, and temporary files. Preserving storage media used can still pose problems due to mis-handling, electromagnetic interference or malware that comes to life when connected, etc.

Tampering may happen during any part of the process, whether the devices are on networks during seizure or being transferred from one place to another or by forensic laboratories. Diggers make reasonably sophisticated use of tools to manipulate or create false evidence or modify existing artifacts.Diggers make reasonably sophisticated use of tools to manipulate or create false evidence or modify artifacts. Such risks are compounded in the context of data out of direct control, such as those of IoT ecosystems and cloud computing systems.

4.3 Legal Barriers to Admitting Digital Evidence in Court

A number of legal obstacles present challenges to admitting digital evidence into criminal trials. To assure reliability and relevance, courts expect strictness. The Daubert or Frye standard in the United States to validate methods and tools from the scientific community. The Indian Evidence Act, 1872 (Sections 65A & 65B for electronic records) requires a responsible person to certify documents in India, but implementation of this requirement is often weak.

But judges and juries do not often have some scientific expertise and therefore can depend on expert testimony which can be debunked. When security personnel make errors in procedure, use the tools are limited or steps are not documented, it is tried to shake creditability of the tools. There are a number of digital forensic tools which are proprietary, and the level of peer-reviewed validation is relatively low; this has raised concerns regarding the reproducibility and potential biases of the tools (Kazaure et al., 2024). However, change in case law adds to the uncertainty. New anti-forensic techniques may mean that what was okay 5 years ago won't be so today. The dependence on automated outputs of tools without any manual verification as well renders an admissible process.

4.4 Cross-Jurisdictional and Cloud Storage Complications

There are significant problems with cross-jurisdictional issues and cloud storage in digital forensics. Cloud data centers may be situated in different countries, with different data protection laws that apply to their data, like the GDPR in Europe or local privacy laws in India.Cloud data centers often store data in different locations in different countries with different data protection laws that apply to that data, such as GDPR in Europe or local privacy laws in India. Such data are not readily accessible, and only via slow Mesis Task Forces or formal requests which are often unsuccessful.

The problems are that come up is data sovereignty in which providers do not provide the data due to local law. Issues surrounding privacy come into play as evidence is isolated while attempting to avoid accessing non-relevant data on shared infrastructure and devices, and encryption makes an impact. Cloud data is "dynamic" users or automated systems can update the files before the investigators are able to, by editing, moving, or deleting them.

In multi-jurisdictional cybercrime cases, there is a conflict over the methods of evidence collection, as well as evidence admissibility. Certain actions that are legally allowed in one country might not be in another because of their procedural differences. Data moving through several borders with VPNs / proxies makes attribution more complex.

4.5 Human Error and Tool Validation Problems

Errors people make and poor tool validation continue to be common pitfalls in classic DF even today. Investigators could accidentally alter data metadata, not utilize write-blockers, or mishandle devices, damaging entire datasets. These are compounded by poor work capacity, lack of training, and the need for high turn-around speed for huge amounts of data. Even a skilled examiner can miss important artifacts or have difficulties interpreting complicated data.

There are many forensic tools for which there is no complete independent validation. There could be undiscovered bugs in proprietary software, or there could be bugs in different versions of the same software. Courts more often doubt and test the reliability of the tool output that is inconsistent with a thorough testing and peer review process. New technologies are emerging too quickly for examiner certifications and the development of new tools. Processes are poorly documented; is difficult to prove due diligence in court. With many agencies facing budget restraints, access to cutting-edge, validated tools and ongoing professional development are limited (Oghazi et al., 2026).

5. BLOCKCHAIN APPLICATIONS FOR STABILIZING DIGITAL FORENSICS

The blockchain's transformative potential for digital forensics is largely driven by its ability to solve key challenges in the industry by being decentralized, open, and secure. In simple terms, blockchain is a distributed ledger that acts as an unalterable record of the evidence lifecycle, providing verifiable evidence and time-stamps, and using cryptographic hashes to secure it. A hash of the digital evidence (such as device images, network logs or files) are recorded on the blockchain at the time of collection. Any subsequent change, no matter how small, would create a mismatched hash, and therefore it would be possible to easily detect tampering. It offers an unprecedented degree of integrity assurance, which traditional chain-of-custody forms can not match.

It has many key applications, such as the management of the chain of custody, where every step in transferring evidence from investigators, forensic labs, prosecutors and courts is automatically recorded on a smart contract. This provides an automated and auditable record which minimises human errors and disagreements. In addition, blockchain technology opens the door to secure evidence storage through hybrid implementations which store sensitive raw data in encrypted, off-chain storage and place metadata and evidence verification proofs on the blockchain. Multiple agencies equipped with the blockchain can share with a consortium of permissioned blockchain, while keeping private with zero-knowledge proofs and role-based access.

Other use cases include tracking evidence in real time during multi-agency operations; capturing, automatically hashing and logging evidence using forensic tools; and evironproofing digital evidence, such as photographs, video footage and IoT information. During cybercrime incidents, blockchain can reliably mark digital evidence of malware, communications and transactions, even when they are manipulated.In the context of cybercrime events, blockchain can reliably time stamp digital data including malware, communications and transactions that may be altered. A few such platforms, like the Hyperledger Fabric and solutions based on ethereum and with improvements in privacy, are being used as a test (Akremi, 2025). Through mathematical proof, blockchain eliminates many difficulties in obtaining evidence that is volatile and easily manipulated. It does take a few areas to consider for successful implementation, however, as it affects scalability of large forensic data sets, interoperability with other tools and training of forensic personnel. Blockchain simplifies digital forensics, transforming it from a trusted system to a verifiable and trustless one and improving the efficiency of investigations and the judicial confidence in blockchain.

6. BLOCKCHAIN SOLUTIONS FOR CYBERCRIME EVIDENCE MANAGEMENT AND COURT ADMISSIBILITY

Blockchain-based solution can serve as an all-in-one evidence management system for cybercrime and address the admissibility issues in court. The good thing about blockchain is that it leaves behind "block" trails, as a digital record, that are inviolable and can be relied upon for authentication purposes to a high degree that is required by legal standards. Blockchain can provide a secure log of volatile data like memory dumps, server logs, cryptocurrency transactions, and communication metadata from seizure to analysis and trial in cyber crime investigations that involve ransomware, phishing, or financial fraud.

Specific functions, such as handling the handing over of custody evidence, logging evidence access, and ensuring data integrity, are automated using smart contracts, thereby reducing the chance of procedural mishandling resulting in evidence being excluded. Blockchain-generated proofs, including timestamps, hash chains, digital signatures, etc., provide objective, verifiable documentation that enhances compliance with requirements of the law in India, Evidence Act Section 65B, Daubert standards, or other reliability tests. Judges will be able to independently review evidence handling without having to rely on possibly contentious expert testimony.

Zero-knowledge proofs, homomorphic encryption, and confidential channels are examples of privacy-preserving techniques that enable the exchange of sensitive data without compromising privacy, yet ensuring the court with the audibility to data integrity. Hybrid models of blockchain also provide a solution to the challenge of verifying the authenticity of evidence, this time in a public manner – without revealing the confidential information of cases – just as is done with the blockchain models. In the real world, blockchain-supported cases have been shown to be more efficient in terms of the time that is needed for litigation and the number of challenges that have to be addressed for admittance.

These solutions also enable information sharing on a cross-Jurisdictional basis, by providing comparable, cross-jurisdictional abstracts that can be verified across the jurisdictions. However, there are challenges still to be overcome, from having blockchain evidence be legally recognized as evidence, legalizing various blockchain protocols to achieving system security from sophisticated adversaries. However, blockchain transforms the often-contested nature of cybercrime evidence into hard-to-dispute assets. It improves prosecution outcomes, boosts public confidence in the justice system and helps the development of evidence regulations to keep pace with new technologies (Abdullahi et al., 2023). In a world in which regulations are moving toward maturity, blockchain is ready to become a dependable evidence management solution for cybercrime around the world.

7. CONCLUSION AND FUTURE DIRECTIONS

As a final thought, the incorporation of blockchain in criminal investigations marks a turning point in the way digital forensics will be conducted and digital evidence from cybercrimes will be admissible. Users can benefit from decentralization, immutability and robust cryptographic features to overcome commonly recurring challenges such as evidence modification, missing or lost links, volatility of data and official scrutiny. It converts frail and tender electronic evidence into business-friendly, court-proof proof with provable audit trails and cryptographic authentication and authentication, thereby beefing up the justice-delivering chain.

The findings of this study have shown the various ways in which blockchain applications are applicable to practical use cases, particularly those relevant to law enforcement, including real-time logging, multi-agency secure communication and architectural designs that protect privacy. On the other hand, consortium and hybrid blockchain seem best suited for certain forensic applications; however, their ability to become viable in practice depends on other issues, such as scalability, interoperability, energy-efficient solutions, data privacy, and compliance with legal and ethical standards.

Future plans should involve building the national and international standards for Blockchain forensics tools, implementing more specialized courses for forensic investigators and implementing blockchain pilot programs in the cybercrime units. The capabilities will continue to grow with integration of new technologies like Artificial Intelligence (AI) for intelligent evidence analysis, quantum-resistant cryptography, and IoT Forensics. Policy supports and investment into infrastructure are needed to facilitate blockchain adoption in policing by governments, especially those with high growth in digital economies, such as India.

Research needs to proceed regarding cost benefit analysis, security analysis of long-term blockchain evidence, and public perception of blockchain evidence. Ethical safeguards need to ensure that the technology complements – and does not supersede – the human element. In the end, the use of blockchain has the power to restore trust in digital evidence, bolstering conviction in cybercrime cases, and furthering the ongoing criminal justice revolution in the digital era. Its transformative vision will require proactively engaging all rhetorians, law enforcement, legal experts, and policy makers throughout.

REFERENCES

. Abdullahi, Z. H., Singh, S. K., & Hasan, M. (2023). Software reverse engineering techniques for evaluating anti-forensic encryption tools: A framework development and analysis. *Int. J. Intell. Syst. Appl. Eng.*

Akhtar, M. S., & Feng, T. (2022). Using blockchain to ensure the integrity of digital forensic evidence in an iot environment. *EAI Endorsed Transactions on Creative Technologies*, *9*(31), e2. DOI: 10.4108/eai.3-6-2022.174089

Akremi, A. (2025). ForensicTwin: Incorporating Digital Forensics Requirements Within a Digital Twin. *Computers*, *14*(4), 115. DOI: 10.3390/computers14040115

Balmiki, V. (2023, October). An evidence collection using blockchain for cybercrime detection. In *2023 4th IEEE Global Conference for Advancement in Technology (GCAT)* (pp. 1-7). IEEE. DOI: 10.1109/GCAT59970.2023.10353259

Daoud, G. (2023). *The evolving nature of financial crime with the increase of internet capabilities. challenge identification, legal considerations and policy recommendations* (Doctoral dissertation, School of Advanced Study).

Haque, E. U., Abbasi, W., Murugesan, S., Anwar, M. S., Khan, F., & Lee, Y. (2023). Cyber forensic investigation infrastructure of Pakistan: An analysis of the cyber threat landscape and readiness. *IEEE Access : Practical Innovations, Open Solutions*, *11*, 40049–40063. DOI: 10.1109/ACCESS.2023.3268529

Igonor, O. S., Amin, M. B., & Garg, S. (2025). The application of blockchain technology in the field of digital forensics: A literature review. *Blockchains*, *3*(1), 5. DOI: 10.3390/blockchains3010005

Kazaure, A. A., Yusoff, M. N., & Jantan, A. (2024). Digital Forensic Investigation on Social Media Platforms: A Survey on Emerging Machine Learning Approaches. [JIStaP]. *Journal of Information Science Theory and Practice*, *12*(1).

Kazaure, A. A., Yusoff, M. N., & Jantan, A. (2024). Digital Forensic Investigation on Social Media Platforms: A Survey on Emerging Machine Learning Approaches. [JIStaP]. *Journal of Information Science Theory and Practice*, *12*(1).

Kiressanth, R. RS, K. R., & Santhi, K. (2025, September). Enhancing Digital Forensics: A Cyber Triage Tool for Streamlined and Efficient Investigations. In *2025 IEEE International Conference on Advances in Computing Research On Science Engineering and Technology (ACROSET)* (pp. 1-6). IEEE.

Muragijimana, E., Shankar, T. N., Kumar, N., Sah, B., & Padhy, S. (2022, October). Digital crimes in cloud environment and the analysis via blockchain. In *2022 IEEE 3rd Global Conference for Advancement in Technology (GCAT)* (pp. 1-6). IEEE. DOI: 10.1109/GCAT55367.2022.9972221

Oghazi, P., Kordestani, A., & Mostaghel, R. (2026). Ecosystem-based framework for organized cybercrime. *The International Entrepreneurship and Management Journal*, *22*(2), 86. DOI: 10.1007/s11365-026-01212-x

. Patrick, H. A., Gujjar, P. J., Prasad, G. M., Kumar, R., & Kumar, N. H. (2025). Issues and Challenges in Emerging Cyber Forensics and Traditional Cyber Forensics Methods. *Cyberology*, 90-102.

Ratul, M. H. A., Mollajafari, S., & Wynn, M. (2024). Managing Digital Evidence in Cybercrime: Efforts Towards a Sustainable Blockchain-Based Solution. *Sustainability (Basel)*, *16*(24), 10885. DOI: 10.3390/su162410885

Sun, P. (2025). On a Multidimensional Framework for Cross-Border Cybercrime Asset Recovery in the Digital Era. *China Legal Sci.*, *13*, 136.

Chapter 6
Cross-Border Evidence Sharing:
Blockchain for International Legal Cooperation

Pooja
http://orcid.org/0009-0004-4463-3317
Reliable Institute of Law, Ghaziabad, India

Saurabh Chandra
http://orcid.org/0000-0003-4172-9968
Symbiosis International (Deemed to be) University, India

ABSTRACT

Cybercrime has gone global, making the exchange of evidence a critical component in the fight against it in criminal investigations. Typical processes like Mutual Legal Assistance Treaties (MLATs) are time-consuming, cumbersome and frequently insufficient for time sensitive digital evidence. In this chapter, the author illustrates how blockchain technology could help transform the way the world enters into international collaboration by answering some of the key questions, including how can blockchain technology enable the secure and immutable exchange of evidence in international legal processes and execute it without compromising the principles of national sovereignty. The use of blockchain can provide a plausible chain of custody, interestingly, requests and requests can be automated using smart contracts, and privacy preserving architectures are also possible, establishing trust between countries.

DOI: 10.4018/979-8-3373-9730-6.ch006

1. INTRODUCTION

The sharing of evidence across jurisdictions is now one of the most intricately complex and important but at the same time difficult components of criminal justice in the digital era. The integrity of the traditional international cooperation tools has been starkly tested as cyber crime evolves in unprecedented speed and scale across countries. This is because conventional international cooperation tools are clearly ill-equipped in the current era of breakthroughs in cyber crime perpetrated across countries at unprecedented speed and scale (Casino et al., 2022). The availability of digital evidence stored or transmitted across borders is a massive burden on law enforcement, as they often experience considerable delays in its retrieval and a diminished chance of timely police action, its preservation, or even the entire case being lost. In addressing sovereignty and privacy concerns, blockchain technology appears to be a viable solution which can offer secure, decentralised and verified methods for exchanging evidence and uphold system integrity and security (Zhang & Gong, 2024).

The chapter discusses how blockchain could help bring about a seamless and yet sovereign respecting international legal cooperation. It explores the ever-changing nature of transnational cybercrime, the shortcomings of current tools such as MLATs and Letters Rogatory, and how these specific and unique attributes of blockchain can provide trust between nations with varying legal systems. Blockchain architectures, integration with existing international (ISO) frameworks, real-world pilot projects are discussed, along with technologies for privacy. The balance between effective information sharing and respect for national data sovereignty, human rights and privacy requirements is a specific focus (Cami & Karsai, 2025). The opportunities and challenges are explored to give an overall picture of the possibilities and limitations of blockchain to transform global criminal investigation and improve global cooperation in the defense against trans-border cyber-crimes. In this study, which examines the technical architecture, legal framework, practical implementation, and obstacles to blockchain adoption in evidence sharing that crosses borders, the Special Rapporteur identifies key constraints and opportunities (Guan, 2025).

Blockchain can support and bolster international efforts against cybercrime through more speedy, reliable, and tamper-proof collaboration, improve prosecution results, and standardize digital evidence practices across legal jurisdictions, etc., which are just a few examples of the blockchain's potential to assist international efforts in combating cybercrime. Some examples of potential blockchain support of international efforts to combat cybercrime are: more speedy collaboration, more reliable collaboration, collaboration that is less likely to be tampered with, improved prosecution results, and harmonization of digital evidence across legal jurisdictions.

1.1 Transnational Cybercrime and Evidence Needs

The growth of the Internet, advanced criminals' networks and increasing digital transformation has led to the transnational cybercrime. The transnational cybercrime has been growing at an exponential rate due to the borderless Internet, the complexity of the group of criminals and the digital transformation (Park & Jeong, 2026). Fraud, ransom, large-scale data breaches, cyber espionage by a nation-state, dark web trafficking for payment of sexual crimes and human trafficking are all regular pan-national crimes that occur weekly, if not daily. Global statistics outline the cost of cybercrime as potentially trillions of dollars each year, of which tremendous parts have international elements. Criminal enterprises capitalise and take advantage of the differences in jurisdictions that can cover their tracks and store evidence far removed from the crime scene and in any corner of the world; VPNs, proxies and cloud services can be utilised from continent to continent to do so (Franssen, 2024).

This increase has spurred the need for speedy and dependable bilateral sharing of evidence. Digital evidence commonly resides within databases or servers located across the globe, as well as in distributed cloud environments such as blockchain, which is accessed and managed by all clients on the blockchain. Digital evidence, that is, databases or server logs, communication metadata, hacked databases and information from IoT devices, is stored in foreign data centres or in distributed cloud (Alvarez et al., 2022). Blockchain data is accessible and managed by every client on the blockchain. It is important that investigators can gain access quickly in order to prevent lost or encrypted volatile evidence. But the classical cooperation channels are time consuming, and in some cases, the MLAT process can be lengthy, taking months or years (Siqi et al., 2024). This can make it easier for the culprit to get away, eliminate evidence, and commit more crimes.

The evidence must not only be collected, but also kept intact, traceable and reliable for use in a variety of legal contexts (Sachdeva et al., 2025). The difficulty can be exacerbated by differences in the acceptance of electronic evidence as evidence, data encryption laws, and data jurisdiction laws. Especially countries such as India which are experiencing an increase in cyber threats from outside the country are in need of effective mechanisms to cooperate with the US, EU and the Southeast Asian region. As ransomware-as-a-service and cyber syndicates have emerged, the demand for live and authentic evidence exchange platforms intensifies, further (Díaz-Perez et al., 2026). The blockchain holds the promise of securing the infrastructure for doing this, providing a technological solution to share securely, respecting the nationality and speeding up justice.

1.2 Role of Blockchain in Addressing Sovereignty and Trust Issues

The shortcomings of trust and sovereignty in cross-border evidence sharing has been a major challenge for which blockchain technology holds great potential to provide solutions. Countries have been reluctant to share sensitive data due to considerations of national sovereignty, for fear that it might be misused, breach their privacy or be beyond their control (Tang, 2023). In carefully designed permissioned networks, every nation who takes part controls the data within their own network and has access to a shared "immutable" ledger that can be used to verify data.In thoughtfully-designed permissioned networks, every nation participating has control of their own chain of data and a shared immutable ledger for verifying the data (Huang et al., 2024).

Countries can store raw sensitive evidence on their own (off-chain or in their private storage) with the cryptographic hashes, timestamps and metadata being recorded on the shared ledger in a hybrid or consortium blockchain architecture (Liang et al., 2025). This allows partner countries to verify the integrity and authenticity of evidence, without having access to the complete evidence, unless they have express permission. Selective disclosure means to show that evidence is correct, but not disclose the evidence itself, through the use of zero-knowledge proofs and certain types of advanced encryption.

Smart contracts also contribute to the trust by automating the verification process, simplifying the approval process, and tracking the chain of custody without the need for dealing with a lot of paperwork and bureaucratic processes (Xiao et al., 2025). All accesses, transfers and modifications are recorded and tracked permanently and are visible to all authorized stakeholders, leading to unprecedented transparency and accountability. This helps to reduce any instances of altering evidence or political manipulation.

The other advantages of blockchain are that it embodies mutual trust by giving the decentralized platform a neutral ground that is not biased to one country or the other. Respects international legal principles and is flexible in implementation. It can, for example, ease the conflicts of diverse EU and non-EU data access preferences and the rigorous privacy regulations in GDPR. In the realms of evidence delivery, blockchain can make the entire evidence sharing process from a diplomatic proceeding into a cryptographic-based technical transaction or system. This non-technological neutrality is vital for nations that have different political systems and legal traditions to gain trust in one another and ultimately enhance the synergies for combating transnational cybercrime through greater cooperation (ALsheyab, 2025).

2. LEGAL AND REGULATORY FRAMEWORKS FOR BLOCKCHAIN-BASED EVIDENCE EXCHANGE

The legal and regulatory aspects of blockchain that are relevant to the exchange of evidence are the pillars for their widespread use in relevant international criminal cooperation. International criminal cooperation's use of blockchain is laid down in the legal and regulatory aspects of blockchain that are relevant for the exchange of evidence. These frameworks need to take into account technological innovation, sovereignty, standards for the protection of data, human rights and the standards of admissibility of judicial procedures. There is currently no international agreement on tangling blockchain evidence, with a collection of national, regional and international laws and regulations necessitating harmonization (Wu, 2024).

At a national level, countries are addressing existing electronic evidence laws to fit blockchain evidence. Many know that blockchain information inherently has the characteristics of being self-authenticating, because of its immutability and cryptographic verification process. But there are certain issues that still remain to be addressed, such as the enforceability of smart contracts, cross-border recognition and the legal validity of records on-chain. Blockchain systems need to respect the privacy by design principles under the privacy rules including GDPR of the EU, the Digital Personal Data Protection Act (DPDP) of India and other privacy laws in various other jurisdictions have strong requirements for how data is processed, stored and transferred.

Internationally, the frameworks put emphasis on mutual assistance with a view to digital realities. As blockchain keeps evolving, protocols are required for different aspects of it, including admissibility, chain of custody and interoperability. Indeed, crucial questions involve existing standards for forensically validating blockchain records, establishing standards for liability to govern smart contract failures and determining how to govern in decentralized environments. These models are being piloted and assessed in real-life situations in different regulatory jurisdictions through regulatory sandboxes.

An effective evidence exchange system requires two things: Legal frameworks need to promote the use of blockchain-based evidence while creating legal clarity and also present some guidelines for hybrid approaches. Future work needs to direct efforts towards creating multilateral cooperation agreements that incorporate blockchain with other cooperation mechanisms with a focus on essential rights (Qasim et al., 2025). An infinite combination of technology and legislation is crucial to realise blockchain's potential in fighting transnational crimes.

2.1 International Legal Standards and Treaties (Budapest Convention, UNTOC)

The Budapest Convention on Cybercrime (2001) and the United Nations Convention against Transnational Organized Crime (UNTOC) are key international tools that support the exchange of evidence using a blockchain. As the first binding international cybercrime treaty, the Budapest Convention brings together the various definitions and laws related to cybercrime at the national level. It offers facilitation for the secure speedy preservation of stored data, manufactured orders and mutual legal aid (MLA). Blockchain applications cannot be overlooked when it comes to the direct cooperation with service providers, streamlined procedures in MLA's, 24/7 contact points, providing cross-border access with the development of, and cooperation with electronic evidence.

UNTOC (Palermo Convention, 2000) is focusing on transnational organized crime, which encompasses cyber crimes. Promotes cooperation in mutual legal assistance, extradition, joint investigations and special investigative techniques. It doesn't cover cyber crimes specifically, but the general evidence-sharing and organized crime which it contains does. Some of these treaties set a foundation that features procedural legitimacy for digital evidence with regards to integrating blockchain. Immutability of audit trail and automated preservation logging are two ways blockchain can support compliance with Budapest Convention. Yet there are also drawbacks: Given the lack of broad usage of blockchains, both are drafted before the advent of specific mechanisms dealing with distributed ledgers, smart contracts or cryptographic proofs.

Challenges lie in the fact that different countries have different statuses regarding ratification, some countries have reservations, and some conflicted laws are issues of data localizations and privacy laws. The Second Protocol of the Budapest Convention moves the ball for quicker disclosure of evidence that will be viable on the blockchain through secure and verifiable communication. Further amendments to the Agreement, supplementary protocols may explicitly ratify the blockchain records as reliable evidence. Seamless and efficient cross-border cooperation in the digital era, and harmonization with future blockchain standards, is essential for establishing trust and making the entire system work.

3. BLOCKCHAIN ARCHITECTURES AND TECHNOLOGIES FOR CROSS-BORDER EVIDENCE SHARING

The blockchain-based architecture for the exchange of evidence at the cross-border level must take into account the issues of sovereignty, privacy, scalability and interoperability. Most appropriate are Consortium and Hybrid blockchain which enable trusted national authorities or international organizations to be nodes whilst still being responsible for sensitive data. Consortium where each country involved shares management rights for the network, granting permission to access certain records, or to validate, only to people authorised to do so.

Hybrid architectures include mixing private chains for evidence storage in other chains for cryptographic anchors (hashed evidence and timestamps). This allows countries to keep raw data at home and show internationally that it is a valid and correct representation of the integrity. Polkadot, Cosmos, and Hyperledger's cross-chain standards are examples of interoperability protocols that enable communication between different blockchain systems in different countries or regions.

Popular enabling technologies include advanced cryptography, such as 'zero knowledge proofs' (ZKPs), which enable parties to verify without having to reveal the underlying data; and secure multi-party computation. These not only preserve privacy, but have an evidentiary standard as well. Very large forensic files are efficiently processed with distributed storage solutions such as combining IPFS with blockchain (Sule et al., 2024).

To make it a reality, it needs to be integrated with existing systems such as INTERPOL's I-24/7 and Europol's platforms. Security measures include quantum-resistant algorithms and strong consensus protocols like Practical Byzantine Fault Tolerance, safeguarding against advanced attacks. These architectures enable real-time evidence tracking, automated compliance reporting and have the ability to provide an auditable trail that could be accepted across jurisdictions. Issues that need to be addressed include standardisation, governance issues in countries, and scale of the amount of evidence.

3.1 Smart Contracts for Automated Evidence Requests and Transfers

Smart contracts are self-executing, and are programs that can be programmed that are rolled out on blockchain and enforce the terms if the conditions are fulfilled. They bring innovation to the traditionally manual, time consuming cross border evidence sharing by automating the request, approval, transfer and logging processes. A general smart contract for evidence exchange can be designed similarly to the MLA, in that a requesting authority can make a formal digital request, offering the specifics of the case and legal grounds for the request. The contract automatically alerts the data holding jurisdiction, checks compliance with mutual agreements (such as dual criminality, proportionality or others) and if approved, sets off secure transfer of the cryptographic proofs or data packages authorized. All actions are permanently recorded and time-stamped, providing an open bookkeeping system.

Advantages encompass significant amounts of time that can be saved between months and hours or even minutes in the processing; the risk of tampering or loss of evidence is reduced. Smart contracts can include privacy rules, which automatically redact sensitive information in fields or even use the zero-knowledge proof. These are generally utilized to provide expiration dates, restrict access to the data, and share restrictions, all of which strengthen compliance with data protection laws (Cao et al., 2022).

Smart contracts are designed to be interoperable with other legal principles, such as those in the Budapest Convention and the UNTOC, which guarantees that automated processes respect international requirements, in practice. They enable conditional releases (sRelease – release on judicial approval – etc.) and the inclusion of multiple stakeholders for multi-signature approvals. The difficulty of obtaining enforceability through various jurisdictions, the challenge of coding mistakes that can be hard to fix after deployment and the updating of contracts to adhere to the intricacies of the law. Contract templates need to be standardised and there must be greater auditing.

4. GLOBAL PILOT PROJECTS IN BLOCKCHAIN EVIDENCE SHARING

Existing pilot initiatives that involve the exchange of evidence through blockchain technology around the world are still in the early stages and show a rising momentum towards the identification of evidence, particularly in the context of criminal investigations and cross-border cooperation (Rashid & East, 2022)). The EU-financed LOCARD Project is a project that is developing a Digital Evidence Management platform, covering the entire range. It leverages blockchain technology to establish an unalterable chain of custody, improving transparency in handling evidence from collection to presentation in court. The project is designed to be seamlessly integrated into existing law enforcement systems and aims to address the common problems in evidence management, such as those encountered in multi-jurisdictional cases.

One major project is the LAW-GAME Project that uses Hyperledger Fabric (a consortium blockchain that is permissionless) to provide integrity and traceability of digital evidence. Capable to effortlessly connect with Digital Evidence Management Systems (DEMS) through API and Smart Contract, enabling various agencies to confirm evidence without compromising confidentiality. Dubai Police has trialed Cardano blockchain timestamping for body camera footage and investigatory files which generate verisimilitude, thereby protecting such files from tampering or deepfake manipulation.

Judicial blockchain platforms in Asia have progressed especially in China, where the Supreme People's Court has developed everything from a secure shared data platform for electronic evidence and archives to an enforcement data platform that allows for streamlined data sharing between courts and government bodies. These systems were mainly internal, but paved the way for later international developments. Conceptual and smaller-scale piloting of docketing Criminal Cases and sharing of evidence through a consortium in other jurisdictions, including South Africa.

Various organisations at the international level, including INTERPOL and Europol, are investigating linking to VAPs like I-24/7 for virtual asset investigation, but the use is still primarily on the tracing of virtual assets such as cryptocurrencies. The sovereignty issue is frequently addressed in projects using the blockchain alongside privacy mechanisms such as zero knowledge proofs.

The following are some of the major advantages displayed by these pilots: faster processing times, enhanced admissibility via cryptographic proofs and greater inter-agency collaboration. Challenges remain, however, such as scalability with large forensic datasets, legal harmonization of jurisdictional integration, interoperability of different blockchain networks, differing maturity of national technological solutions, and so on. The majority of projects are still at the proof-of-concept or pilot deployment stage and few fully functional global systems are focused on comprehensive evidence exchange. Standardization, Regulatory Support, and Trust-building among participating Countries is vital to Success. As these pilots grow, they will be a source of wider learning, building closer to the learning of more efficient, verifiable digital processes for shareable, slow traditional MLA processes.

4.1 Indian Perspectives on Cross-Border Cybercrime Cooperation

India finds itself in a special place across the globe when it comes to cross-border cybercrime cooperation, given a number of unique reasons like its rapidly-digitizing economy, high volume of cyber incidents, and geopolitical positioning. Global cyber crimes such as ransomware threats, financial crimes, cryptocurrency fraud, and Southeast Asia and Eastern European cyber trafficking of humane are big risks. Indian agencies including the Ministry of Home Affairs's Indian Cyber Crime Coordination Centre (I4C) have emphasised cooperation internationally and other bilateral deals such as the 24/7 network of the G8, as well as with INTERPOL, where immediate data preservation is an urgent concern.

India is progressively moving toward improved data transparency by getting involved in the OECD's Crypto-Asset Reporting Framework (CARF) that will enable automatic exchange of cross-border crypto transactions from April 2027. The regulation marks a significant progress in terms of transparency for virtual asset investigations. Joint-operations, victim-repatriation and evidence requests are strong with the country, such as the USA, UK, UAE, Singapore and Thailand. In recent times, the MoUs signed by I4C with various institutions such as the Reserve Bank Innovation Hub to exchange information on mule accounts and financial fraud have to be mentioned.

In spite of the progress, there is no Budapest Convention being ratified in India, and its bilateral treaties are favored over an overall treaty.Although India has already established some measure of progress, regarding ratification of the Budapest Convention, they have chosen the bilateral treaties over an overall one and also have chosen the UN-centric options based on UNTOC. Such a stance sometimes hinders cooperation but ensures the safeguarding of data localization interests per legislation in countries, including the Digital Personal Data Protection Act. Traditional approaches leading to the production of electronic copies of evidence are time consuming, typically stretching out over a number of months (months), which has led to a need for a more technological based approach.

Blockchain is seen as a potential solution to this. There is a cluster of research and agency initiatives underway in India for secure recording and chain of custody documentation in cybercrime cases via permissioned blockchain options.A group of research and agency activities are emerging in India for secure documentary purposes through environment like evidence logging/custodial control on the blockchain for a cybercrime case with a permissioned ledger-based proposal (Eyo-Udo et al., 2024). There are no large scale national evidence-sharing pilots using blockchain, but there is a discussion about linking with the existing initiatives such as National Cyber Crime Reporting Portal and cyber lab. Technology gaps between states, capacity development, privacy issues, and integrating blockchain applications with the Indian Evidence Act are among the challenges.

When it comes to future directions for India, investing in platforms that enable fast adoption of MLA, engaging with global standards development efforts and building capacity by training with international partners will be considered. Greater connection with QUAD countries and BRICS could ease the way for region-specific blockchain solutions addressing Asian cyber threats. The push for sovereignty and innovation is the balance that India hopes to strike to make itself a proactive force in the world of cybercrime, while ensuring the interests of the nation and the privacy of its citizens.

5. CHALLENGES AND ETHICAL CONSIDERATIONS

The introduction of blockchain to share verification across borders poses great challenges in the fields of technology, law, politcs and ethics. Scalability continues to be an issue, albeit technically,'". Digital evidence can come in many formats, from high-resolution video footage, complete images of devices, to vast quantities of log files and more.There is often a huge amount of digital evidence involved in criminal investigations: high resolution video footage, complete images of a device, transcripts of log data, and more. Efficiently processing and storing the amounts of data required to run such a large network, while maintaining low transaction costs and acceptable speeds on the network, is difficult in most blockchain networks. Another challenge highlighted is Interoperability between national or regional blockchain systems, as different countries could use different technologies, consensus mechanisms, and standards, causing interoperability to be fragmented instead (Oliveira, 2023).

Chain security issues, such as a 51% Attack risk on public chains, smart contract vulnerabilities and the threat of quantum computing to existing cryptographic security methods, also pose serious concerns to the integrity of evidence which will go through a well rigorous examination of judicial authorities. On the legal side, there is lack of clarity regarding the recognition of blockchain evidence under international law. Implementation complexities include the different rules for admissibility and inconsistencies in accepting electronic records, along with regulatory issues between data localization laws and needs for data sharing. Not all countries have updated their evidence laws to make evidence from decentralized ledgers or smart contract outputs specifically fit into Prima Facie evidence.

Sovereignty issues are foremost politically. One of the main concerns is that countries may be hesitant to join a cross-border blockchain network because of concerns about ceding control over sensitive data, or the risk of it being misused for political surveillance purposes. Unequal participation and benefits from technological development may ensue due to power imbalances between technologically advanced and developing countries (Lindeman et al., 2024). From an ethical point of view, the application of blockchain creates ethical challenges concerning human rights and privacy. Great efforts are being made with the "right to be forgotten" regulation like GDPR, which contradicts the blockchain's "right to forget," but that is not enough. The danger of mission creep also exists, that systems set up to spook billies in cybercrime may learn to affect "normal citizens or prospective political dissidents. How does the legal community deal with the problem of accountability arising when smart contracts act on their own?

Cost, difficult training of law enforcement and judicial staff, and digital divide problems, which can keep smaller, less-developed countries from being included, are among the other difficulties encountered. It is vital to ensure equity of access and to avoid the technology being used as a tool of "digital colonialism. Ensuring transparency for the purposes of justice and yet maintaining confidentiality for sensitive operations, vulnerable populations, and to prevent algorithmic bias in evidence validation systems is a tricky ethical fist-off-hand, and requires adequate governance measures, proper supervision and regular ethical oversight. Solve these complex problems is essential for blockchain to be trusted and legitimate across the globe in evidence sharing.

6. CONCLUSION

Blockchain functions have the potential to transform the way information sharing and collaboration takes place across borders and to bolster international efforts in combating transnational cybercrime. Through the immutable record, streamlined workflows with smart contracts, cryptographically guaranteed traceability of the origin of data and the necessary transactions, and privacy protection, blockchain solves problems, delays and lack of trust in traditional methods of cooperation, including so-called mutual legal assistance treaties, or MLATs. Designed on sound consortium or hybrid solutions it allows to share evidence faster, more securely and in a manner that is respectful of sovereignty, and improve the quality of digital evidence for use in courts the world over.

While international laws and conventions are evolving to account for technological innovations, and the novel approaches piloting blockchain internationally are evolving, this chapter has pointed out the ways in which both have been merged to cover the gaps.International laws and conventions are progressively adapting to technological advances and innovation, while blockchain innovations are being experimented globally; this chapter has focused on the ways in which technological advances and innovation have been caught up by both international laws and conventions as well as international experiments with blockchain innovations. Yet, to realize that possibility, it will take significant technical, legal, political and ethical hurdles (described above) to overcome. Finally, it will require cooperation between governments, internationally working organisations and technologists and legal professionals to agree on standardised protocols, build capacity and create strong governance models for success.

7. FUTURE TRENDS

The future of the domain has bright prospects, with some exciting trends in the near future. The convergence of Artificial Intelligence and Machine Learning with blockchain will facilitate engaging in intelligent evidence analysis, large data anomaly detection automation, and predicting and identifying cross-border crime patterns. As such, quantum-resistant cryptography is needed to build future-proof systems in the face of future computational risks. Seamless multi-chain ecosystems, and the potential creation of a global "Evidence Blockchain Federation" under neutral, international leadership and oversight, could greatly improve participation and trust.

It can expect more experience with regulations, as more countries update their evidence laws to include blockchain evidence and new treaties or protocols tailored to digital evidence are developed. Combined with the rise of blockchain and decentralized identity systems and enhanced privacy technologies, this blockchain evolution will further tilt the balance in favor of the security requirements and the rights of individuals. The potential of increased cooperation within the I4C, inclusion of crypto assets in CARF and other plans for aligning – in the Indian context – with enhanced Budapest Convention mechanisms would support the country's place in the regional and global blockchain evidence networks.

Blockchain technology for handling and sharing evidence across borders is a more than just a technological advancement; it's a new age of digital justice that's quicker, more equitable, and more durable. If and when it is invested in for research, ethics, international exchange, and capacity development, this technology could greatly contribute to the rule of law in the digital world. The next 10 years will tell if that's the case for the court to decide whether blockchain is the accepted eggshell for a secure and trustworthy international criminal cooperation or it takes a hit. Building it safely, inclusively and proactively will be essential to realizing its potential to provide a safer digital world.

REFERENCES

ALsheyab, M. S. A.ALsheyab. (2025). Legal analysis of the merits of electronic transferable records: Toward cross-border trade digitalization. *International Journal of Law and Management*, *67*(1), 145–163. DOI: 10.1108/IJLMA-09-2023-0209

Alvarez, O. P., i Vidal, O. V., & Vallespinós, L. D. (2022). Unlocking Blockchain evidence in international arbitration. *Iurgium [previously Spain Arbitration Review], 2022*(43).

Cami, G., & Karsai, K. (2025). International Cooperation Mechanisms in Criminal Justice: Human Rights Implications and Sovereignty Constraints in Cross-Border Access to Electronic Evidence. *Balkans Legal* [BLESS]. *Economic and Social Studies*, *2*(2), 93–110. DOI: 10.14232/bless.2025.2.93-110

Cao, S., Boyen, X., Deane, F., Miller, T., & Foth, M. (2022). Enabling cross-border trade in the face of regulatory barriers to data flow–the case of the blockchain-based service network. In *Blockchain for Industry 4.0* (pp. 285–303). CRC Press. DOI: 10.1201/9781003282914-15

Casino, F., Pina, C., López-Aguilar, P., Batista, E., Solanas, A., & Patsakis, C. (2022). SoK: Cross-border criminal investigations and digital evidence. *Journal of Cybersecurity*, *8*(1), tyac014. DOI: 10.1093/cybsec/tyac014

Díaz-Perez, L. C., Quintanar-Reséndiz, A. L., Vázquez-Álvarez, G., & Vázquez-Medina, R. (2026). A review of cross-border cooperation regulation for digital forensics in LATAM from the soft systems methodology. *Applied Computing and Informatics*, *22*(1-2), 115–128. DOI: 10.1108/ACI-01-2022-0010

Eyo-Udo, N. L., Agho, M. O., Onukwulu, E. C., Sule, A. K., Azubuike, C., Nigeria, L., & Nigeria, P. (2024). Advances in blockchain solutions for secure and efficient cross-border payment systems. *International Journal of Research and Innovation in Applied Science*, *9*(12), 536–563.

Franssen, V. (2024). Cross-border gathering of electronic evidence in the EU: toward more direct cooperation under the e-Evidence Regulation. In *Research Handbook on EU Criminal Law* (pp. 184–211). Edward Elgar Publishing. DOI: 10.4337/9781800886438.00016

. Guan, C. (2025). Cross-Border Cybercrime Digital Evidence: Current Research and Fundamental Categories. *Modern Law Research, 6*(4).

Huang, L., Zhao, C., Chen, S., & Zeng, L. (2024). Blockchain: A promising technology for judicial translation services in cases with foreign elements. *Aslib Journal of Information Management*, *76*(5), 713–735. DOI: 10.1108/AJIM-11-2022-0485

Liang, Z. Y., Liu, G. Y., Ren, Y., Yang, M., Jiang, R. W., Luo, Y., & Ma, Y. S. (2025). Trustworthy data space collaborative trust mechanism driven by blockchain: Technology integration, cross-border governance, and standardization path. *Information (Basel)*, *16*(12), 1066. DOI: 10.3390/info16121066

Lindeman, J., Luchtman, M., & Van Toor, D. (2024). Admissibility of Evidence in EU Cross-Border Criminal Proceedings: Electronic Evidence, Efficiency and Fair-Trial Rights in the Netherlands. In *Admissibility of Evidence in EU Cross-Border Criminal Proceedings: Electronic Evidence, Efficiency and Fair Trial Rights* (pp. 103-126). Hart Publishing.

Oliveira, N. B. (2023). *The role of international arbitration in resolving cross-border smart contract disputes: opportunities and challenges*. PQDT-Global.

Park, Y., & Jeong, D. (2026). A blockchain-based digital evidence management system: Integrating forensic procedures and multi-party authorization. *Information Processing & Management*, *63*(5), 104654. DOI: 10.1016/j.ipm.2026.104654

Qasim, M., Rehman, I. U., & Malik, H. (2025). Cross-Border Enforcement of IP Rights in the Digital Era. *Frontiers*, *21*, 49–58.

Rashid, H., & East, C. M. (2022). Implementing Blockchain for Enhanced Transparency and Efficiency in Cross-Border Logistics. *International Journal of Core Engineering & Management*, *7*(3), 181–192.

Sachdeva, C., Kaur, P., Gangwar, V. P., & Jasrai, L. (2025). Cross-Border Collaboration in New Digital Era with Blockchain Integration. In *Blockchain in the Tourism Industry: A New Era of Secure and Transparent Travel Solutions* (pp. 235–266). Springer Nature Switzerland. DOI: 10.1007/978-3-031-95341-5_12

Siqi, C., Rajamanickam, R., Manap, N. A., & Zahir, Z. M. (2024). Application of Blockchain Technology in Cross-Border Telecommunications Network Fraud to Ensure China's Judicial Justice. *Jurnal IUS Kajian Hukum Dan Keadilan*, *12*(3), 472–486. DOI: 10.29303/ius.v12i3.1554

Sule, A. K., Eyo-Udo, N. L., Onukwulu, E. C., Agho, M. O., & Azubuike, C. (2024). Implementing blockchain for secure and efficient cross-border payment systems. *International Journal of Research and Innovation in Applied Science*, *9*(12), 508–535.

Tang, Z. (2023). Smart Courts in Cross-Border Litigation. *Rabels Zeitschrift für ausländisches und internationales Privatrecht/The Rabel Journal of Comparative and International Private Law*, (H. 1), 118-143.

Wu, S. (2024). The Legal Problems of Blockchain Technology in Cross-border E-Commerce. *J. Econ. Law*, *1*(4), 20–28. DOI: 10.62517/jel.202414403

Xiao, S., Qin, X., Tian, Y., & Dang, Z. (2025). Blockchain-Based Framework for Secure Sharing of Cross-Border Trade Data. *Computers, Materials & Continua*, *83*(2), 2351–2373. DOI: 10.32604/cmc.2025.062324

Zhang, H., & Gong, X. (2024). The research on an electronic evidence forensic system for cross-border cybercrime. *The International Journal of Evidence & Proof*, *28*(1), 21–44. DOI: 10.1177/13657127231187059

Chapter 7
Data Security and Vulnerabilities:
Hacking Brains, Unauthorized Access, and Cloud Storage Risks

Mohd Faiz Khan
School of Legal Studies, CGC University, Mohali, India

Saurabh Chandra
http://orcid.org/0000-0003-4172-9968
Symbiosis International (Deemed to be) University, India

ABSTRACT

This chapter discusses the most important issues related to data security and vulnerabilities in blockchain assisted criminal investigations, particularly in relation to "hacking brains", unauthorized access vectors, and potential risks of cloud storage in a hybrid setup. Blockchain is a solution that is unalterable & transparent but has allowed incorporation of humans, instructions/executable smart contracts and cloud solutions, creating enormous attack surfaces. A thorough analysis of social engineering attacks, insider threats, authentication vulnerabilities, smart contracts exploits and the unique vulnerabilities within the cloud computing environment that may impact the integrity and chain of custody of digital evidence. This chapter analyzed and a focus is laid on the importance of using comprehensive security measures, including those centered on humans, policies and technologies, to safeguard sensitive forensic data in the current threatening cyber landscape.

DOI: 10.4018/979-8-3373-9730-6.ch007

1. INTRODUCTION

Data security is a main reason for concern in using blockchain technology for criminal investigations and digital forensics. Although blockchain itself is inherently secure with information that is extremely hard to manipulate, it becomes vulnerable through many layers – such as human actors or hybrid architectures, smart contracts, or cloud storage.Even with blockchain's inherent ability to be immovable and cryptographically protected, the broader blockchain ecosystem paved with human actors, hybrid architectures, smart contracts and cloud storage presents multiple layers of vulnerabilities capable of exploiting the entire system by a sophisticated adversary. The risks directly impact the integrity, confidentiality and availability of digital evidence and can impact the chain of custody and court admissibility.

The most powerful and hardest-to-prevent attack vectors is "hacking brains" or exploiting the vulnerabilities in humans. Social engineering attacks are especially attractive to law enforcement, forensic analysts, prosecutors and judges. Phishing, spear-phishing, vishing and pretexting are becoming more deceptive and frequently make use of the data that's publicly available online, like from social media or other earlier breaches. With deep fake technology, it is now possible to swap the voice and video with that of an officer in a saga to grant the access of evidence or access to sensitive nodes on the blockchain for granting access. This is exacerbated by insider threats as well: If someone in the organization is unhappy or corrupt or is forced to do something, they can circumvent the security measures. Good-for-nothing training does not stop civil servants from being manipulated, stressed and rushed, or manipulated by authority it's always been proven in human factors studies, which raises questions about how those researchers were trained.

There are many layers of technical vulnerabilities to unauthorized access. Commonly, attackers in a permissioned network can successfully block by exploiting weak identity and access management (IAM) systems with brute force, credential stuffing, or password spraying. Although it's a must-have, multi-factor authentication (MFA) isn't infallible, with a number of high-profile failures including SIM swapping and push notification fatigue, in addition to compromised hardware tokens. Smart contracts can create new risks by eliminating the need for paperwork for evidence requests, transferring custody and keeping track of access logs. In the wider blockchain sector, coding mistakes like re-entrancy, integer overflow, and lack of proper access modifiers have caused multi-million-dollar losses in the industry and thus could be devastating when they are exploited to alter evidence logs or to leak sensitive information in a forensic application (Nikesh et al., 2025).

However, hybrid derivations of blockchain structure with on-chain metadata and off-chain cloud storage present challenges in security more than any others. The cloud environment is "shared responsibility" as the cloud service provider's infrastructure is protected, customers of the service are responsible for data encryption, access policies and configurations. Old vulnerabilities like public storage buckets with sensitive data, tedious IAM role permissions and lack of logging are still around the world at the top of the data breaches list. There's another layer when talking about one country and integrating with another things stored in a cloud data center in another country might be subject to different types of access requests or subpoenas, meaning there may be a backdoor access to evidence.

Other risks associated with cloud have to do with advanced persistent threats (APTs) attacking forensic data lakes, side channels on virtual machines and supply chain weaknesses in cloud forensic tools. The management of encryption key becomes very important and difficult; the poor practice of the rotation of encryption keys or weakness of the key generation system or the fact that the keys are saved alongside the encrypted file makes an effective encryption system useless. In a blockchain-forensic system, if the attacker is able to obtain off-chain storage containing raw evidence and still has on-chain hash, he/she might be able to develop convincing fake evidence in case of certain compromises of the keys that washes out the blockchain information if he/she manages to develop its evidence during the off-chain storage phase.

All these weaknesses present synergies that generate compounded risks. If a social engineering attack is successful, and you are able to steal credentials this could cause the compromise of your blockchain access and manipulation, and cloud-exfiltration of evidence. This undermines on-going investigations, as well as the overall integrity of the entire court-based blockchain evidence landscape. If defense attorneys can establish that these blockchain records are vulnerable, they can argue that these records are unreliable.

Moreover, nation-state hackers and financially well-backed cybercrime deals are targeting police blockchain projects. The incentive is very high it's an opportunity for criminals to beat their rivals in court, and to avoid prosecution if they get caught. Geopolitical standoffs may result in state-supported attacks trying to vitiate cooperation platforms in trans-border situations. Dealing with these risks calls for defense in depth and a zero-trust approach. This encompasses ongoing security awareness initiatives geared toward forensic users, smart contract auditing and the execution of formal verification, hardware security module (HSM) network application to key management, and periodic penetration testing of the entire ecosystem. Cloud-blockchain need to rely on privacy-enhancing technologies like zero-knowledge proofs and confidential computing.

2. HACKING BRAINS: SOCIAL ENGINEERING AND HUMAN FACTOR VULNERABILITIES: SOCIAL ENGINEERING TECHNIQUES TARGETING LAW ENFORCEMENT

Social engineering, often dubbed as the "weakest link in the security chain", is one of the most common and most severe flaws in blockchain-based crime investigation systems and is one of the most critical deceptive attacks. As opposed to technical exploits that aim for code or infrastructure, social engineering focuses on people, their psychology, trust and authority, along with human emotions and it can outsmart the most advanced blockchain security. Law enforcement, digital forensic analysts, prosecutors, blockchain network administrators and judicial personnel handling evidence are particularly appealing because of their access to very sensitive information, decision-making power and time-sensitive operational needs (Omotade, 2025). A successful social engineering attack can lead to the compromise of credentials, to the execution of unauthorized smart contracts, private key leaks, and the alteration of the chain-of-custody, all of which can derail the integrity of digital evidence and result in its non-admissibility in court.

The sophistication of social engineering against police has advanced a long way in both complexity and sophistication. The top two entry points continue to be Phishing and Spear-Phishing. Most phishing emails are now replaced by highly customised and targeted spear-phishing emails. The attackers do a great deal of 'googling' by gathering public data, LinkedIn, court records, and data breaches and use it to create convincing messages. For example, a legitimate e-mail message from someone in the top ranks of the police or a collaborating agency might claim it is from a high priority cross-border ransomware case, with a link or attachment that contains credential harvesting malware. Such attacks are dangerous in blockchain systems as they could compromise multi-signature wallets or admin accounts in charge of evidence gathering.

The use of Vishing (Voice Phishing) and Whaling also is becoming more successful against Police. Persons disguised as senior members of the police, judges, or INTERPOL afterservice members.Impersonation of key staff – by providing spoofed callers or through deep-fak technology. They impose the sense of urgency by suggesting an investigation is in danger or some evidence in the blockchain ledger should be quickly verified or even transferred. The officials could unknowingly divulge one-time passwords, grant access requests, and even provide some of the private keys. The ability to deepfake video calls has been added to the arsenal as a powerful new move for the real-time "maven to maven" virtual coordination meetings between agencies in different countries.

A method of data collection and/or a procedure in which false scenarios are developed to obtain information or actions. An attacker could make a call for installation of a "critical security patch" that is required by a trusted blockchain vendor. Then they lead the victim along the way, secretly setting up backdoors or stealing identities. Other excuses are fake court orders and fake MLA requests that are legal in appearance and are exerting pressure on the officials to allow access to certain types of evidence vaults.

The old biting and tailgating methods used physically continue to be effective. Malware may be placed on USB drives that are left on police parking lot stations or computers in conference rooms with the label "Confidential Cybercrime Evidence-Joint Operation". Tailgating enables unauthorized people to gain access to systems and places in secure facilities. An example being exploited on the Quid Pro Quo attacks are risks to hold up updated blockchain platforms in exchange for "temporary" information. They've also used Honey Traps and had personnel with access privileges targeted, particularly in long-term investigations which create personal stress.

These vulnerabilities are aggravated by certain human factors, especially in law enforcement. Manipulation takes place in the context of high workload, emotional strain in handling serious crimes, hierarchical command, and a fast pace of the cybercrime response (Kittappa et al., 2025). Few officers have received cutting-edge cybersecurity education for blockchain applications. While familiar with some aspects of phishing, they are not sufficiently familiar with new methods for attacks such as smart contract, zero-knowledge proof, and hybrid cloud-blockchain.

The impact to blockchain forensic systems is profound. Malicious parties can edit metadata prior to it being hashed onto the blockchain, add fraudulent entries using hacked smart contracts, or steal sensitive information from cloud-based storage off a compromised investigator's machine. The violations in cross-border cooperation platforms can damage the trust between States and cause diplomatic problems and/or delays in investigations. Central blockchain protocol might stay unchangeable, but should there be an apparent compromise, courts may reject evidence based on admissibility rules.

These cases show the dangers this threat poses in the real world. Several such instances of global law enforcement successfully playing the part of a social engineer have been reported in which they were able to trigger a ransomware attack or leak data. To follow, a series of blockchain-related attacks that started with social engineering of employees and progressed to technical attacks had targeted several cryptocurrency exchange platforms and decentralized finance (DeFi) platforms. The same approach is now being employed against other pilots of blockchains in the public service and police sectors.

"Hacking Brains" needs to be addressed at multiple layers, and in considering the human factor. Security awareness training in a continuous and scenario-specific manner is crucial. They should be required to simulate phishing exercises, run "red team" social engineering tests and analyze user behavior to identify unusual user behavior and activities. Strict least-privilege access, hardware security keys, just in time permissions and implemented AI-powered anomaly detection can minimize the potential risk of human errors. Any request for verification of information in an organizational culture should be encouraged and no punishment should be given when information is given with caution.

Although blockchain offers solid technical countermeasures to the manipulation of data, it does not safeguard against good social engineering of the people that operate it. To ensure the security of blockchain technology's role in criminal investigations in the future, it is crucial to focus on the human element as a critical attack surface, not an afterthought (Abdulrahman Satam & Szabolcsi, 2025). Extensive coverage requires a multi-layered approach involving investment in people, processes and technology all functioning together to weather the ongoing and ever-changing challenge of “Hacking Brains.”

3. UNAUTHORIZED ACCESS AND AUTHENTICATION WEAKNESSES

Unauthorized access and authentication are significant threats that pose a security concern for a blockchain-based criminal investigation system. But, despite the solid cryptographic layers, the blockchain as a whole is only as secure as its access controls and identity verification systems, meaning that without proper controls, it can be weak. The potential unethical use in Forensics includes evidence evidence metadata tampering, violation of chain of custody, illegal access to sensitive case information, and operation/manipulation of smart contracts. The vulnerabilities are especially precarious since more than one organization, entity, or agency may be involved in a blockchain system, and they may have different levels of security culture and technical IQ.

Generally, blockchain forensic platforms use multi-factor authentication, role-based access control (RBAC), public-private keys and digital certificates to ensure the proper authentication process. But, practical challenges often give rise to implementation weak spots. There is a potential risk of over-privileged accounts, weak session management and no continual authentication on poorly designed permissioned networks. Cloud blockchain-hybrid architectures lack the defenses required to protect only against compromised credentials affecting raw evidence storage while keeping on-chain metadata intact (Farooq et al., 2025). The decentralized structure of blockchain is different to centralized systems, and makes it harder to deceive and remove illegitimate users from the blockchain, which can mean that forks continue to exist in the network.

Moreover, numerous police blockchain projects are handed over with old authentication systems that weren't engineered for the level of security required for immutable evidence systems. This results in a problematic paradox, with the evidence of a crisis of high stakes and relatively low access control (Kamble et al., 2025). Besides data theft, however, there are serious legal ramifications of any breach, and even if access is suspected, a court might doubt the reliability of an entire blockchain evidence ledger. With the growing number of platforms emerging for thematic evidence sharing across borders, authentication issues take on an even greater importance as a disruption in one country can impact the trustworthiness of all of them. Effective solutions include strong identity management, continuous monitoring, adhering to the principle of least privilege, and regular security audits, as well as performing audit-specific security checks on a forensic blockchain system.

3.1 Weak Access Control Mechanisms in Blockchain Networks

Poor access control mechanisms in blockchain systems is a key area of risk in digital forensics and evidence handling infrastructure. Law-enforcement-specific permissioned (consortium) blockchains are built on the concept of proper role-based access control (RBAC) and attribute-based access control (ABAC) that enable only certain participating parties to read, write or validate certain evidence records. But many deployments have overly permissive permissions, poorly-defined roles and under-enforced policies.

Some of the frequent failings are default administrator accounts that are given too many permissions, inability to fine-tune access control granularity of smart contracts, and insufficient segregation of duties. For instance, an investigator who requires only evidence upload could have rights for approving custody transfers or edit metadata (Wan, 2025). Hyperledger Fabric or other blockchain platforms can have unauthorized nodes obtain sensitive channel access via improper configuration, or recommendation policies, for the evidence channels. Access modifier errors in smart contracts leading to improper access restrictions make it easier for an attacker to bypass these security measures and escalate privileges to execute malicious code.

Another major problem is that a lot of the access control lists are static. Access rights could become invalid, or be revoked prematurely, in such an environment as has a dynamic mix of team members, which means that there are windows of vulnerability. There is extra complexity when incorporating different identities over into the other country, which each have bequeathed different security standards (Mohammad et al., 2025). Weak access controls (and safety measures) are especially problematic because the immutability of the blockchain means that if the secure information of a specific account is compromised and any data is written or even altered, the data is written into the blockchain and is irreversible, which creates a risk of contaminating the entire chain of evidence.

Indeed, blockchain breaches in the real world, like unauthorised access rights on DeFi protocol, demonstrate the potential threat posed to forensic apps. In criminal justice fields, weaknesses may give defense lawyers grounds to reject a piece of evidence as being plagiarized, due to the inability to rule out virtual admission by others. Bad practices might give defense lawyers reason to claim that evidence is untrustworthy in criminal justice fields because they can show that it could have been produced through virtual admission even if a defense may not be able to establish that it was indeed internally produced. To achieve effective mitigation, dynamic access controls, "just in time" permissions, routine audits of access rights, multi-signature approval chains for sensitive activities and ongoing monitoring must be used to track all activity on the blockchain (Murlidharan et al., 2025). The importance of having robust access control cannot be overstated, as it is an essential factor to ensuring the judicial faith in blockchain-based evidence.

3.2 Credential Attacks and Multi-Factor Authentication Failures

Some of the vulnerabilities in blockchain forensic systems are top attack points including credential attacks and multi-factor authentication (MFA) system failures. The most common entry points for attackers are session tokens, private keys, passwords and usernames. Here are some of the more common methods: credential stuffing with leaked credentials from other breaches, password spraying, weak endpoint security, and phishing campaign targeting MFA codes.

Even when done well, MFA has been found to be vulnerable. SIM rewiring exploits recent SMS-based two factor authentication and "MFA fatigue" or "push bombing" involve tricking the user to accept a malicious login attempt. Although hardware tokens and authenticator apps are more secure, they can be compromised via session hijacking, and malware on the motivator device can break them. The same credentials employed by people in police, security, or other related fields are used in several different systems, creating more of a target.

Private key management is a particular and challenging challenge in blockchain systems. If a proper key of an investigator is stolen and clandestine evidence is entered onto the blockchain, it allows the entity whose key is stolen to then sign those entries as the official thus forging the account, or to sign the changes for custody transfers that were not approved by the investigators. Nonetheless, a large number of systems continue to use software wallets, or poorly secured key stores, instead of hardware security modules (HSMs) or secure enclaves (Said, 2025).

When credential compromise is coupled with weak MFA, devastating attack chains are created. Generally, a successful attack begins with the process of social engineering to get initial credentials and then MFA bypass ultimately culminating in complete network entry. In forensic blockchain, it can lead to tampering with evidence prior to hashing, undue compromise of sensitive information from victims and or of the service of sharing evidence across borders.

Working with shift systems, remote access needs and a requirement to respond swiftly during large-scale incidents frequently result in security short cuts that make security risks worse. The best protection can be achieved through a combination of methods: Phishing-resistant MFA (FIDO2/WebAuthn), Behavioral biometrics, Continuous authentication, and Regular credential rotation, complemented by strict device management policies (Malaraju, 2025). The deployment of zero-trust architecture is also important and imperative to train personnel to identify credential phishing attempts. Even the most sophisticated blockchain systems can be easily breached when they lack effective defense measures against credential attacks and MFAs.

4. CLOUD STORAGE RISKS IN HYBRID BLOCKCHAIN ARCHITECTURES: DATA RESIDENCY, SOVEREIGNTY AND THIRD-PARTY RISKS

When a hybrid blockchain architecture is applied as a cloud service, the transmission of evidence across jurisdictions, and blockchain security in general, are some of the most challenging and critical areas of digital forensics and cloud computing. The hybrid models protect owners of sensitive evidence up to this point by securely off-chain storing device images, full forensic duplicates, videos and logs while securely on-chain storing cryptographic hashes and metadata, which increases the attack surface featuring vulnerabilities of centralized cloud providers and complexities of decentralized ledgers.

Data residency and sovereignty risk are top of the list of these risks. Most cloud service providers (AWS, Azure, Google Cloud or regional cloud providers) have data stored in multiple geographic regions, for redundancy and performance. In terms of law enforcement, this can present major problems. Physical evidence from a case in India can be located in data centres in Singapore, U.S. or Europe where the evidence will be exposed to Singaporean, U.S. or European legal regimes and subject to requests from the government. This directly violates data sovereignty policies and local laws and regulations like in India, the Digital Personal Data Protection (DPDP) Act, which recommend a strict guideline for data localizing sensitive data, or similar laws in other jurisdictions. In some cases, in cross-border investigations jurisdictions may have conflicting laws in place to request and block access to evidence, resulting in legal arguments between jurisdictions and evidence being suppressed in court.

The risks from third party are related to the high reliance agencies have to make on commercial cloud providers (Malve et al., 2025). These providers are also entitled to special access to infrastructure, which can become a point of vulnerability and/ or compliance issues. Despite robust contractual safeguards, even inside an agency there is only weak insight and control into how the provider treats its own security, employee screenings or government obligations under the U.S. CLOUD Act. A third serious incident where the government's data was breached at the cloud service provider has the possibility of exposing huge amounts of raw forensic information, while the blockchain ledger records "intact" hashes, unwittingly giving users the false sense of security.

Other cons are user-relevent misconfigurations of cloud storage buckets, over-sharing Identity and Access Management (IAM) roles, weak of poor management of encryption keys, and weak or poor accounting. However, for hybrid configurations, if the attackers successfully access the cloud storage where the real evidence files are stored, they can swap existing evidence files with files containing altered metadata and checksums for evidence files that have identical blockchains, as long as they have enough care not to notice the changes and effectively manage the reference lists or signatures that reference the files. Add to that the risk of attacks on specialized forensic tools that rely on a cloud-based solution. Threats in the supply chain to cloud based forensic solutions also exacerbate these threats.

Not only is the shared responsibility model in cloud computing complex on its own, but it also brings yet another layer of complexity. The law enforcement agencies are responsible for data classifications, encryption, access policies and monitoring while providers will provide the physical infrastructure and hypervisor. A lot of agencies overlook this aspect and end up with major security breaches. When it comes to multi-jurisdictional blockchain platforms, it is particularly challenging to implement a consistent security standard, especially when using various cloud providers and regions to do so.

The Risks have direct relevance with regards to admissibility of evidence. In the event that any evidence has been tampered with, defense counsel can question the reliability of such evidence by pointing out that third parties may have accessed such evidence through unauthorized means or if there was a violation of data residency. The integrity of the chain of custody could be called into question by Courts where the evidence has moved through commercial infrastructure abroad (Nazir et al., 2026).

Successful risk management depends on making the right choice of cloud provider with good cloud sovereignty guarantees, introducing confidential computing and encryption-in-use, securing the use of Hardware Security Modules (HSMs), frequent 3rd party audits, policy adherence, and clear data residency policies. For some advanced architectures, decentralized storage solutions such as IPFS and pinning on blockchain presents an alternative and/or complementary solution to the use of cloud storage.

5. POLICY TRAINING AND GOVERNANCE FRAMEWORKS

The final three areas mentioned as policy, training, and governance are crucial to ensuring blockchain-powered forensic solutions are secure and to helping curtail some of the multitude of human, technical and operational risk variables highlighted above. The ability to develop and maintain strong, consistent evidence management practices into reliable, court defensible practices hinges on strong governance – strategic oversight, accountability and standardization.

Good blockchain governance needs to start with an organizational policy, setting out roles and responsibilities of all stakeholders in the process of blockchain evidence systems. This covers evidence custody, forensic examination, operations in the evac network, prosecution, and trial institutions. The policies need to be explicit about classifications of data, principles of access to data (particularly least privileged and need to know), the procedures to act in the case of an incident involving blockchain systems, and rules for giving evidence to the other party to a transaction, where required and appropriate. Frequent periodic reviews and changes of policy are essential in order to deal with the new threats and new technologies.

More efforts with training programs need to be made in providing more role-based training than general awareness for cyber security (Zeb & Lodhi, 2025). The blockchain is novel enough that investigators and analysts need extensive experience with concepts unique to the blockchain like exposure to how to manage the private keys, interact with a smart contract, spot attempts at social engineering into blockchain platforms, and understand how to use a hybrid cloud blockchain interface. Senior officials and decision-makers should undertake specific training on the nature of risk, legal considerations of blockchain evidence and their roles and responsibilities in the context of blockchain evidence. Simulated exercises, such as on red-team social engineering, mock breach scenarios and table top exercises in the event of cross-border cooperation failures, can be very effective at increasing institutional resilience (Shahid et al., 2025).

For instance, the governance settings should be designed to contain independent governance committees or ethics boards looking over deployments of blockchain platforms, especially cross-border initiatives. They should have Law Enforcement officials, Technical Experts, Investigators with experience and members of civil society (for privacy issues). Having clear audit trails, third party security audits regularly, mandatory reporting of security incidents to oversight authorities helps maintain transparency and accountability.

Human rights are also key concerns for cross-border platforms in this context. This also highlights the need for international governance. Nations to participate must agree upon the set of standards for evidence handling procedures, handling of data, processes of dispute resolution and minimum security standards (Ikegwu et al., 2025). This encompasses policy harmonization in the areas of smart contract auditing standard, vulnerability disclosure policies and liability sharing in case of an exploit.

Effective frameworks also integrate cultural issues and behaviours. Organizations should encourage 'security first' mentality in employees that they feel free to report any suspicious activity or possible policy violation without any fear of retaliation. Case resolution speed should not be the sole metric used for performance measures, they should also incorporate security compliance metrics into the measures. It is imperative to maintain all documentation of policies, training and governance decisions, and to have a version control in place to ensure appropriate due diligence in court. When evidence admissibility is thrown into doubt and the defense objects to or doubts the genuineness and integrity of the blockchain system.

Problems arise with these models, such as limited agency resources, opposition to changes in the procedures, difficulties in keeping up with the rapidly changing technological environment and the dilemma between security and efficiency. It is important to ensure that the implementation has strong leadership commitment, appropriate funding have been allocated, and collaboration has been established with the academic world and experts from the private sector to get up to date knowledge (Varsha et al., 2025).

6. CONCLUSION AND EMERGING TECHNOLOGIES FOR ENHANCED SECURITY AND RESILIENCE

Blockchain has been shown to enhance evidence integrity beyond what can be achieved with traditional methods, but certainly does not abdicate security duties. The organizations which are in consideration of these solutions must regard security as an ongoing process instead of an optional feature to be deployed once in a while. New advances in blockchain technology that are necessary for its future success in criminal investigations rely greatly on innovative solutions to these security issues across the human, technical and cloud domain, with a focus on early deployment in order to facilitate changes. A number of new advances that will need to be made in the near future to the success of blockchain in criminal investigations are heavily reliant on innovative solutions to human, technical and cloud-related vulnerabilities proactively and early. Without it, there may be world-class failures that will not only stall the adoption efforts years but also cause the public and courts to lose faith in technologies and practices for digital evidence. A comprehensive, all round security approach that meets the ever constant attack of 'hacking brains,' access and cloud threats are thus essential.

REFERENCES

Abdulrahman Satam, I., & Szabolcsi, R. (2025). Ethical and Safety Challenges of Implantable Brain-Computer Interface. *Interdisciplinary Description of Complex Systems: INDECS, 23*(2), 82–94. DOI: 10.7906/indecs.23.2.1

Farooq, M., Younas, R. M. F., Qureshi, J. N., Haider, A., & Nasim, F. (2025). Cyber security risks in DBMS: Strategies to mitigate data security threats: A systematic review. *Spectrum of engineering sciences*, 268-290.

Ikegwu, A. C., Uzuegbu, V. C., & Alo, U. R. (2025). Review of embedded systems and cyber threat intelligence for enhancing data security in mobile health. *J Electron Inf Syst, 7*(1), 98–120. DOI: 10.30564/jeis.v7i1.10050

Kamble, T., Ghuge, M., Jain, R., & Sarbhukan Bodade, V. (2025). Secure data transmission in cloud computing using a cyber-security trust model with multi-risk protection scheme in smart IOT application. *Cluster Computing, 28*(2), 79. DOI: 10.1007/s10586-024-04847-z

Kittappa, T., Snehal, S. M., Amrutha, J., & Mageshwaran, D. R. (2025, November). Emerging Cyber Threats in the Quantum Era: From Neural Hacking to Space. In *Information System Design: Communication Networks and Internet of Things: Proceedings of Ninth International Conference on Information System Design and Intelligent Applications (ISDIA 2025),* Volume 2 (Vol. 2, p. 29). Springer Nature.

Malaraju, S. K. (2025, August). An Overview of Cybersecurity Risks and Threats in Cloud Computing. In *International Conference on Computing and Communication Networks* (pp. 447-458). Cham: Springer Nature Switzerland.

Malve, D., Kumar, R. C. K., Meenal, H., & Hagaldivte, V. (2025). Cybersecurity vulnerabilities and threat mitigation strategies in the Metaverse. In *Defending the Metaverse* (pp. 94–114). CRC Press. DOI: 10.1201/9781003581659-6

Mohammad, S., Sajid, A., Abbasi, U. S. A., Razzaq, H., Yadav, S., & Khademizadeh, S. (2025). A Review on Analyzing Cloud Computing and Network Cyber Security Threats: Issues and Challenges With Solutions. *Iraqi Journal of Information and Communication Technology, 8*(1), 38–49.

Murlidharan, S., Ravulakole, V., Karnati, J., & Malik, H. (2025). Battery management system: Threat modeling, vulnerability analysis, and cybersecurity strategy. *IEEE Access : Practical Innovations, Open Solutions, 13*, 37198–37220. DOI: 10.1109/ACCESS.2025.3543249

Nazir, R., Laghari, A. A., Dahri, F. H., Shoulin, Y., Alhakeem, Z. M., Hakim, H., & Mughal, Z. A. (2026). A review on machine learning techniques for network security. *Journal of Cyber Security Technology*, *10*(1), 1–45. DOI: 10.1080/23742917.2025.2480730

Nikesh, M., Bharathi, M., Naaz, S. H., & Srinivas, T. A. S. (2025). IoT's Biggest Headaches: Privacy, Security, and Data Management Challenges. *J. IoT Secur. Smart Technol*, *4*, 1–23.

Omotade, A. L. (2025). Neurotechnology and Human-Machine Interfaces: Securing Brain-Computer Interfaces (BCIs) Against Hacking. *World Journal of Advanced Research and Reviews*, *27*(01), 2761–2771. DOI: 10.30574/wjarr.2025.27.1.2534

Said, G. (2025). Brain-Computer Interface 5.0: Potential threats, computational law and protection of digital rights. *Legal Issues in the digital. The Age (Melbourne, Vic.)*, (2), 134–160.

Shahid, U., Kanwal, S., Bano, M., Inam, S., Abdalla, M. E. M., & Shaikh, Z. A. (2025). Blockchain driven medical image encryption employing chaotic tent map in cloud computing. *Scientific Reports*, *15*(1), 6236. DOI: 10.1038/s41598-025-90502-5 PMID: 39979488

Varsha, A., Kumar, N. A., Bichanga, S. N., & Chakraborty, P. (2025). Future Direction in Digital Forensics and Cyber Security. *Emerging Threats and Countermeasures in Cybersecurity*, 467-493.

Wan, J. (2025, November). Research on the Application and Risk Control of Cloud Computing in Accounting from the Perspective of Network Security. In *2025 IEEE 11th International Conference on Edge Computing and Scalable Cloud (EdgeCom)* (pp. 183-188). IEEE. DOI: 10.1109/EdgeCom66327.2025.00037

Zeb, S., & Lodhi, S. K. (2025). AI and cybersecurity in smart manufacturing: Protecting industrial systems. *American Journal of Artificial Intelligence and Computing*, *1*(1), 1–23.

Chapter 8
Ensuring Transparency and Accountability in Right to Information Regimes:
The Role of Blockchain in Legal Evidence Justification

Malvika Pandey
Amity University, Gwalior, India

Vijay Srivastava
http://orcid.org/0000-0002-3034-9903
Amity University, Gwalior, India

Priyansh Samadhiya
Amity University, Gwalior, India

ABSTRACT

The Right to Information (RTI) is a fundamental pillar of democratic governance, providing citizens with access to public information and helps them hold public authorities accountable. Conventional models of RTI typically have a variety of problems, however: evidence is stripped or embellished, documents are tampered with, there is bureaucratic opacity, and they don't really hold up in court. The Blockchain technology has unique characteristics, such as immutability, decentralization, and cryptographic security, which make it a revolutionary solution. Blockchain can offer end-to-end transparency with legal evidence for requests, answers, as well as all supporting documents, to ensure all stakeholders are transparent and to produce

DOI: 10.4018/979-8-3373-9730-6.ch008

strong legal records. This chapter examines the possibilities of applying blockchain to RTI systems, arguing that the distributed ledger can help to reduce corruption risks, boost public trust and improve the admissibility of judgments.

1. INTRODUCTION

The Right to Information (RTI) regime is one of the most important legislative efforts to advance open government and participatory democracy. These laws are among those in different jurisdictions, including India's groundbreaking RTI Act 2005, which require disclosure of information from public institutions when requested, with reasonable exemptions (Mustafa et al., 2025). Though well-meaning and theoretically sound, conventional paper-based or centralized digital information systems often fail to provide the level of transparency that the "new." information, the MESO, and its applications strive for. Changes to documents can be made, documents can get lost, delayed responses to the document can occur, and the chain of custody of evidence may be suspect at trial. In sum, blockchain technology offers a promising solution to these problems, presenting a decentralized and immutable ledger that can hold great promise for improving the process and evidentiary integrity of RTI and related processes in legal situations. It is through conceptual frameworks, as well as potential architectures, and policy insights that it makes an argument to modernize the mechanisms that enable transparency in the digital age, attributing to citizen rights and accountability by the government (Jain et al., 2024).

Blockchain essentially works as a "chain of blocks," with each block representing a new entry of data in the blockchain. As part of it, blockchain is simply a replicated database where every part of the data in a block is made a round date bound to the earlier one in the block chain, to such an extent that it is hard to change retroactively without consensus among the chain. This aids in addressing a key problem in the RTI systems, which is the ability to manipulate request, acknowledge, or retrieved documents. An RTI application submitted on such a portal via a ledger on the blockchain will be registered on a blockchain-based ledger thereby being immobilized and recorded. When an application for an RTI is submitted through such a portal, via a blockchain-based ledger, it will be immobilized and recorded on a ledger available to authorized nodes (governmental agencies, regulatory agencies and even independent auditors). Final responses and follow-up (after PIO receipt/ consultation, etc.) is a new transaction (Azeem et al., 2023). Citizens and watchdogs will be able to independently confirm authenticity of the entire process, without the help of any one party.

This is very effective traceability and helps to build accountability. Low compliance with RTI, frivolous rejection of RTI applications and harassment of applicants is experienced by many countries in the implementation of RTI (Angon, 2024). Smart contracts can automate workflows, such as recording clearly defined and important deadlines for response, and alerting or escalating to appeal authorities if these are not met. Smart contracts might additionally choose to alert exempted data routinely based on pre-determined legal principles, minimizing discretion and guaranteeing that there is information that is properly confidentialized using zero-knowledge proofs or other methods. Less human involvement at points where it tends to be prone to corruption or inefficient minimises the number of such points.

The echoes with legal evidence through blockchain are very interesting. Digital records are growing in increasing recognition by the courts around the world, but issues regarding authenticity and integrity have detracted from the probative value of the records. This is where blockchain comes in.This is where blockchain comes in. If the record exists in that form at that time when a government response or a disclosed document is hashed and recorded on-chain, then that's prima facie evidence as to how it is recorded.When the disclosed document hashes and is recorded on-chain, or a government response, then it's prima facie evidence of how the record is recorded at that time (Laukyte, 2023). Blockchain audit trails are an alternative to disputed affidavits in litigation where there are alleged omissions or misrepresentations of information. This helps to send a clear message that the burden of proof is theirs and does not shift to the plaintiff and thus prevents the malpractices.

1.1 Historical Evolution and Global Adoption

There are some conceptual architectures that facilitate this integration. The hybrid approach can use a public permissionless blockchain for general audit logging and a private or consortium blockchain for confidential information. A combination of public permissionless blockchain for general auditing logs and private or consortium blockchain for confidential information can strike a balance between transparency and privacy. For instance, the documents could be stored in encrypted systems off-chain and their related transaction history and metadata would be recorded on the blockchain. This is in line with the data protection regulations and meets the goals of RTI. The framework of e-governance in Estonia (e-residency, e-court) with the incorporation of the blockchain components is an inspirational example, while RTI-specific deployments are still forthcoming.

While all this may sound great, there are still some difficulties involved. Technological obstacles are scalability – While most public blockchains, such as Ethereum, charge steep fees to process transactions and have lower speeds, it is being addressed by scaling solutions like layer-2 on Ethereum and the introduction of newer consensus protocols like Proof of Stake or Directed Acyclic Graphs. Some different types of blockchain use energy that need alternative approaches to sustainable energy use

(Enyiorji, 2023). It is still vital that blockchain records are acknowledged by law, just as electronic signatures were billed by lawmaking.Furthermore, it is essential for many jurisdictions to critically consider amendments in their evidence laws to allow blockchain records, as is the case for electronic signatures.

1.2 Core Principles of Transparency and Accountability

Integration with legacy government systems is a challenge in terms of interoperability. In order to achieve adoption, it is important to build capacity of officials and raise awareness among citizens on the topic. It is important to reduce privacy risks appropriately—a desire for transparency must be balanced against the rights that are being infringed by the indiscriminate release of personal information in the RTI responses. Regulatory sandboxes and phased implementation (non-sensitive departments first) can be used to put the technology to the test and to update the technology's definitions and functions. These policies can be tested and updated through regulatory sandboxes and through a phased implementation (i.e. starting with departments not sensitive to the technology).

As a cross-cutting governance aspect, blockchain in RTI represents the cross-over between technological and constitutional values (Alyas et al., 2025). It is a realisation of the slogan, "Power belongs to the people, and should be held responsible to them. It increases transparency of governmental actions, mitigates 'information mismatch' that leads to corruption and cynicism in governance. Creating standards for blockchain-based governance transparency mechanisms by international organisations such as the UN or the World Bank, which are pushing for OGD releases, would enable mutual learning and provide opportunities to harmonise.

1.3 Persistent Challenges in Implementation

From an economic perspective, the up-front cost of infrastructure for the blockchain could pay off in so many ways, from decreased litigation, quicker grievance resolution, to enhanced ease of doing business with trustworthy public records. So, nothing can substitute political will or institutional reforms from blockchain, but it offers a solid technical underpinning that allows for transparency to be enforced not merely desired or uttered in Lady Gaga's stage presence. Blockchain records set a bar for governmental transparency and allow citizens to have a stake in that that can lead to legal verifications. Blockchain records set a bar at governmental transparency and give the citizen a tool to be able to exercise meaningful oversight. To explore and create free software systems with open-source RTI blockchain protocols, empirical evaluation of impact on transparency and to design still more model noraml regulation which combines existing transparency regulation with distributed ledger technology. In the end, the blockchain and democratic spirit of RTI can together usher in the age of radical transparency: accountability that does not just come and go, but for which the guarantee is always in place operating and perceptible from the core of governance itself (Khlifi & Zouari, 2025).

2. LIMITATIONS OF TRADITIONAL RTI SYSTEMS: ISSUES OF RECORD TAMPERING AND DATA INTEGRITY

Traditional Right to Information (RTI) systems, which aim to create open governance, face inherent inefficiencies in their systems which hinder the effectiveness of the RTI. In most, methods are manual, on paper or a central digital database controlled only by government departments (Zhang, 2025). This design provides numerous areas of weakness, where the principles of transparency can be undermined because of the subjectivity of humans, the slowness of administrative action and pressure from outside. Citizens frequently receive arbitrary answers, delays in answering their appeals and a lack of trust in the truthfulness of information that is released. Even in a more developed democracy, good compliance with the regulations is not guaranteed, and a lot of information commissions are overdue. Lack of proven audit processes renders it hard to effectively challenge the process when information is denied or only partially disclosed.

In traditional RTI systems data integrity and data tampering are the most severe vulnerabilities. While physical files can be manipulated, lost or destroyed, centralized digital files systems can be hijacked, manipulated by insiders, and attacked by hackers. At times, the Public Information Officer (PIO) or higher official has unrestricted authority to amend PIO's response(s) or supporting documentation prior to release. From around the globe, major files are lost or altered in history on matters that have raised issues of corruption, environmental offenses or human rights (Karisma & Moslemzadeh Tehrani, 2023). When converted to a digital format, it's hard to determine whether a document had been altered from its original format even if you have cryptographic hashing or immutable logs. This poses problems when the responses are utilised in a court of law, where unauthentic responses are easy to challenge.

2.1 Bureaucratic Delays and Lack of Traceability

The feasibility of RTI regimes is hampered by inefficiencies in bureaucratic procedures and low level of traceability. Many laws have internal movements, interdepartmental consultations and make-do and-do-proofs that push the applicants past the prescribed time lines (for example 30 days). Manual tracking systems provide limited visibility into an application in progress and there is little information to help citizens know what is "happening" to their application or where is it in the system. This obscurity allows harassment, multiple app transfers and silly exemptions. Dolleying process is also frequently delayed: Appellate process may also be slow, featuring a lot of delay till final resolution. Not having end-to-end traceability leaves no way to track specific officials' performance and ensure accountability for any delays or compliance problems. These delays can obviate the usefulness of the information obtained in cases where the future of general dollars and policy decisions are at stake.

3. BLOCKCHAIN TECHNOLOGY: FUNDAMENTALS AND RELEVANCE

The adaptability of blockchain technology the root of all cryptocurrencies has made it a useful tool for governing and managing public administration. It's simply a ledger that is distributed as it records transactions across many computers, securing, verifying and forgoing any ability to delete that record or tamper with it. It is relevant to the Right to Information systems because it has the potential to address some major issues of trust, transparency, and evidence-centered public records management. The blockchain's ability to store and share a single source of truth, bypassing the need for a middle man, has the potential to revolutionize the way citizens have access to government data. It provides a way to record each stage of an information request from the filing to the final disclosure in an RTI setting in a tamper-proof way. This technolab fits perfect with the values of democracy: openness, transparency (Simanjuntak et al., 2025). The extension to RTI is an obvious application of blockchain that governments around the world are considering for land records, voting, procurement, etc.It is an obvious extension to other applications governments are thinking of using blockchain for, such as land records, voting or procurement.

3.1 Core Features – Immutability, Decentralization, and Transparency

The core features of blockchain immutability, decentralization and transparency make blockchain very well suited to bolstering RTI regimes. Immutability means that data is once recorded and confirmed by the network, it can't be deleted or altered without its trace being left permanently. If any attempt towards the modification was made, then all the other blocks ahead moving from the distributed nodes would need to be modified which would be sheer computational workload. Decentralization eliminates single points of failure and control, as opposed to one government department owning the database, multiple authorized nodes (government departments, oversight bodies and independent auditors) hold copies of the ledger. From now on, there's no unilateral manipulation. It relies on openness of the transaction history – either in public or permissioned visibility. Citizens can validate the authenticity of the RTI applications that they make, and the integrity of the responses, without relying on any one entity. All these features combine to provide an "auditable and trustworthy" set, with all actions being time stamped and connected.

3.2 Types of Blockchains Suitable for Public Governance

Permissioned and consortium blockchains are typically better suited for public governance and RTI applications.Public governance and RTI applications are primarily more suited to permissioned or consortium blockchains. Public permissionless blockchains (such as Bitcoin or the mainnet of Ethereum) provide the highest degree of transparency and, ironically, suffer from problems of speed, cost, and privacy of their data. Permissioned blockchains, by contrast restrict the participation to those who have been approved like government departments, information commissions and recognised auditors. Ensures increased security and greater control of sensitive information in this model. Organisations-based consortium blockchains have just the right balance, e.g. a group of ministries could each operate these nodes, and an independent body can be responsible for consensus (Spano et al., 2025). Another potential architecture seems to be interesting: sensitive RTI content can be stored "off-chain" i.e. in secure databases (encrypted) or in IPFS (hashed, timestamped), while transaction records, metadata and content hashes will be kept in the blockchain. Internal resource departments can work with private blockchains while selectively info is made available to citizens on public blockchains. There are also a number of emerging federated models that further enable interoperability at different levels of government.

3.3 Smart Contracts and Automated Compliance

Smart contracts are automated programs that are stored on the blockchain and execute themselves when the conditions are realised. In RTI systems, they can revolutionise compliance via eliminating discretionary delays, and by eradicating people biases. The smart contract can automatically create an RTI information and notify the involved PIO on its filing, and initiate a countdown period of 30 days from the date of filing. When there is no response on the due date, automatic escalation to the first appellate authority could be triggered and pull in oversight mechanisms. Exemption clauses can also be coded into smart contracts.Smart contracts can also contain consistent logic for exemptioning information, and provide clear rationale. Compliance verifiers can use privacy-enhancing technologies, such as zero-knowledge proofs, to ensure that the data being processed meets the necessary standards for privacy and security. Inform the departments of timed accounts and/ or assign automated penalties or show performance dashboards can further encourage prompt actions. They're programmed with code that is immutable so that they execute correctly, so the code cannot be changed and all parties know exactly what should be done. They make sure there is a clear, traceable history of all automated decisions (for legal evidence).

4. INTEGRATING OF BLOCKCHAIN IN RTI AND LEGAL EVIDENCE

Blockchain technology in the Regime of Right to Information (RTI) signify a paradigm shift in making laws and mechanisms of transparency and accountability verifiable and technology-sceptile than the traditional trust-based approach. Distributed ledger technology can be employed to develop a digital end-to-end ecosystem in which all phases of any information request, from filing of the request through the decision-making, disclosure and appeal processes, is secured in a way that makes it impossible for any information to be changed and ensures that it is auditable. This integration fills up monumental gaps in the past regarding evidence integrity, response time and integrity of records for judicial proceedings. A good RTI platform based on the blockchain would be a combination of one or more user facing interfaces, private off-chain storage mechanisms, and public on-chain verification mechanisms (Hakimi et al., 2024). Citizens would be able to request through a single portal where a cryptographic hash and a block time stamp would be automatically generated from the application, providing it with anchor on blockchain. The permissioned or consortium blockchain would record each transaction made on the request by public authorities, which would provide an open and transparent audit trail, visible to the applicant and overseeing body.

This technological marriage does a lot to improve the quality of the evidence presented in court. Problems of authenticity occur to responses and documents to RTI in many jurisdictions when presented to court. This is addressed by blockchain, which offers cryptographic evidence of existence, integrity and chain of custody. Judges and parties can independently verify that information has not been tampered with since installation by permanently putting the disclosed information's unique digital fingerprint (hash) on the blockchain. Timestamping provides another safeguard of admissibility, since it provides an indispersion timeline, which is particularly relevant in time-related issues such as statutes of limitations, allegations of suppression, or late compliance. Smart contracts can help with rote tasks of compliance without replacing the human element for some tough choices, ensuring consistency and with minimised arbitrary rejections.

Most of the time strategies used for integration are most close to the hybrid, where transparency is maintained and privacy is preserved, and the scalability can be balanced. The core metadata, request IDs, timestamps, status updates, and document hashes are recorded on the blockchain, while the core actual content of the documents is kept off-chain, either in a decentralized storage solution like the IPFS or in an encrypted government database (Oliveira, 2023). Zero knowledge proofs and other sophisticated security methods allow to provide verification without revealing restricted data. High volume, low sensitivity departments, like public works, education, environmental clearances, etc., may be first targets for pilot implementations, before expanding to other government entities. A seamless integration with the other RTI portals (e.g. India's RTI Online) would provide for the smooth transition and not a replacement.

Its possibilities go past the chance of individual requests to seismic change in governance. All these technologies would increase the level of accountability, such as real-time dashboards for information commissions, self-verifying performance indicators for public services and verification algorithms for the end citizen. But for proper integration, it is finally crucial for legal frameworks to change, such as updating evidence laws to include blockchain evidence as main pieces of evidence, importing similarities and capacity-building of officials. There are different international examples that can be influential, like Estonia's e-governance system using blockchain or Georgia's Land Registry on blockchain. When properly designed, blockchain makes it a democratic governance backstop that can never be denied simply used through the bureaucratic channel (Nguyen, 2025). It provides the judicial arena with the ground for peer-to-peer judicial review and gives people the technology to hold judiciary to account. The whole thing is a bridge between the letter of transparency laws and implementation of those laws in the digital age.

4.1 Secure Storage and Timestamping of Information Requests

The base layer of blockchain interactions in RTI systems is the secure recording and recording of info requests. An application for an RTI submitted via their blockchain-based application generates an immediate digital record of the applicant's details (where they can be shared), what information they are requesting, the supporting documents that are provided to CTB online, and metadata related to the application itself. This record is then cryptographically "hashed" with secure hash funcyields like sha256 and "timelimited" with the network consensus time at which it is added. The final result, after adding the hash and key non-sensitive identifying information, is then recorded within a permissioned blockchain ledger which becomes part of an unalterable chain from the time of its submission. In a traditional systems, this means that it would not be possible to post-date, modify, or only register applications, providing a clear advantage over traditional systems.

Secure Storage Mechanism: The method by which information is stored is usually a combination of both architectures for optimal performance and privacy. The entire content of the application could be encrypted and placed out-of-chain on a distributed file system, such as the InterPlanetary File System (IPFS) or a secure file repository in the government's cloud repository, while only the content hash, timestamp, unique transaction ID and status flags would be recorded on the blockchain (Mezzi et al., 2025). This design leads to the availability and integrity of the data on the ledger, while not bloating the ledger size with large files. The ledger is synchronized to authorized nodes, which contain concerned departments, appellate authorities and information commissions, making sure an information single point of failure will never be created and offering redundancies. Later access or changes to the stored record would result in additional transactions clearly related to the original, which would produce a chain of transactions that is totally traceable with no chance that someone could tamper with it.

The process of RTI is made more time-sensitive by adding "timestamping." Each milestone – from the receipt, to the next department, to higher level office, to the final answer – is given its own 'stamp of authority'. This is inherent to the ability, and addresses chronic delay right away by providing unarguable evidence of time and actions. For legal proceedings, these activities are recorded with a certain date which can be used as solid evidence when claiming that the procedure was not adhered to or that there were delays. Judicial systems have access to precise and scientifically proven facts, not official versions, from blockchain timestamps.

Moreover, this safe and secure environment is resistant to internal tamper and external threats. The blockchain works based on the consensus mechanisms, and changing one record would take a bigger security step that at the moment would be getting together a greater majority of the network nodes (Bernards et al., 2024). The use of role-based access control and cryptographic keys guarantees that only authorized users have access to certain requests; while audit logs are kept clear of oversight institutions. A straightforward mobile application or web dashboard enables instant monitoring of the status of an applicant's request by referring to the transaction hash of the original request, giving the applicants the sense of security and eliminating the need to chase up re-questioning.

There are challenges to address when implementing, particularly with regard to offline filings and legacy records. Historical RTI data can be bulk migrated using batch hashing and anchoring to the blockchain. To meet privacy law, data minimisation principles should be used to determine information to be stored. With proper execution, secure storage and timestamping will enable RTI requests to become real, permanent, verifiable digital assets.

4.2 Audit Trails for Government Responses and Disclosures

The entire idea of accountability lies in audit trails in an eRTI system where the blockchain is incorporated. Once the public authorities have completed the information request in a secure way, each further step they take is a subsequent transaction on the distributed ledger. This establishes a continuous cross-sectional link of events leading to document disclosure, such as the first PIO mentioning the document, consultation within the Legal Department, the document being passed to another Department Office for further consideration, an application to include an exempt document, the documents being disclosed, and reasons for disclosing (or denying) the exempt documents. Every action is time stamped, signed cryptographically by the official concerned using his keys and then tied to the prior action, hence everything can be reconstructed and verified.

Actually, every response of government build has own unique hashes of content, which are connected to the blockchain. Even if the actual files are kept of-chain, any modification, no matter how trivial, would result in the hash changing, and the hash would be immediately be recognised as tampered. This is one area of particular concern in existing RTI models because lots of citizens can feel that anything was sanitised or possibly a document was edited in a biased way. Authorised stakeholders (information commissions, appellate authorities) can readily view the audit trail, both physically and in real time or near-real time (no request for physical records required). Citizens can easily obtain simplified views or verification proofs, through an accessible dashboard based on their original request hash, allowing citizens to keep track of progress for themselves.

This open bookkeeping nature of these audit trails gives a huge incentive against bureaucratic abuse. Officials have an awareness that each delay, transfer, and/or exemption results in a permanent, traceable, digital notation. This can also be further improved using smart contracts, which can automatically alert if statutory deadlines have been missed, or identify different uses of the exemption in the same type of cases. In business environments where high volume procurements, environmental clearances or public expenditure are a key concern, such auditability shifts from reactive supervisory functions to a proactive approach to business governance (Silva, 2025). An aggregated and anonymized data can be used by oversight bodies to benchmark and detect on a systemic level, whether there is a slowdown or a trend to non-compliance on a ministry-by-ministry basis. Furthermore, by having thorough audit trails increases the coordination across departments. Where information is shared across agencies, the blockchain ledger gives one shared knowledge view of the movement and status of a request. This helps to minimize multiple "file not traceable" returns.

4.3 Blockchain as Tamper-Proof Legal Evidence in Courts

The technology of blockchain has deparalleated potential to become tamper-proof legal evidence in judicial proceedings which deal with disputes of RTI. The standard practices of maintaining RTI records can present admissibility issues as the courts may have to rely on an affidavit and testimony to certify the authenticity of the record, which can be subject to problems with the chain of custody and integrity of evidence. Blockchain eliminates the need for these caveats by building a cryptographic barrier to any tampering: if that transaction is stored in any particular form at some specific time, and has never been modified since it was made, proof of these facts follows as a chain of secure blocks.

An RTI response and/or a disclosed document has a digital signature, timestamp and hash value that can be independently verified by any party to the transaction against the disclosed ledger (public or permissioned). Courts can and should confirm evidence through primary sources other than government submissions. The acceptance of blockchain evidence is spreading around the world. A number of jurisdictions have updated or are looking to update their Evidence Acts to accommodate distributed ledger records, electronic forms of signatures and timestamping services. For example, this could be based on the provisions under the Information Technology Act in India with regard to electronic records. Judges may be given easy-to-use proof Validation tools or reports from blockchain certified proof validators to verify the integrity of the evidence related to the RTI.

When facing Appeals courts and Writ courts, Blockchain audit trail can be key evidence if a procedure was followed or not. In public interest litigation related to environmental and corruption cases, for instance, it will be possible for the petitioners to file RTI docs verified by blockchain, thereby increasing their probative value. This helps to cut down on time consuming evidentiary hearings and expedites justice. The automated compliance steps can also be illustrated via smart contract logs, to give an extra level of trust. Judicial capacity development continues to present a challenge. Especially the education of judges, attorneys and court personnel in blockchain forensics (Grijalva-Salazar et al., 2025). Blockchain-admissibility standards must be codified, including audit certificates, the reliability of the consensus mechanism and node security.

5. CONCLUSION: CHALLENGES, OPPORTUNITIES AND FUTURE DIRECTIONS

The use of blockchain in the context of "it tech" in the context of RtI provides a powerful future option to increase the transparency and accountability of democratic governance. It has the potential to provide strong options with data that cannot be manipulated or changed, secure audit trails, and legal proof, but there are a few related issues that must be addressed to make it work. One of the challenges with technical implementation is that almost every application requires millions of times more requests per year than an RTI can process, and some implementations are expensive, costing considerably more than light nodes. Another challenge is the power consumption of certain consensus algorithms. However, working interoperably with legacy government systems is still a complex challenge and will present some data migration nuances and hybrid architecture requirements. Despite the progress in blockchain adoption, there still exist legal and regulatory challenges and uncertainties in many jurisdictions with respect to the admissibility of blocks, lack of compliance with privacy regulations (such as GDPR in Europe or DPDP in India), and the liability framework for the failure of smart contracts. The digital divide issue may obstruct the marginalised population of being able to make use of the blockchain-based RTI portal; and capacity building of public officials in thousands requires long-term investments in training and infrastructure.

Long-term plans to proceed with implementation in phases and steps are suggested. Pilot projects in high-impact areas (e.g. land, public procurement and environment) can provide important learning that will help inform the broader implementation process. The knowledge sharing and interoperability between the lines would be enhanced thanks to the development of open-source RTI blockchain protocols and international standards. Specific policy suggestions are to introduce dedicated legislation on recognising Blockchain records as primary evidence, design regulatory sandboxes and set up independent blockchain governance bodies for its use. Zero-knowledge proofs, secure multi-party computation, and other privacy-enhancing technologies will play a pivotal role in achieving a balance between transparency and data protection.

The assessment of the impact of the blockchain RTI efforts on compliance rates, levels of citizen satisfaction and corruption perception index-based research are recommended. Human centric design will result from a combination of technologists, legal experts, policy makers and civil society organizations. The more advanced technologies emerging, such as AI systems, will be able to further add to the blockchain, creating further complex levels of transparency. Blockchain does not address the governance challenges out of the box, but is a powerful fabric to strengthen accountability systems. Governments are increasingly approaching the principle of openness towards citizens when introducing RTI systems at the core of their processes, instead of as an optional program. When used at the core of specific systems and processes for producing RTI, governments can get closer to a democratic vision of openness towards citizens.

REFERENCES

Alyas, T., Abbas, Q., Niazi, S., Alqahtany, S. S., Alghamdi, T., Alzahrani, A., Tabassum, N., & Ibrahim, A. M. (2025). Multi blockchain architecture for judicial case management using smart contracts. *Scientific Reports*, *15*(1), 8471. DOI: 10.1038/s41598-025-92842-8 PMID: 40069277

Angon, O. C. (2024). General Data Protection Regulation, Right to Be Forgotten, Blockchain Technology and Human Rights. *The Age of Human Rights Journal*, (23), e8702–e8702. DOI: 10.17561/tahrj.v23.8702

Azeem, H. M., Sheer, A., & Umar, M. (2023). Unveiling the power of the right to information: Promoting transparency, accountability, and effective governance. *Al-Kashaf*, *3*(3), 26–39.

Bernards, N., Campbell-Verduyn, M., & Rodima-Taylor, D. (2024). The veil of transparency: Blockchain and sustainability governance in global supply chains. *Environment and Planning C. Politics and Space*, *42*(5), 742–760.

Enyiorji, P. (2023). Blockchain-enforced data lineage architectures with formal verification workflows enabling auditable AI decision chains across regulated fintech compliance regimes and supervisory reporting. *International Journal of Science and Research Archive*, *9*(2), 1201–1217. DOI: 10.30574/ijsra.2023.9.2.0559

Grijalva-Salazar, R. V., Caicedo-Mendoza, J. A., Zúñiga-Castillo, A. J., Olivas-Valencia, E., & Fernández-Bedoya, V. H. (2025). Bridging Regulation and Innovation: A Systematic Review of Cryptocurrency Taxation and Fiscal Policy (2020–2025). *Journal of Risk and Financial Management*, *18*(12), 720. DOI: 10.3390/jrfm18120720

Hakimi, M., Rahmani, K. R., Ezam, Z., & Shahbazi, H. (2024). Integrating blockchain technology for secure e-government services: Opportunities and challenges. *Journal of Social Science Utilizing Technology*, *2*(3), 317–335.

Jain, H., Jain, K., Paliwal, V., Begmal, C., & Girdhar, P. (2024). Towards Transparent Justice: Promoting Integrity and Efficiency in the Judicial System with Blockchain. *Available at SSRN* 4847643. DOI: 10.2139/ssrn.4847643

Karisma, K., & Moslemzadeh Tehrani, P. (2023). Blockchain: legal and regulatory issues. In *Sustainable Oil and Gas Using Blockchain* (pp. 75–118). Springer International Publishing. DOI: 10.1007/978-3-031-30697-6_4

Khlifi, S., & Zouari, G. (2025). The moderating role of corporate ethics on the relationship between blockchain technology and classification shifting: European evidence. *EuroMed Journal of Business*, •••, 1–30. DOI: 10.1108/EMJB-12-2024-0357

Laukyte, M. (2023). Blockchain and the right to good administration: Adding blocks to or blocking of the globalization of good administration? *Indiana Journal of Global Legal Studies*, *30*(1), 195–225. DOI: 10.2979/gls.2023.a886167

Mezzi, E., Mertzani, A., Manis, M. P., Lilova, S., Vadivoulis, N., Gatirdakis, S., . . . Hmede, R. (2025). Who owns the output? bridging law and technology in llms attribution. *arXiv preprint arXiv:2504.01032*.

Mustafa, G., Rafiq, W., Jhamat, N., Arshad, Z., & Rana, F. A. (2025). Blockchain-based governance models in e-government: A comprehensive framework for legal, technical, ethical and security considerations. *International Journal of Law and Management*, *67*(1), 37–55. DOI: 10.1108/IJLMA-08-2023-0172

Nguyen, M. D. (2025). Towards a comprehensive land use rights management system: Blockchain and semantics integration with legal compliance in Vietnam. *Artificial Intelligence and Law*, •••, 1–26. DOI: 10.1007/s10506-025-09486-2

Oliveira, N. B. (2023). *The role of international arbitration in resolving cross-border smart contract disputes: opportunities and challenges*. PQDT-Global.

Silva, S. R. (2025). Blockchain evidence versus the State: RAIMUNDO as a case study. *Oñati Socio-Legal Series*, *15*(4), 1473–1498.

Simanjuntak, E. L., Trinaili, Y., & Said, M. H. M. (2025). The Convergence of Classical Punishment in Money Laundering: Follow the Money Principle Using Blockchain Approach. *Lex Publica*, *12*(1), 264–290. DOI: 10.58829/lp.12.1.2025.298

Spano, R., Zampella, A., Serino, L., & Campanella, F. (2025). *(Un) accountability of crypto assets exchanges: evidence from a slippery financial field*. Qualitative Research in Financial Markets.

Zhang, T. (2025, November). A Neuro-Symbolic and Blockchain-Enhanced Multi-Agent Framework for Fair and Consistent Cross-Regulatory Audit Intelligence. In *Proceedings of the 2025 International Conference on Digital Society and Intelligent Computing* (pp. 254-261). DOI: 10.1145/3788910.3788948

Chapter 9
Exploring Blockchain in Criminal Investigations for Protecting Evidence and Digital Forensics

Vinod Kumar
Amity University, Jaipur, India

Abhijay Chakraborty
http://orcid.org/0000-0003-4228-1931
Amity University, Jaipur, India

Sanjiv Bhadauria
http://orcid.org/0000-0002-2885-3668
Amity University, Gwalior, India

ABSTRACT

As cybercrime continues to grow in size and scope, the problem of receiving and maintaining the integrity and admissibility of digital evidence is growing larger in criminal matters, with greater complexity. The traditional approach to digital forensics can face problems like data volatility, weak chain of custody, cross jurisdiction sharing, and tampering. The key characteristics of blockchain technology immutability, decentralization, transparency and cryptographic time stamping are key attributes that make it a transformative solution. The Blockchain's hashes, evidence metadata and custody transfers are stored in a decentralized way, creating a way to improve the trustworthiness of records and maximize chances of their being usable in court.

DOI: 10.4018/979-8-3373-9730-6.ch009

It sheds light on the potential of blockchain to fortify evidence preservation, tackle privacy and scalability issues, and pave the way for more sound and dependable cybercrime investigations in the digital age.

1. INTRODUCTION

As cybercrime has developed to unprecedented levels, from ransomware and phishing attacks and identity theft to crypto currency crimes, it is far overloading the law enforcement agencies and judicial systems. The Digital information is intricately bound up with its durability, and includes logs, files, images, IoT data, and transaction records all of which are prone to modification, deletion, or contamination. The Traditional forensic methods involve a centralized database handling and manual documentation of chain of custody which is not always with irrefutable evidence for establishing integrity. This defect often has the effect of compromising evidence or making it completely inacceptable in court. This is where blockchain technology comes in as a powerful solution to tackle these challenges, by providing a decentralized, consensual, and immutable system of records through cryptographic hashing, distributed consensus, and tamper-resistant features (Popal et al., 2025). The chapter discusses recent digital forensics blockchain applications, blockchain architectures to support digital forensics, real-world implementations, legal challenges, and ongoing challenges. The Blockchain is essentially a distributed data base of blocks, which include a cryptographic hash of the block just before them, a timestamp, and transaction data. When it is saved, there's no way to change the information that has been saved without a unanimous agreement the whole network. When the evidence is obtained in criminal investigations, it is obtained in accordance with normal evidence collection procedures (such as NIST or ISO 27037). This generates a cryptographic hash (e.g., SHA-256) of the original data that is then recorded along with metadata such as who the collector was, when it was collected, and other important details. The real evidence could exist on the cloud (although never in the blockchain) or on local storage with some sort of data protection, and the chain only points at this location. Any further access, transfer or analysis will result in a new transaction, thus leaving an audit trail and chain of custody.

The main uses is the ability to form the chain of custody. The Conventional paper-based or centralized logs can easily be inaccurate or tampered with by users or due to disagreements. The Blockchain technology enables such systems to automate it, creating smart contracts that establish rules for the handling of evidence, such as needing participation from multiple parties to access evidence. The Coding platforms such as Forensic-Chain on Ethereum or permissioned networks using Hyperledger Fabric have shown that all interactions among the investigators, forensic analyzers, prosecutors and the courts are stamped down non-repudiably (Yadav et al., 2026). It not only guards against tampering, but can offer a legal defensible cryptographic proof too.

The relevant domain is in IoT and multimedia forensics, which often creates a large amount of volatile evidence that is needed to be preserved. The Interested area is the preservation of evidence in IoT and multimedia forensics, where a lot of volatile evidence is generated. For example, in a BEvPF-IoT arrangement, the data from the sensors or surveillance cameras is real time timestamped and real time hashed using blockchain technology, maintaining the authenticity of the data even in distributed settings. Likewise, cloud forensics can take advantage of hybrid approaches, such as, on-chain metadata validating off-chain data integrity, a safeguard against establishing data sovereignty and trading partners' reliability (Kreso, 2025).

1.1 Overview of Cybercrime and Digital Evidence Challenges: The Role of Emerging Technologies in Modern Forensics

The Practical viability is reinforced through real world pilots and research implementations. The notion of "lawful evidence management" with blockchain and cloud computing offer solutions that allow for transparency of the whole evidence management process while eliminating the opportunity for forgery. The Insertions such as LEChain combine blockchain technology with cloud computing, allowing for a transparent examination of the evidence management process without the possibility of falsification. Police or law enforcement agencies of different jurisdictions have been playing with private or consortium blockchains to trade the evidence with a new level of security, while at the same time protecting sensitive information from being compromised. A few U.S. states have started to accept blockchain-backed record as evidence alongside electronic signatures. There are several states in the U.S. have started to accept blockchain-backed records as proof along with electronic signatures. Previously, ransomware and frauds involving multiple countries failed to be easy to trace and lessened stakeholder confidence. But with these case simulations, that is no longer the case.

An Implementations usually use hybrid architectures, a mixture of techniques, in order to balance security and efficiency. The privacy and cost concerns for important investigations are raised by the public blockchain platforms such as Ethereum that provide good decentralization. Private or permissioned blockchain offer controlled access, improved speed and meet the needs of data protection laws like GDPR. Workflow automation can be automated using smart contracts, such as either a policy for evidence expiration or a conditional release. Existing tools, including forensic imaging software, can seamlessly integrate for easy hashing and ledger updates.

Scalability is an issue, though: a large evidence file (such as a terabyte disk image) will be kept off-chain and only pointers and hash to that file will be kept on-chain:

1.2 Blockchain as a Solution for Evidence Integrity

While this is beneficial, there are some obstacles. When dealing with a large volume of cases, there may be an increase in storage and transaction fees. The Standardisation is needed to achieve interoperability between various tools and blockchain platforms used in forensics. Privacy is essential: transparency can enhance auditability but should be weighed against the importance of keeping details of victims confidential and ensuring the details of currently ongoing investigations remain confidential; approaches such as a 'Zero-Knowledge Proof' or 'Selective Disclosure' are being considered. In addition, there are legal and regulatory challenges to overcome, as courts must be educated on the reliability of the blockchain, and there is a need for standards to be developed for its validation. The risks of quantum computing are a far-reaching threat to existing cryptographic methods, and there is a need to seek out post-quantum cryptographic methods.

Yet ethical issues add complexity with regard to adoption. However decentralization means that there are no single points of failure, but who would govern the network, in a law enforcement environment? An excessive dependence on technology may have an impact on smaller agencies that aren't well-funded. Furthermore, compared to traditional forensics, blockchain provides improvements to integrity but is not a panacea for all forensic concerns, including evidence collection from tampered devices at the beginning and anti-forensic techniques devised by advanced criminals.

The future holds potential for further enhancements in associating blockchain with AI and machine learning, including things like computerised anomaly detection in the evidence logs or predicting potential issues with custody procedures. International cooperations could create and maintain jointly-developed consortium blockchains to enhance the proactive response to cybercrime across the globe (Igonor et al., 2025). Future research is needed on delving into this area of usability, performance benchmarking, lab studies, and court validation, on to gain wider acceptance.

In conclusion, blockchain is going to be a paradigm shift in saving digital forensics and cybercrime evidence. It offers a bulletproof, transparent and verifiable root for the chain of custody that directly tackles previous gaps in the chain. Technical, legal and operational challenges still lie ahead, but still, continuous progress holds blockchain out there in the future prospect of being the cornerstone to future criminal investigations. By adopting proactive solutions like these, law enforcement can better ensure evidence integrity, improve judicial success and effectively deal with increasing cyber threats. The technology not only protects individual cases, it also generates an overall trust in processes of digital justice.

2. FUNDAMENTALS OF BLOCKCHAIN TECHNOLOGY: DECENTRALIZATION, IMMUTABILITY AND CRYPTOGRAPHY

The essence of blockchain is that it is a distributed digital ledger that can be used to keep records in a secure, transparent, and verifiable way without relying on any central authority. Because of its decentralizaton, immutability and cryptography pillars, it is also of great value for applications with high trust requirements and integrity such as Digital Forensics and criminal investigation. In terms of the distribution of information and control, decentralisation means that data and control is spread throughout a network of nodes, not just a single server or institution (Chakraborty, 2026). Each participant (node) holds a full copy of the ledger. This eliminates single points of failure, decreases predispositions to any sort of censorship or manipulation by any kind of one party and increases resilience to cyber attacks. Decentralisation provides foramin the forensic context, that although evidence records cannot be modified by a corrupted insider agent or by a single server within a single agency

The Data on the blockchain is imputable which means that data once it is written on the blockchain can never be deleted, and if it is attempted to be changed it can be discovered. This is done through cryptographic linking of the blocks, with the hash value of each block in the previous block's block added in the form of a chain. If one block gets changed, all of the following blocks automatically get rejected as well, and they must be verified by the network to accept a change, negating the value of a large secure network for this application. Immutability offers tamper-proof tracing of all changes to digital evidence in criminal investigations, helping to make digital evidence more admissible in court. The Immutability ensures that there is an audit trail of digital evidence, that no changes have occurred to the evidence, and that it has been preserved in a tamper-proof way, making it more admissible in criminal investigations.

The Cryptography is the bedrock of the security of blockchain. It can be used in combination with various hash functions such as SHA-256, to generate unique digital fingerprints of data objects, public-private key pairs, to ensure digital signatures and identity, and encryption, to ensure confidentiality.

2.1 Types of Blockchains: Public, Private, Consortium and Hybrid

A blockchain from the others based on the four types of access control, management and participation: public, private, consortium and hybrid. Every type has its own particular strengths and weaknesses in the application to preserve digital forensics and cybercrime evidence.

The public chain such as Bitcoin and Ethereum are open and permissionless. Consensus and reading data also happens in the public domain: anyone can participate, read data, and participate in consensus. They are highly resistant to tampering and are provided with maximum decentralization and transparency. They have, however, large barriers that make them difficult for investigations, and with respect to the records, they are public and have high transactions, slow transactions, and lack of privacy of sensitive case information.

The permissioned private blockchains are blockchains under the control of one organization. For better privacy, more transaction speeds, and lower costs they are only accessible to those with authorization. They offer excellent control and compliance functions at the expense of some level of centralization, which is appropriate for the internal law enforcement proof management role. What it has going against it is that any entity that is controlling is never trusted if they are known to be biased.

A consortium (also known as federated) blockchain is one that's managed by a collection of organisations, possibly multiple law enforcement or international groups. They strike a balance between decentralized and controlled. Pre-approved nodes validate transactions and are ideal for cross-jurisdictional evidence sharing. Consortium models are not only helpful in improving cooperation, but also in keeping things confidential and compliant with regulations such as data protection laws.

2.2 Key Mechanisms: Hashing, Consensus Algorithms, and Smart Contracts

This is called hashing: it's the process of applying a mathematical function to any input data to produce a fixed-size string of characters, such as a hash, which is typically the case for digital signatures. Just as with any other file, even the slightest alteration leaves a different hash; it's a superb integrity verification method (Khazem et al., 2025). When acquiring evidence, a hash of the evidence is calculated instantly and saved on the blockchain by a digital forensics investigator. The original hash will provide them with a means to verify any future access and analysis to prove that the evidence is unchanged.

The Consensus algorithms facilitate distributed nodes to share an agreement of the actuality of transactions and maintain one version of the actuality. Known algorithms rule out spam and attacks in Bitcoin, and use computational effort to ensure faster finality such as Practical Byzantine Fault Tolerance (PBFT) in permissioned networks, which are faster for finalizing transactions. In forensics applications, permissioned consensus is recommended because it is faster to receive confirmation, and the participation in the process is limited, keeping transactions in logaries where it matters most – reliable custody transfers of evidence.

2.3 Blockchain Platforms Relevant to Forensics

The Ethereum ecosystem, its developer community and smart contract functionality, through its Solidity, make it one of the most popular platforms available. It is public, which makes it suitable for timestamping and hashing services, and the layer 2 solutions aim to solve scalability issues. However, the cost of gas and privacy are often a reason to take the road to private forks and sidechains when considering forensic use.

For law enforcement, it's also ideal to use Hyperledger Fabric, an open-source Linux Foundation framework. It is a permissioned, modular platform which provides confidential channels, flexible consensus and high throughput. It enables agencies to join a consortium and with its architecture, have separate access to sensitive information without intermingling it. There are also other interesting platforms like Corda, developed with a heavy focus on legal enforceability and privacy, which is suitable for business and legal applications. Quorum is a permissioned Ethereum with improvements to private transactions.

Foremost, new technologies and frameworks that are specifically designed for forensics, like the IPFS (Inter Planetary File System) decentralized file storage with blockchain anchoring. Research prototypes use Polkadot or Cosmos for interoperability with other agency chains, but these projects were limited. An interoperability between different agency chains is achieved with some research prototypes using Polkadot or Cosmos.

2.4 Time-stamping and Distributed Ledger Technology

The Distributed Ledger Technology (DLT) is the umbrella term for blockchain, which describes a "database shared, replicated and synchronized across several participants with consensus. On top of that, without a central administrator, DLT achieves transparency and resilience that is different from traditional databases. The more formidable features for DLT forensics is timestamping. It includes a precise date and time that a data item (or hash of it) was added to the ledger. Blockchain timestamping is a technique that generates verifiable proof-of-existence via cryptographic proof. The services provided by organizations such as open time-stamps can be used to "timestamp" a data element at little cost to the user, to show that a copy of a particular element existed in a certain form at a specific time, and that it stood on some public blockchain (like Bitcoin). In criminal investigations, accurate time stamping can establish the time of collection of digital evidence, the time of custody transfer and if there were any time gaps.

3. DIGITAL FORENSICS AND CYBERCRIME EVIDENCE: CONCEPTS AND CHALLENGES

This course teaches students about the concept of digital forensics and the challenges of collecting digital evidence, such as that encountered in cybercrime investigations.

The scientific method used to identify, collect, preserve, analyze and present electronic data in a legally admissible way is known as digital forensics (Rani et al., 2025). It has a central role to play in investigations of cybercrime processes in relation to computing evidence from computers, mobile devices, networks, cloud storage, Internet of Things (IoT), and other digital artifacts. Unlike physical evidence, cybercrime evidence can change, be spread out and volatile.

With various types of cybercrimes, from ransomware attacks to phishing, and state-sponsored attacks becoming increasingly complex and numerous, digital evidence is now available in huge quantities and has significantly complicated the learners' lives. In recent years, the volume of digital evidence has significantly expanded and its complexity has now made it easy for the learners to find themselves overwhelmed, ranging from ransomware and phishing to complex state sponsored attacks. The top threats are staying malware attacks and phishing attacks, which are facilitated by using AI-powered tools, deepfakes, and cloud exploits, as per the latest reports. This evidence can comprise logs, files, metadata, network traffic, encrypted communications and crypto-currency transactions (Prasad et al., 2026).

Despite this crucial importance, there are huge challenges for using digital evidence: data degradation, cross-border jurisdictional issues and the vast amounts of data involved (big data concerns), and anti-forensic technology capabilities of criminals. Centralized approach to storage and handling of records, combined with manual operations, frequently cannot ensure record integrity and this may create authenticity and chain-of-custody issues.

To tackle these issues, the blockchain technology has received considerable attention, as it offers immutable records and verifiable timestamps. Successful integration needs to consider other technical challenges, as well as privacy issues (particularly given GDPR and related laws), scalability of the integration, and legal notice and consent. In this section, the essential principles and evidence forms, preservation challenges, admissibility requirements, as well as current and future risks are explored to cultivate an understanding of blockchain's potential to enhance forensic processes in contemporary investigations of crime.

3.1 Principles of Digital Forensics (Identification, Preservation, Analysis, Presentation)

A difficult task is to find a possible sources of useful digital information. While engaged in investigation within legal boundaries (e.g., search warrant), Investigators shall be mindful of devices, networks, cloud accounts or media that may hold evidence. This is a stage that calls for instant response because digital data is not likely to be stable.

The Preservation is concerned with the provision of irrefutable evidence, which does not involve changes. Important practices include the use of write-blockers, maintaining complete chain-of-custody documents, and making a bit-for-bit copy of the drives (forensic images). The first ACPO principle is there has been no material alteration of data upon which court action may be taken. Using hashes, such as hash values (for e.g. SHA-256), to check integrity.

An Analysis involves looking into the information on hand using dedicated equipment and tools to get useful information. This involves file recovery, reconstruction of timelines, keyword search and reverse engineering of Malware. The Examiner should be competent (ACPO Principle 2) and complete records of all processes must be maintained.

3.2 Common Cybercrimes and Associated Digital Evidence Types

Some of the most commonly seen cybercrimes are ransomware-as-a-service, business email compromise (BEC) attacks, deep fakes and fraud, data breaches, and AI-powered phishing. Some other major crimes include crypto-currency hackers, online child pornography, intellectual property theft and Distributed denial-of-service (DDoS) attacks.

The Evidence can be anywhere, including endpoints, servers, mobile devices, on the cloud or as proof distributed across several networks. Data in RAM (volatile data) and network traffic that is transient (passing through the network) must be captured immediately, with terabytes of data to handle, there are big data challenges and that's where data triage and AI analysis comes into play.

3.3 Traditional Evidence Preservation Issues: Tampering, Chain of Custody, and Volatility

The Tampering is a critical issue as in the case of digital files, there are no visible physical signs that the files have been tampered with. It is easy to edit and alter content without any changes to visual appearance of the file undermining authenticity. There's the possibility of inside job opportunities or hacker attacks to centralized storage systems.

The Chain of Custody (CoC) tracks evidence from evidence collection to courtroom. This is typically based on manual tracking in systems, paper documentation, or simple databases that can be prone to human mistakes, loss, or manipulation. Breaks in the CoC can make evidence inadmissible and/or impact its probative value.

The data in a Digital Data is continually changing; it is in a dynamic state. Only data in RAM exists even after that power off, logs can be altered and data stored in the cloud cloud can be be deleted or modified by cloud providers. Data from networks and IoT streams is dynamic and changing and must be captured in real-time, which is often impractical.

Often these problems result in smear campaigns against the evidence in court, stalled investigations and missed prosecutions. The cross-border situation perpetuates issues related to incomparability of systems and slow approval process of mutual legal assistance treaties. Criminals make these challenges easier to overcome with the use of anti-forensic tools, which can allow them to delete information in a systematic way (Shami et al., 2025).

3.4 Legal and Admissibility Requirements for Digital Evidence

Digital evidence is accepted in court only if it meets the high standards of law on authenticity, integrity, reliability and relevance. According to the Federal Rules of Evidence (Rules 901 & 902), authentication is required in the United States. The Daubert Standard for scientific reliability of methods and expert testimony is followed by many jurisdictions.

Key requirements include:

Authenticity: assurance that data is what it says it is; with metadata, hashes and a linking of the devices.

A set of properties demonstrated by cryptographic hashes that the evidence has not been manipulated since it was collected. Complete, documented trace of handling, storage and transfers

Legal Collection: Collecting through a WARRANT, consent or legal exceptions to prevent the "fruit-of-the-poisonous-tree" exclusion.

Relevance and Reliability: The evidence should be relevant and derived from good forensic practice.

Digital evidence handling is guided by International standards like ISO/IEC 27037. Data protection regimes also, such as GDPR and CCPA, are crucial to compliance to prevent suppression.

As blockchain evidence becomes more accepted in judicious ways and the technology is explained by experts, courts are accepting it in increasing numbers.

3.5 Emerging Threats: Anti-Forensics Techniques and Data Manipulation

All these techniques take advantage of the easiness of digital data and of the fact that the conventional forensic tools have only limited capabilities. When multiple techniques are used, it becomes very difficult to attribute and reconstruct a threat as advanced attack (APT). They are met with counters specializing in tools designed for artifact recovery, building timelines, and finding anomalies with the use of AI machine learning. These are arrested by counters who specialize in tools that enable them to make timelines, to recover artifacts, and to find anomalies using AI/machine learning. But the arms race goes on, with technologically-enhanced methods being embraced by criminals.

4. BLOCKCHAIN APPLICATIONS IN PRESERVING DIGITAL FORENSICS EVIDENCE

The primary issues of blockchain technology in digital forensics are understood, oral consensus is building, and collaboration is taking shape. The foundation of blockchain technology in digital forensics evidence preservation is revolutionizing by tackling key vulnerabilities in conventional systems. As for the future, oral consensus is growing and collaboration efforts are beginning to materialize. Its fundamental properties immutability, decentralization, transparency and cryptographic safety make it feasible to establish tamper-evidence records that highly improve the reliability and court-admissibility of electronic evidence. Blockchain offers a strong solution for ensuring evidence integrity across the entire evidence lifecycle for criminal investigations that involve volatile evidence and face strong challenges to its integrity such as ransomware, data breaches, and online fraud. The distributed ledger keeps a record of metadata, hashes, and transfers of custody, making good audit trails and bolstering judicial trust and reducing disputes.

A key use is in tracking the chain of custody ensuring that the product's history is secure. Traditional chain of custody methods use manual log books or a centralized database filled by manual entry, which can lead to human errors, tampering by insiders or data loss. This process is digitalized and automated by using Blockchain-based systems (Mishra et al., 2025). The data is cryptographically hashed (usually SHA-256), which is captured together with timestamps, collectors' identity and case data and stored in the blockchain. All accesses and analyses thereafter are then recorded as new transactions, so that an unbroken trail of accesses and analysis is maintained, and can be traced back. For example, Forensic-Chain (currently being developed in the Ethereum and Hyperledger ecosystems) establishes this, providing law enforcement authorities with cryptographic security to ensure the seamless following of evidence transfers between investigators, analysts, prosecutors and courts. Smart contracts can have rules imposed upon them, like network access may require multiple party approval, which minimises tampering by unauthorised parties.

Immutable timestamping, in addition to hash-based evidence authentication, also contributes to preservation efforts. Based on a distributed ledger, blockchain offers a decentralized and trustworthy way to establish a precise time and place for a document, piece of data or content. This is a priceless fix regardless of whether it is to prevent claims to tampering or to backdate. In practice, investigators attach evidence hashes to public blockchains such as Bitcoin or Ethereum (hashes attached through a service akin to OpenTimestamps) and/or private chains so they can leverage the privacy afforded to them. Large evidence files are stored off-chain (in safe cloud storage, IPFS, etc.) and only singular hashes and metadata are kept on-chain in a hybrid model. This way, no data is lost in order to ensure integrity verification. In this way, research prototypes, for example, BEvPF-IoT for multimedia and IoT evidence, have managed to preserve surveillance footage and sensor data in real time in very good practice.

Using the decentralised storage and verifiable integrity features of evidence keeps against single points of failure. Blockchain divides up records between multiple nodes, rather than relying on centralized servers that can be breached or suffer from ransomware. Individuals can choose to verify authenticity of evidence themselves through comparing computed hashes to on-chain records (Naseer et al., 2026). This would be useful in an inter-jurisdictional investigation in which there are lack of mutual trust or trust with agencies or where the flow of JLA is delayed. Participating law enforcement organizations share securely and verifiably information associated with the evidence, but keep sensitive evidence raw data within their own control by sharing through Consortium blockchains.

An Automated evidence handling protocols are made possible by Smart Contracts, which decrease human involvement and risks. These programs can be automatically executed to let users register evidence, log access, set expiration periods or conditionally release access to authorized users, to name just a few. For example, a smart contract can automatically alert stakeholders to evidence accessed, or can flag potential issues when evidence if accessed—a transfer of custody for example. This can be further improved with integration with AI, which can identify patterns in access logs that may be suspicious. Reccnt deployments have successfully validated high levels of integrity using Hyperledger Fabric and AI anomaly detection and enhanced the speed and effectiveness of forensic workflows.

Ideally, integration with existing forensic tools and frameworks is needed for use. There are modern solutions which connect blockchain with both tools that are compliant with NIST and ISO 27037. Forensic Imaging Software can auto-calculate hashes and upload them to the BCC once they are acquired. Cloud forensics means that the cloud-based platform runs as a hybrid architecture with an anchoring via blockchain on top of data kept in cloud entities such as AWS or Azure. The popularly used permissioned platforms (like Hyperledger Fabric) have a high throughput, way of channel communication is also confidential and allows the very flexible modularization, that's why they are most applicable for enterprise level law enforcement. For public timestamping services, there is an exploration of Ethereum and its layer two solutions.

The Experience based on actual pilots and academic prototypes highlights the potential. Ransomware and fraud cases have been tested under projects such as LEChain, and with other Hyperledger-based systems, this has resulted in enhanced traceability. Blockchain-encrypted records are now starting to be accepted by some jurisdictions as evidence with supporting expert testimony about blockchain technology's reliability (Alotaibe, 2025). The key area of pain in current cross-border cyber investigation is how to share the evidence securely, securely and with confidence with partners across the globe and this could be overcome by a consortium approach.

While all this is good, there are still some problems. High volume (TB data) situations can cause scalability problems, but can be addressed by hybrid on/off chain designs. However, with privacy regulations such as GDPR, it becomes imperative to use privacy-enhancing methods like zero-knowledge proofs or selective disclosure. Other challenges include: transaction costs on the public chains; and standardization across agencies. Judicial or legal education is needed, as are the creation of validation standards.

The over-all blockchain applications in the field of digital forensics have changed the way of evidence preservation from trusted and to cryptographically verifiable model. Blockchain fortifies the entire forensic chain of custody, possibility of sharing inaccessible artifacts, time-stamping, and integrity verification, as well as automating the process. With the growing maturity of technology and the increasing ability to integrate it more easily, it will have a substantial impact on combating Cybercrime and building trust in cyber justice systems. Its transformative impact will be further realized through ongoing research, standardization and pilot deployments.

5. TECHNICAL IMPLEMENTATION AND ARCHITECTURES

Implementing blockchain in the context of digital forensics necessitates careful design of the architecture to ensure security, performance, privacy, and legal compliance. The standard forensics workflow supported by a blockchain system involves the evidence collection that takes place using standard evidence collection tools which automatically create a cryptographic hash (SHA-256 or SHA-3) and metadata (Kumari, 2025). The data is later pushed to the blockchain network through APIs and/or middle layers. Most architectural patterns are based on the idea of a layered structure, with the acquisition layer, hashing and metadata extraction layer, blockchain interaction layer, storage layer, and query/presentation layer as the different layers. These consensus mechanisms can be modular, indemodifiable,-and pluggable, allowing for configurations like Raft or Kafka. IPLX is favored for most law enforcement implementations because it has this modular nature as well as confidential channels and pluggable consensus mechanisms. These enable several agencies to join a Consortium, and then ensures the data is segregated.

This has led to the development of hybrid architectures, which are the most feasible option. For a hybrid model, only light, on-chain material is stored on the chain (minimal disk images, video content, custody logs, and transaction records), with the bulkier off-chain data (logs, disk images, videos) being kept in secure (encrypted) cloud-based storage locations or content-addressed decentralized systems like IPFS (Inter Planetary File System). Smart contracts include protocols that automatically validate data flows, validate access rights and alert for integrity issues. To give an example, when the investigator logs in to evidence, the smart contract will log this action and verify the evidence hash is worthy of being decrypted before releasing the evidence decryption keys.

The standardized APIs and middleware provide interoperability with legacy forensic suites (Autopsy, EnCase, FTK) as well as with new or emerging forensic capabilities such as IoT ecosystems, cloud platforms and mobile device management. Real-time blockchain anchoring of sensor data streams is helpful for IoT forensics, and blockchain's data integrity and provenance for multi-tenant cloud setups is useful for cloud forensics. Acquisition reports can be directly pushed by Mobile forensics tools to the ledger.

It is secured via multiple factors of authentication, role-based access control (RBAC), and end-to-end encryption and privacy-preserving verification with zero knowledge proofs. Private keys are controlled through the use of hardware security modules (HSMs) to ward off any compromise (Padma et al. 2025). The principles of privacy by design directly respond to GDPR and other laws and regulations with the selective disclosure and storing of sensitive information on the off-chain.

It's important to take performance and scalability factors into account. However, public blocks are low performance either have high latency or are costly and can only be used for timestamp anchoring. Permissioned networks are able to deliver hundreds to thousands of transactions per second with low latency. Sharding, layer-two solutions, and sidechains contribute to the ability to deal with hefty workloads. Analysis of costs demonstrates that although initial set-up will be costly, running the same system will be far more affordable with automation and subsequently less disputes involved. Issues such as change and access to keys, network control and public communications, and availability of data long-term can be a challenge. The technical solutions striking for this combination of blockchain and trusted execution environments (TEE), applications for anomaly detection and standardized solutions are forensically sound and come with the next court-ready system.

6. CONCLUSION

The blockchain technology is an important development in maintaining the digital forensic and cybercrime evidence. It overcomes the shortcomings of traditional approaches, such as problems of tampering, volatility, and admissibility concerns, with verifiable timestamps, automated chain of custody and decentralized trust. During this research it has been shown how blockchain can support all phases of the digital forensic workflow, from evidence acquisition, to courtroom presentation. The advantages of hybrid architectures, smart contracts, and permissioned ledgers illustrate feasible solutions for trusted and transparent evidence management for law enforcement institutions that are also reliable and verifiable.

The incorporation of blockchain will not only make each case more secure and secure, but it will also promote more inter-agency and inter-border cooperation. The implementation of real-world pilots and research prototypes has been noted to have measurable improvements in evidence trustworthiness, decreased litigation regarding authenticity and speed up to the resolution of cybercrime cases. But it's not a cure-all for blockchain. There are a number of technical issues, including scalability, storage costs, interoperability; legal concerns over the challenges of admissibility standards; and ethical ones in regards to privacy and governance that need to be systematically addressed before mass adoption of AI can be considered.

There are a number of areas Future Work should concentrate upon. The first is to create international standards and certification procedures for blockchain forensic tools to ensure their uniformity and acceptance in different countries. Second, pushing further the development of privacy enhancing technologies like zero-knowledge proofs, homomorphic encryption and secure multiparty computation, specifically for sensitive investigative data. Thirdly, the integration of blockchain with AI and machine learning, for automated evidence triage, anomaly detection in custody logs, and predictive analysis on verifying potential custody misuse.

Post-quantum algorithms must be studied to create systems that are secure in the future against imminent threats. Large-scale pilot deployments in real police settings, and empirical performance metrics will lead to useful information about practical viability. In addition, studies with users will be essential for the successful transfer of technology to training investigators and judicial officers.

With the increasing sophistication and volume of cyber threats, blockchain can provide a revolutionary platform for a new cyber trustworthy ecosystem of digital evidence. The future of blockchain integrated forensic systems looks promising, as further interdisciplinary studies, drafting policies and advancements in technology would result in blockchain forensic systems being the ultimate benchmark in criminal investigation. However, law-enforcement agencies and policymakers need to act proactively to leverage this technology, so that justice systems continue to be effective and accountable in what is becoming a digital world. Blockchain-enabled, decentralized, intelligent evidence and cryptographically verifiable evidence ecosystems are the key to the future of cybercrime investigations.

REFERENCES

Alotaibe, D. Z. (2025, April). Blockchain-Based Forensic Investigation Metamodel (BBFIM) for Investigating IoT Cybercrimes. In *2025 4th International Conference on Computing and Information Technology (ICCIT)* (pp. 32-37). IEEE.

Chakraborty, S. (2026). Next-Gen Digital Forensics: Investigating Cybercrime in the Era of AI, Blockchain, and the Dark Web. *The Science of Criminal Investigations*, 286.

Igonor, O. S., Amin, M. B., & Garg, S. (2025). The application of blockchain technology in the field of digital forensics: A literature review. *Blockchains*, *3*(1), 5. DOI: 10.3390/blockchains3010005

Khazem, M. M., Al Okagaili, S. M., Jassim, B. M., Hasan, M. S., Ahmed, S. A., Khalaf, I. Z., & Mohammed, A. A. (2025, July). Real-Time Detection of Cybercrime and Digital Forensics Automation Using AI-Based Legal Evidence Collection and Preservation Mechanisms. In *2025 3rd International Conference on Cyber Resilience (ICCR)* (pp. 1-7). IEEE. DOI: 10.1109/ICCR67387.2025.11292443

Kreso, I. (2025). Using blockchain technology for preserving digital evidence in digital forensics. *KNOWLEDGE-International Journal*, *68*(3), 331–336.

Kumari, S. (2025). Securing Evidence in Digital Forensics Using Blockchain. *Advances in Data Science and Artificial Intelligence: Proceedings of ERCICA 2024,* Volume 1, *1*, 395.

Mishra, R., Arya, P., Narwaria, M., & Kaur, I. (2025, October). Blockchain-Enhanced Chain of Custody for Digital Forensic Evidence Management. In *2025 IEEE International Conference on Blockchain and Distributed Systems Security (ICBDS)* (pp. 1-5). IEEE. DOI: 10.1109/ICBDS67396.2025.11379799

Naseer, M., Gusdevi, H., Rahayudin, R., & Guterres, A. (2026). Blockchain-Based Evidence Legality in Indonesia's Criminal Justice System. *Jurnal Hukum Indonesia*, *5*(1), 40–65. DOI: 10.58344/jhi.v5i1.2351

Padma, U. R., Gnanaprakash, T., Karthik Roshan, R., & Saravanan, G. (2025). Unyielding Integrity & Safeguarding In Digital Forensics Through Blockchain Integration. *African Journal of Biomedical Research*, •••, 28.

Popal, M., Ahmad, A., & Arshad, M. (2025). The Significance of Blockchain Technology in Preserving Digital Evidence Integrity in Forensic Investigations. *Journal of Computing & Biomedical Informatics*, *9*(02).

Prasad, V. L. S., Srivastava, V., & Singh, H. (2026). Cyber-Crimes in AI-Enabled Green Platforms: Legal Hurdles in ESG Investing, Prosecution, and Financial Loss Mitigation. In AI Governance, Law, Policy and Ethics in Green Finance and ESG (pp. 265-282). IGI Global Scientific Publishing.

Rani, D., Gill, N. S., Gulia, P., Yahya, M., Ahanger, T. A., Hassan, M. M., Abdallah, F. B., & Shukla, P. K. (2025). A secure digital evidence preservation system for an iot-enabled smart environment using ipfs, blockchain, and smart contracts. *Peer-to-Peer Networking and Applications*, *18*(2), 5. DOI: 10.1007/s12083-024-01855-z

Shami, A. Z. A., Saleem, M., & Ashraf, J. (2025). Cybercrime and Digital Evidence: Investigating the Challenges and Opportunities in Prosecuting Cybercrime and Handling Digital Evidence. *Research Consortium Archive*, *3*(2), 401–411.

Yadav, A., Srivastava, V., & Singh, H. (2026). Enhancing Green Investment Through AI and Automation: A Critical Legal Study of Regulatory Frameworks Effectiveness in Tackling Cybersquatting in India. In AI Governance, Law, Policy and Ethics in Green Finance and ESG (pp. 149-166). IGI Global Scientific Publishing. DOI: 10.4018/979-8-2600-1308-3.ch009

Chapter 10
Exploring Privacy-Preserving Techniques in Blockchain:
Zero-Knowledge Proofs and Confidential Evidence Handling

Arunima Shastri
http://orcid.org/0000-0002-6260-1253
Christ University, Bangalore, India

ABSTRACT

The transparency of the blockchain technology makes privacy issues acutely challenging in certain highly sensitive applications such as IP protection and contractual arguments. This chapter is an overview of privacy preserving methods and in particular Zero-Knowledge Proofs (ZKPs) and confidential evidence handling mechanisms. ZKPs are set to transform notarization by allowing parties to prove that information or statements are true without disclosing the information that they have associated with them. The study covers the concept of use of blockchain and how they can be used to combine with smart contracts for privacy-preserving IP access rights governance and dispute resolution. It also covers confidential computing, homomorphic encryption, and secure multi-party computation for processing privacy sensitive evidence on the blockchain. In regulated industries, these technologies hold the promise of increasing prevalence, but encounter challenges relating to regulations and trusted setup, as well as computational overhead issues.

DOI: 10.4018/979-8-3373-9730-6.ch010

1. INTRODUCTION

The most essential blocks to the widespread adoption of blockchain has proven to be privacy, which is especially relevant in areas that involve confidentiality, like protecting IP, entering into contractual arrangements, and notarisation. A trade secret, personal data, and proprietary evidence are pivotal considerations in today's business environment, and public blockchains such as Bitcoin and Ethereum provide such transparency that they pose a tension between the need for transparency and protection of business sensitive information, trade secrets, personal data, and proprietary evidence. To circumvent this, techniques that support privacy-preserving disclosure and verifiable computation are adopted (Majdoub & Atmani, 2025). Of these, Zero-Knowledge Proofs (ZKPs) are a novel cryptographic technology which allows one party (the prover) to convince another party (the verifier) that a statement is true without communicating any extra information than just a confirmation that the statement is indeed correct.

A Zero-Knowledge Proof consists of three basic properties: completeness, soundness and zero-knowledge. Completeness is its counterpart: It is guaranteed that an honest prover can make the verifier believe that a statement is true, if it really is. Because of soundness, provers who say something untrue to their verifiers, cannot prevent the verifiers from knowing that something is amiss. Zero knowledge means the verifier does not even learn the truth of the statement of the assertion (Mbimbi et al., 2025). This is ideal for blockchain notarisation, where users are required to prove the contents of a document or IP ownership or integrity without revealing the contents of that object.

Some of the most popular variants are zk-SNARKs, which are succinct proofs impressively small and fast to verify that have been adopted by the privacy coins Zcash and, as of recently, layer-2 scaling solutions like Polygon-Hermez, zkSync and StarkNet. Here, a creator could create a zk-SNARK which proves that they have the original file (by privately hashing it), and created it prior to a specific date, without uploading the file. This allows for the safe and secure timing and identification of Computer Programs that is essential in Copyright suits.

Another potent variant is called zk-STARKs (Scalable Transparent Arguments of Knowledge) and it removes the need to stage a trusted setup ceremony, which is necessary to build many zk-SNARK constructions, thus lowering any security concern related to bad actors discarding any sort of setups. zk-STARKs generate a longer evidence, but they are post-quantum resistant and hence have some transparency which makes them attractive for long-term evidence handling in the legal system. In some situations, parties may require a range proof system that allows them to prove a value is in a specified range, without divulging the exact value, such as in asset valuations or royalty settlements. Bulletproofs are an efficient range proof system appropriate for such cases.

Complementary techniques can be used with ZKPs to handle information in a way that is confidential. The private input in smart chains that compute private IP licensing terms, or dispute parameters, without decrypting the input data is made possible by homomorphic encryption. Secure Multi-Party Computation (MPC) is suitable for collaborative IP development similar to multiple parties computing functions on their own private inputs where they can prove they did so but without revealing full designs (Albalwy, 2026). Trusted Execution Environments (TEEs) such as those offered by Intel SGX contain secure environments to conduct confidential computation, the premise being: off-chain security and on-chain verification.

When resolving contractual disputes, these tools help with "confidential evidence anchoring" and during notarization. Parties can hash sensitive contracts and/or evidence, produce ZKPs that certify that certain clauses or conditions were satisfied, and record the ZKPs on-chain rather than the contracts and/or evidence. For example, when a business enters a licensing arrangement, the licensee may demonstrate that he or she has paid the licensing fees, or has adhered to the usage limits, without revealing exact numbers. Alternatively, settlement platforms based on decentralization can also verify claims in private way with confidentiality in settlement provision ensuring fairness. This method drastically decreases the threat of information leaking as is present with regular notarization and court filing.

Potential uses include IP management applications. Prototype / prior art / creation timelines can be proven in confidence by the artist and/or the inventor to maintain confidentiality and protect its competitive edge. ZKPs can be used to verify that members of patent pools or licensing consortia meet certain conditions and/or have the rights to use the patented technology without revealing proprietary portfolios. Private ownership transfers and selective disclosure of NFT metadata are possible thanks to the introduction of privacy-enhanced variants in the NFT ecosystems, such as zk-NFTs. Confidential traceability is particularly good for supply chain IP protection, as the assets of the brands can be only shared with their authorized persons.

In a process of security analysis the compromises are exposed. ZKPs offer robust cryptographic assurances, yet issues such as side-channel attacks, vulnerabilities in implementations, or oracle vulnerabilities compromise privacy. Post-quantum friendly schemes and quantum computing threats. Careful design is required for regulatory compliance with GDPR, CCPA and new laws, privacy techniques have to empower the "right to be forgotten", or select disclosure for legal audits.

Progress is making rapid strides in the real world. The zk-EVM support of private smart contract deployments is part of Ethereum's roadmap.zk-EVM private smart contract deployment support is part of Ethereum's roadmap. Programmable privacy is the subject of entire ecosystems, such as the project's Aztec, Aleo and

Secret Network. In the legal sector, we are experimenting with the use of confidential evidence in arbitration, and with e-discovery. Governments are considering ensuring public transparency whilst also protecting commercial confidentiality with a privacy-preserving blockchain technology for IP registries.

In the future, hybrid and advanced tryouts of Hybrid ZKPs, off-chain storage (content addressing) and advanced encryptions will be the most successful. Embedding AI to generate proofs automatically and identify anomalies in private systems will simplify the use of the system. Regulatory sandboxes and standardization bodies will be vital to ensuring alignment between privacy innovations and the admissibility of confidential evidence on the blockchain for legal purposes. Regulatory sandboxes and standardization bodies will play a crucial role in ensuring alignment between privacy innovations and the ability of confidential evidence to be legally admissible.

So, privacy-enhancing methods, such as Zero-Knowledge Proofs and confidential evidence methods, play a vital role in blockchain's future in such applications. They are able to balance the seemingly contradictory objectives of transparency, verifiability and confidentiality in order to pave the way for the wider institutional adoption. As these technologies develop, they have the potential to introduce efficiencies and safeguard sensitive data that fuels innovation and commerce. As cryptographers, lawyers, and policymakers continue to investigate, optimize, and cross-fertilize their ideas, the extent to which blockchain can provide a secure and trusted platform for the digital economy will be measured.

2. ZERO-KNOWLEDGE PROOFS: CORE CONCEPTS AND MECHANISMS

ZKPs are one of the greatest advances in cryptography of the late 20th and early 21st century, where a prover can prove ownership of a bit without revealing any details beyond the proof of the bit itself to a verifier. First reported on in a game-changing 1985 seminal paper by Shafi Goldwasser, Silvio Micali, and Charles Rackoff, "The Knowledge Complexity of Interactive Proof Systems," ZKPs have grown from theory to practical implementations in blockchain systems, facilitating privacy in confidential notarization, IP protection, and secure contractual enforcement (Khalid et al., 2026).

ZKPs come with three basic properties: completeness, soundness, and zero-knowledge. If the statement is true, and prover and verifier are playing the protocol honestly, then with high probability the verifier will be convinced under conditions of completeness. The soundness is guaranteed by the fact that whenever the statement is false, then no provers can make an honest verifier accept the statement, except with a negligible probability. The Zero Knowledge property is the most revolutionary says that verifier learns nothing except the truth of the statement. Roughly speaking, any verifier can be simulated by a simulator, even if it is without having access to the secret witness, so that it is possible to produce a transcript, indistinguishable from a transcript of a real interaction with the prover. The Property may be Perfected (Information-theoretically secure), Statistical or Computational, depending on the assumption used.

The typical classification of ZKPs is into interactive or non-interactive. An interactive proof includes several rounds of challenge-response. The prover has to prove his knowledge of an isomorphism between two graphs; the classic example is called the Graph Isomorphism protocol. In each round, the verifier attempts to ask the prover to reveal a copy of the original graph, or a permuted form of it, at random; repeated rounds of this constitute a form of statistical confidence building exercise (Myeong & Ram, 2025). Though interactive proofs are necessary, but they don't work for the blockchain because parties can't be online at the same time and they're supposed to be verifiable in public.

This is where Non-interactive Zero-Knowledge Proofs (NIZKs) come in handy. The Fiat-Shamir heuristic turns interactive protocols into non-interactive protocols simply by eliminating the verifier challenge processes and using outputs of a cryptographic hash function on the transcript of the protocol. This forms only a single possibility of proof that is publicly verifiable. In light of their efficiency on decentralized networks, non-interactive constructions are the major construction approach for contemporary blockchain ZKP.

zk-SNARKs (Zero-Knowledge Succinct Non-interactive ARguments of Knowledge) are the most widely used one today. Proof size and verification time are very compact with zk-SNARKs, often a few hundred bytes, and very fast regardless of the underlying computation – usually the verification takes less than a second. zk-SNARKs generally express computations as polynomial equations using elliptic curve pairings or Rank-1 Constraint Systems (R1CS). Arithmetic Circuit Compilation: The statement to be proven (e.g., "I know a preimage to hash equal to X, and it was made before timestamp T") is translated into an arithmetic circuit. There is a one time ceremony to generate structured reference strings (SRS) or common reference strings (CRS) in Trusted Setup.

zk-STARKs (Zero-Knowledge Scalable Transparent Arguments of Knowledge) overcome some of the shortcomings in zk-SNARKs. STARKs were developed by Eli Ben-Sasson and his colleagues, and they are essentially based on the use of collision-resistant hash functions, together with Reed-Solomon codes, over finite fields, which obviate the need for trusted setup. Though more scalable than SNARKs if larger computations are required, they require larger proof sizes (in the tens to hundreds of kilobytes) and are slower to verify than SNARKs are, but are post-quantum resistant (Maheshwari & Prasanna, 2025). The transparency and flexibility they offer are appealing in scenarios such as sensitive evidence management in legal and IP proceedings where security is a primary concern.

Another important mechanism is the bulletproofs, which are very useful when proofing that a specific value is within a range (e.g., if proving that a specific value is in the range 0 to the so called maximum value without disclosing it), of which range proofs are a special case. The sizes of their proofs are logarithmic and do not need trusted setups. Inner-product arguments facilitate additional compression, which is handy for privacy in smart contract transactions and confidential transactions.

Technically, the modern ZKPs are typically based on the Polynomial Interactive Oracle Proof (PIOP) framework and polynomial commitment schemes. Computations are simplified to polynomial identities, proved with techniques such as Sumcheck protocols, multivariate polynomial commitments. Recursive proof composition (RPCO) is a recently developed method to enable an efficient verification of proof by proof, as developed in Halo, with extensions in Halo2. This allows for obtaining "proofs of proofs": essential for the scalable layer-2 rollups and long and complicated IP management processes that require multiple proofs to be verified in succession.

The blockchain also has some strong privacy properties in blockchain notarization and IP applications; these properties are enabled by the ZKPs. Powered by a preimage known only to the asset owner, or without his or her disclosure, a creator of digital assets can establish proof that he or she has created an asset. In contractual conflicts, parties are able to establish compliance with the terms of the license (e.g., that the limits of usage were not exceeded) and payment of royalties; meanwhile, they avoid releasing confidential business information. Smart contracts may be used to verify ZKPs on the blockchain, which will cause an automatic operation without providing the proof.

There are still performance compromises that to be considered. Generation of proofs is very demanding computation, which is in most cases not feasible with large circuits, unless some specialized hardware is used, such as GPGPUs or FPGAs. Although quick, verification still costs gas on public blockchains. Current research includes work in the areas of recursive proofs, folding schemes (as Nova), and hardware acceleration to minimize these costs. Developers have reduced the effort involved in implementing systems based on ZKPs with libraries such as libsnark, circom, Halo2, and Starkware's toolchain.

The security analysis of ZKPs should take into account several attack vectors: soundness from several points of view (discrete log, knowledge of exponent etc.), real world extractability from practical security considerations and resistance to quantum adversaries. Side-channel attacks on implementations are also demanding in terms of precautions to be taken during the setup of a trusted implementation with constant-time program and secure multiparty computing.

The essence of Zero Knowledge Proofs is to change the paradigm of trust in digital systems. They offer cryptographic certainty, with minimal leakage of information, rather than relying on trusted third parties, or the disclosure of full data sets (Krishappa et al., 2025). The mechanisms are expected to lay the groundwork for a more efficient, usable, and universal blockchain notarization, confidential IP registries, and new-generation smart contract platforms in terms of privacy protection. The potential of ZKPs to strike a balance between transparency and confidentiality makes them a key technology for the future of secure, private and verifiable digital economies.

3. ADVANCED ZERO-KNOWLEDGE PROTOCOLS AND VARIANTS

From basic zk-SNARK and zk-STARK, Advanced Zero-Knowledge Proofs have expanded to tackle the issues of scalability, security, and user-friendliness in the realm of blockchain technology. A notable advance is the PLONK (Permutations over Lagrange-bases for Oecumenical Noninteractive arguments of Knowledge) protocol that is used to build Universal Trusted Setups and Updatable Trusted Setups. PLONK offers a one-time reference string to support multiple circuits, one of the key factors that lowers the complexity and costs of deploying zk-SNARKs in practice. Another key aspect in making zk-SNARK deployments more practical compared to previous offerings, like Groth16, was the ability to share a setup string for multiple circuits. The effect of its permutation argument on its ability to efficiently represent arithmetic circuits makes it very popular in state-of-the-art L2 solutions, such as zkSync Era and PolyGon zkEVM.

Halo and Halo2 are new developments in recursive proof composition. In inner-product recursive setting, Halo removes the need of trusted setup with elliptic curve cycles to achieve this. Proving with customized gates and lookup arguments, Halo2's highly performant PLONK-based proving established a new frontier in Zcash. Recursive proofs can check other proofs, making it easy to combine thousands of transactions or complex IP rights into a small proof—a vital problem for high throughput notarization systems (Berrios Moya et al., 2025).

Some folding schemes are alternatives to the traditional SNARKs, including Nova folding and HyperNova folding. They perform incremental verifiable computation with proofs being "folded" together in an iterative fashion. Better sequential performance, coupled with efficient recursion without any excessive pre-processing, makes these a promising choice for verifiable smart contracts and confidential evidence chains.

zk-STARKs keep making progress as both proof size and verification time is reduced. STARK technology is a cornerstone of StarkNet's solution and is instrumental in achieving the platform's promise of scalability, transparency, and resistance to quantum computers. Developers can write typical code which is automatically verified, abstracting away the low-level design of circuits, in their STARK friendly virtual machines (zkVMs) Cairo and RISC Zero. This makes it more accessible and user-friendly for developers of ZKP applications that do not necessarily require extensive cryptographic knowledge, such as those involved in ownership verification, where complex operations depend on simple ZKPs.It makes it more accessible and user-friendly for developers that come with various applications of ZKPs such as IP management, where complex algorithms rely on simple ZKPs, which can be proven without in-depth cryptographic expertise.

There are several other notable variants that are efficient for a range proof (Bulletproofs, extensions of Bulletproofs), efficient arithmetic proofs (zk-SNARKs with transparent setup such as Sonic, Marlin), or post-quantum security (Multi-Party Computation in the Head MPCitH constructions). Succinct Non-interactive Arguments of Knowledge from Lattice assumptions are developing popularity in quantum resistant arguments. Plus, functional commitments and vector commitments add some more flex with statements about large data.

The complex processes in blockchain notarization allow smart contracts with enhanced privacy, ensuring that the details of the contract's execution are kept confidential whilst its results are made public (Li et al., 2026). They help create zk-VMs that are capable of proving the whole computations of programs, so that confidential timestamping of IP asset or contract payments without revealing sensitive content.

There was a progress, but there are still some compromises: Proofs are still costly to generate, horsepower is required, and to accelerate that, it requires dedicated hardware accelerated (GPUs, ASIC, FPGA). The data sizes of proofs differ greatly across protocols, which impacts on-chain costs. The IETF and the Ethereum Foundation have been working on the standardization which is expected to make things more compatible (Bounveur et al., 2025). These sophisticated technologies grow in sophistication, and as they do, work their way toward blurring the boundaries of theoretical privacy and enterprise-class IP and contractual confidential systems.

4. CONFIDENTIAL EVIDENCE HANDLING IN BLOCKCHAIN NOTARIZATION

Confidential Evidence Handling in blockchain notarization is a group of methods that enable the placement of sensitive information on-chain without compromising privacy while ensuring high levels of verifiability. The traditional way to notate blockchain records cryptographic hash of the object publicly, proving that it exists and is unaltered, but also introducing an indirect way to leak out metadata or perform correlation attacks. Modern privacy technologies get the best of both worlds by leveraging data security and computation methods along with Zero-Knowledge Proofs.

The main workflow process starts with off-chain storage of evidence (usually on decentralized platforms, such as IPFS or Arweave, or Filecoin), which involves encryption and storage location based on the blockchain's content hash. It's only a commitment (cryptographic digest) that gets treated in the form of a commitment, it is placed on-chain. The owner is then able to prove specific properties of the evidence, without showing the underlying data: existence at a certain time, authorship, conditions on data subject to a contract, and authenticity, etc. In the case of one owning the patent, it is possible to verify a private design file satisfying a public disclosure date by a zk-SNARK that can confirm a private design file is equal to a publicly known commitment.

Similar to these is homomorphic encryption (HE) and fully homomorphic encryption (FHE) that allows one to compute the evidence without it being decrypted. Smart contracts are permitted to monitor licensing demands or even issue disputes, supplying encrypted outcomes stripped of party accreditation only equipped to decipher them (Nazir et al., 2025). It can be essential in an IP partnership with lots of parties that each party contributes to a project but doesn't reveal trade secrets.

Secure Multi-Party Computation (MPC) allows multiple parties to collaborate and sign or confirm a transaction keeping their contributions confidential. For contractual issues, MPC has the ability to calculate if all obligations have been met but no one party has seen any performance data of others parties. Hardware-backed inclined areas referred to as Trusted Execution Environments (TEEs), like Intel SGX or AWS Nitro Enclaves, produce verifiable attestations anchored to the blockchain that are processed in an enclave without being revealed to anybody else.

Confidential evidence systems are helpful for dispute resolution by facilitating selective disclosure. Parties may intimate particular passages or documents metadatas to an arbitrator and/or a court without disclosing the others. Data sourced from decentralized identity solutions with verifiable credentials (VCs) and ZKPs can be used for privacy-preserving attestations, or proving credentials (e.g., ownership rights, professional qualifications) without revealing the full identity or document.

In the field of intellectual property management, confidential notarization serves to prevent competition from "taking over" or stealing your ideas. Creators can give works private timestamping and uncover them selectively later on enforcement actions. For example, IP licenses can use ZKPs to prove the conditions before payments and access to the code can be unlocked from an escrow in the smart contract.

Key management, long-term availability of off-chain storage, and regulating privacy and auditability while handling the evidence are all challenges in confidential evidence handling. The implementation of a "right to be forgotten" mechanism must be designed for such cases, e.g., by including commitment field chameleons or by permitting editors to withdraw from a permissioned network (Sezer et al., 2025).

Confidential smart contracts are seen in realworld projects such as Aztec Network, Secret Network and Aleo. Hybrid on-chain/off-chain evidence admissibility is a practice being explored via Legal Technology Projects. The integration of AI with these technologies holds promise for future advancements, making confidential notarization a more prevalent way to safeguard sensitive IP assets and establish contractual agreements in an increasingly trustworthy, secure, and efficient manner.

5. APPLICATIONS IN INTELLECTUAL PROPERTY AND CONTRACTUAL SYSTEMS

The known as privacy-preserving technologies, these innovations, especially Zero-Knowledge Proofs (ZKPs) and confidential evidence handling, are revolutionizing the intellectual property (IP) landscape and contractual frameworks by facilitating secure trust without sharing sensitive data. For the copyright protection, creators can use zk-SNARKs to provide proofs of creation dates, authorship, and ownership without disclosing the entire work or content, and anchor cryptographic commitments on a blockchain (Ramya et al., 2025). This is crucial in the digital economy as early release could otherwise result in infringement of a patent or loss of competitive advantage. The strong evidentiary value in Court and the protection the platforms may give against idea theft are assured when a submitted work matches a previously notarized private file during the dispute resolution process.

Homomorphic encryption or ZKPs are used in patent systems to securely and privately record the information of the invention and evidence of its reduction-to-practice. This provides priority dates that will not be publicized until formal filing, thereby minimizing risk of the usual provisional patent filing. There are great advantages for collaborative R&D environments: multiple parties can prove to a joint invention without disclosing proprietary algorithms or data sets, using an MPC and a ZKP. For IP assets (patents or trademarks), for example, a token can include smart contracts that automatically grant licenses and maintain privacy about the asset's usage or monetary weight, allowing its owner to maintain control while avoiding the high costs associated with different licensing deals (Ghanta et al., 2026).

Confidential traceability is used for protection against counterfeiting and trademark registration. Products can be powered with customized product-specific metadata, which will enable authorized verifiers, such as customs or retailers, to verify product authenticity using a ZKP without revealing the details of supply chains. Through zero-knowledge attestation, companies can share information that is sensitive and subject to a company's trade secret rights, effectively establishing evidentiary trails of compliance and/or misappropriation, therefore enforcing their most defensible interests in trade secret misappropriation situations.

The use of such systems increases the efficiency of contractual systems further. ZKPs (sometimes referred to as zk-contracts) are smart contracts that can be used for complex agreements, but are still private because they are placed in a smart contract. In royalty arrangements, for example, if the use of a product falls short of stipulated limits, the licensee can assert that this standard was not met and as a result no or a lesser royalty will be paid, short of giving details of the actual volume of sales. This is greatly minimizing disagreements caused by opacity. As a part of cross-border licensing agreements, confidential evidence handling enables parties to demonstrate the performance of evidence obligations (proof of delivery/quality/limit of use etc.) and complying with the different data protection regulations and frameworks (GDPR etc.).

These tools are perfectly utilized on decentralized dispute resolution platforms. Arbitrators can check confidential claims without having to access raw evidence, that helps accelerate resolutions and reduces costs. Funds are held in an escrow until they are transferred under 0-knowledge completion of the milestones (for IP transactions). When participants enter into contracts with one another for use of IP, compliance with its licensing conditions is demonstrated privately, increasing the level of trust among competitors in the supply chain (Mummidi & Srinivasan, 2025).

They can be applied to new domains like selectively disclosing NFTs, assets in the metaverse, AI generated content ownership. Collective IP rights CDEs can utilize with contribution tracking and privacy preserving voting. In conclusion, the blending of cutting-edge ZKPs and anonymous methods is creating a more accessible landscape for SMEs and individual creators, democratizing the protection of IP rights, decreasing the expense and burden of enforcement, and promoting innovative practices by contributing to a more secure digital environment. Nevertheless, hybrid systems that integrate on-chain proofs with off-chain storage will need to be implemented for successful deployment, along with careful legal integration.

6. CONCLUSION AND FUTURE SCOPE

In summary, the use of techniques for privacy preserving such as Zero-Knowledge Proof and confidential evidence handling are a disruptive and promising step towards utilizing blockchain for sensitive use-cases like intellectual rights and contractual systems. These technologies overcome this inherent dichotomy between transparency and confidentiality that exists with the public ledgers, allowing for verifiable computation and notarization without revealing all data. The cryptographic toolkit has come a long way from fundamental concepts such as zk-SNARKs and zk-STARKs, to high-profile protocols like PLONK, Halo2, and folding schemes, which have provided a wealth of practical applications related to secure timestamping, proof of ownership, automated royalty tracking, and private resolution of disputes.

From the applications discussed above, creators see improved and robust IP rights and privacy capabilities, brands love low-friction licensing and collaboration capabilities, and legal systems obtain more reliable, tamper-proof evidence capabilities that are still confidential. These innovations mitigate the need for trusted intermediaries and minimize transaction and litigation expenses while also improving access to global markets, in response to the regulatory requirements concerning data protection.

However, there are a few issues to address. This overhead of proving is still cumbersome, hence not widely adopted for resource poor users. There should be standardization of interoperability between various ZKP systems and blockchains. The acceptance of zero-knowledge attestations in judicial proceedings varies by jurisdiction and extends the need for dialogue among technologists and policymakers. Zero-knowledge attestations are not universally accepted as admissible evidence, adding to on-going dialogue between technologists and policymakers. Practical considerations such as resistance to emerging quantum dangers, long-term data availability and key management are also important and need sustained monitoring.

These technologies have future potential of great promise. By integrating AI technologies, complex contracts could be automatically generated and audited, providing efficient and accurate ZKPs.The integration of AI technologies could enable automation in generating and auditing ZKPs for complex contracts, resulting in efficient and accurate ZKPs. Specialized ZKP accelerators, emerging hardware, and TEEs will further help to reduce the costs and enhance performance. Post-quantum ZKPs variants will make them more secure for the long haul. At the patent office, collective rights management organizations and courts, we expect to see privacy-preserving blockchain registries covering all use cases.

The mix of public verification with prioritizing selective privacy will predominate enterprise solutions. Future advancements in Verifiable Credentials, SBT and De-Fi will further strengthen these confidential IP ecosystems. Stimulating institutional acceptance could be achieved by the regulatory sandboxes and international standards (potentially WIPO or ISO).

With the advancement of blockchain towards Web3 and decentralized knowledge economies, privacy-preserving notarization will no longer be a luxury but will become essential infrastructure. Further interdisciplinary studies, including from the industry community, cryptographers and in the legal arena, are vital. In the end, harnessing these skills will empower individuals to fully capitalize on blockchain's potential as a secure, private, and efficient digital innovation, commerce, and creative expression platform. These powerful tools hold the promise of revolutionizing next-generation secure digital contracts and even IP regimes thanks to their cryptographic strength combined with ease of use.

REFERENCES

Albalwy, F. (2026). Zero-Knowledge-Based Policy Enforcement for Privacy-Preserving Cross-Institutional Health Data Sharing on Blockchain. *Systems*, *14*(4), 385. DOI: 10.3390/systems14040385

Berrios Moya, J. A., Ayoade, J., & Uddin, M. A. (2025). A zero-knowledge proof-enabled blockchain-based academic record verification system. *Sensors (Basel)*, *25*(11), 3450. DOI: 10.3390/s25113450 PMID: 40968974

Ghanta, S., Pradhan, A. K., Boyapati, P., Biswas, S., & Mohanty, S. P. (2026). Security and Verifiability in Federated Learning: A Zero-Knowledge Reputation-Based Blockchain Framework. *IEEE Transactions on Network Science and Engineering*, *13*, 8005–8022. DOI: 10.1109/TNSE.2026.3676154

Khalid, L., Akhtar, M. U., Khalid, M., & Ahmed, I. (2026). Zero Knowledge Proofs Enabling Ethical AI and Privacy-Preserving Verification in Distributed Systems. In *Ethical AI Applications for Software Engineering and Development* (pp. 123–154). IGI Global Scientific Publishing. DOI: 10.4018/979-8-3373-6038-6.ch005

Krishappa, N., Shivappa, G. G., Zachariah, S., Pattan, K. I., Paria, A., Hiremath, S., & Vaithiyanathan, R. (2025). A Blockchain-Based Framework With Zero-Knowledge Proof Incorporated for Safeguarded Sharing of Genomic Data Through Health Record Systems. *Blockchain in Healthcare Today*, *8*, 10–30953. PMID: 41623334

Li, H., Oza, D., Yoshida, M., & Noguchi, T. (2026). Privacy-Preserving Emergency Vehicle Authentication Scheme Using Zero-Knowledge Proofs and Blockchain. *IoT*, *7*(2), 35. DOI: 10.3390/iot7020035

Maheshwari, V., & Prasanna, M. (2025). Privacy-preserving authentication for 5G healthcare with HBZKP: Hierarchical blockchain-based zero knowledge proof for secure edge devices. *Ain Shams Engineering Journal*, *16*(8), 103463. DOI: 10.1016/j.asej.2025.103463

Majdoub, I., & Atmani, K. (2025). Privacy paradigm shift: Zero knowledge proofs in criminal e-evidence collection. In *Cybercrime Unveiled: Technologies for Analysing Legal Complexity* (pp. 151–175). Springer Nature Switzerland. DOI: 10.1007/978-3-031-80557-8_7

Mbimbi, B., Murray, D., & Wilson, M. (2025). Preserving whistleblower anonymity through zero-knowledge proofs and private blockchain: A secure digital evidence management framework. *Blockchains*, *3*(2), 7. DOI: 10.3390/blockchains3020007

Mummidi, S. S., & Srinivasan, S. (2025, November). Enhancement of Cybersecurity with Blockchain-Based Identity Authentication Systems: Zero-information Evidence Procedures for Secure Access, Biometric Encryption, and Decentralized Trust. In *2025 IEEE 7th International Conference on Computing, Communication and Automation (ICCCA)* (pp. 1-6). IEEE.

Myeong, G. E., & Ram, K. S. (2025). Blockchain based zero knowledge proof protocol for privacy preserving healthcare data sharing. *Journal of Technology Informatics and Engineering*, *4*(1), 171–189. DOI: 10.51903/jtie.v4i1.296

Nazir, M. A., Hussain, N., Hamid, K., Rasheed, M. D., Akhter, M., Ibrar, M., ... & Zafar, F. (2025). The Silent Guard: ML-Based Zero-Knowledge Proofs in Blockchain Security. *Spectrum of Engineering Sciences*, 1659-1678.

Ramya, M., Anuvarshini, B. S., Kanika, G., Lohith, A., & Barath, B. (2025, September). Enhancing Decentralized Identity Management with Zero-Knowledge Proofs for Selective Disclosure. In *2025 6th International Conference on Electronics and Sustainable Communication Systems (ICESC)* (pp. 727-732). IEEE. DOI: 10.1109/ICESC65114.2025.11212333

Sezer, B. B., Akleylek, S., & Nuriyev, U. (2025). Pp-pqb: Privacy-preserving in post-quantum blockchain-based systems: A systematization of knowledge. *IEEE Access : Practical Innovations, Open Solutions.*

Chapter 11
Harnessing Blockchain for Legal Evidence Preservation:
A Cyber Law Perspective

Vedullapalli Leelakrishna Sai Prasad
http://orcid.org/0009-0001-8159-0131
Amity University, Gwalior, India

Vijay Srivastava
http://orcid.org/0000-0002-3034-9903
Amity University, Gwalior, India

Priyansh Samadhiya
Amity University, Gwalior, India

ABSTRACT

The use of blockchain in legal evidence preservation is a paradigm shift in the domain of cyber law, and it is a solution to a long-standing vulnerability in the field of digital forensics that includes tampering, chain of custody breaches, and admissibility challenges. The essence attributes of blockchain such as the impossibility of being tampered with due to the cryptographic hashing, the decentralization of record keeping to allow transparent audit trails, and the time stamping allow recording evidence handling, including its collection, and its presentation in the courtroom in an impeccable manner. This chapter examines the transformative effect of blockchain as an enhancement of the reliability of evidence, the reduction of risks of manipulation, and the establishment of trust in the judicial system, offers models of hybridization and policy changes that can lead such practices to be smoothly integrated into legal systems across the globe.

DOI: 10.4018/979-8-3373-9730-6.ch011

1. INTRODUCTION AND BACKGROUND

The physical objects and documents used in legal cases are progressively giving way to the electronic ones, including emails, social networking platforms, metadata, IoT devices and sensors, video surveillance, and even blockchain transactions. This revolution, which is hastened by the spread of cybercrimes, including hacking, data attacks, online fraud, deepfake manipulations and cryptocurrency offenses, has left the maintenance and verification of digital evidence with demands it never had. The conventional evidence management strategies, which are based on centralized data repositories, handwritten records, and chain of custody, are prone to human error, insider interference, unauthorized modifications, and breakages of the chain of custody. Any unnoticed alteration will make the evidence inadmissible and affect the justice and confidence of people in the court procedures. This improves integrity, non-repudiation and traceability especially where volatile digital artifacts are used in cybercrimes involving IoT, deepfakes, and multimedia (Ratul et al., 2024).

Chain of custody (CoC) is still the most basic element of evidentiary reliability in both common law and civil law jurisdictions. It records the evidence confiscation, transportation, examination, and storage to demonstrate that it is not changed or corrupted. The digital forensics pose a greater challenge of having a continuous CoC because data is easily copied, edited, or deleted without necessarily leaving any trace. The forensic standards like the ones provided by NIST (National Institute of Standards and Technology) require a high level of documentation of who accessed evidence, when, why, and how to render them intact and authentic to be accepted in court. However, the traditional method is not always effective in decentralized high-volume digital settings where evidence can be distributed such as cloud servers, mobile devices, or blockchain networks.

1.1 Core Features of Blockchain Technology: Immutability, Decentralization, Transparency and Cryptographic Hashing

The concept of blockchain technology popularized by Bitcoin in 2008 is a radical solution since it is a distributed, append-only registry with cryptography and consensus. A cryptographic hash of the previous block, transaction data (or metadata) and a timestamp are stored in each block creating an unchangeable chain, which is hard to modify without a consensus across the network. This irreversibility provides tamper-evidence: any modification to a record would render later hashes invalid, warning participants. Decentralization removes any points of failures and transparency enables audits that could be verified by the authorized parties. Smart contracts may automatic code, registry custody incidences, imposed access controls, and raise warning of anomalies.

Since the middle of the 2010s, the use of blockchain in preservation of evidence has become popular in digital forensics and cyber law. Initial ideas centered on blockchain as a distributed registry of CoCs, in which hashes of digital evidence (or the evidence in small scale) are written to-chain, and full files are written off-chain through systems such as IPFS (InterPlanetary File System). This type of hybrid approach guarantees provenance: a special hash is used to connect the preserved file to some immutable timestamped record, which guarantees the existence and integrity of the preserved file at a certain point in time (Ghasemi & Mahmoudi, 2024). Frameworks such as Forensic-Chain, BEvPF-IoT to IoT devices and LO-CARD (an EU-funded project) are practical examples and shown to be auditability, non-repudiable and resistant to tampering.

1.2 The Growing Role of Digital Evidence in Cyber Law and Modern Litigation

Cyber law wise, blockchain comes in with major admissibility challenges. Cryptographic proofs can make blockchain records self-authenticating, and thus meet a standard of reliability of a testifier under the Daubert standard, in the United States under Federal Rules of Evidence. The NIST guidelines are becoming more aware of blockchain in CoC documentation, which is in line with traceability and integrity needs. Jurisdictions such as China have been the first globally to accept judicial acceptance, with courts admitting blockchain-preserved evidence as early as 2018 in copyright cases through platforms.This change is intended to make admissibility straight forward, but introduces a certification dilemma of a decentralized, distributed blockchain evidence: who is the person in charge in a permissionless system? There are proposals to consider cryptographic consensus in blockchain to be inherent certification or permissioned chains where certificates are issued by an authority. Recent discussions underscore BSA silence regarding blockchain-specific provisions and call on amendments to be made to include decentralized authentication and to be in line with IT Act validations.

Regardless of these opportunities, issues are numerous. Immutability does not comply with privacy, including the right to be forgotten in GDPR or similar principles since one is not allowed to erase the data without forking the chain. High transaction costs and slow processing of public blockchains such as Ethereum are limits to scaling, but it can be mitigated by permissioned blockchains (e.g., Hyperledger) or layer-2 solutions (Sakshi & Sharma, 2024). There are still input vulnerabilities: garbage-in-garbage-out is true when bad evidence is hashed before handing over garbage. Technical risks are difficult to occur in well-established networks bugs in smart contracts, and the issue of jurisdiction in cross-border scenarios. The obstacles to adoption are institutional resistance, deficiency in the forensic expertise to verify the blockchain, and possible excessive dependence on technology without human supervision.

1.3 Objectives and Scope of Harnessing Blockchain in This Domain

Recent events indicate increased impetus as judicial evidence platforms, AI incorporation in deepfake-detection, and legislation studies in several jurisdictions illustrate how blockchain can help in combating the new threats such as AI-generated manipulations. Blockchain creates a sense of reliability in evidence ecosystems, facilitating their safe exchange between law enforcement, prosecutors, and courts and maintaining audit trails in case of an appeal or cold case, which would be discussed in a legal case regarding cyber law.

This discussion does not place blockchain as a panacea but as a basic tool that can be used to strengthen legal evidence preservation. It will bring more robust, transparent and just justice systems in an ever more digitized world by bringing together technology immutability and the cyber law requirements of authenticity, reliability, and procedural fairness. The future involves interdisciplinary cooperation between technologists, law scholars, policy makers, and forensic experts to establish standardized protocols, hybrid architectures and specific reforms that will resolve certification tensions and privacy paradoxes and eventually achieve the full potential of blockchain in assuring truth in the digital era.

2. CHAIN OF CUSTODY CONCEPT IN CYBER LAW

Chain of custody (CoC) is the pillars of cyber law and digital forensics because it is the written and chronological record of evidence handling that traces the evidence since its discovery and capture through analysis, storage, and transfer, and finally in court. The CoC is relevant in the domain of cyber law, where electronic evidence is the norm in the investigation of hacking, data breach, cyber fraud, deepfakes, and cryptocurrency crime, to guarantee that the data stored in the logs, metadata, device photographs, or blockchain transactions has not been altered or modified (Rani et al., 2025). The CoC helps to avert substitution, tampering, contamination, or misidentification by specifying who handled the evidence, the date/time of the transfers and what happened by documenting this information in a process documenting every individual who touched the evidence.

This traceability becomes essential in cyber investigations as digital evidence is volatile and vulnerable by nature; it can be easily changed or damaged by a third party with no trace left. Cyber law systems all over the world focus on CoC in order to maintain evidentiary reliability, non-repudiation, and accountability. In India, the CoC is aligned with the requirements of electronic evidence admissibility, under the Bharatiya Sakshya Adhiniyam, 2023 (BSA), as additional requirements to demonstrate provenance and avoid manipulation to the certification requirements. It advocates such standards as those in the UNODC and ISO/IEC 27037 that include the identification, collection, acquisition, and preservation phases. Strong CoC cultivates judicial trust when it proves that evidence has not been contaminated throughout its lifecycle, and thus reducing the risks in the decentralized digital environment (Malik & Sharma, 2023).

The absence of it can lead to the exclusion or the weighting down of evidence by courts, which can lead to the derailment of prosecutions based on cybercrimes where evidence depends upon digital evidence. Due to the ever-changing cyber threats, continuous CoC is necessary to balance the technological instability with the law of fairness and due process, as well as keeping justice on the verifiable, tamper-evident grounds, and not necessarily on the assumptions of integrity. The chain of custody is an important legal term that defines and provides the integrity of evidence in legal cases by establishing its physical location throughout the legal proceedings and merits of the case.

2.1 Legal Definition and Importance of Chain of Custody for Evidence Integrity

In law, the chain of custody is the orderly, documented procedure that will track down the seizure, custody, control, transfer, examination and disposition of evidence to confirm its authenticity and integrity during the lifecycle. In cyber law, it has been defined by NIST as the record of evidence movement through recording of handlers, dates/times, and transfer purposes and described by such authorities as the U.S. Department of Justice as the record of checking evidence movement to ensure it has not been tampered with, replaced, or falsified. Such definition can be applied to the digital forensics, where CoC includes electronic trails of volatile data such as network logs or IoT outputs (Sanjalawe et al., 2024).

The most significant aspect about it is its role in preserving the integrity of evidence- the guarantee that the item presented is the one that was taken at the location. Evidentiary value is based upon integrity where any breach causes an implication of uncertainty whether it is genuine or not, which may make evidence inadmissible or less dependable. Cyber law CoC offers non-repudiation and accountability through manipulation being easy (e.g. modifying metadata or adding fake logs) in contexts such as cyber law, a record of who, when, and why someone has accessed something is documented. Such transparency discourages insider threats, unintentional changes or malicious interventions, which are paramount in prosecuting cyber crimes of great importance (Sathe et al., 2024). Courts also use CoC to prove relevancy, reliability, and procedural fairness, without which the triers of fact cannot be able to authoritatively make attribution of findings to the crime scene.

2.2 Traditional Vulnerabilities in Physical and Digital Evidence Handling

Conventional evidence management, both in the physical and digital form, is plagued with insecurities that compromise the chain of custody and integrity (Dhabliya et al., 2024). Among the physical evidence dangers are the insufficient packaging resulting in contamination or tampering at the crime scenes, loss during the transfer because of improper labeling, human factor in the manual logging, insider access to the physical evidence without supervision, and environmental degradation (e.g., degradation in unsecured storage). Manual procedures are also dependent on paper trails, signatures and witness accounts which are prone to forgery, gap that needs to be filled with unreliable memories as well as labor which is resource intensive and encourages inconsistencies.

Digital vulnerabilities increase because data is intangible: it can be copied, edited, or deleted easily and without evidence; it can be changed by accident during the imaging or analysis process; its storage is centralized, leaving it vulnerable to a single point of failure; therefore, there is no redundancy and the evidence can be corrupted or lost. Some of the most common traps include incomplete documentation, unauthorized access on unsecured systems, failure to use write-blockers during acquisition, the presence of hash-mismatches as a result of unlogged changes and excessive dependency on manual reporting that can be forged or omitted. Among the risks mentioned by NIST are evidence pre-hashing, hash-overwriting, and weak algorithms (e.g. MD5 collisions). These problems are exacerbated in cyber law by sources which, such as cloud information or temporary communications, can be volatile, with overwrites automatic due to delay in acquisition. Traditional techniques are not inherently immutable, transparent, and automatically verifiable, and may rely on human care, which breaks down under the workload stresses or malice. Physical-digital hybrids are vulnerable to attack by either being physically snatched and mismanaged, or by being digitally attacked without the ability to notice until a forensic package is installed (Igonor et al., 2025). These weaknesses often lead to broken chains, and the exclusion at the court, as in the cases where the gaps present challenges to defense.

2.3 Requirements for Evidence Admissibility in Courts

The admissibility of evidence in courts must pass test of relevance, authenticity, reliability and proper foundation and certain provisions regarding electronic evidence under cyber law. To establish that there was no tampering, the courts require continuous chain of custody records (seizure memos, imaging with hashes, transfer logs, seals). The case laws of the Supreme Court such as Arjun Panditrao Khotkar underscore guaranteed certification as a result of reliability. Incorporating U.S. Federal Rules of Evidence around the world, authentication is required through testimony or self-proving techniques and a rule 702 and Daubert standard that expert testimony must be reliable, tested, peer-reviewed and known error rates and generally accepted. NIST guidelines emphasize on hashing, secure storage and CoC to integrity. The admissibility depends on the relevance (relevant to the facts), exception of hearsay, as well as laying foundation (establishing the source and managing it). In the case of digital evidence, the courts examine the protocols of collection (write-blockers, forensically sound images), preservation (offline storage), and transparency in the analysis (Zou & Chen, 2024). Violation of CoC or certification is likely to result in disqualification or demarcation. Newer issues such as deepfakes require further investigation, but when such requirements are followed, such as proofs of integrity, expert authentication, and provenance, it is reasonable to admit such evidence, and the balance between technological innovation and procedural security to ensure a fair trial.

3. HOW BLOCKCHAIN ENHANCES EVIDENCE PRESERVATION MECHANISMS

The central aspect of blockchain technology is that it is changing the concept of preservation of evidence in cyber law by providing mechanisms that defeat the barriers of the conventional centralized systems. The distributed ledger architecture of its architecture makes sure that evidence handling records are stored impartially, transparent, and are verifiable by various parties without necessarily using a trusted party. Blockchain in digital forensics ensures an audible trail of logs, photos, videos, or IoT data, used in evidence, between the collection and the courtroom due to the possibility of loss or modification of this evidence. It offers provenance and integrity at the integrity of evidence files (hashed), as well as metadata (e.g. timestamps, handler identities, actions) recorded on-chain, which indicates tamper-evident integrity.

The recent models such as blockchain-based BEvPF-IoT that implements multimedia in IoTs and Custody-Chain-Guardian indicate that blockchain can be used to create a chain of custody that can never be broken with the help of decentralized consensus and cryptographic connectivity. This improves non-repudiation because the participants cannot refute activities recorded in the ledger (AlKhanafseh & Surakhi, 2024). However, in the context of cyber law, e.g. investigations under the Bharatiya Sakshya Adhiniyam, 2023, of India, blockchain is compatible with admissibility rules, providing verifiable authenticity through hashes and timestamps and potentially lowering the costs of certification. Decentralization helps to reduce the risks of insider manipulation or institutional failures, and transparency allows working with multi-agency (e.g. police, prosecutors, courts) controlled access. Smart contracts are compliance checks which are automated therefore less prone to human error. On the whole, blockchain transforms preservation into cryptographically proven models where trust does not play a crucial role and provides the judicial system with more confidence in digital evidence despite the increasing rate of cybercrimes such as deepfakes and information breaches.

3.1 Immutable Ledger for Tamper-Proof Records and Timestamping

The immutable ledger of blockchain is the key to the preservation of tamper-proof evidence, which creates an append-only document and it is impossible to change or delete the data in this case without network-wide consensus. The blocks are connected in a chain by cryptographic hash to the one before, and if a block is altered, the following blocks will be invalid and this will result in their detection. In digital forensics, this guarantees the non-corruption of evidence records time stamps of collection, access logs or transfer details, which gives an unquestionable integrity. Blockchain is time-stamped (usually by a trusted oracle or network consensus), so that it is impossible to backdate or fake a moment an action is taken.

In the case of cyber law implementation, this is used to overcome difficulties on admissibility by providing demonstrable existence and unchangeability at a certain point, which is essential to volatile digital evidence. This is used in frameworks such as those in IEEE studies and judicial preservation schemes, where evidence files are used to produce unique fingerprints on-chain in hashing, and the entire data is stored off-chain (e.g. in IPFS), connected in some way. Any attempt to tamper with it ends up failing since any changes made will be detected as hash mismatches immediately. Where there is evidence of multimedia or of IoT, immutability can neutralize the threat of manipulation and improve court admissibility according to such criterion as BSA Section 63 in India or NIST guidelines. In its favor are non-repudiation: actors can never refute any actions logged; and auditability to make appeals or reviews.

3.2 Decentralized Storage and Distributed Verification to Prevent Single-Point Failures

evidence-related data or metadata Decentralized storage in blockchain spreads the data or metadata of evidence-related data to a network of nodes, removing single points of failure that existed in centralized databases (Atlam et al., 2024). Blockchain will ensure availability unlike in traditional systems where servers can crash or be hacked or compromised by insiders, blockchain facilitates record replication through consensus mechanisms (Proof-of-Work or Proof-of-Stake) and makes the records available even when nodes go down. Multiple independent parties can participate in the process of distributed verification and increase resilience and trust without a central authority.

In evidence preservation, such as hashes, timestamps, and custody logs are stored and cross-checked redundantly, which does not allow any loss or unauthorized alteration. The forensics models emphasize the role of decentralization in mitigating risks in multi-agency sharing of information, police, labs, courts access the same immutable trail, and no middlemen. This aids in preserving cross-border or collaborative investigation safely and tamper-resistant in cyber law, such as global standards such as UNODC guidelines. IPFS integration (off-chain solutions) distribute large files, and on-chain pointers are used to make sure that files are linked together and their integrity is verified. This resists individual threats: no single party can have power of the system, making corruption or destruction difficult. The decentralization is useful in IoT forensics or cloud-sourced evidence where the centralized clouds are prone to breaches. Permissioned blockchains are also controlled and have the advantages of distribution, which are best suited to courts.

3.3 Cryptographic Techniques as Hashing, Digital Signatures for Integrity Assurance

Hashing and the application of digital signatures serve as the foundation of assurance of integrity in evidence preservation using blockchain. The technique of hashing (e.g. SHA-256) transforms evidence into a fixed-size unique digest; any modification results in a totally different hash thus allowing detection of tampering instantly (Vaghela et al., 2024). Forensics Data in forensics, evidence files are hashed when they are collected, the hashes are recorded on-chain to verify the file or file on-chain to prove the file has not been changed. Action-at-identity:

identities are bound with asymmetric cryptography (e.g. ECDSA), where a private key is used to sign records, and these can be verified by any public key in order to obtain authenticity and non-repudiation. Signing custody events by handlers is not forged or denied. These combine to form powerful evidences: hashing to integrity of content, signatures to origin and authorization. This is used in cyber law, where admissibility is granted by self-authenticating evidence such as U.S. FRE 901 or India certification of BSA, where hashes are used as digital fingerprints. Frameworks Merkle trees are used to verify batches efficiently and blockchain linking is used to verify chain-wide integrity. In the context of deepfake or manipulated media, hashing identifies the differences at the granular levels. These are highlighted in CoC documentation approaches that are NIST-aligned.

3.4 Smart Contracts for Automated Chain of Custody Logging and Access Control

Self-executing blockchain code known as smart contracts automate chain of custody logging and access control and reduce human error and intervention. They represent regulations of evidence processing: when uploaded or transferred, contracts automatically record timestamps, identities of the handler (through signatures), and actions on the immutable ledger. Events are caused by conditions, such as raising an alarm when somebody gains unauthorized access or performing steps in sequential custody. Role-based logic is applied to access control: privileges are taken away and given back dynamically, only authorized addresses (e.g., investigators, experts) are allowed to execute functions. In a forensic system, it generates audit-friendly automated trails: evidence hash collection logs, analysis status updates, transfers need approvals (Verma et al., 2023). The judicial schemes use contracts to register cases, upload/download evidence, share, and energy through review of the law. With cyber law, automation would guarantee compliance with admissibility (e.g. BSA certification proxies through logs) and minimize challenge of handling. Implementations based on Ethereum or the Hyperledger are used to enforce complicated processes, such as conditional disclosure or partial redaction. Advantages are efficiency, lower costs and error-free enforcement- contracts are deterministic. In the case of multi-agencies, the intermediaries are avoided by means of contracts. Audits are necessitated by issues such as code bugs, yet formal verification suppresses the risks. In general, smart contracts bring CoC to the next level and make it programmable and tamper-proof, increasing its transparency, accountability, and judicial efficiency in the maintenance of digital proofs.

4. BLOCKCHAIN APPLICATIONS IN DIGITAL FORENSICS AND EVIDENCE MANAGEMENT

The blockchain technology has become an influential instrument in digital forensics and evidence management providing a response to the most critical gaps in the existing systems by offering immutable, transparent, and decentralized ways of manipulating digital artifacts. Blockchain assures provenance, integrity, and traceability in digital evidence in cyber investigations of volatile datatypes such as IoT devices, cloud environments, mobile forensics and multimedia evidence, between acquisition and presentation in court. The current literature reviews up to the year 2025 emphasize the increased use of blockchain as a solution to prevent evidence tampering, lack of transparency, and admissibility in the sphere of cyber law. Core applications are concerned with creating chains of custody (CoC), the hash of evidence files, timestamps, identity of the handler, and events of transfers are registered on distributed ledgers, and retroactive changes are not permitted (Salih & Ibrahim, 2023). The Hyperledger Fabric, an example of permissioned blockchains, should allow secure recordkeeping with cryptographic signatures and automated logging with smart contracts, such as crime scene evidence management prototypes that digitize CoC operations and improve their trustworthiness and transparency.

Specialized frameworks represent real-world applications: BEvPF-IoT, a multimedia evidence preservation system based on blockchain that supports IoT devices, preserve digital artifacts through the immutability and off-chain storage (e.g., IPFS) through on-chain metadata connections, resistant to single-point failure and tampering in smart city or IIoT contexts. Likewise, Forensic-Chain as well as LOCARD (an EU-funded project) apply blockchain to record evidence metadata, allowing auditability and non-repudiation of multi-party investigations. In a decentralized structure, ZAKON is more propositional to the admissibility of the courtroom with the automation of validation of smart contracts, with privacy-preserving query resolution and multi-dimensional checks, other than CoC. Other systems represent evidence as tokens through schemes such as Ethereum ERC-721 of unique tracking, making verification times many times lower (e.g. 12 to 2 seconds in some prototypes) and allowing a secure sharing of documents between law enforcement, forensic laboratories, and the judiciary.

Blockchain has a solid reputation in the field of cybercrime, particularly by protecting evidence of ephemeral sources, such as deepfakes, network logs, cryptocurrency transactions, or AI-generated manipulations, by timestamping and hashing on intake, making it lifelong auditable. It is further enhanced by integration with deep learning to detect integrity or steganography to preserve it covertly, which is outlined as supporting the usage in heterogeneous environments. Permissioned networks provide a balance of transparency and confidentiality and public chains have a higher level of immutability when dealing with high-stakes cases. Non-repudiation (it is hard to deny actions), automated audit trails to appeal, and insider resistance to insiders, or institutional breakdown are all benefits.

Such developments notwithstanding, even with these developments, there exist gaps such as malware forensics, blockchain-specific forensics (on-chain data analysis), and the initial stages such as identification and examination, the role of blockchain is under-scope. This is hampered by scalability, computational overhead, compatibility with legacy forensic tools and complexities in jurisdiction, but progress with hybrid frameworks and standard protocols is being achieved. On the whole, the application of blockchains will turn the digital forensics process into a proactive and cryptographically secured system and increase the reliability of the evidence in cyber law and help administer justice fairly in the face of increasing digital threats.

5. LEGAL AND EVIDENTIARY IMPLICATIONS FROM A CYBER LAW VIEWPOINT

Cyber law Cyber law The implementation of blockchain in evidence preservation has significant legal and evidentiary effects that redefine admissibility, authenticity, and procedural standards and introduce new challenges. Blockchain records: hashes, timestamps, smart contract logs, custody events are self-authenticating schemes with cryptographic proofs, and would help reduce the work required in courts of frameworks that focus on integrity and reliability. Federal Rules of Evidence (Rule 901) in the United States permit authentication using digital signatures or hash, which is consistent with Daubert standards of scientific validity, and NIST standardisation recommends the use of blockchain to document CoCs. International Jurisdictions such as China have accepted evidence preserved using blockchains as early as 2018 in copyright and contract cases as credible because of immutability. New systems, such as ZAKON, are based on courtroom admissibility rather than the conventional CoC, with smart contracts that are automatically-validated and privacy-guaranteed after-trial queries.

The Bharatiya Sakshya Adhiniyam, 2023 (BSA) in India raises electronic records to first-level evidence under Section 63 where it is stated that the record is certified (Section 63(4)) and signed by a responsible person and expert stating the identity of that record, how it was produced, how it functions, and whether it is intact (Batisha et al., 2023). This is improved by blockchain which offers intrinsic proofs (e.g. hash chains as digital fingerprints) although this generates a certification conundrum, since in decentralized or permissionless systems, there is a conflict of interest between identifying a single person in charge and distributed consensus. Permissioned blockchains alleviate this by assigning powers to certify, whereas proposals support admitting cryptographic validation as synonymous. The theory of mandatory certification to prevent the unreliability of the hearsay is supported by the previous case law of the Supreme Court (e.g., Arjun Panditrao Khotkar), but the absence of blockchain-specific regulations in BSA raises the demand to revise the law to align with IT Act verifications.

The main implications are enhanced non-repudiation and auditability, minimization of risks of manipulation of cybercrimes that engage deepfakes or volatile data. Nonetheless, obstacles still exist: immutability contradicts the rights such as the right to be forgotten of GDPR or other similar rules, as it must be erased with chain forking. Scalability restricts the feasibility of public chains to volume evidence, but permissioned ones solve this. Input vulnerabilities (garbage-in-garbage-out) imply that bad initial data compromises the benefits, whereas cross-border cases have technical risks (e.g., smart contract bugs, 51% attacks) and the problem of jurisdictional fragmentation. The challenges to admissibility include demonstrating the reliability of consensus mechanisms, demonstrating that blockchain forensics is the testimony of an expert, and the hearsay or authentication objection in a conservative court.

Current 2025- 2026 overviews also note the application of blockchain in counteracting the dangers of the AI era (e.g. deepfakes) through provenance trails, but note the necessity of standard legal acceptance and validation procedures (Singh & Kaunert, 2024). In cyber law, blockchain leads to the development of trust, as it provides the ability to share data across multiple agencies and offer verifiable integrity, but requires interdisciplinary changes, such as changes to the law to provide decentralized certification and privacy-protecting methods (e.g. zero-knowledge proofs) and judicial education. Finally, blockchain has a tremendous potential to achieve systemic evidentiary trust, but to fully achieve immediacy, certification tensions, privacy paradoxes, and barriers to adoption must be resolved to clarify how technological immutability might be reconciled with the tenets of fairness, due process, and justice during the digital proceedings process.

6. SCALABILITY, PERFORMANCE AND COST BARRIERS IN LARGE-SCALE ADOPTION

Aggressive implementation of blockchain as a digital preservation of legal evidence in digital forensics has considerable obstacles in terms of scalability, performance, and costs that prevent its transition to prototyping to a broader implementation in judicial and law enforcement functions (Verma, 2024). Scalability will also be a priority since blockchain networks should be able to process exponentially increasing amounts of digital evidence - IoT sensors and mobile devices, cloud logs, multimedia files and artifacts of cybercrime, but retain low latency to support real-time logging and retrieval. Public blockchains such as Ethereum have a low throughput (typically 15-30 TPS historically, though better with upgrades), which contributes to congestion, slowness in ingesting evidence during incidents with a large volume of evidence, and storage of terabytes of forensic data. In forensic use cases where evidence needs to be hashed, timed and recorded, hashing speeds are important to maintain chain of custody, and therefore in volatile settings, evidence may be destroyed during hashing or lost in volatile media.

A private or permissioned blockchain is more scalable due to a controlled consensus mechanism, such as Raft or PBFT, reaching thousands of TPS with optimized configurations, but even here a large evidence set still causes storage bloat over time as all nodes store data. The work on structures such as ZAKON has demonstrated up to 8320 TPS of throughput on 1.85-second latency with linear complexity, 70 times higher than previous systems, but only with structured large files such as videos and disk pictures.

The issue of degraded performance worsens the scalability issues: a high computational cost of consensus, cryptographic functions (hashing, signatures) and network synchronization have an adverse effect on real-time forensic processes. The shared mining model used with private chains will allocate nonce ranges to miners to produce blocks faster, but some of the models implement energy-intensive Proof-of-Work variants, which manifests environmental and operational costs. Latency in retrieval varies, blockchain is good at append only writes but can be inconsistent when it comes to queries of large chains and off-chain solutions such as IPFS help to ease the storage burden but add dependency and single point failure risk if not fully integrated. In court settings, where access to evidence is required to be fast to either carry out trials or to appeal the verdict, such delays are counterproductive to the efficiency. The cost barriers are also prohibitive: it is operational costs, electricity to run the consensus, and transaction fees (gas in public networks) and distributed networks maintenance. Small agencies or developing jurisdictions are expensive to set up (between $50,000 and millions to install enterprise-quality systems), need constant fees to store data on the blockchain, and have resource needs that are already bone-throbbing to many budgets due to the traditional forensic tools (Patil et al., 2024). The validation is expensive to compute and the economic model of the public chains discourages adoption, especially when ROI is not clear-cut in the circumstances of regulatory challenges.

Mitigation solutions concentrate on hybrid designs: moving the entire evidence off-chain (IPFS, distributed file systems) but anchoring metadata, hashes and logs on-chain minimises on-chain bloat and expenses. Rollups and sidechains (layer-2 solutions) enhance throughput in a non-security-degrading manner. Efficient consensus in permissioned blockchains (e.g. zero-knowledge proofs to preserve privacy) trades-off performance and control. Open-source facilitates easier entry into the collaborative structures, whereas standardization (protocols based on NIST) ensures interoperability. There has been a focus on consensus that is energy efficient (Proof-of-Stake) and resource allocation optimized by AI to reduce costs. Regardless of these, full-scale implementation needs to respond to integration with the legacy systems, training forensic personnel, and policy support of the subsidized infrastructure in the public sectors. By addressing these barriers with specific innovations, blockchain can scale reliably in order to become trusted in management of evidence in cyber law ecosystems (Onyeashie et al., 2023).

7. CONCLUSION AND FUTURE DIRECTIONS: TRANSFORMATIVE POTENTIAL OF BLOCKCHAIN FOR TRUSTWORTHY LEGAL EVIDENCE SYSTEMS

Blockchain has a disruptive potential to transform the system of trustful legal evidence and to introduce in digital forensics and cyber law practice the element of immutability, transparency, and cryptographic assurance. Being able to build tamper-evident chains of custody, automate logging with smart contracts, and permit distributed verification solve fundamental weaknesses in the traditional evidence management: risk of tampering and broken provenance, and admissibility debate, in the face of soaring cybercrimes, deepfakes, and AI manipulations. In some jurisdictions such as under the Bharatiya Sakshya Adhiniyam, 2023, hash based proofs and timestamping of blockchain provides a way to meet the certification requirement, which may solve the issue of decentralized certification with a permissioned model or accepted consensus as implicit validation. International agreements with NIST recommendations, Federal Rules of Evidence, and new judicial precedents (such as blockchain evidence acceptance) show that blockchain can improve the electronic records to primary and self-authenticating status, minimizing the use of fallible human testimony and manual records.

This technology is a guarantee of fair and resilient justice systems: non-repudiation of insider threats, audit trails contribute to the appeal and cold-case, and secure multi-agency sharing can speed up the investigation without compromising the integrity. Immutability-privacy conflicts can be addressed through hybrid means (such as IPFS integration) and anomaly-detecting AI and privacy control (zero-knowledge proofs) to ensure that neither data protection regulations are violated nor that the evidence is compromised. With the looming volumes of digital evidence with the proliferation of IoT and blockchain forensics itself becoming a subdiscipline, the framework presents blockchain as the basis of combating contemporary threats.

The further directions should focus on eliminating the still existing hurdles by interdisciplinary efforts. High throughput forensic applications will be supported by scalability improvements through the use of advanced Layer-2 protocols, sharding and optimized consensus. Amendments on blockchain-specific admissibility rules, international standardisation of certification and decentralised authentication are necessary, especially in India to make BSA more in line with the technological reality. The use of blockchain in evidence categorization, correlation, malware analysis, and initial stages of forensic (identification/examination) needs to be expanded with the research that would include emerging technologies such as AI-based pattern recognition and quantum-resistant cryptography. Training initiatives will create forensic skills in blockchain verification, and legal platforms, cross-border engagements, and open-source ecosystems will initiate feasible implementation.

Recommendations that could be suggested to the policy are permissioned networks in governmental sectors, uniform protocols in hybrid storing, and structures in dealing with interjurisdictional cases in international situations. It is possible that by 2026 and later that convergence of AI, IoT forensics and tokenized evidence tracking will result in automated, smart evidence ecosystems. Finally, the revolutionary nature of blockchain is in moving towards trust-based to cryptographically-enforced systems, in which the reliability and validity of digital proof is equal to its probative weight. To achieve this vision requires a concerted effort, the technologists to perfect architectures, legal academics to develop regulations, policymakers to facilitate adoption and communities of forensic workers to embrace change in order to create reliable infrastructures of legal evidence, capable of upholding justice in the digital era.

REFERENCES

AlKhanafseh, M., & Surakhi, O. (2024). Evidence preservation in digital forensics: An approach using blockchain and lstm-based steganography. *Electronics (Basel)*, *13*(18), 3729. DOI: 10.3390/electronics13183729

Atlam, H. F., Ekuri, N., Azad, M. A., & Lallie, H. S. (2024). Blockchain forensics: A systematic literature review of techniques, applications, challenges, and future directions. *Electronics (Basel)*, *13*(17), 3568. DOI: 10.3390/electronics13173568

Dhabliya, D., Veeraiah, V., Dari, S. S., Kumar, J. R. R., Dhabliya, R., Gupta, A., & Pramanik, S. (2024). An Investigation on the Utilization of Blockchain in the Field of Digital Forensics. In *Revolutionizing the Global Stock Market: Harnessing Blockchain for Enhanced Adaptability* (pp. 1-28). IGI Global Scientific Publishing. DOI: 10.4018/979-8-3693-1758-7.ch001

Ghasemi, J., & Mahmoudi, N. (2024, October). The application of IoT devices in evidence collection and preservation In legal investigations In the common law legal system of Western countries. In *2024 11th International Symposium on Telecommunications (IST)* (pp. 120-124). IEEE. DOI: 10.1109/IST64061.2024.10843627

Igonor, O. S., Amin, M. B., & Garg, S. (2025). The application of blockchain technology in the field of digital forensics: A literature review. *Blockchains*, *3*(1), 5. DOI: 10.3390/blockchains3010005

Malik, A., & Sharma, A. K. (2023). Blockchain-based digital chain of custody multimedia evidence preservation framework for internet-of-things. *Journal of Information Security and Applications*, *77*, 103579. DOI: 10.1016/j.jisa.2023.103579

Onyeashie, B. I., Leimich, P., McKeown, S., & Russell, G. (2023, October). An Auditable Framework for Evidence Sharing and Management Using Smart Lockers and Distributed Technologies: Law Enforcement Use Case. In *International Conference on Big Data Technologies and Applications* (pp. 156-167). Cham: Springer Nature Switzerland.

Patil, C. S., Patil, A. P., & Patil, V. B. (2024). Evolution of technologies: A comprehensive analysis of AI, blockchain, and big data analytics. In *AI and Emerging Technologies* (pp. 1–26). CRC Press. DOI: 10.1201/9781003501152-1

Rani, D., Gill, N. S., Gulia, P., Yahya, M., Ahanger, T. A., Hassan, M. M., Abdallah, F. B., & Shukla, P. K. (2025). A secure digital evidence preservation system for an iot-enabled smart environment using ipfs, blockchain, and smart contracts. *Peer-to-Peer Networking and Applications*, *18*(2), 5. DOI: 10.1007/s12083-024-01855-z

Ratul, M. H. A., Mollajafari, S., & Wynn, M. (2024). Managing Digital Evidence in Cybercrime: Efforts Towards a Sustainable Blockchain-Based Solution. *Sustainability (Basel)*, *16*(24), 10885. DOI: 10.3390/su162410885

Sakshi, M., Malik, A., & Sharma, A. K. (2024). A survey on blockchain based IoT forensic evidence preservation: Research trends and current challenges. *Multimedia Tools and Applications*, *83*(14), 42413–42458. DOI: 10.1007/s11042-023-17104-z

Salih, K. M. M., & Ibrahim, N. B. (2023, December). CustodyChainGuardian: Blockchain of Custody Digital Evidence Preservation System. In *2023 IEEE Asia-Pacific Conference on Geoscience, Electronics and Remote Sensing Technology (AGERS)* (pp. 168-175). IEEE. DOI: 10.1109/AGERS61027.2023.10490757

Sanjalawe, Y., Makhadmeh, S., & Alqudah, H. (2024, February). Digital forensics meets blockchain: Enhancing evidence authenticity and traceability. In *2024 2nd International Conference on Cyber Resilience (ICCR)* (pp. 01-06). IEEE.

Sathe, A., Yadavade, H., Shetty, R., Singh, J., Kashilkar, M., Pangarkar, P., & Deshpande, K. (2024, April). Comprehensive Blockchain-Enabled Web Framework for Evidence Management. In *International Conference on Information and Communication Technology for Intelligent Systems* (pp. 257-268). Singapore: Springer Nature Singapore. DOI: 10.1007/978-981-97-6681-9_23

Singh, B., & Kaunert, C. (2024). Reinventing Artificial Intelligence and Blockchain for Preserving Medical Data. In *Ethical Artificial Intelligence in Power Electronics* (pp. 77–91). CRC Press. DOI: 10.1201/9781032648323-6

Vaghela, R., Gowda, V. D., Taj, M., Arudra, A., & Chopra, M. (2024). Digital evidence collection and preservation in computer network forensics. In *Handbook of Research on Innovative Approaches to Information Technology in Library and Information Science* (pp. 42–62). IGI Global Scientific Publishing. DOI: 10.4018/979-8-3693-0807-3.ch003

Verma, S. (2024). Digital Forensics: Using Blockchain in Cryptocurrency Investigations. In *Fintech, and Blockchains Trends in The Financial Sector* (pp. 84-96). Bentham Science Publishers.

Verma, S., Kumar, A., Pandey, S., & Negi, P. (2023, July). Blockchain and Cloud Computing used in Preservation of Crime Scene Evidences. In *2023 2nd International Conference on Edge Computing and Applications (ICECAA)* (pp. 7-11). IEEE. DOI: 10.1109/ICECAA58104.2023.10212110

Zou, L., & Chen, D. (2024). Using Blockchain Evidence in China's Digital Copyright Legislation to Enhance the Sustainability of Legal Systems. *Systems*, *12*(9), 356. DOI: 10.3390/systems12090356

Chapter 12
Intellectual Property and Contractual Disputes:
Blockchain as a Notarization

Arunima Shastri
http://orcid.org/0000-0002-6260-1253
Christ University, Bangalore, India

ABSTRACT

Blockchain's decentralized ledger is a game-changer for processing and documenting contracts, while also offering a solution to the long-standing problems in intellectual property (IP) protection. It ensures consistent and secure proof of creation and ownership using cryptographic hashes, minimizing risks of infringement, forgery, and dispute over ownership, without needing non-dependant archives or centralized trust. Minimal human intervention and intervention conflicts, thanks to the automation of smart contracts involved with the licensing, royalty payment and enforcement process. This chapter dives into various technical, legal and practical issues surrounding the application of blockchain in IP management and identifies how it can boost transparency, security, and efficiency in managing IP assets and agreements.

1. INTRODUCTION

While the adoption of blockchain is rising, it holds the potential to enhance IP ecosystems in the global scope, promote trust amongst creators and parties, and greatly revolutionize the way disputes are settled, although integration is important high standards for efficacy globally. Some of the reality is intellectual property or contractual issues are long-term thorns in the feet for creators, inventors, the

DOI: 10.4018/979-8-3373-9730-6.ch012

corporate world and legal fields around the globe. The traditional means to protect copyright, patents, trademarks, and trade secrets are often slow, expensive, too costly for enforcement, easily forged, and rely on centralized registries, notaries, and courts, and are therefore restricted by geographical boundaries (Alqarni, 2025). Ambiguous terms, uncorroborated date stamps and establishing proof of performance and ownership transfer are all common contractual disputes covered by these potential contract clauses. The blockchain technology comes in as a potent notarization option providing unalterable and transparent history, ownership, and transactions in a decentralized and unchangeable ledger. This capacity essentially revolutionizes the way IP is managed and/or potential disagreements ultimately handled.

Blockchain notarization is actually the generation of a cryptographic hash, or a distinctive electronic fingerprint, of any document, digital asset or code, with the creation and recording of the hash on a distributed ledger, linked to a point in time. When put in the record is not changed without coming to an agreement on the network, thus, immutability of the record. This is the process itself which constitutes evidence of date and authorship, important for an IP claim. An artist making an e-artwork or a software developer adding software codes, for example, can tag a time on it immediately and give an indelible snapshot proof superior to that of conventional copyrights, in accessibility and speed. Creators can reduce the intermediaries and costs of notating works with platforms (Johri, 2025).

Blockchain helps solve these challenges in the realm of IP management. Digital media are plagued by copyright violations; it is easy to copy and distribute. With blockchain, users can trace the origins of NFTs, images, music, or designs; ensuring that buyers can trust the authenticity of their NFTs. Tokenization of IP assets involves converting IP assets into electronic tokens that provide for fractional ownership and licensing. Royalty payments are automated with smart contracts: payments are automatically triggered off, based on pre-programmed terms, whenever a licensed work is used or sold and the smart contract is executed automatically, and royalty payments are accurate and predictable, eliminating the need for calculating payments from either end and avoiding disputes.

The advantages are also for patents and trade secrets. Even though it is essential to patent for legal monopoly, it is possible on blockchain to comply with fair record keeping of the timeline of invention or prior art, or collaborative development logs, which would make it easier to establish evidence in the case of infringement or priority action. In partnerships, access to trade secrets can be controlled, and with the possibility of audit trails, there is less chance of leakage when using permissioned blockchains to share. Examples of companies like IPwe have begun to exploit the potential of blockchain by establishing patent trading and management platforms, where a large part of world patents is kept on the blockchain, which brings transparency.

Common problems in contractual disputes are often about differing expectations, lack of clarity or issues with enforcement (Dombrovska, 2025). Volatile contracts, ambiguous wording, and third-party notary/witnesses are problems with traditional contract. Using blockchain notarization however, can soften this trend by fixing on the ledger full agreements or important sections. Contract can be hashed and timestamped by parties leaving a proof of existence and content of the contract at a certain moment in time. Far more impactful, smart contracts can have logic built into them and if, for example, the conditions are payment received on delivery, or milestones, these are automatically carried out, moving assets or monies without the use of any intermediaries. This lessens conflicts that might occur due to non-performance since execution is verified by code, and can be seen by all.

Chain of custody or licenses related to electronic materials/parties can be kept on the blockchain, ensuring that every action in the chain of materials and parties is recorded for traceability. On-chain evidence is far more accurate than paper and emails, in the event of a dispute. To effectively resolve smart contract disputes, with decision-makers appointed through a crowd-based, game-theoretical incentives structure and blockchain tokens, players of decentralized dispute-resolution platforms can find smarter solutions than traditional litigation at a lower cost and faster time (Maesa et al., 2025). To weave together on-chain and off-chain worlds, there are also specific arbitration rules for blockchain, such as the UKJT Digital Dispute Resolution Rules or JAMS' Arbitration Rules.

These are demonstrated in the real-world applications. The music industry is leveraging blockchain, for example by platform Audius, to pay directly artists and prove their ownership. Photographers take advantage of systems similar to KodakOne to keep track of the rights to images. To deter fake images and articles in media, articles and images are notarized. Real estate and wills have tamper-proof title and asset records which has limited ownership disputes. First, these cases demonstrate less litigation and shorter transactions, and create greater trust within both scenarios.

There are some challenges and promise as yet. The big uncertainty is legal: although many jurisdictions now accept the use of blockchain times themselves, it is yet to be established as a true evidence or notarisation, and there are only a handful of precedents and some injunctions. High-value IP adoption is hampered by scalability constraints on public chains with congestions (such as high fees on the network), based on the number of devices (Wagner et al., 2025). Public chains have scalability constraints that hinder adoption for high-value IP as the number of devices grows (outside of congestion such as public networks with high fees). Technical challenges are faced in terms of interoperability of other blockchains and the integration with legacy IP offices. Public ledgers have privacy implications and hybrid or permissioned are required for sensitive data. Proof-of work chains are energy consuming and have environmental troubles leading to migration to proof-of-stake verification. Still, in many instances, physical enforcement of an on-chain outcome must be taken up by an off-chain legal matter, because it's not always possible to force an off-chain compliance with an on-chain action.

2. TRADITIONAL CHALLENGES IN IP PROTECTION AND CONTRACTUAL DISPUTES

Protection of intellectual property (IP) rights and contractual agreements traditionally has proved difficult and have lost their value in promoting innovation and commercial trust. One of the major issues in IP protection is territoriality. The provision and enforcement of patents, copyrights, trademarks and trade secrets are national phenomena, resulting in a different picture of world patent law. Despite the international legislation, such as TRIPS agreement, there are different legal norms, legal enforcement methods and judicial efficiency available in each country. Effective institutions do exist in developed economies, but in many developing markets, existing systems are weak with resources limited and corruption rampant, which leads to below-average examination, registration delays and weak enforcement (Kumar & Suthar, 2025). This provides room for unlawful and counterfeit products and piracy leading to significant economic losses of hundreds of billions of dollars a year and loss of consumer safety and brand values.

These problems have been magnified by digitalisation. Content is widely replicated and distributed via file sharing, social media and eCommerce platforms and is hard to track and prevents infringement. Monitoring unauthorized music, movie, software, designs and text usage is continuous and expensive and can be complicated by anonymous servers and cross borders. There's patent trolling and trademark “squatting” adding to the legal hassle for owner (Al Husseini et al., 2025). However, the protection of trade secret is highly dependent on confidentiality, which can be compromised in a collaborative setting, a supply chain or due to employee movements and cyber spying. Ownership and first creation as part of the dispute is costly and time consuming, and traditional methods of notary or copyright-based solemnization of the date of work creation can be forgery and loss prone.

These issues are aggravated by contractual conflicts. Traditional contracts, which are typically paper based or digitally signed on centralized platforms, can create problems with language, version control, and verifying performance or delivery. Conflicts often occur regarding what “must be done” in the agreement, whether something was actually completed, when a payment must be made, or simultaneously, in case a termination condition is satisfied (Hanif et al., 2025). In many situations the preferred choice is litigating, but it is often slow, costly and contentious requiring a lot of time and resources sometimes years and final results that vary depending on jurisdictional differences in cross-border deals. Due to backlogged courts, the exorbitant legal costs and requirement to have physical evidence or witnesses further slows delivery of justice. International contracts add layers of complexity and possibility of conflicting laws, choice-of-forum-type agreements and enforcement of foreign judgments.

Other barriers are administrative requirements related to IP registration and IP portfolio management, particularly for SMEs and individual creators, who may not have the resources of large companies. Like AI content, cultural and legal mismatches are heightened due to globalization and emerging technologies (Perdana et al., 2025). Overall, these traditional systems lead to mistrust and high transaction costs, slow innovation in some areas, and disproportionate affect on smaller players, which shows the need for more efficient and transparent systems using verifiable means for rights and conflict resolution.

3. BLOCKCHAIN TECHNOLOGY: FUNDAMENTALS AND NOTARIZATION MECHANISMS

Blockchain technology is a decentralized, distributed ledger system that securely, transparently and permanently records transactions on a network of computers. It is based on a block chain, a record of transactions that are linked in series with cryptographic hashes connecting each block to the one before it. Because in this structure, if data is added, it would make changes in all the following blocks, and for that, the consent of the majority of the network would have to be obtained, making it difficult to tamper among this community split. Pivotal features are decentralized (no central control), transparent (all users can access the ledger, depending on access permissions), and using cryptographic security with hash functions and digital signatures. Consensus mechanisms like Proof of Work (PoW), Proof of Stake (PoS), or Practical Byzantine Fault Tolerance (PByFT) allow for network consensus without the need for a central authority to validate transactions (Yadav & Singh, 2026).

These attributes make the notarization on blockchain a valuable solution for ensuring that all documents and digital assets are impossible to tamper with, are in owners' possession, and have remained unaltered and in an acceptable state. Document, image, code, or any other digital file is usually processed with an algorithm, such as the SHA-2 algorithm, to create a uniquely defined, fixed-length "digital fingerprint" or hash. A slight modification in the input file results in a completely different hash. This hash is then logged on the blockchain, not the actual document, and the record of the documents is fixed.This hash is then written to the blockchain, not to the actual documents, preserving document privacy, while providing a fixed record of the documents. Permissionless or hybrid blockchains achieve high security with large networks, and permissioned blockchains allow enterprise access.

Timestamping is an important aspect of blockchain notarizations. Because it gives it a verifiable time from the network that can not be erased from it, it provides irrefutable evidence that the content existed in its current form at a precise time – much more reliable and accessible than traditional notary stamps or registry deposits. Verification is simple – re-hashing the original file can be done by anyone and it can be compared with what is on-chain. If it matches, then integrity and timing is confirmed (Walters, 2025). This process can be used in IP to instantaneously and universally proof authorship and creation date. Smart contracts, which are self-executing pieces of blockchain code, further the notarization by automating rules required to adhere with preset conditions, including royalty payouts or access controls.

Without relying on trusted third parties, incorporating blockchain lowers the cost of operation, points of failure, and risk of fraud. Being open-source, using protocols such as Open Timestamps, which reduces fees and is optimized for scalability, proves to boost the efficiency by having multiple hashes combined in Merkle Trees and then anchoring the root onto the blockchain. Security is provided by public-key cryptography-based authentication and economic motivations in consensus (e.g., mining rewards or staking). Factors such as trade-offs are also important for fundamentals: Public chains are the most immutable, but are less scalable and have less energy efficiency; Private chains are energy efficient and faster, albeit less decentralized.

In actual application, blockchain notarization is compatible with current systems via APIs and hybrid solutions, with the aim of being able to seamlessly time stamp without completely overhauling the legal landscape. It offers mathematical securely [where traditional methods give procedural assurance] that brings in a change in the processes of constructing evidence and eliminating conflicts. With the development of zero-knowledge proofs and layer-2 scaling solutions, this notarization function can become even more robust, private, centric in any IP or contractual usages, making the use of the zk-byzantium scaling solution even more desirable.The technology continues to improve with the evolution of zero-knowledge proofs and layer-2 scaling, making its privacy-preserving, robust, more robust capabilities for notarization even more desirable for wide use and adoption in IP and contractual scenarios.

4. APPLICATIONS OF BLOCKCHAIN IN INTELLECTUAL PROPERTY MANAGEMENT

The IP landscape has been plagued by inefficiencies and uncertainty, but the rise of blockchain technology is poised to change all that.Blockchain technology is making its way into the realm of intellectual property (IP) management, offering a new range of immutability, transparency, and decentralization that solves many traditional problems with IP frameworks. The more obvious, yet equally significant application is copyright protection, as creators, from digital artists and musicians to authors and software developers, can cryptographically hash any interestable creation, for instance art, music, literature, software code or photographs, and then bind the hash to the blockchain ledger to timestamp their creation (Wang et al., 2026). This offers irrefutable proof of creation date, ownership and integrity, that is accessible without relying on slow and expensive central registries such as copyright offices. Signing online works directly on the chain does not require any platform to provide documentation, as genuineness is ensured by the chain.Content can be copied and distributed online globally in seconds and platforms like Blockai allow writers, artists and developers to register works on-chain, therefore providing verifiable content documentation, which further helps to enhance the enforcement to infringement in the online age.

Within the field of visual arts and collectibles, non-fungible tokens (NFTs) have proven to be an effective solution for the tokenization of IP assets. Artists issue one-of-a-kind metadata and licensing information along with digital certificate of origin on-chains, such as Ethereum or specialized layers, that describe the licensing terms and discuss the tokens' origin. Not only does this make sales and transfers more secure, but also it allows for automated royalty payments via smart contracts, thanks to blockchain technology. Blockchain technology makes this possible and makes sales and transfers more secure, along with smart contract automated royalty payments. The notable example illustrated the use of NFTs and distribution of profits to the initial creator when he sold his work later on, as there is a chance to track the sale on secondary markets and distribute predefined percentages to the initial creator – meaning there are no intermediaries involved, unlike a gallery or licensing agreement that leaves the initial creator without compensation for later re-sales as it would be difficult to track. Verisart can also generate a tamper-proof digital Certificate for Artworks that ensures secure conversion to their next phase, NFTs, without compromising authenticity, and prevents artworks from being copied and creating a loss of buyer trust in high-value art sales.

Blockchain can be done to the benefit of the music market immensely. Delays and unexpected payments due are the result of long-standing fragmented rights ownership, complicated royalty tracks that include labels, publishers, performers and songwriters, and murky distribution processes. Royalty sharing on blockchain platforms and smart contracts is automated: each stream, download or sync license unlocks a stream of instant, clear and equitable royalty distribution based on proven ownership rights. Standards such as EIP-2981 integrate standards into NFT's, and more complex music technology ecosystems are developing tokenized music rights so that each smart contract becomes a song's or catalogue's fractional asset, in order to unlock novel funding mechanisms and unlock new areas of liquidity for artists. This should ease the accounting disputes and help independent creators to keep more control in their hands and more revenues.

Another crucial application domain is patent management. Although they still need to be examined by governmental offices, blockchain is ideal for documenting the timeline, prior art, collaborative development communications, and proof of reduction to practice of an invention. Priority dates in areas of innovation that move quickly can be established with immutable timestamps that will strengthen a position in interference and/or infringement proceedings. Businesses are investigating patent marketplaces with, for example, tokenization of patents for better trading, licensing, and even collateralization (Wang et al., 2025). By tokenizing patents as digital assets, only small pieces of an IP portfolio are transferred and instead of a complete patent assignment, a share ownership agreement is executed. Platforms are designed to become "transparencies" in which the number of duplicate claims is minimized, and searches for prior art are facilitated through on-chain records.

The traceability capabilities of Blockchain can also be applied to Copy/Patent Protection and Anti-Copying efforts. Luxury brands and manufacturers put a unique characteristic or a digital twin of a physical product on the ledger to facilitate verification by the consumer and partners in the supply chain until the end user. This establishes an accountability chain of events that can help stop the sale of counterfeit goods such as those in fashion, thousands and medications. Smart contracts can also be used to automate licensing models for trademarks in order to grant access or pay accordingly based on use, after successfully verifying the use (Bingyuan & Zhaoxun, 2025). The role of blockchain in supply chains is to record each movement, help ensure adherence to licensing conditions and act as a tool for prosecution in enforcement proceedings.

Permissioned or hybrid blockchains are ideal for sharing restricted access information and proprietary data, such as trade secrets, through controlled, cryptographically secured access with access keys that enables partners, employees, or collaborators to access the data without worry. Any access or modification that is not authorized is easily identified, offering a greater evidential value in misappropriation disputes. For collaborative innovation environments (as in open innovation project or research consortia), blockchain can track those contributing with secure activities assignments, guaranteeing the data origin and distribution of the gains, in addition to allowing the secure storage of sensitive information either with a zero-knowledge proof or by out-of-chain storage linked to the commitment on-chain.

In addition to the individual types of IPs, blockchain can also enable full-fledged digital rights management (DRM) systems. Fine-grained content access permissions, viewing, modification, and commercial, can be automatically enforced using smart contracts. This is especially useful in the media, publishing and software sectors, where licensing conditions are intricate and often violated. Blockchains in architecture, engineering, and construction (AEC) quests with NFTs to safeguard building blueprints and the IP they convey all through the lives of designs.

Applications in real life are becoming increasingly more mature. IPwe has created tools for patent trading and management to make this once murky market now transparent. Bernstein generates certified version histories for innovations, thus establishing a trace of development in digital form. For instance, in the metaverse and gaming industry, companies such as Nike are starting to take steps to use the trademark to protect virtual goods and virtual sneakers, allowing them to go further than protecting their product names and create new revenue streams. Both governments and organisations are trialling blockchain registries in order to lower administrative burden on the traditional IP offices and enable hybrid legal recognition of IP through new paths.

The technology also enables new business models, including fractional ownership of valuable IP, collective management by a DAO, and evidence of infringement on-chain supported by AI. Blockchain simplifies the process of IP protection, offering a platform for individual creators and small businesses who have been disadvantaged due to the high costs and complexity of acquiring an IP. Transaction costs drop significantly, data is transparent and enforceability on a global scale is now possible, and trust is created based on verified data, not on the presence of intermediaries (Widya & Santoso, 2025).

However, there are still challenges for integration with these applications. This means that legal recognition of on-chain records can differ across jurisdictions, while interoperability between various blockchains is still limited and if a public chain is used, it can fall short for high volume use cases due to scalability challenges. Given the need for privacy concerns, careful design with hybrid or enterprise solutions are required, and smart contract vulnerabilities need to be thoroughly audited. Even with some challenges, the visions of blockchain-based integration with AI, IoT and 'smart' cryptography may offer yet more complex tools for managing IP, including automated global licensing, real-time IP infringement detection, and enforcement across borders. Indeed, blockchain can be used throughout the IP lifecycle process, not only in the creation and registration process, but also in IP commercialisation, IP enforcement and even monetisation, providing unparalleled security, efficiency and integrity.

5. SMART CONTRACTS FOR AUTOMATED CONTRACTUAL ENFORCEMENT AND DISPUTE MITIGATION

Smart contracts are automated programs that run on the blockchain that trigger an agreement's terms when specific conditions are fulfilled. They are usually written in languages such as Solidity on a platform like Ethereum and converted to code so the contractual clauses may be executed without any intermediaries, like a lawyer, a bank or a notary. Smart contracts are a powerful tool in intellectual property (IP) and contractual settings that can be programmed into the blockchain's immutable ledger to automate, make transparent, and help avoid disputes.

The further application of smart contracts in the field of IP management can transform the licensing and royalty sharing processes. For instance, if a music license agreement stipulates the following splits – 30% to the performer and 20% to the publisher and 50% to the song writer, every stream or download on the platform could cause these royalty payments to be made on a real-time basis to the rights holder(s). This will remove the downfalls of traditional systems that include the delay and lack of transparency in the accounts and controversy regarding revenue division. NFT marketplaces incorporate resale royalties (generally 5-10%, which activate automatically at second hand trades, letting creators reap profits for good enough future sales of NFTS (Chopra & Naqshbandi, 2025). Smart Contracts can be widely used in software and patent licensing to track usage data through oracles and revoke rights, such as access for warehouses or renewal if any access is terminated. In software and patent licensing, smart contracts can use oracles to track the data required for tracking software usage, automatically revoke Rights or carry out other actions when it is breached, thus decreasing the enforcement costs significantly.

Smart contracts are great for conditional logic, which will help with more widespread enforcement of contracts. Payment releases are made in supply chain or collaboration agreements when goods have been delivered confirmed by IoT sensors or third-party oracles and/or when milestones have been met and/or quality thresholds satisfied. That results in automation that functions as "if-then": If goods are available, and if they're acceptable, then it's a "then" money transfer. With IP co-development agreements, smart contracts can keep record of contributions, assign ownership portion and fairly provide reward without any dispute over rewards or credit.

There is currently no good way to avoid dispute except through its prevention. Smart contracts eliminate ambiguity by ensuring there is unambiguous, actionable code, and there is on-chain documentation of the events. The code and transaction history can be audited by all parties in real-time, creating trust. But when disputes do arise, whether it's because of coding bugs or the failure of oracles or off-chain events, it's customary to mix on-chain automation and off-chain dispute resolution to get the best of both worlds. A service such as Kleros employs a game theory informed system of jurors provided by the crowd, and incentivized by tokens, to be able to resolve cases quickly and effectively and to enforce resolution through smart contracts that replace conventional, slower and more costly litigation.

Benefits: cost and time reductions are achieved as manual processing, intermediaries are eliminated and the court proceedings are minimised a dramatic opportunity to cost and time reduce. Cryptographic Security and Immutability also contribute to better security, and Cross-Border Accessibility facilitates cross-body business transactions without any jurisdictional issues. But there are disadvantages: the "oracle problem" (supplying correct 'real world' data); code defects (as in early hacks); and only limited power to deliver on subjective and complex disagreements and forced physical performances. Smart legal contracts sometimes incorporate natural language along with code to fill the missing gaps, to make legal contracts work as well as technical contracts (Bacon et al., 2018). In general, smart contracts change the paradigm of contracts from dispute resolution to proactive and automatic compliance. Their efficiency will be further enhanced by integration with AI, IoT, and other oracles, but obtaining legal recognition and standardization to facilitate widespread adoption are crucial.

6. CASE STUDIES, BENEFITS AND REAL-WORLD IMPLEMENTATIONS

The use of blockchain and smart contracts for IP and contracts has proven effective in real-world applications in a variety of sectors. In the music industry, Audius is a decentralized streaming system for both music and artists, allowing them to enter track information and establish royalty rates through smart contracts. It also features automatic, invisible payouts with a revenue split of up to 90%, as opposed to lower payouts of traditional platforms. This model eliminates the need for labels and middlemen, and ensures transparency on earnings and verification of ownership in real time, thereby minimizing and simplifying royalty conflicts.

With the support of IBM, IPwe developed a patent marketplace based on blockchain to enable tokenization of patents and make them easy to trade and license and clearly visible. It automates transactions and royalty payments, and adds transparency to a historically opaque market, with smart contracts also adding the ability to fractionalize ownership. This has made patent management much simpler to smaller innovators and corporations.

The visual arts are a prime example of areas where platforms such as Verisart are issuing blockchain-encrypted digital certificates to works created in the art medium which can be converted to NFTs with embedded blockchained smart contracts that track the original art work's changing hands and allow for automatic royalty payments to the creator during exchanges. This helps to reduce forgery and gives an unalterable record of ownership to benefit artists and collectors. Kleros is a case in point of decentralized dispute resolution: it has already dealt with thousands of cases involving IP disputes, smart contract disputes, and more, with crowdsourced jurors. A notable hybrid case in Mexico involved enforcement of an arbitral award which was also substantially adjudicated through Kleros. Yet, substantial recognition of the Kleros protocols in judicial proceedings has been achieved, as in a notable hybrid case in Mexico, an arbitral award was enforced with adjudication taking place via Kleros. With the help of blockchain smart contracts, the Home Depot is able to save processing time and costs when handling conflict with its vendors quickly (Corneli et al., 2025). But companies such as Walmart are also using the same technology to enable traceability and compliance - ensuring that products are not counterfeited in the supply chain.

All transactions are auditable, and this provides key benefits of unprecedented transparency and trust. Reduce administration and accelerate the execution of tasks from days/weeks to seconds with automation. The cost savings come from both disintermediation and a decreased amount of litigation. To help prevent tampering, advanced security and immutability are put in place; and global reach makes foreign IP management easier. Monetization will be enhanced for creators through direct, fair-authority compensation, and efficient licensing and minimised risk for companies. Fractional ownership provides new lines of capital to IP assets.

In practice it has resulted in reduced rates of disagreement because the terms are self-explanatory and self-enforceable and there is solid evidence on which any remaining discord is based. Early criticisms have been met by improvements to the environment and solution scalability with the help of layer-2 solutions and proof-of-stake. But problems remain such as regulatory issues, interoperability concerns, and the necessity of intermediate solutions of a cross-coded and cross-legally nature. There is a need to fill the lack of education and fluctuating gas prices to prevent limiting adoption.

Governments and organizations are implementing trial blockchain IP registries and/or DAOs are experimenting with collective rights management. Connecting AI to smart contract creation and monitoring adds to potentiality. Such deployments validate the change from the hype around blockchain to its effective utilization for value creation with quicker innovation cycles, leveler reward creation and more efficient market. A more widespread use of something like this could have an impact on the worldwide IP and contractual landscape and significant economic and creative value for the world (Singh et al., 2025).

7. CONCLUSION AND FUTURE PROSPECTS

There is no standardization as without having uniform global protocols issues can complicate between nation. Smart contracts can have bugs caused by programming errors; these may cause them to be executed unintentionally as in the case of some early DAO hacks, so there is a need for thorough auditing and the development of smart legal contracts that combine both an ATM-like interface and the use of legal contracts and smart contracts. The regulation is still in progress, and organisations are studying how blockchain technology fits into current IP frameworks, such as Berne Convention or TRIPS. Lack of knowledge by both lawyers and creators/ innovators slows the adoption of the mainstream.

The future shows great potential, and blockchain as notarization could become a tool to revolutionize IP law and ensure creators receive proper rights and protection from the large infringers and spell an environment of collaborative innovation. Powered by AI, automated infringement detection, privacy-respecting zero-knowledge proofs, and innovative layer-2 scaling solutions will improve their capabilities. IP registries using blockchain are being experimented with by governments and organizations, with the potential of making patent offices more efficient. Hybrid approaches that link self-executing code with traditional ADR will represent the ultimate compromise between the two options for contractual disputes, somewhere between automation and humans in the mix for reasons of fairness.

REFERENCES

Al Husseini, A. A., Alasadi, A. Y., Alsadi, A. M., Hasan, M. H., Jehad, M. T., Hussein, A. M., & Muhamad, M. N. (2025, July). Scalable Blockchain-Based Smart Contract Enforcement Framework for Cross-Border Protection and Verification of Intellectual Property. In *2025 3rd International Conference on Cyber Resilience (ICCR)* (pp. 1-7). IEEE. DOI: 10.1109/ICCR67387.2025.11292063

Alqarni, A. (2025). A blockchain-based solution for transparent intellectual property rights management: Smart contracts as enablers. *Kybernetes*, *54*(13), 7380–7407. DOI: 10.1108/K-04-2024-1074

Bacon, J., Michels, J. D., Millard, C., & Singh, J. (2018). Blockchain demystified: A technical and legal introduction to distributed and centralized ledgers. *Rich. JL & Tech.*, *25*, 1.

Bingyuan, M., & Zhaoxun, C. (2025). Theory of Interest Jurisprudence for the Development of the Notarial System. *Journal of Advanced Research in Social and Behavioural Sciences*, *38*(1), 15–26. DOI: 10.37934/jarsbs.38.1.1526

Chopra, N., & Naqshbandi, M. Q. (2025). The role of blockchain and smart contracts in business law. *Journal of Scientific Research and Technology*, 28-40.

Corneli, A., Carbonari, A., Spegni, F., Pieroni, T., & Naticchia, B. (2025). On-site safety inspections through marker-less augmented reality and Blockchain notarization of BIM-based processes. *Buildings (Basel, Switzerland)*, *15*(13), 2318. DOI: 10.3390/buildings15132318

Dombrovska, A. (2025). Blockchain Enabled Governance of Intellectual Property: Evidentiary Integrity, Licensing Automation, and Enforcement Design. *Public Administration and Law Review*, (4 (24)), 37–49. DOI: 10.36690/2674-5216-2025-4-37-49

Hanif, M., Munir, E. U., Rehan, M. M., Ahmad, S. G., Khan, I., & Setchi, R. (2025). Tiered blockchain framework: A secure, trustworthy, and cost-efficient solution for the digital rights protection. *Blockchain: Research and Applications*, 100308.

Johri, P. (2025). Legal Issues and Models of Ownership for Intellectual Property Materials within Blockchain Systems. *J. Intell. Prot. Stud.*, *9*, 108.

Kumar, D., & Suthar, N. (2025). Assessing the prospects and constraints of blockchain technology for intellectual property management. *The Journal of World Intellectual Property*, *28*(1), 124–140. DOI: 10.1111/jwip.12324

Maesa, D. D. F., Loporchio, M., & Tietze, F. (2025). Privacy-preserving and automated intellectual property license agreements over heterogeneous blockchain networks. *Blockchain: Research and Applications*, 100288.

Perdana, M. R. A., Bhakti, R. T. A., & Maileni, D. A. (2025). Validity of Electronic Signatures in Digital Agreements: An Analysis of the Application of the Intellectual Property Law and the Civil Code in E-Commerce Transactions. *Jurnal Mahkamah: Kajian Ilmu Hukum dan Hukum Islam*, 565-578.

Singh, B., Wongmahesak, K., & Chandra, S. (2025). Transforming digital ownership and assessing role of blockchain technology and NFTs in future economy. In *Practical Strategies and Case Studies for Online Marketing 6.0* (pp. 343–368). IGI Global Scientific Publishing. DOI: 10.4018/979-8-3373-2058-8.ch015

Wagner, S. M., Fink, A. A., Ehrnsperger, J. F., & Düpree, P. (2025). Supporting Intellectual Property Protection: Blockchain Technology as a Catalyst for Open Innovation. *California Management Review*, *67*(3), 164–185. DOI: 10.1177/00081256251320366

Walters, R. (2025). Smart contracts and international commercial arbitration. In *Routledge Handbook on Transnational Commercial Law* (pp. 390–414). Routledge. DOI: 10.4324/9781003394822-25

Wang, Y., Xu, K., Wan, Q., Huang, Y., & Guan, Q. (2026). OChain: A blockchain oracle system for dynamic plagiarism detection of software copyrights. *Computer Networks*, *281*, 112175. DOI: 10.1016/j.comnet.2026.112175

Wang, Y., Zhou, Y., Yang, D., & Guo, H. (2025, May). Innovative Pathways for Blockchain-Enabled Intellectual Property Pledge Financing: A Case Study of the "Zhiyirong" Platform. In *International Conference on Blockchain and Trustworthy Systems* (pp. 404-417). Singapore: Springer Nature Singapore.

Widya, G. M., & Santoso, B. (2025). Notary's Authority in Making Deeds of Agreement to Protect Trade Secrets. *Widya Pranata Hukum: Jurnal Kajian dan Penelitian Hukum*, *7*(1), 18-36.

Yadav, S., & Singh, R. R. (2026). Decentralized Dispute Resolution in International Trade with Blockchain and Smart Contracts. *Journal of Legal Affairs and Dispute Resolution in Engineering and Construction*, *18*(2), 04526006. DOI: 10.1061/JLADAH.LADR-1470

Chapter 13
Mediation in the Digital Age:
Ensuring Justice Through Blockchain Technology

Vijaishree Tiwari
RKDF University, Bhopal, India

Nilesh Verma
RKDF University, Bhopal, India

Sheersha Saxena
http://orcid.org/0009-0009-7214-6192
Vivekananda Global University, Jaipur, India

ABSTRACT

The Blockchain technology offers a truly revolutionary framework for Online Dispute Resolution (ODR), lends transparency, security and enforceability to the process. This paper examines the advantages and disadvantages of these different blockchain platforms, as measured by their technical features, and their potential for mediation and arbitration. The capability to execute smart contracts, manage evidence and handle settlements automatically is considered on public blockchains like Ethereum, permissioned networks like Hyperledger Fabric as well as specialized solutions like Kleros and Aragon. The research is informative on how these platforms help to overcome a number of problems that hinder the application of the digital mediation process such as the problem of trust, the problem of enforcement, and the problem of confidentiality, among others, and investigates the problem of the legal recognition of these platforms and the issue of its practical application.

DOI: 10.4018/979-8-3373-9730-6.ch013

1. INTRODUCTION

In today's era of digital information, where lengthy courts, slow response times and expenses have become a major issue, mediation has become an essential tool for voluntary and collaborative dispute resolution. This growth of e-commerce, remote working practices, cross-border business and digital relationships has resulted in more and more contractual, family, consumer and IP-related disputes. Although successful, traditional mediation has its own set of drawbacks: problems of establishing trust, inadequate records, problematic enforcement and location. As a result of this, blockchain technology arises as a potent enabler that can revolutionise mediation in the way it becomes a more secure and transparent process, thereby becoming more efficient and enforceable and thus more access to justice.

In essence, blockchain is decentralized, immutable, and has been made secure through a cryptographic process. Online Dispute Resolution (ODR) platforms can be blockchain-enabled, with all communications, exchanges of documents and agreements being recorded on a distributed ledger. This results in a virtually impossible-to-tamper record of events which gives parties, possibly not known by or trusting of one another, confidence. Smart contracts self-activating code that resides on the blockchain can automatically carry out the terms of a settlement when conditions for both sides are fulfilled, like cashing out escrow if the parties agree. This is a huge step toward diminishing the issue of non-compliance, a major challenge in the traditional mediation process (Kovalchuk et al., 2024).

The Blockchain has made one of the greatest impacts in blockchain applications related to evidence management and preservation. Mediation digital evidence (e mail, chat, contract, transaction records), etc., frequently has challenges with respect to authenticity. Blockchain does this by using cryptographic hashing and timestamping. Documents can be uploaded and the system generates an easily verifiable digital fingerprint on the ledger in real time. If there is any modification done later, it will be immediately known. It is undeniably very useful in family conflicts, business negotiations or customer disputes where evidence tampering charges frequently crop up. Large on-chain files near impossible to compromise, but with EIP-7291, efficient storage is ensured with hybrid architecture using on-chain anchoring of these file hashes.

The Smart contracts will transform the post mediation process. Once parties to a settlement agree, the settlement can be encoded in a sort of smart contract that places assets into an escrow account and releases the assets in exchange for the party's performance. For instance, in a business dispute, if the delivery confirmation is verified using IoT sensors or from an oracle from another party, then the payment is released. This automation sector reduces post-settlement legal process and boosts finality. Smart contracts help decrease reliance on time-consuming and costly international enforcement in cross-border mediations.

The Powerful privacy capabilities uphold confidentiality, a key part of mediation. The Proofs and permissioned blockchains enable parties to make a claim without disclosing details that would be sensitive. The Private channels are used to display certain information to only certain participants. This technical balance seeks to reconcile data protection issues raised by various data protection laws including GDPR and India's DPDPA so as to ensure blockchain mediation is compliant and trusted (Zhao & Chen, 2024).

Another key benefit of blockchain in boosting access to justice is that it brings down costs and makes it more accessible. The common approach to mediation is highly expensive because of high venue and travel costs and high legal representation costs. Blockchain technologies help bring high-functioning completely remote and low-cost processes to smartphones. This is revolutionary for businesses, consumers and the individual in the remote areas. The Reputation systems that are exploited openly on the blockchain can be used to identify neutral mediators for legal proceedings, decrease prejudice and improve fairness throughout the procedure. AI tools can also be beneficial for mediators by analyzing the communication dynamics of the relationship and making informed recommendations for a balanced resolution. AI tools can also be useful for mediators in the analysis of conversational patterns and make reasoned decisions to suggest a fair resolution for the relationship, while maintaining the control of human mediators.

Although there are benefits to it, there are a number of issues that remain. Many jurisdictions don't support legal enforcement of blockchain-based agreements. But doubts about the ability of smart contracts to be legally enforceable, the admissibility of smart contracts in court, and the liabilities for coding mistakes should be addressed with some guidance. There need to be technical hurdles overcome (scalabilty, energy usage in public blockchains, lack of digital literacy etc.). Strong mitigations are needed to deal with the dangers lurking in the cyber world, such as private key compromises. Furthermore, it is crucial for just blockchain systems to not amplify the “digital divide” phenomenon.

A number of early platforms showcase the application opportunities. Medication features make use of blockchain for decentralized resolution of paperwork and disputes, including Kleros or Aragon. There are platforms which combine mediation and smart contract execution, such as Kleros or Aragon for decentralized resolution of paperwork and disputes. In family and community cases, pilot projects have been effective in making use of blockchain to document agreements on kid custody, alimony and house sharing. When compared to traditional applications, these applications deliver faster resolution times, higher compliance and higher levels of participant satisfaction.

The prospects for the future are even more promising as blockchain technology is expected to further integrate with AI, machine learning, and other sophisticated tools to enable complex mediation procedures. AI can help to find common ground, help formulate agreements and predict what the court will decide; blockchain will make sure that the whole process is accurate. International harmonisation of standards, facilitated on an intergovernmental basis by, e.g., UNCITRAL, will be an important factor towards cross-borders effectivity. The governments or judicial bodies should treat blockchain settlement like an arbitral award under the New York Convention, as binding.

2. BLOCKCHAIN PLATFORMS SUITABLE FOR DISPUTE RESOLUTION

In the digital era, blockchain platforms are a central component to develop effective, trustworthy, and scalable means of dispute resolution. Each platform provides specific features that are available to address mediation, arbitration and Online Dispute Resolution (ODR) needs. Dispute resolution platforms offer various advantages, including, but not limited to, scalability, privacy and anonymity, governance arrangements, smart contracts, speed of transactions, costs and compliance.

Ethereum continues to be one of the more popular options for dispute resolution applications. It has powerful features with smart contracts, which are set up with the Solidity language, to ensure complex automatized agreements (Kadioglu Kumtepe, 2025). Systems such as Kleros use Ethereum to setup a decentralized courts platform that has jurors committing tokens to the vote to reward it according to game theory. In terms of public dispute resolution, Ethereum offers a strong and recognisable ecosystem, developer community and user base that makes it appealing. However, high gas fees, scalability issues (which are mitigated by layer-2 solutions like Polygon, Optimism) and privacy concerns become an issue with sensitive disputes like family mediation or commercial negotiations where privacy is key.

The most suitable platforms for running dispute resolution at an institutional and enterprise level is Hyperledger Fabric, an open-source permissioned blockchain framework, hosted by the Linux foundation. Modular architecture, confidential channels, flexible consensus mechanisms, such as Raft, Kafka, support Fabric. These functions enable multiple entities or individuals to participate, acting as mediators, disputants, attorneys and arbitrators, all under the utmost data confidentiality. It's also optimized for use in real-time mediation sessions, with a high volume of transactions and low latency. In mediation settings, Fabric allows for documents to be shared securely, the negotiation to be logged completely, and auto-enforcement of mediation agreement terms, while ensuring that no sensitive information is thrown out into the public sphere.

Designed by ConsenSys, Quorum is a permissioned version of Ethereum, which features the privacy capabilities of Ethereum along with smart contract capabilities. It can enable private transfers and offer zero knowledge proofs, which makes it appropriate for monetary and commercial conflicts that require privacy (Shmyndruk et al., 2025). Quorum has been piloted in the arbitration and escrow sector in a way that has proven effective when it comes to blockchain-based arbitration.Quorum has successfully been tested in pilot projects in the escrow and arbitration sector.

Corda, launched by R3, is tailored for the business/legal use case. Unlike the traditional blockchains, with their “need-to-know” approach, in which only the parties involved view the transaction data. It is an option that is highly appealing for correspondence when business contracts, IP or family dispute resolution are utilized with disregarded components. Corda's robust and legal footing and interoperability with current legal systems are an advantage for enforcability.

Polkadot and Cosmos are regions of interoperable blockchain infrastructures that facilitate the ability of different chains for communication. These platforms can be useful when disputes arise between different blockchains and parties involved in it. The parachains feature in Polkadot support specialized dispute resolution modules within it, and they also provide with shared security.

There are also specialized types of Dispute Resolution Platforms. Kleros can be known as a decentralized autonomous group (DAO) for dispute resolution that very well works within ecommerce, freelance or small-value online transactions. In Aragon, conflict can be managed with resources designed for decentralized organizations. While Jur runs the firms specialty (legal smart contracts) Sagewise specializes in drafting collaborating contracts, including dispute-resolution components. Permissioned platforms are being created to meet local regulatory requirements, as stipulated in Information Technology Act, as well as local ODR polices, in India and Asia (Poncibo et al., 2024).

Instead, hybrid Blockchain Solutions are growing in popularity when it comes to mediation. Public blocks-based anchoring for immutability (e.g., Bitcoin or Ethereum does the timestamping) but actual operation is private or consortium chain. This design serves as a good approach in court to provide evidence, maintain confidentiality. For example, evidence and negotiation logs can be placed on public chains and anchored; the full content of the negotiation is on permissioned chains. The essential aspects to take into account about disputes resolution platform are:

Scalability: Being able to manage large numbers at complex multi-party mediations.

Finality: Transaction's finality that happens by fast and irreversible transaction confirmation.

Governance: Platform changes and dispute resolution procedures clearly defined within the system.

Motivation: Making it possible for all legal and payment systems to interoperate.

Resist attacks, key management for parties.

Challenges remain significant. Volatility, cost uncertainty, and lack of privacy are problems associated with public platforms. Permissioned platforms may be less decentralized and are subject to certain centralization risks, but may be more appropriate. Uncertainties about the cross-border enforceability of the results from smart contracts remain an issue. Energy use by proof-of-work systems is also a sustainability issue for applications such as fair justice.

The outlook for the future is towards further specialization in the Adventist church. To usher in neutral outcome predictions, robust cryptography to ensure privacy, and oracles to validate real-world data, next-generation platforms are adopting AI capabilities. Whether governments or judicial institutions are increasingly experimenting with court-annexed mediation by using sovereign blockchain networks is ultimately up to interpretation (Bennet et al., 2024).

3. BLOCKCHAIN-ENABLED ONLINE MEDIATION SYSTEMS

The blockchain technology can transform online mediation platforms, combining essential elements of the mediation process with the power of blockchain technology. The Online mediation platforms powered by blockchain technology are a massive development of modern dispute resolution, encompassing crucial facets of the mediation procedure with blockchain technology. These mechanisms may be used to resolve disputes securely, transparently, and in a way that is enforceable in a digital world. Through the use of Blockchain, parties can send themselves for a mediation without sacrificing trust, transparency in evidence and accountability for the process. These platforms are especially useful in scenarios such as an international dispute, an issue in e-commerce agreements, a family-related issue, or a commercial disagreement where geographical distance and an absence of trust is a significant element. They facilitate video conferencing, document exchange, negotiation, record-keeping, execution of smart contracts, and cryptographic verification while maintaining the immutability of the document record. This creates a more effective, protected and user friendly mediation process which would improve access to justice, save costs and time (Salger, 2024).

3.1 Architecture of Blockchain-Based Mediation Platforms

The Commodore's Architecture is usually multi-layered hybrid structured for security, scalability and usability, in line with blockchain based mediation solutions. The backbone is the blockchain layer, which may be permissioned (e.g., Hyperledger Fabric) or hybrid, and is used for all critical actions, such as evidence uploads, evidence timestampping, logs of negotiations, settlement agreements, and more. The application layer enables user friendly interfaces, including secure video/audio conferencing, real-time chat, and co-editing of documents using web or mobile applications.

The Decentralized systems for storing large files, such as IPFS; only cryptographic hashes are stored on the blockchain. Smart Contracts are used for automating workflows like escrow, conditional payments, and ensuring compliance with agreements between various parties. End-to-end encryption, role-based access control, zero-knowledge proof, multi-factor authentication are elements reinforcing security. An Oracle layer is used to add real world data if necessary. This architecture is modular in nature, which has the advantage of ensuring confidentiality of sensitive discussion and unchangeability of evidence and agreements. The governance modules also establish guidelines for mediator selection, updates of platforms and escalation of disputes in the system.

3.2 Integration of Blockchain with ODR Platforms

Combining blockchain with the current Online Dispute Resolution (ODR) platforms boosts their legitimacy and usability. Most traditional modes of ODR are communication- and case-management-based, like Modria or SAMA and CADRE in India. By applying the blockchain, this layer of immutable trust can be added to these systems.

Connecting the ODR front-end interfaces with the blockchain backends is done using APIs and middleware that enable and simplify integration. Every time a document is uploaded or every time a step is taken for a negotiation, a hash is generated and added to the blockchain at a certain time. Smart contracts are also packaged in to change these kinds of mediated deals into actionable ones. If parties agree to a settlement, for instance, the amounts of funds in blockchain escrow are immediately released based on the agreed conditions.

The most common integration models are hybrid, whereby sensitive negotiation materials stay away from the public blockchain or from public channels, but key milestones (agreement reached, evidence submitted, settlement signed) are recorded on the open, public blockchain for legal enforceability. This partnership also will mean there will be a seamless transition into mediation to arbitration or court proceedings, should that be desired, thanks to verifiable digital records. Properly integrating this necessitates taking a cautious approach with data protection, user experience, and electronic signature legislation.

3.3 Advantages over Conventional Online Mediation Tools

The Online mediation platforms that utilize the blockchain have some interesting advantages over traditional online mediation tools. The first attribute is immutability and trust: All communications, whether of evidence or final agreement, are unwritable and untamperable, which eliminates the problems disproportionately facing typical ODR systems of proving authenticity and/or trustworthiness. Second, smart contracts facilitate automated enforcement, which will increase compliance with the contract, since payments and obligations are handled automatically (with fewer post-mediation litigation) than they are with traditional contracts (Waseem et al., 2023).

Third, improved transparency and privacy parties can have assurance of process while maintaining privacy enabled by an increasingly complex and sophisticated means of facial cryptographic verification. Fourth, improved evidence management through cryptographic timestamping and chain of custody provides more solid evidence that can be used in court if mediation unsuccessful.

Moreover, these platforms streamline the process and minimize the involvement of intermediaries and paperwork, which contributes to significant cost reduction. They also advocate for improved cross-border and small-value dispute resolution. The blockchain-based reputation mechanisms facilitate the selection of qualified and independent mediators. Blockchain mediation offers several advantages over traditional methods that can be subject to manipulation or hacks, such as centralized servers.Overall, blockchain mediation is more efficient, more accountable, and more final than traditional mediation processes that may be rife with manipulation or breach.

4. SMART CONTRACTS IN MEDIATION AND SETTLEMENT AGREEMENTS

The smart contracts are one of the most remarkable use-cases of blockchain technology in contemporary dispute resolution. Medication-wise, they're utilized as electronic contracts that execute automatically when details are fulfilled, offering unparalleled efficiency, openness, and enforceability in mediation negotiations. The problem with traditional mediation is that often, the parties do not comply with the resolution, the enforcement of the resolution is lengthy, and the mediation is not as well-trusted. In contrast, mediated agreements can be defined as contracts, which are now being realized as smart contracts – which can be automatically executed and automatically enforced, and are stored on an unalterable distributed ledger.

The blockchain Mediation is a type of mediation in which parties negotiate the conditions with the help of a mediator with blockchain technology. After consensus is agreed, the settlement is recorded in a smart contract, one that collects the money, property or responsibility. This is an expression of a technological transformation which from mediation become finalizing/performance. Smart contracts are especially useful in cases involving commercial disputes, family settlement, consumer disputes and eventual cross-border cases where enforcement is difficult. They minimize the need for participation in the courts by parties, keep mediation confidential and non-voluntary. But, there are key considerations when it comes to the successful implementation of it, including balancing automation with the human element, legal compliance, and adaptability for the unexpected. The use of smart contracts is transforming mediation by making the leap from agreeing to actually performing, ensuring the current age of mediation is bringing justice to the people.

4.1 Concept And Functionality Of Smart Contracts

The Smart contracts are computer programs self-executing and on a blockchain that execute the terms of an agreement when certain conditions are met. They were initially envisioned by Nick Szabo in 1994 and were practically implemented with the creation of Ethereum in 2015. Smart contracts use code and cryptographic techniques, instead of legal enforcement, to provide their power.

The role of smart contracts in mediation is that they serve as the digital agent of a settlement, the impartial arbitrator, and the guard. These are essentially split into three parts: the code (or the terms and conditions), the condition or trigger (oracles, or data from the real-world), and the blockchain ledger that guarantees that the data is unalterable. Automatic execution, transparency (anybody can review the code) and tamper-resistant capabilities are key capabilities.

The Smart contracts can also contain intricate dispute resolution logic like multiple party approvals, tiered payment structures, milestone-based releases, and penalty clauses. Their working rule is based on "if this then that": If the goods are confirmed, payment is released (Wang et al., 2024). This eliminates subjectivity and interpretation conflicts. The Modern smart contracts also introduce "escape hatches" or an oracle-facilitated degree of flexibility to arrange with unusual circumstances. They offer enhanced transparency for obligations, and this can be seen in real-time in mediation platforms, particularly when there is no previous relationship between the conflicting parties.

4.2 Drafting and Executing Enforceable Settlement Agreements

When it comes to mediation, it is crucial for mediators to work in collaboration with lawyers and blockchain development teams to draft smart contract agreements. It involves the normal mediation procedures to discuss and reach a settlement on the substance. These terms are then translated into unambiguous, clear code, but are also left in a form understandable by human and accessible to everyone who has access to the code.

The best practice is to utilise smart contract libraries that are templated, reviewed and audited which are legally approved. Payment schedules, asset transfers, confidentiality requirements, and escalation processes for disagreements are translated into code.Payment schedules and transfers of assets, confidentiality requirements, and processes of escalating disputes are translated into code. A natural language contract and the code version are examined by the parities before they enter into an agreement with digital signatures. When everyone involved (and the mediator) gives cryptographic approval on the blockchain, execution takes place.

The execution phase is fully traceable. All of the signing and performance stages are recorded and timestamped and cannot be altered. In practice, most platforms employed a 'multi-signature' method where they need to be approved by all those involved before they are activated. This way, voluntariness is ensured, but unilateral changes are not acceptable. Hybrid models are expected to help resolve monetary issues via on-chain execution but to resolve off-chain obligations (such as “behavioral” requirements in family-related cases), a softer approach ought to be adopted. The quality of draft acts as a great leverage to the likelihood of court recognition and to avoid litigation risks in the future.

4.3 Automated Performance and Conditional Releases

There are several advantages to smart contracts in mediation, among them automated performance. The contract is activated through oracles (trusted data sources) or by party confirmations and operates automatically. This automation particularly helps in financial settlements whereby the savings that can be secured are automatically unlocked when milestones are achieved (Dylag & Smith, 2023).

Conditional releases provide sophistication to Mediation Outcomes. In a construction conflict, for example, the first steps of the project may be paid after successfully meeting verified project milestones that are monitored by IoT sensors or independent certification bodies. Child support payments can be drafted to be automatic monthly in family mediation. Clauses of penalization and/or incentive clauses can also be programmed (bonuses for early performance, penalties for late performance).

This process can drastically decrease enforcement costs and delays. Parties immediately and transparently know their obligations. However, there must be safeguards – most advanced systems have "Pause" or "Override" functionalities provided by multiple parties' consensus system – for true unanticipated situations. Smart contracts, in other words, are able to be automated and thus transform mediation from reaching agreement to real realization and compliance.

4.4 Legal Enforceability of Blockchain-Based Agreements

One of the biggest key areas to mediations and smart contracts is their legal enforceability. The code can be executed on the blockchain but it can not always be enforced by judicial recognition in classical courts. Currently, electronic agreements and smart contracts are recognised in a growing number of countries, including the USA, the UK, Singapore and many countries in the EU, via existing e-transaction laws.

The recognition of electronic records and digital signatures in India is supported by the Information Technology Act 2000 and the Bharatiya Sakshya Adhiniyam 2023. However, it is not always enough that the smart contract conform with the formal elements of a contract i.e accepting an offer, countering with an acceptance, providing consideration, and in the domain of most contracts, a lawful object. Parties and agreements based on natural language are typically considered in courts.

The Challenges involve trying to prove the purpose of the code, coding errors, and cases where the coding is automated too "rigidly" so that the results aren't fair. The Best practices suggest using audited code from trusted developers, legally reviewing the contract or obtaining legal opinions, and having a parallel traditional contract which references the smart contract for added enforceability. There are some jurisdictions which are proposing specific legislation that will predicably validate the smart contracts. Blockchain integrated mediated settlements are gaining support due to their growing knowledge of the judiciary. Knowledge of blockchains is growing and the blockchain mediated settlements being upheld is a big move towards digital justice.

5. ENSURING FAIRNESS, IMPARTIALITY AND ACCESS TO JUSTICE: ADDRESSING POWER IMBALANCES THROUGH TECHNOLOGY

Maintaining fairness, impartiality and access to justice is central to a successful mediation. Power differentials tend to detract from the mediation process in traditional mediation formats. Weaker parties (such as those with less financial means, legal information, social standing and/or technological access) may be forced to accept the decisions of stronger parties by intimidation or by depriving them of access to information. Blockchain-based mediation can provide significant technology solutions to help equalize some of these disparities and provide a more even playing field.

There are several important ways in which technology can mitigate the power differential. By providing anonymity and pseudonymity in the early negotiations phases, it helps minimise the gender, caste, economic, and reputation biases. For the weaker side of a dispute, like an employee or the victim of a landlord/tenant dispute, they can join the process without imminent fear of any negative action. Second, the power of the parties who are able to afford the time required for lengthy litigation or enforcement is significantly taken away as a result of smart contracts and automated escrow (Arnone & Giacalone, 2025). The funds and/or assets get locked and unlocked automatically by agreement, circumventing the capacity of strong individuals or entities to delay or refuse compliance.

Furthermore, blockchain platforms encourage transparency with controlled visibility. Each step of negotiations, evidence presented and mediations conducted are all listed and stored immutably in a way that protects confidentiality by using private channels and zero-knowledge proofs. This establishes an audit trail which discourages manipulative ways of doing things. Completely integrated on the blockchain, reputation systems based on past mediations assist parties in picking out really neutral and competent mediators, mitigating the chance of a skewed or inexperienced facilitator.

The blockchain mediation has an amazing impact on access to justice. Mediation and litigation are traditional, and are time-consuming, expensive, and location-specific. By eliminating physical locations, several attorneys, and reoccurring court cases, blockchain-based platforms massively cut down on expenses. Linking up to basic mobile phones from any location, offering justice for small businesses, people living in rural areas and for marginalized groups. The use of AI-powered tools can enable real-time translation services, making legal jargon easy to understand, and fairness scoring of proposed settlements, benefiting those who may be less informed.

Additionally, properly applied algorithmic support (with human oversight) could be used to determine whether a proposal is fair, and to identify unbalanced terms and suggest alternative, equitable paraphrases based on similar cases that have been resolved in the past. This diminishes the power of "aggressive negotiating". In cross-border conflicts, blockchain removes the ability to wield jurisdiction-based power plays, delivering a technology-based framework that is accepted on a border agnostic basis.

But the deployment of technology needs to be done carefully. The possibility arises of forming new "digital divides", with technologically adept parties benefit-ing. Strengthening platform design requires design interfaces that are easy to use for users, voice assistance and assistance for digitally illiterate users. Information privacy serves as a shield against the misuse of collected data by formidable actors (Chen, 2022). Information privacy helps to guard against the misuse of collected information by powerful actors.

The blockchain mediation has proven to be effective in achieving a delicate balancing between power in family disputes, consumer disputes and even employment conflicts. These relationship independent trust and cryptographic fairness systems enable the weaker parties to negotiate with greater confidence. In the end, instead of being replaced by blockchains, human mediators are enhanced and adopt more sense of fairness, with an unprecedented level of procedural justice. By handling the goals of equity and access to justice in the digital age with the platform of blockchain technology in a well-thought-out way, it becomes a potent potential for democratizing the dispute resolution.

6. LEGAL AND REGULATORY FRAMEWORKS: INTERNATIONAL AND INDIAN STANDARDS FOR DIGITAL AND BLOCKCHAIN MEDIATION

The legal and regulatory framework for digital and blockchain mediation is still dynamic, rapidly evolving and adapting to technological progress, along with maintaining fairness, enforceability and adherence to public policy. Around the world and in India, frameworks are slowly starting to recognize electronic proceedings and electronic based on blockchain agreements. International Standards are important indicators. The Model Law on Electronic Commerce (1996) and Model Law on Electronic Signatures (2001) of UNCITRAL provide for the functional equivalence between paper and electronic records. Singapore Convention on Mediation (2019) is a historic piece which paved the way for cross-border enforcement of agreements for settlement by mediation, which resembling New York Convention for arbitration. There are many countries who are synchronizing local laws so that it can enable this convention.There are many countries saying that they should sync up their local laws in order to help enable this convention.

The EU's eIDAS Regulation (Electronic Identification, Authentication and Trust Services) makes electronic signatures and qualifications electronic timestamps legal. If a blockchain record and a smart contract are not only accurate, but also secure and meet strength requirements, they could also serve as strong legal presumptions (Bhushan, 2023). The strict GDPR data protection requirements mandate that blockchain mediation platforms have to follow a "privacy by design" strategy, which includes off-chain nodes and zero-knowledge proofs as examples.

The Digital dispute resolution is encouraged in the United States by the Uniform Electronic Transactions Act (UETA) and the Federal Arbitration Act (FAA).

Many states have passed blockchain record and smart contract enabling legislation. Platforms such as Kleros run somewhere between the legal limbo, but they are being accepted on a worldwide scale with hybrid solutions that integrate between traditional contracts and code.

The Indian Legal Framework has been evolving in a progressive way. According to Section 4 and 5 of the Information Technology Act, 2000 (amended in 2008), electronic records and digital signatures are recognised. The Bharatiya Sakshya Adhiniyam, 2023 (BSA) updates the evidence rules by providing for admissibility of an electronic record, properly certified, as evidence.

Online Dispute Resolution (ODR) is encouraged through the Consumer Protection (Mediation) Regulations, 2020 and by the Ministry of Consumer Affairs. The roadmap of NITI Aayog for ODR in India makes it clear that technology is to be encouraged. At this time, there does not exist any specific legislation regarding mediation by blockchain, however the Digital Personal Data Protection Act, 2023 (DPDPA) regulates the taking care of of the information in mediation platforms. If smart contracts fulfil the provisions of the Indian Contract Act, 1872 like free consent, legality of consideration, and competent parties, they can be considered as valid contracts.Smart contracts can be seen as valid contracts if they demonstrate the conditions of the Indian Contract Act, 1872 namely free consent, lawful consideration, and competent parties.

There's a growing sense of acceptance from judges. In a time of electronic agreements, especially after COVID, Indian courts have validated electronic agreements and video-conferencing the whole process. Issues remain around the enforceability of purely code-based smart contracts and that the blockchain is definitely not identified as proof in the absence of a unique "person in charge" to certify it.

Some of the key regulatory gaps are the lack of clarity regarding the legal nature of on-chain settlements, liability for smart contract coding mistakes and standards for blockchain platform accreditation. Even with the Singapore Convention, it's complicated to enforce cross-border. Way Forward includes in-depth policy-making. Indian policy should specifically include rules on blockchain ODR, as it is in Singapore or Dubai. Essential elements include judicial training, standards for platform certification and linking to the court's mediation process.Judicial training, standards for certification of the platform, and linkage with court-mediated systems in the court are essential. To what extent blockchain mediation can provide a "scaleable platform for delivering justice" will be a function of the extent to which this can be achieved via a process of harmonization between international best practice and the domestic requirements. If the regulations are there, blockchain can place India at the forefront of technology for dispute resolution in the global scenario (Kumar & Singh, 2024).

7. CONCLUDING REMARKS

The blockchain technology can play a game-changing role in mediation in the digital era, offering in its way improved trust, assurance of evidence integrity, automation, and increased access to justice. It evolves mediation from trust-based to cryptographic certainty approach without compromising upon the confidentiality and voluntariness of the process. Despite the technical, legal and cultural hurdles, proactively developing policies, standards and engaging with stakeholders can open the door to the potential of blockchain. With growing intensity, conflicts are now happening in digital spaces, and blockchain-based mediation provides the answers for a future-proof dispute resolution system that brings justice into the 21st century, while improving the three key features of speed, fairness and accessibility.

Although no single mediation platform will be perfectly suited in every scenario, Hyperledger Fabric and Corda (as of now) seem to be the best options for enterprise usage for mainstream mediation because of their privacy, scalability and enterprise suitability. Ethereum-based solutions are outstanding for decentralized, public dispute resolution. The best solution frequently is hybrids, depending on the type of dispute – commercial, family, consumer, or international. The usage of blockchain platforms will become even more prevalent in providing faster, more inexpensive and more trustworthy justice in the future as regulatory frameworks are progressing and technical capacities are developing. In the dynamic field of dispute resolution, finding the right platform is essential for ensuring transparency, confidentiality, efficiency, and legal strength.

REFERENCES

Arnone, G., & Giacalone, M. (2025). Redefining Dispute Resolution Mechanisms for Digital Assets in the Metaverse: Exploring the Role of Blockchain and Emerging Technologies. *European Journal of Law and Technology*, *16*(2).

Bennet, D., Maria, L., Sanjaya, Y. P. A., & Zahra, A. R. A. (2024). Blockchain technology: Revolutionizing transactions in the digital age. *ADI Journal on Recent Innovation*, *5*(2), 192–199. DOI: 10.34306/ajri.v5i2.1065

Bhushan, T. (2023). The Impact of digital technologies on alternative dispute resolution. *Revista Brasileira de Alternative Dispute Resolution-Brazilian Journal of Alternative Dispute Resolution-RBADR*, *5*(10), 329–352. DOI: 10.52028/rbadr.v5i10.ART16.Ind

Chen, J. W. (2022). Dispute resolution in the new digital era-exploring arbitration as a suitable mechanism to resolve disputes over crypto assets. *Contemp. Asia Arb. J.*, *15*, 255.

Dylag, M., & Smith, H. (2023). From cryptocurrencies to cryptocourts: Blockchain and the financialization of dispute resolution platforms. *Information Communication and Society*, *26*(2), 372–387. DOI: 10.1080/1369118X.2021.1942958

Kadioglu Kumtepe, C. C. (2025). Unpacking the technology of trust: Establishing trust and fairness in online dispute resolution through blockchain and smart contracts. *International Journal of Law and Information Technology*, *33*, eaaf017. DOI: 10.1093/ijlit/eaaf017

Kovalchuk, O. Y., Dovhopolyi, Y. I., & Shliakhovchuk, M. V. (2024). Digital Technologies in Justice: Blockchain as an Innovative Way of Dispute Resolution. *JE Eur.*, *L*, 56.

Kumar, D. R., & Singh, P. (2024). The rise of the robo-mediator: AI's transformative role in alternative dispute resolution. *White Black Legal*, *3*(1), 1–11.

Poncibo, C., Gangemi, A., & Ravot, G. S. (2024). Blockchain justice: Exploring decentralising dispute resolution across borders. *JL, Mkt. &. Innovation*, •••, 14.

Salger, C. (2024). Decentralized dispute resolution: Using blockchain technology and smart contracts in arbitration. *Pepp. Disp. Resol. LJ*, *24*, 65.

Shmyndruk, O., Ustrytska, N., Serkevych, I., Baltadzhy, P., & Yasin, I. (2025). ICT and modern technologies for training professional mediators in restorative justice and related processes. *Revista Eduweb*, *19*(4), 175–187. DOI: 10.46502/issn.1856-7576/2025.19.04.11

Wang, S., Li, Y., & Khaskheli, M. B. (2024). Innovation helps with sustainable business, law, and digital technologies: Economic development and dispute resolution. *Sustainability (Basel)*, *16*(10), 3910. DOI: 10.3390/su16103910

Sharma, A., & Kumar, A. (2023). Transforming access to justice in the digital age: The role of e-courts. NUJS Journal of Regulatory Studies, 8(2).

Zhao, Y., & Chen, H. (2024). Enhancing access to digital justice: Digital governance of dispute resolution and dispute prevention in online commercial activities. *Journal of International Dispute Settlement*, *15*(2), 273–304. DOI: 10.1093/jnlids/idae001

Chapter 14
Regulatory and Admissibility Challenges:
Blockchain Evidence in Courts

Pradip Kumar Kashyap
http://orcid.org/0009-0007-8156-2767
School of Legal Studies, CGC University, Mohali, India

Nirbhay Kumar Sharma
http://orcid.org/0009-0003-5304-6387
Mohammad Ali Jauhar University, Rampur, India

ABSTRACT

The chapter critically analyzes regulatory and admissibility issues arising from the use of blockchain evidentiary in court. However, as blockchain is increasingly being adopted in the field of digital forensics and criminal investigation, law enforcement and judicial authorities around the globe are encountering considerable challenges in assessing blockchain technology's reliability, authenticity and compliance with current evidentiary rules and procedures. The chapter discusses how the nature of digital evidence has changed over time, the new legal issues that blockchain immutability and decentralized structure creates, and its significant impact on cybercrime prosecutions. It covers a range of admissibility considerations, regulatory deficiencies, authentication issues, privacy concerns and precedent. The main objective of this study is to fill the gap between technological innovation and judicial acceptance, so evidence collected via blockchain can be withstand in strict court procedures, and enhance the global combat against cybercrime.

DOI: 10.4018/979-8-3373-9730-6.ch014

1. INTRODUCTION

While blockchain offers new possibilities and difficulties in criminal investigations, it also provides a chance to enhance forensic methods and solve complex cases.The application of blockchain technology in criminal investigations is fraught with both opportunities and complexities for the judiciary worldwide and can be a way to improve forensic processes and tackle complex cases. In the days of growing attention to digital evidence that has been secured via blockchain, courts become more and more forced to tread into uncharted legal waters about the admissibility, reliability, and probative value of blockchain-secured digital evidence. Such features of blockchain as immutability, decentralization, cryptographic verification, distributed ledgers, and others are putting traditional rules of evidence under severe tests, which were adopted primarily for physical or easier electronic records (Park & Jeong, 2026).

The chapter offers in-depth coverage of the challenges for blockchain-based evidence in court, the regulation, and admissibility. It explores the impact of this disruptive technology on judicial systems, how they are changing to meet this challenge, and the very essence of justice, fairness, and due process. The discussion covers different legal traditions, in particular common law and civil law countries and has a specific focus on India's developing common framework based on the Indian Evidence Act and the Indian Information Technology Act.

The real conflict comes when presenting blockchain technology with existing legal frameworks. The key conflict is between the technological attributes of blockchain and legal rules. Compared to traditional digital evidence, blockchain provides greater tamper resistance and auditability, but still has a lot of challenges that need to be resolved in regard to authentication, chain of custody, expert testimony requirements, etc., and compliance with data protection laws. The problems are exacerbated when the case is of transnational cybercrime. In addition, there is currently no specific legislation on blockchain evidence that has been put in place to clarify the requirements for assessing such evidence, leaving how to do so under laws in force, open to interpretation and therefore uncertain. Judges, prosecutors and defense attorneys by themselves may not have the technical expertise required for the adjudication process. This opening section lays the groundwork, explaining the dynamic nature of digital evidence, the unique challenges presented by blockchain, and its importance in addressing these to ensure a successful digital criminal justice system.

1.1 The Evolving Landscape of Digital Evidence in Judicial Systems

Digital evidence is no longer a side issue in the modern-day court case, but has instead become an integral component of the judicial process. In the last 20 years, even as courts have increasingly turned to physical documents and oral testimony, they have also become increasingly accepting of emails and social media records, along with information captured on surveillance cameras, cell phones and via cloud storage. The changes have required periodic changes in evidence laws and procedures all over the world (Chamim et al., 2025).

The Information Technology Act, 2000, in India, introduced Section 65A and 65B of the Indian Evidence Act, to legally base the admission of electronic records. The same adaptation has been seen all over the world, with various regulatory bodies creating their own procedures and guidelines on digital forensics. The vast scale, complexity and dynamism of digital evidence today has however highlighted many shortcomings of the traditional methods applied to it. Problems such as easy manipulation, metadata changes and chain of custody issues have decreased the occurrences of authenticity and reliability issues.

The judicial systems have faced a new generation of digital evidence enabled by the new technologies, such as artificial intelligence, IoT and distributed ledger systems. The technology used to produce or secure evidence will also need to be taken into account by courts when assessing evidence. It has necessitated development of the technical expert testimony and constituted more responsibility for the judges to be familiar with sophisticated technological issues.

1.2 Unique Challenges Posed by Blockchain Technology

Blockchain technology has some unique issues raised that are different from traditional digital evidence. While its basic property (decentralization, immutability, cryptographic hashing, and distributed consensus) provides excellent security, it also presents particular interpretation challenges for courts. The authenticity and reliability of blockchain records is one of the main challenges of this technology (Goel et al., 2026). Older evidence rules depend upon the proper working of the system and that the system has not been tampered with. Understanding of advanced topics like consensus mechanisms, hashing algorithms, public/private/consortium blockchain chains etc. is required which is not the case with the regular court. Technical challenges with most judges and lawyers in determining if the blockchain implementation is reliable to meet the reliability standards.

There's another substantial drawback that springs out from the faint, and that is the discentralized nature of the ledger. A centralized database with a single control authority does not exist on blockchain. The blockchain is not a centralized database with one authority controlling it and asking the question who should take responsibility for what? For hybrid architectures, where raw data is stored in the cloud while hashes are on-chain, it is especially challenging to achieve a full chain of custody.

The next level of challenge is introduced with the use of smart contracts. Courts need to determine whether automated code executions can be used in court as sound evidence and who is responsible for the coding mistakes or unintended consequences. The non-refudiability, one of the services most touted benefits, also poses problems on the rights of privacy, especially the "right to be forgotten."

1.3 Importance for Criminal Justice and Cybercrime Prosecutions

The successful acceptance of blockchain evidence is crucial for the future of criminal justice, and it can play a key role in the fight against cybercrime. The cyber threat landscape, including ransomware, financial fraud, identity theft, and the abuse of the dark web, creates exponentially large amounts of unique digital evidence that's easy to manufacture in case a dispute arises in the future. The potential of blockchain to give cryptographically verifiable timestamps, immutables audit trails, and unlocking 'chain of custody' for such evidence can make it a much harder case to crack.

For cybercrime prosecutions, where the attribution and timeline can be challenging, blockchain can provide objective, unalterable evidence that can improve the results for prosecution. It can allow you to find out at what point the evidence was gathered, who has handled the evidence, and whether there has been any tampering or alterations all of which can often be essential to making or breaking the case. A legally sound blockchain record can quell protracted admissibility battles, cut down on the use of on-demand expert testimony, and enhance prosecutors' certainty in regards to conviction in technology-enabled crimes. Apart from each specific instance, international cooperation platforms and contemporary law enforcement forensic technologies would gain further traction if it was no longer an obstacle in judicial adoption (Zhuk, 2025).

2. LEGAL STANDARDS FOR EVIDENCE ADMISSIBILITY

The underlying basis for determining admissibility of evidence, particularly relevant to criminal trials, is legal standards for evidence generated by blockchain. Legal standards for evidence generated by blockchain constitute the foundation to address admissibility of evidence – especially relevant to criminal cases. These standards are used to assess the reliability, relevance, authenticity and probative value of evidence. As blockchain technology has entered into the legal space, courts around the globe have been using and adapting blockchains as a new mode of digital evidence. The central hurdle is the need to compare blockchain's technical attributes, like immutability and cryptographic hashing, with the historic evidentiary tests created for bodily records or more easily, digital ones.

The evidence must be admissible if it is considered to be relevant to the facts in issue, that it has scientific reliability, that it had been collected and preserved in proper procedure, and that the prejudice caused (or) does not exceed the probative value. When it comes to blockchain evidence, courts will need to evaluate specific information involved in the blockchain usage - whether public, private or consortium, consensus mechanism, security protocols and system integrity. Expert testimony is a key element in communicating these science–based concepts to the court. There are differing tests in different jurisdictions which can be inconsistent, particularly in cross-border cybercrime cases. Some systems value the reliability and consistency of the procedure and others have a higher focus on meeting statutory requirements for an electronic record. Lack of specific blockchain legislation presents a challenge to the courts in applying existing laws in novel ways (Adinda et al., 2025).

2.1 Daubert and Frye Standards (United States)

For blockchain records and other scientific and technical types of evidence, the Daubert standard adopted by the Supreme Court in Daubert v. Merrell Dow Pharmaceuticals (1993) dominates admissibility in federal court in the United States. The Daubert test calls on judges to serve as gatekeepers and determine whether the evidence is relevant and reliable. The significance of these factors for courts is as follows: (1) Can the theory or technique be (and has been) tested; (2) Has the theory or technique been peer reviewed and published?; (3) What is the rate of error known or potential?; (4) General acceptance in the relevant scientific community, and the maintenance of standards controlling technique operation?

This poses both opportunities and challenges for blockchain evidence. The underlying principles of cryptography (sha-256, digital signatures, merkle trees) have been proven and are commonly used in computer science. Implementations, however, and particularly private or consortium blockchains in police activities may not have broad peer-reviewed studies or known error rate. Courts might require specifics concerning the blockchain platform, consensus strategy, access measures, and security audits.

Under the older (and still used in some state courts) Frye test, the scientific methodology must be "generally accepted" in the relevant scientific community. Frye might otherwise pose problems with blockchain evidence, considering the term is relatively new to the judicial system and is still slowly being accepted by judges. In reality, U.S. courts have started to consider blockchain evidence in cases involving tracing cryptocurrencies and verifying the supply chain. Proponents will generally introduce expert witnesses to discuss such imutability, the accuracy of the timestamping, and the chain of custody process. Issues are often encountered around the "51% attack" (as in a public chain privacy restrictions), whether the smart contract is vulnerable, or whether there are human errors within the off-chain data processing.

2.2 Indian Evidence Act, 1872 (Section 65A & 65B) and IT Act Provisions

In India, the use of blockchain evidence is subject to the admissibility of evidence in general, which is subject to Sections 65A and 65B of the Indian Evidence Act, 1872 that were added by the Information Technology Act, 2000. If any part of an electronic record is proved by virtue of Section 65A, this section may be used to prove its contents. Printed on paper or recorded, or copied, in optical or magnetic media, or produced by a computer, section 65B(1) declares any information to be a document and admissible as evidence without needing to prove that it is the original information in print, record, or magnetic media, etc (Saputra & Kusumah, 2025).

The qualifying conditions of section 65B (4) must be met and a certificate, issued by a person holding a responsible official position is required. This certificate should indicate the electronic record, its source, and certify that the computer was being used in an appropriate manner during the period in question. In the case of blockchain evidence, this asks questions of practicality: who is going to issue the certificate when about to operational channels are decentralised or consortium? How to certify operation of a distributed network?

The Information Technology Act, 2000, also acknowledges the electronic records and digital signing (Section 4 and Section 5) and provides the definition of 'secure electronic signature' and 'hash' function. Using cryptographic hashing, as blockchain does, is well-suited to these surlivability terms. But blockchain and distributed ledger technology is not specifically mentioned in the law, which creates some gaps in interpretation.

2.3 Common Law vs. Civil Law Jurisdictions

When it comes to the use of blockchain evidence, common law and civil law regions boom altogether. The admissibility of blockchain evidence differs greatly among common law and civil law jurisdictions, stemming from fundamental differences in legal philosophy and differing approaches to evidence. Common Law systems are adversarial systems (USA, United Kingdom, India, Australia). Rules on evidence admissibility are carefully framed, and pay close attention to the reliability of the evidence, relevance of the evidence, and fairness of the evidence. US judges rely on precedent and cross-examination and expert testimony, and are considered as gatekeepers (Daubert/Frye). Evidence of blockchain is expected to be met with stringent challenges on the issues of authenticity and chain of custody. Common law permits development over time via case law: If enough case law develops, help for blockchain may just end up being there. The burden of proof involved, however, can often result in an extended admissibility battle and the confrontational style can strain relationships.

Most of continental Europe, China, Japan and many Latin American nations adopt an inquisitorial system. Judges are more involved in the fact-finding by themselves and are less governed by the strict rules of evidence that exclude evidence. Increased focus on allowing the courts to "free evaluate" evidence. This may enable blockchain evidence to be better admitted, even if not based on stringent technical requirements, if the judge is convinced of the overall reliability of the blockchain evidence. Often there is less clarity about how blockchain evidence is being marked up for use, however, due to the absence of detailed cross-examination and precedents.

In many civil law countries, the civil procedure law has been revised to include the notion of electronic evidence, but a special provision on the blockchain is not common. The Electronic Identification and Trust Services (eIDAS) regulation by the European Union could serve as a basis for electronic evidence, including blockchain evidence.

3. REGULATORY GAPS AND LEGAL RECOGNITION OF BLOCKCHAIN EVIDENCE

Despite its maturity and widespread adoption in the industry, blockchain evidence is not yet recognized as legal proof in most judicial systems across the world and its potential application to these areas are still grappling with legal hurdles. Its promise of increased data security, transparency and auditability is ideal for blockchain technology, but most legal frameworks predate the advent of distributed ledger technology. This forms a huge disproportionality between technology and law. At this moment, few countries have laws concerning the admissibility, validity and evidence of blockchain records in criminal or civil proceedings.

The big problem is that there is no clarity and agreement on what is legitimate blockchain evidence. Legacy laws, designed to apply to traditional paperwork or simple electronic submissions, are tasked with assessing very complex decentralized systems in court. It often means that cases are not certain, not consistent and that law enforcement have not been willing to commit to blockchain-based solutions. The key challenges for regulators are the need for common benchmarking tools to assess various blockchain types (public, private, consortium, and hybrid), establishing criteria for smart contract validity as proof, establishing a framework for cross-border recognition of blockchain records, and providing guidance on hybrid architectures that combine on-chain and off-chain data.

Legal recognition has several prongs: the first being whether blockchain records are evidence according to evidence laws, the second requiring that they display high evidence of authenticity and reliability, and the third whether they have a presumptive evidentiary value. While in many jurisdictions, electronic evidence still must be certified or expertly validated, these demands may also lead to some problems employed to decentralized ledges. There are tons of questions unanswered regarding livability and liabilities regarding character, violation of rights, and jurisdiction in relation to distributed nodes, and what occurs if they crash?Questions concerning character in relation to jurisdiction, legal status of consensus mechanisms are only a handful of other concerns that are unanswered.

In addition, data protection and privacy laws, like GDPR in Europe and the DPDP Act in India, contrary to the immutability principle of a blockchain (Santillan-Lima et al., 2025). The "right to forget" directly questions the idea of having records that cannot be deleted from the blockchain. There are other regulatory issues that are unclear, including the standardization of the evidence collection process for blockchain technology, requiring security and audit protocols for use as evidence in court, and accreditation of platforms for blockchain use in laws enforcement.

The lack of broader regulation makes it difficult for the judiciary to accept blockchain evidence as valid, because they do not necessarily mean it is invalid, but that they don't know the rules of the game. This results in a slower rate of progress with technology that can prove very valuable in crimes, and gives more creative criminals an opportunity to make use of leaks that may exist in the evidence. To fill such regulatory gaps, there has to be a coordination between legislatures, judiciaries, technologists and law enforcement agencies. There is a need to better balance innovation with protections for fairness, privacy and due process in future regulations. If that is not the case, using blockchain technology in resolving cybercrime in the absence of development will be largely underutilised to its potential of enhancing digital evidence and improving the cybercrime prosecution.

3.1 Absence of Specific Blockchain Evidence Laws

Blockchain lacks any specific blockchain evidence laws, and this is the most elementally missing piece in the regulation that still holds back the judicial acceptance of this paradigm-changing technology. While the number of countries with specific laws concerning blockchain technology is rising, most nations still have general provisions for electronic evidence from laws enacted early in the internet era, before blockchain entered the picture. The lack of legislation leaves courts only with technological solutions that rely on an old model of data storage, verification, and governance (Siddharth, 2025).

For example, blockchain, distributed ledgers, cryptographic hashing, and smart contracts are not explicitly referenced in India; its Electronic Records and E-Signature Regulations envision such items but lack the specificity or breadth needed to make the regulations practical for those who wish to adopt blockchain technology and smart contracts to achieve these goals. Again, there is no specific treatment of blockchain in either the federal or state evidence rules in the United States, and judges are left to come up with case-by-case Daubert decisions. While there has been progress with eIDAS regulations on electronic trust services, the rules don't go far enough in fully accommodating blockchain evidence in criminal proceedings.

This lacuna in the law constitutes several, real-world challenges. First, there is no clarity over what is the minimum level of technical standards which blockchain system needs have to have to be seen as reliable for court use. What is not clear are the requirements for the consensus algorithm, who is allowed to join the network, how it will be governed, or how secure it is. Second, it's a bit confusing how much weight should be given to blockchain records. Can they get a presumption of reliability like government issued documents or must all the time be backed by substantial expert testimony?

Cross-border evidence sharing is also difficult due to the absence of specific laws. It becomes much harder to provide mutual assistance when the courts of one country are likely to accept evidence from blockchain transactions and another country's courts won't. In most legal systems, there are still unanswered questions about which jurisdiction's law would apply to a specific distributed ledger, how the laws would be interpreted in case of a conflict, and what weight would foreign blockchain records be given in a way? The major obstacles is the lack of a standardised process for the collection, preservation and presentation of blockchain evidence. Unlike the standard digital forensics where set standards are available and there are specific digital forensics best practices and required protocols, blockchain evidence handling does not have universal best practices nor required protocols (Popal et al., 2025). This heightens exposure of need for proper handling which might result into evidence rejection.

In addition, by being immutable, blockchain directly challenges current laws regarding privacy and data protection. Today most of the regulations can't keep pace with permanently recorded data that can't be erased or adjusted. If no legislation outlines specific exceptions, or offers more practical solutions (such as zero knowledge proofs, or "editable" It also stifles investment due to the lack of legislation.

While mocha and coffee are popular in coffee shops, providing the chain of custody evidence is questionable is the equivalent of a dream of a different kind.When the evidence in court is not clear, it's like mocha and coffee in a coffee shop: agencies and tech providers wouldn't want to deploy or build blockchains on a large scale. This leads to a slow progress in the modernization of digital forensics, even though there is a growing need to fight the growing cybercrime situation.

Countries therefore, must develop stand-alone legislation related to blockchain evidence or general amendment of the evidence acts. These should establish criteria for what is admissible, requirements for security and audit, international cooperation frameworks and a definition of key terms, as well as mitigate privacy issues. Until specific blockchain evidence laws are put in place, it is likely that each case will be individually handled by a judge using evidence rules and expert testimony that will stay piecemeal and inconsistent.

4. AUTHENTICATION AND CHAIN OF CUSTODY CHALLENGES: PROVING AUTHENTICITY OF BLOCKCHAIN RECORDS IN COURT

One of the most difficult and important issues when blockchain will appear in court as evidence in criminal investigations is substantiating it as a true record. For authentication, it is necessary to establish that the document is the document being presented, that it does not contain alterations that lie outside the scope of the existence and/or knowledge of a person, and that it connects with the facts in issue. The technology behind blockchain could, in principle, provide greater authenticity by securing cryptographically that no one alters the data or that participants in the chain (admittedly a small group) are not the ones under suspicion of wrongdoing. The idea of blockchain technology is to be more authentic through cryptographic security, decentralized verification as well as set-up to make sure that no one would be able to tamper with the data or that a smaller group of people (Badkul et al., 2025). Blockchain participants were targeted by those in charge of the verification process. Instead of the standard physical or digital evidence that has easily visible stamps or a server log to back them up, blockchain offers a completely different type of evidence. To call it a type of evidence without looking at it is an understatement: blockchain evidence operates on abstract mathematical rules that most lawyers know nothing of and are unable to independently evaluate.

So the essence of blockchain is cryptographic hashes—cryptographic functions that produce "hash" codes or digital fingerprints of the different blocks, forming this unbreakable chain. If Redmond attempted to modify one letter of the record stored in the database, the hash sum would change and the record would be immediately known to be changed. Timestamps from the network also set the date of when each piece of evidence was recorded. Public-key cryptography based digital signatures can enable verification of the identity of the party that added the record. In concept, these features take into account that they make blockchain records extremely reliable. But, realistically, any court will require stringent evidence that the target blockchain actually enabled the behavior that the party is alleging, that evidence was properly ingested, and that vulnerabilities were not exploited in the process.

The first type of problem is the difference between various blockchain types. Public Blockchains such as Bitcoin or Ethereum are the most transparent and decentralized, but they come with risks that include 51% attacks (which is very difficult in large networks), transactions being malleable, and there is no control over who joins the network. Permissioned or consortium blockchains offer higher levels of control and privacy, a desirable feature for law enforcement, but with increased concerns over centralization (Bhattacharjee et al., 2025). A consortium blockchain involving a limited number of primary trusted nodes (police agencies, forensic labs and judicial authorities) may be questioned at court, with regard to its decentralized trust model designed to represent this credibility. Defenders can also contend that where all nodes are under the investigative control of the same agency, there is no independence and the system is effectively open to infiltration or collusion among its members.

Having plain evidence files on fileshare servers in the cloud and just hashes and metadata on the blockchain raises even greater authentication challenges. Prosecutors can be required to demonstrate, in addition to the integrity of on-chain data, that the off-chain data is a perfect match for the blockchain hash. This involves the proper establishment of linking mechanisms, like content-addressed storage (IPFS for instance with pinning), real-time integrity checks, and verifiable evidence of lack of substitution of file contents. Any flaw in crucial management, account access or content synchronization can lead to suspicion regarding authenticity.

It's just as hard to build a reliable chain of custody in blockchain systems. The traditional method of chain of custody uses signoffs, manual documentation, physical seals. Blockchain does this automatically by storing every access, transfer, and change in the blockchain through smart contracts, which are non-hackable. Courts have to be sure, however, that the steps taken from the very time the evidence was seized at the crime scene, to the imaging of the evidence, hashing, uploading to the blockchain, analysis, and presentation in court, have been properly recorded and protected. This not only establishes that the private keys were maintained with security, but also meant that only authorized personnel had access to it and that no private keys were modified before the data was anchored onto the blockchain. Decentralized means there is no "original custodian" unlike in traditional law, thus questioning the idea of possession and control.

This means that expert evidence is essential to proving blockchain evidence when used in this field. Experts should break down topics that involve a lot of information, such as Merkle trees, consensus protocols (Proof of Work, Proof of Stake, Practical Byzantine Fault Tolerance), zero-knowledge proofs, among other things, and the security assumptions of the selected blockchain platform (Jaradat & Rabab'ah, 2026). It is the Daubert standard in the US or the requirement of Section 65B in India that the expert is required to establish that the technology is reliable, tested and properly applied in the specific case. Defense counsel may question the credentials of the expert, its peer-reviewed status of the blockchain implementation, or how difficult it may be to mount a sophisticated attack, including a smart contract compromise, an eclipse attack on nodes or a social engineering attack on key personnel.

The major challenge is the lack of transparency in the blockchain technology sphere within the eyes of judges and juries. If no non-technical explanations are provided backed by a proof, it's possible that courts will deem blockchain records less probative or evenworthy of being dismissed.If a non-technical explanation is not explained, there is a risk that explanations based on blocks could be rejected or even be assigned low value. The effective presentation of blockchain evidence frequently involves the presentation of visual aids, simplified analogies, demonstration of hash verification in real time, and independent compliance assurance of the system. Some progressive courts have designated technological assessors. or other government-certified forensic laboratories to certify blockchain platforms.

Choices of authentication are compounded in cross-border situations. There is a potential for conflicts between jurisdictions as a result of the different standards there might be with regard to the recognition of foreign blockchain records. A blockchain record that is accepted in country A is accessible in country B might be challenged more strongly, especially in regards to data sovereignty or residency. This makes international cybercrime investigations on the basis of shared evidence platforms difficult.

All that is required to make successful authentication possible, however, is careful preparation to overcome these difficulties. Best practices consist of incentivizing court-approved or independently certified blockchain sites, maintaining detailed system documentation, regular system penetration testing and security audits, multi-signature controls for critical operations, and backup and storing every raw data set with verifiable links to the blockchain. Several jurisdictions are slowly taking the first steps towards establishing the presumption of validity for blockchain records created by government-authorized record-keeping systems, akin to the status of validated government documents.

The final steps in adopting blockchain evidence within court proceedings are the willingness of judges to recognize and trust this form of evidence. Ultimately, judicial acceptance of blockchain evidence relies on bridging the gap between

Technological reality and Legal understanding. As the number of cases goes into the courts and precedents are set, it is likely that the procedure to establish authenticity will be made easier (Bhatti, 2026). Until there is new legislation hammered out and standardized procedures established, however, obtaining the authenticity of blockchain records will likely be an undertaking of considerable resources, quality expert testimony and case preparation.

5. PRIVACY, DATA PROTECTION AND HUMAN RIGHTS CONCERNS

Some of the most complex issues in the adoption and enforcement of blockchain evidence in court are related to privacy, data protection, and human rights issues. The immutability is core to the blockchain and in turn, conflicts with fundamental rights to privacy and data protection during crime investigations while ensuring unparalleled integrity and transparency within investigations. This conflict has created an important regulatory and ethical issue in numerous countries.

The biggest problem is the legal obligation for the right to be forgotten in norms like the General Data Protection Regulation (GDPR) of the European Union and Digital Personal Data Protection (DPDP) Act, 2023, in India. With the append-only principle of blockchain, the data that has been recorded is technically difficult or impossible to delete or erase once being added. When data subject rights are detected, it's tricky if sensitive personal data, like victim information, suspect biometrics, or communications, is secured via a blockchain connection. Courts and regulators are concerned that some customers might be permanently stigmatized or have their right to privacy violated if immutable ledgers are implemented, notably because they may be exonerated or found not guilty of the crimes at a later point in time (Igonor et al., 2025).

These concerns are heightened in cross-border platforms for sharing evidence. Data may be gathered in one country that falls outside the privacy laws of another. Data gathered in a country, may not conform to another Country's stricter privacy laws. It is very difficult to define DPDP and GDPR requirements on a consortium blockchain when sharing evidence with agencies of different countries in the Indian and European zone, for instance. Two key principles of the modern approach to data protection, such as data minimization, purpose limitation and storage limitation, are hard to reconcile with blocks which are transparent and have no limits.

The implications of privacy go far beyond human rights. Use of mass surveillance, creep and possible misuse of blockchain evidence systems by the state are real harms that require concern. A lack of a proper regulatory regime on the law enforcement blockchain systems could turn these systems into the powerful tools to track citizens outside the legal process of a criminal investigation. There could be increased risk for vulnerable groups such as journalists, activists and political dissidents in authoritarian-oriented regimes. In an adverse scenario, the use of blockchain evidence might lead to skewed sentencing, with blockchain evidence believed and trusted more than other pieces of evidence that may fail to be accepted, potentially resulting in greater conviction than warranted and disregarding the presumption of innocence.

Some methods like anonymization and pseudonymization can be used, and are improved by certain methods like zero-knowledge proofs, ring signatures and the confidential transactions, but these are not always effective for the full purpose. Identities can still be revealed by sophisticated de-anonymisation techniques and identifying the on-chain and off-chain data. Also, informed consent may also be questioned when the usage of blockchain in forensics entails that information concerning victims or third parties is stored on distributed ledgers.

These considerations need sound architectural decisions, such as the use of permissioned and hybrid blockchain that are well protected with privacy enhancing technologies, as well as strong legal protections, independence in oversight, frequent privacy impact reviews, and clear judicial instructions. In essence, finding a balance between effective law enforcement and basic human rights would be one of the most important challenges for policymaker and courts as blockchain evidence becomes more commonplace in the courtroom. When these do not receive careful attention these are likely to be the cause of constitutional challenges, backlash by the public and delayed implementation of the technology (Apsimet et al., 2026).

6. CONCLUSION AND FUTURE DIRECTIONS

To summarize, today the advent of blockchain technology into the realm of criminal evidence offers a promising opportunity for the advancement of digital forensics and cybercrime cases; however, certain legal and evidentiary hurdles, together with regulation and human rights concerns remain to be addressed. The three key aspects of blockchain which make it effective in addressing longstanding issues of evidence tampering, authenticity claims, and poor audit trail - immutability, cryptographic verification and automated chain of custody. As explained in the chapter, though, significant gaps in the law, case law, privacy, and international alignment of legal frameworks, judicial interpretation, and privacy protections still exist, and need to be overcome if blockchain evidence is to reach its maximum potential in courts.

The main challenges covered are the lack of specific blockchain evidence legislation, challenges in satisfying existing evidence-admissibility requirements (such as Daubert, Section 65B, etc.), authentication issues in intended types of hybrid systems, and the dual nature of "immutability" and privacy and enforcement. All these challenges are made even more difficult, if encountered in a trans-border setting, where two competing legal traditions coexist with sovereignty issues. However, despite these obstacles, early judicial decisions, and government pilots suggest there is a moderately positive trend toward acceptance.

In the future, there are a series of directions that should be focused on. To begin with, countries should take steps to clearly define the nature of blockchain record-keeping with specific legislation or overall amendments to evidence acts to ensure admissibility of these records, establish minimum security standards, and respond to privacy concerns. Second, global collaboration between entities such as the Budapest Convention, INTERPOL and UNCITRAL needs to grow around establishing a greater degree of harmonisation of the evidence exchange practices regarding Blockchain and mutual recognition.

Thirdly, capacity building is essential. The implementation of judicial academies to provide compulsory training on blockchain technology, digital forensics and privacy issue for judges, prosecutors, lawyers, etc. Fourth, there should be technical requirements and certification systems for blockchain systems that can be used in court, which can be established in collaboration with public and private parties. Advanced privacy-enancing technologies like zero-knowledge proofs and homomorphic encryption, as well as selective disclosure mechanisms, will play an important role in addressing privacy concerns.

Fifthly, there needs to be larger pilot initiatives or 'sandbox' regulatory regimes focused on blockchain proof that can be deployed in genuine judicial contexts to create precedents and best practices. Last but not least, there is a need for ongoing monitoring and third party evaluations of blockchain forensics technologies to preserve public confidence and safeguard human rights.

Whether blockchain will become a major force in the field of criminal justice will rely on the cooperation of technologists, legal experts, law enforcement and policy makers. By proactively addressing these challenges, blockchain evidence has the potential to greatly improve criminal justice systems globally in terms of efficiency, fairness, and credibility. Over the next ten years, it will be clear whether or not blockchain will become an integral part of digital evidence or a promising and still underused technology. If wisely regulated, technologically enhanced, and judicially adapted, blockchain can be a key enabler to a new age of fair and effective digital justice.

REFERENCES

Adinda, F. A., Rahmawati, E., Suparman, E., Arifin, R., & Ezzerouali, S. (2025). The challenge of admitting electronic evidence in civil procedure law. *Jurnal IUS Kajian Hukum dan Keadilan, 13*(3), 656-680.

Apsimet, N., Alimkulov, Y., Konysbay, B., Zhanibekov, A., & Muratova, A. (2026). Challenges of using digital evidence in pretrial investigations of online fraud: Lessons for Kazakhstan from international practice. *IDP. Revista de Internet. Derecho y Política*, (44), 1–17. DOI: 10.7238/idp.v0i44.433072

Badkul, S., Kishor, A., Juchnevicius, E., & Madvariya, S. (2025). Blockchain and the Future of Digital Evidence: Opportunities and Challenges for Law Enforcement. *Rethinking the Police for a Better Future: Navigating Policing Challenges with Accountability and Trust*, 287-297.

Bhattacharjee, T., Mahapatra, A. S., De, D., & Chowdhury, A. (2025). JudicBlock: Judicial Evidence Preservation Scheme Based on Blockchain Technology. *Blockchains, 3*(4), 11. DOI: 10.3390/blockchains3040011

Bhatti, N. (2026). The Use of Digital Evidence in Criminal Proceedings. *American Journal of Society and Law, 5*(1), 10–19. DOI: 10.54536/ajsl.v5i1.7211

Chamim, M., Widodo, K., Riyadi, S., Achyarsyah, P., & Faisal, F. (2025). The role of digital evidence in criminal law enforcement: Challenges of authentication and admissibility in court. *Research Horizon, 5*(6), 2987–2998. DOI: 10.54518/rh.5.6.2025.950

Goel, V., Ranjan, R., Baxtiyarovich, R. D., Ibragimovich, S. S., Reymbayevich, S. K., & Zafar, K. (2026, February). Blockchain-Based Evidence Management Systems for Judicial Integrity and Transparency. In *2026 5th International Conference on Innovative Practices in Technology and Management (ICIPTM)* (pp. 1-6). IEEE. DOI: 10.1109/ICIPTM69057.2026.11465195

Igonor, O. S., Amin, M. B., & Garg, S. (2025). The application of blockchain technology in the field of digital forensics: A literature review. *Blockchains, 3*(1), 5. DOI: 10.3390/blockchains3010005

Jaradat, M. S., & Rabab'ah, M. M. (2026). FinTech and AI technologies for Enhancing Evidence Verification and Dispute Resolution in Financial Litigation. *International Journal of Advances in Soft Computing and its Applications, 18*(1), 434-452.

Park, Y., & Jeong, D. (2026). A blockchain-based digital evidence management system: Integrating forensic procedures and multi-party authorization. *Information Processing & Management*, *63*(5), 104654. DOI: 10.1016/j.ipm.2026.104654

Popal, M., Ahmad, A., & Arshad, M. (2025). The Significance of Blockchain Technology in Preserving Digital Evidence Integrity in Forensic Investigations. *Journal of Computing & Biomedical Informatics*, *9*(02).

Santillan-Lima, J. C., Díaz, J. F., Piccirilli, D., Haro-Tufiño, K. A., Urgirles-Rodríguez, B., & Molina-Granja, F. T. (2025, October). Admissibility of digital evidence: integration of technical and legal standards in forensic and judicial contexts. In *International Conference on Advanced Research in Technologies, Information, Innovation and Sustainability* (pp. 252-266). Cham: Springer Nature Switzerland.

Saputra, D. H., & Kusumah, F. (2025). Blockchain Forensics and the Evidentiary Challenges of Crypto-Based Corruption in Developing Countries. *Indonesian Journal of Criminal Law Studies*, *10*(2), 615–658.

Siddharth, E. (2025). Time-Stamping in Blockchain for Legal Evidence Submission. *Sci. J. Artif. Intell. Blockchain Technol*, *2*(2), 34–42. DOI: 10.63345/sjaibt.v2.i2.205

Zhuk, A. (2025). Beyond the blockchain hype: Addressing legal and regulatory challenges. *SN Social Sciences*, *5*(2), 11. DOI: 10.1007/s43545-024-01044-y

Chapter 15
Regulatory and Admissibility Challenges in Male Victimization in Domestic Violence:
Blockchain Evidence in Courts

Sakshi Bhatnagar
Amity University, Gwalior, India

Vijay Srivastava
http://orcid.org/0000-0002-3034-9903
Amity University, Gwalior, India

Govind Singh Rajpal
http://orcid.org/0000-0002-3078-311X
MIT Art, Design, and Technology University, Pune, India

ABSTRACT

The social stigma, gender stereotypes, and systems biases experienced by men who have been victims of domestic violence (DV) extend underreporting to their cases, limiting access to justice. Threatening messages, contacts, financial documents, and videos are important pieces of evidence, but easily tampered with, or questioned as to authenticity, in these cases. The Blockchain technology is a potentially helpful solution as blockchain technology ensures immutability, no tampering, chain of custody and verifiable integrity of digital evidence. It aims to discuss the regulatory frameworks and the admissibility of the blockchain evidence in court, specifically in

DOI: 10.4018/979-8-3373-9730-6.ch015

the context of a typical male victimisation case. It studies legal rules (Daubert/Frye tests), privacy issues related to data protection laws, that judges don't consider, and that additional male bias adds to the difficult hurdle of evidence.

1. INTRODUCTION

The violence against women is a hugely underfunded area of domestic violence, with particular issues being male victimisation. There are number of forms of domestic violence recognised under DV Act in which adultery is also recognised as one of the forms of domestic violence come in the category of mental abuse (Singh & Naruka, 2019). The Research has shown that around one in ten men is physically or sexually abused or are stalked by an intimate partner, and probably many are psychologically abused as well. Although victimization rates are similar in some surveys, male victims are less likely to report victimisation because of the stigma (may be ashamed to admit to being a victim), others may not believe they were a victim of domestic violence, and there is a perception that domestic violence that is against women only (Harris, 2023). This underreporting results in inadequate protection, high rate of unreported abuse and systemic disadvantages in legal matters. The Digital evidence is the focal point of these cases from SMS threats and financial transaction data evidencing economic control to audio/video recording, emails, and social media posts. But in the case of traditional digital evidence tampering and lack of provenance is easily contested. Blockchain could boost the victim's rights; however, regulations and procedures are still not in place, nor is there judicial awareness. There is a pressing need to reform the policy, consider uniformization and training, to make justice accessible and available in an equitable manner, the study points out.

The blockchain technology comes to the rescue as a game-changing solution for safeguarding such proof. Blockchains provide an audit trail that is impossible to alter or fake, as it generates an immutable hash and a timestamp as soon as evidence is captured, giving an account of when the evidence was captured and by whom and making it verifiable. Sensitive files are left off-chain and blockchain eliminates the need to trust in the security of the systems and apps that rely on it, by recording incidents on the blockchain, with cryptographic proof on the distributed ledgers (Kumar et al., 2023). This is a useful tool in male DV cases to rebut false counter-allegations or establish patterns of coercive control which are often overlooked because of issues of gender bias. However, there are significant hurdles to regulators, for blockchain evidence to be adopted.

There is a lack of harmonisation around the regulation of digital and blockchain evidence. Admissibility is governed by Federal Rules of Evidence (FRE) 901 (authentication), 702/ Daubert (expert testimony), and 803(6) (business records) but there is no single federal rule particular to blockchain. There are some states, such as California, Arizona and Vermont which have a law recognizing blockchain records as electronically signed or admitting to evidence but each state has different laws. Other regulations, such as the EU's eIDAS at the international level, and GDPR at the national level, put an extra level of regulations and privacy features on top of blockchain's transparency, which are actually counterproductive. The Existing DV laws or policies have tended to be targeting women as the victim and the evidence requirements are different for boys and men, with a risk that blockchain evidence may be discarded if matched with an incomplete or incorrect context.

There are many aspects to admissibility challenges. The Daubert test is being used in courts to determine if blockchain technology and expert testimony is generally accepted, testable and reliable in the scientific community. Defence lawyers often put forward arguments about the technology's complexity and its lack of probative value, since jurors may be less familiar with the technology, such as hashes, consensus mechanisms, and smart contracts (Naseer et al., 2026). In male victimization cases, these technical issues converge with beliefs in the society, specifically that judges and jurors might be more skeptical of the testimony, and may believe that male criminals are more likely than female ones to be primary aggressors. When the first capture process is not forensic sound, there are issues with the chain of custody, while hearsay objections can be raised using the blockchain records for the truth of alleged abuse.

The added complexity is the privacy laws and data protection legislations. Sensitive information, like health and location data as found in DV cases, is important to work with legally, as GoBDP and other laws dictate. In a public blockchain, the identities of victims may be compromised, and compliance for a permissioned or hybrid blockchain must prove its worth. While the technology is developed, blockchain evidence can include information that could cause further damage to the male victim, who is already being doubtfully treated. But, the practice of cross jurisdictional cases only fuels further issues due to the incompatibility of the blockchain evidence standards with the underlying basis of mutual legal assistance treaties.

There is still a high degree of not being familiar with the court. The Judges and legal practitioners don't necessarily have strong technical expertise of blockchain, resulting in ineffective rulings. Added to this is the problematic role of gender stereotypes – research indicates that, for male victims, there is likely to be disbelief or a greater expectation of proof and less likelihood of receiving protection orders. Even strong evidence of a blockchain may be denied in court if it has a less vulnerable impression in the eyes of the court. Expert testimony is a critical component but is costly and complex, and for men, can be even harder to get because they may not have other resources to help.

The judicial precedents are in their beginning stages in the context of blockchain in the DV. While timestamps and hashes have been accepted by the courts in commercial and cryptocurrency cases, there are less frequently found cases using the DV. Past haste cases highlight the importance of a proper foundation, through experienced witnesses who will be able to explain immutability and system reliability. The successful admission of evidence often involves using blockchain evidence to fit a pattern of abuse for male victims and/or addressing the counterclaim about the fabrication of blockages.

The Targeted reforms are needed to overcome these challenges. Legislatures should craft gender neutral DV policies that have a specific position of blockchain-secured evidence. The need for judicial training programmes on use of digital forensic and blockchain is of the utmost importance (Lesiuk, 2023). However, to improve the admissibility of blockchain evidence, there is a need for standardisation of protocols for capturing such evidence, particularly with regards to mobile applications that victims might use. Naturally, in the future, privacy-preserving yet transparent architectures, based on zero-knowledge proofs, can mitigate regulatory disputes. Support groups for male victims ought to incorporate blockchain instruments and legal advocacy to create more robust cases.

Although blockchain holds great promise for confirming digital evidence in male gender domestic violence, the fragmentation of the regulatory landscape, combined with the technical difficulties of admissibility, and compounded by gender biases substantially capsits its effect. There is a need for cross-sectoral collaboration between the legal, technological and social fields in addressing these. With the right structures, blockchain can now help to balance the worlds, decrease wrongful dismissals and provide a fair justice for male victims (El-Kady, 2025). This potential must be fully achieved through future policies that focus on inclusiveness, technological competence of courts and on a design of crime victimization that prioritizes victims.

2. BLOCKCHAIN TECHNOLOGY FOR DOMESTIC VIOLENCE EVIDENCE: TECHNICAL IMPLEMENTATION IN DOMESTIC VIOLENCE CONTEXTS

The Technical implementation of blockchain for domestic violence (DV) evidence should be victim-centered, privacy first, with focus on safety of use, usability and legal acceptance. Situations of surveillance, device compromise or retaliatory actions are prominent features in DV contexts and are not just part of general digital forensics (Singh et al., 2025). In order to keep every system, there need to be discreet capture mechanisms, minimal exposure for potential abusers and strong encryption and a chain of custody that complies with court requirements for evidence.

A typical blockchain architecture is a hybrid setup. Thc victim takes pictures, videos, records conversation, visualizes and/or records screenshots of threats or call logs using a mobile application (e.g., HeHop or other prototypes). The app hashes the media file and associated metadata such as time stamp, GPS if safe; and received ID of the device that acquired it upon capture.The app hashes the media file and associated metadata (time stamp, GPS if safe, device ID on which the media file was captured). It is then, on the victim's local system, locally encrypted with high security standards, AES-256 or even stronger, and uploaded to the secure off-chain storage, such as IPFS (InterPlanetary File System), or an encrypted cloud fileshare, with a redundant backup of the file. These data elements of hash, timestamp and a unique evidence identifier are the only ones that are stored on the blockchain and provide proof-of-existence and proof-of-integrity that can't be changed.

The Permissioned and consortium blockchains, such as Hyperledger Fabric are better suited to the needs of DV applications, as compared to public ones. These are designed for controlled participation by properly-empowered individuals (the victim, support organizations, the police and the courts) in the group, with confidentiality expressed through private channels. Nodes can be managed by a trusted NGO, government agency or forensic service providers. In the case of smart contracts, the following functions are performed automatically: Critical functions such as evidence registration, access logging, and integrity verification are performed automatically by smart contracts. A smart contract can, for instance, mandate several forms of authentication before allowing access and record each view or transfer – leaving no scope for tampering and for an audit trail to be created.

It is important to have features that are discreet yet safe. Apps can use camo apps (stimulating like calculators or weather apps), record using voice or trigger words (such as in EviSafe) and operate even when the device is locked. Inert files can be used to carry evidence in the guise of a steganography technique (Alketbi, 2024). To prevent forensically compromising evidence from being transferred to and deleted from locally stored logs, some devices also offer "panic" modes that upload/modify evidence silently and remove evidence at a later time. Zero-knowledge proofs (ZKPs) allow for the verification of the integrity of evidence, yet without divulging sensitive contents unless the law calls for it.

The Connects to existing processes to improve uptake. Victims can report to authority and provide a secure access token, or QR code, to enable forensic teams to verify hashes of the transactions on the blockchain without revealing anything completely. Similar systems could be used by medical records generated, documenting injuries, to connect the photographic documentation and reports to the same ledger as demonstrated in California with the Domestic Violence Report and Referral (DVRR) for medical evidence integrity. Elements of technology are the following:

Private keys are controlled by victims through HW Security Module or Trusted Enclave on mobile devices; it is called Secure Key Management. Multi-factor, or trusted guardian mechanisms but not centralized custodial mechanisms are used for recovery options.

For critical situations: Timestamping: Anchoring to public blockchains (e.g., Bitcoin or Ethereum) is offered by services like OpenTimestamps, for increased immutability.

Access Control and Role Based Permissions: Limiting the amount of data access given to support workers and a full package given to courts.

Scalability and Performance: Off-chain storage for large media files Layer 2 solution or sidechains for real-time uploads in order to reduce costs and latency.

Implementing in DV situations is very difficult. Victims should be made technically illiterate and dependent on the internet and internet for solving their problems, which would deal a blow to battery drain, and this should be done using simple interfaces, offline queuing (that is, uploads when there is safety) must be solved through very simple interfaces. Data minimization for privacy is of paramount importance under GDPR/CCPA - PII remains out-of-chain (Susilowati & Frans, 2025). Not easily accessible costs for NGO and victims require a subsidised or open source solution. There is a need for interoperability between different support organisations or jurisdictions, indicating a need for common protocols on the export and verification of evidence.

The feasibility is illustrated with examples of the real world. The HeHop app records on the blockchain in a way that protects privacy and is impossible to alter, ensuring that they cannot be used in court. Identical projects also have been able to integrate blockchain and AI-based danger pattern discovery, keeping the anonymity of victims. Medical and Police evidence custody in abuse scenarios have been tested with Hyperledger Fabric research prototypes, which have delivered good results in maintaining the integrity of the evidence in the custody of different institutions.

The security is not just about the technical aspects of things. Vital factors are regular audits, penetration tests for common DV attacker tactics (for example, ability to access devices), and to integrate with existing safety planning. Encouraging and empowering victims and advocates through training to use safely in the first place, prevents accidental exposure. Preserving the evidence for the long-term will also require ways to move across blockchain upgrades or across platforms.

Looking at the bigger picture, embedding blockchain in domestic violence evidence collection is about to empower victims by offering a cryptographically secure, and easily-evident-to-the-court proof that's hard to dislodge. These can be highly effective if implemented in a trauma-informed manner that focuses on safety, control and accessibility, and can greatly facilitate prosecutions and confidence in victims' ability to seek revenge. Ongoing partnership work will be key to further develop these implementations and address the remaining barriers, between technologists, experts, anti-violence institutions and survivors (Ng et al., 2024).

3. REGULATORY FRAMEWORKS GOVERNING BLOCKCHAIN EVIDENCE IN DOMESTIC VIOLENCE CASES: INTERNATIONAL AND INDIAN LEGAL STANDARDS FOR DIGITAL EVIDENCE

The Regulatory regimes governing the use of blockchain evidence in domestic violence (DV) situations exist where various laws relating to digital evidence, data protection, and victim protection come together. Such frameworks need to strike a balance between the potential need for an inalterable record of inquiry and privacy, safety and the right to a fair trial rights. Blockchain's immutability and timestamping can improve claims in DV contexts, in which evidence can take the form of messages, call logs, video, and GPS locations, where they may also be subject to particularly high levels of scrutiny and stigma that are faced by the male victim. But there are issues of implementation because of disjointed global standards, and changing Indian legislation.

An International Standards are guidelines which apply at a basic level, but do not conform to a single standard. The primary basis for international cyber-crime intellectual property evidence gathering and cooperation is laid out in the Budapest Convention on Cybercrime (2001) and its Second Additional Protocol. It highlights the procedural rules and precautions needed to maintain integrity of electronic evidence without infringing on human rights. For blockchain evidence, the convention provides sides assistance requests with information on the ledger, however in a decentralized system it becomes troublesome to determine a single custodian (Prasad et al., 2026).

The eIDAS Regulation (910/2014) as an update (eIDAS 2.0) is key in the European Union. Increases legal presumption of integrity, accuracy and chronological order for electronic timestamp and electronic ledger received as qualified. The mere fact that the Blockchain timestamps are electronic should not preclude their admissibility (Vismiha & Chinnu, 2026). Presumptions favour the use of qualified electronic ledgers, which are useful for DV evidence e.g. for actors to video threats. But GDPR (2016/679) brings tensions: blockchain is immutable and the right tcybero be forgotten (GDPR, Article 17) is a data minimisation principle. In DV cases, personal data (such as location, health data) needs hybrid architectures (raw data off-chain, hashes on-chain), as well as other technology, such as zero-knowledge proofs. Public blockchains are susceptible to non-compliance, which will drive by DV applications the adoption of permissioned or consortium blockchains.

According to ISO/IEC 27037, best practice is defined in terms of the identification, collection, acquisition and preservation of digital evidence, including blockchain evidence. It highlights the importance of chain of custody, integrity verification via hashing and documentation, all of which can be leveraged for blockchain-based DV evidence. In the U.S., the Federal Rules of Evidence (FRE) control admission: FRE 901 calls for authentication; FRE 902 offers self-authentication alternatives and the Daubert standard applies to testimony by experts on blockchain technology, to test for reliability. Several States (such as Vermont) have singular statutes in regards to blockchain records being authentic. In other parts of the world, UNCITRAL rules and regulations and arbitration rules (IBA/ ICC) have increasingly recognized the blockchain as a reliable documentary evidence.

This pioneering effort is exemplified by the methods of the People's Republic of China, which since 2018 have allowed blockchain evidence to be accepted in court proceedings, especially in criminal cases, for which the Supreme People's Court has included this as one of its new guidelines. If a blockchain platform complies with integrity requirements, the evidence so created can be used in accordance with the rules of presumption of authenticity. These developments impact on norms across the globe, and yet in the case of DV, jurisdiction-specific adaptation of the norm is essential when dealing with personal data deemed sensitive in nature.

This is the right of Indian Legal standards for digital evidence, which are based on three acts, the Information Technology Act (IT Act), 2000, the Bharatiya Sakshya Adhiniyam (BSA) which replaces Indian Evidence Act (1872) and Protection of Women from Domestic Violence Act (PWDVA) 2005 (gender neutral in nature despite the name) (Lane & Adam, 2022). The term "electronic records" is broadly worded in Section 2(t) of the IT Act and Section 4 and 5 provide legal validity for electronic records on par with paper documents. A new section was created in the IT Act: the admissibility of electronic evidence, as Sections 65A and 65B (now Section 63 of BSA) were inserted into the IT Act.

If blockchain is present, it can be included in physical records in compliance with Section 63 of the BSA (formerly 65B), provided the proof of blockchain is included with a certificate of identification, production method and signature. The certificate should be signed by an individual in a responsible role. This requirement, which is upheld in cases such as Anvar P.V. v. P.K. Basheer (2014) and Arjun Panditrao Khotkar v Kailash Kushanrao Gorantyal (2020), gives rise to some special challenges for decentralised blockchain systems, where there is no single 'person in charge.' The courts may order expert evidence or the expertise of hybrid system retainees, such as NGOs or forensic labs, to get off to a start.

The BNSS, 2023 and BNS, 2023 are also found to modernize the procedure, with a strong reliance on electronic evidence for investigations. Blockchain evidence may be used in DV proceedings under PWDVA Sections 18 - 23 (protection, residence, monetary relief orders). In the case of male victimization, however, Indian courts show extra caution given to these perceptions of society. However, this can be addressed by the use of blockchain, which can deliver objectivity, tamper-resistant evidence of abuse behaviors.

There is the issue of privacy and Data Protection. The principles of consent, purpose limitation and data security are mandated under the Digital Personal Data Protection Act, 2023 (DPDPA) of India, which is consistent with the GDPR principles. The Blockchain use in DV should follow a Privacy-by-design approach where only sensitive contents should be stored on-chain whilst the rest can be stored in an off-chain format and disclosed selectively. Cross-border DV cases raise issues under the mutual legal assistance agreement as the standards are different on their applicability, such as EU GDPR Requirements vs Indian DPDPA Requirements, which makes it difficult to get evidence from the other country.

Including the following Key Challenges in DV Contexts are:

Decision: Certification versus De-centralized – Part 63 BSA.

Gender Bias: By determining a stricter limitation for admissibility, the male victim is not considered.

Victim Safety: The public ledger risks victim identity; permissioned ledgers are better.

Judicial capacity: Judges and prosecutors, limited knowledge of blockchain.

Interoperability: There are differences among international standards that affects handling of cross-border DV cases in NRI marriages or migrant victim cases (Worsley et al., 2023).

4. ADMISSIBILITY CHALLENGES OF BLOCKCHAIN EVIDENCE IN COURTS

The inclusion of blockchain evidence in criminal cases of domestic violence, especially when there are victims who are male, raises a myriad of legal, technological, and social issues. Reliability, relevance and fairness are held to high standards for electronic evidence before courts all over the world. Blockchain evidence faces many unique challenges in many jurisdictions, such as India and common law countries, as well as being subject to authentication, integrity and hearsay requirements.

The biggest challenge is the authentication and base requirements. In India, seeking a certificate from a responsible person regarding the devices from which the electronic record was drawn and how it was created, as well as the accuracy of the electronic record, constitutes a requirement of Bharatiya Sakshya Adhiniyam, 2023 (previously Section 65B of the Indian Evidence Act). With a distributed blockchain system, it is sometimes difficult because there is no single "person in charge." Courts after Arjun Panditrao Khotkar v. Kailash Kushanrao Gorantyal (2020) make it difficult for hybrid blockchain as evidence is captured by the victim and securely stored on permissionless ledgers. In the United States, an introduction to the evidence under Federal Rule of Evidence 901 must be supported by sufficient proof that the evidence is "what it is said to be. Origin, hashing process and custody trails behind blockchain records of DV evidence are often appealed by defense counsel.

Another major hurdle to reliability under Frye is the standard. The Judges will be asked to judge whether blockchain technology fulfills the following criteria: scientifically valid, peer-reviewed, generally accepted. Immutability and cryptographic hashing are academically well-developed concepts, but there remains uncertainty in application for DV subject contexts involving mobile apps used by non-technical victims with regards to rates of error, testing and potential vulnerabilities. The testimony of experts is required and is expensive especially for male victims as they are more likely to lack the means and institutional backing of female victims.

Even though blockchain has numerous advantages, chain of custody issues is still very important. The chain of custody is unchangeable on the ledger, however the first capture (pre-hash) is vulnerable. Courts might scrutinize all the chain if a victim is compromised or if the app is not forensically sound. This vulnerability is litigated in cases in which the allegations of fabrication are explored in male DV cases, where it occurs more frequently (prasha et al., 2023). Documented evidence of all transfers of files and/or hashes from victim to support organization, support organization to forensic lab, forensic lab to court, and victim to court is critical with Hybrid architectures (on-chain hashes and off-chain files).

Acceptance is also hindered by the technical complexity and lack of familiarity by the Judiciary. There aren't a lot of judges and lawyers who actually understand what a distributed ledger system is, or a consensus mechanism, or smart contracts, or a zero-knowledge proof is. This disconnect causes flawed decisions to be made, or outright rejection. But in DV cases, it may take a long time to explain the concept of a blockchain with precedential cases that come from courts with a high volume of cases. Female victims are already subject to the social bias that makes their testimony more closely examined in court, and male victims are even more susceptible to this bias, often being believed to be less at risk, or more likely to be the primary aggressor.

An Admissibility problems are aggravated by the fact that the evidence is often tainted by bias and is frequently subject to common sense objections as to its reliability or admissibility (Wilson et al., 2022). The Data from all studies run consistently through that male victims of domestic violence face distrust, reluctance or lack of support from the police, prosecutors and courts. If the court sees the male complainant with traditional gender perspective, the evidence of the Blockchain showing repetitive psychological abuse/repetitive economic control/repetitive threats may not be upheld. The Probative value and prejudice come into play and complex evidence which can confuse the jury may be given less weight under the Rules of Evidence.

There are further challenges arising from issues of privacy and data protection. The GDPR (Europe) and the Digital Personal Data Protection Act (India) both require minimizing data and consent, but blockchain is transparent. While GDPR (Europe) and the Digital Personal Data Protection Act (India) both call for minimum data and consent, blockchain provides transparency. Public blockchains run the risk of victims being doxxed, permissioned blockchains have to demonstrate compliance. Hearsay objections can occur if blocks are offered as evidence that damaging statements are true instead of just existing. Individuals who practice in a multiple jurisdiction setting with either NRIs or migrants are required to deal with recognition issues arising from the arbitrary differences between countries.

5. OVERCOMING CHALLENGES AND FUTURE DIRECTIONS

To get blockchain evidence accepted in male DVs requires a combination of law reform, technaronia, capacity building and societal shifts. Although blockchain provides an unprecedented level of evidentiary strength, it is yet propped up by deliberate interventions to attain the promised potential. Legal and Policy Reforms should upsurge. The government of India, or other legislatures worldwide, could include provisos for blockchain evidence of prescribed standards in their respective guidelines, not unlike the rules of China's Supreme People's Court or the eIDAS framework of the European Union. The Bharatiya Sakshya Adhiniyam could point out the conditions to become a certified system, enabling qualified custodians forensic labs or accredited NGOs to issue certificates for decentralized systems (Yadav et al., 2026). The technology as evidence in case of male victimisation should be explicitly covered in the gender neutral domestic violence laws and there should be a requirement to consider records held on blockchain (Al-Mulla et al., 2026).

The Judicial and Law Enforcement Training is a must. Judicial academic training, prosecutor training and police training should be accompanied by extensive courses on blockchain and digital forensics. Mock trials with blockchain DV evidence help to establish familiarity and confidence. Complex hearings might be better directed to a specialized 'technical' court with special experts and the result would minimize wrongful exclusions.

Many of the challenges faced today will be tackled by technological developments and standardisation. Permissioned blockchains containing built-in compliance features and developing the DV evidence platforms in accordance with the nation's standards would facilitate admissibility. Advanced steganography, homomorphic encryption and zero-knowledge proofs can help overcome privacy issues.

Especially for male victims, support ecosystem strengthening is important. Resources should be provided to NGOs who work with male survivors to adopt blockchain tools and ensure male survivors receive legal-technical assistance. The Tech firms, forensics labs and victim groups can all help to subsidize and maintain proper chain of custody of access from the moment of capture.

Promoting ethical applications and protecting victims should be a guiding principle for all developments. Victim safety, agency and informed consent shall be key considerations in systems (Garrett et al., 2024). That data minimization is a must, as well as access that is revocable, and protection from a retaliation. Women on average one in ten male victims will have misused blockchain evidence in false counter cases and require special protection to prevent it from being misused.

Future Research Directions involve empirical research to establish the effectiveness of the blockchain evidence on convictions in male domestic violence cases, comparison of different architectures on the blockchain, and the creation of postquantum secure solutions. For international collaboration, organisations such as the Budapest Convention can standardize cross-border evidence for DV in the interest of harmonisation.

The short-term actions of Roadmap for Integration include deploying pilot programs in certain districts, conducting judicial sensitization workshops, while the long-term goals encompass the development of a national blockchain-DV infrastructure and legislative amendments by the year 2030. Awareness-raising initiatives that undermine gender stereotypes in the context of domestic violence will set the courts in a more conducive setting. Blockchain can be a tool that gives women justice by empowerment giving a fair chance to the males who are victims of domestic violence due to supplying credible, tamper evidence.

6. CONCLUSION

There are emerging solutions comprise introduction of a set of standardised forensic procedures, training of the judiciary and amendments of laws that recognise qualified blockchain ledgers (inspired by eIDAS). Presumption of reliability of certified blockchain platforms can be taken by Indian courts, as is done in China or EU such presumptions. It is necessary that an App developed through collaboration among researchers from MEITY, Forensic Labs and DV SUPPORT is victim friendly and can produce a court-ready blockchain evidence.

There are emerging frameworks and standards such as eIDAS and ISO 27037 that are rising to the occasion, but Indian legal frameworks, like the IT Act and the Budapest Convention, serve as a solid base with still some varations to cover in the context of blockchain evidence in DV cases and matters of record management. For ameliorating the strength of blockchain such as immutability and verifiability, along with safeguarding susceptible victims and ensuring equitable trial, harmonization, guidelines on hybrid architectures and capacity building of the blockchain are all essential. Whether blockchain proves to be a helping technology to fair justice or yet another obstacle in Domestic Violence suits will be decided by the pro-active policy changes and reforms in the near future.

REFERENCES

Al-Mulla, M. S., Hammoud, M., Moussa, A. F., & Barafi, J. (2026). The impact of cybercrimes on the achievement of sustainable development goals: An analytical study. *International Journal of Electronic Security and Digital Forensics*, *18*(2), 240–259. DOI: 10.1504/IJESDF.2026.152245

Alketbi, S. K. (2024). Emerging technologies in forensic DNA analysis. *Perspectives in Legal and Forensic Sciences, 1*(1).

El-Kady, R. (2025). Unmasking virtual crimes: Investigating and proving evidence in the Metaverse. In *Unveiling Social Dynamics and Community Interaction in the Metaverse* (pp. 389–444). IGI Global Scientific Publishing. DOI: 10.4018/979-8-3693-8628-6.ch018

Garrett, B. L., Gutierrez, R., & Scurich, N. (2024). The impact of defense experts on juror perceptions of firearms examination testimony. *Jurimetrics*, *64*(3), 223–248.

Harris, M. (2023). Blockchain-Based Evidence in Courts: Standards, Reliability, and Admissibility Challenges. *Legal Studies in Digital Age*, *2*(3), 49–63.

Kumar, D., Kumar, S., & Joshi, A. (2023). Assessing the viability of blockchain technology for enhancing court operations. *International Journal of Law and Management*, *65*(5), 425–439. DOI: 10.1108/IJLMA-03-2023-0046

Lane, A. M., & Adam, L. (2022). Crime and cryptocurrency in Australian courts. *Monash University Law Review. Monash University. Faculty of Law*, *48*(3), 146–190.

Lesiuk, N. (2023). Ushering in a new era: Assessing the reasonable expectation of privacy vis-a-vis cryptocurrency and blockchain data. *Man. LJ*, *46*, 1.

Naseer, M., Gusdevi, H., Rahayudin, R., & Guterres, A. (2026). Blockchain-Based Evidence Legality in Indonesia's Criminal Justice System. *Jurnal Hukum Indonesia*, *5*(1), 40–65. DOI: 10.58344/jhi.v5i1.2351

Ng, M., James, J., & Bull, R. (2024). "What you say in the lab, stays in the lab": A reflexive thematic analysis of current challenges and future directions of digital forensic investigations in the UK. *Forensic Science International Digital Investigation*, *51*, 301839. DOI: 10.1016/j.fsidi.2024.301839

Prasad, V. L. S., Srivastava, V., & Singh, H. (2026). Cyber-Crimes in AI-Enabled Green Platforms: Legal Hurdles in ESG Investing, Prosecution, and Financial Loss Mitigation. In AI Governance, Law, Policy and Ethics in Green Finance and ESG (pp. 265-282). IGI Global Scientific Publishing.

Singh, C., Gautam, S. K., Khajuria, H., & Nayak, B. P. (2025). Integrated blockchain-based framework for investigating child sexual exploitation materials (CSEM) in India. *International Journal of Information Technology : an Official Journal of Bharati Vidyapeeth's Institute of Computer Applications and Management*, •••, 1–19. DOI: 10.1007/s41870-025-02852-y

Singh, H., & Naruka, R. (2019). Decriminalisation of adultery in India: Issues and challenges. *Universal Review*, *8*(5), 957–964.

Susilowati, C. M. I., & Frans, M. P. (2025). Interpreting power, grooming, and deception in sexual violence cases: a hermeneutic study on legal challenges in Indonesia. *International Journal for the Semiotics of Law-Revue internationale de Sémiotique juridique, 38*(3), 1061-1078.

Vismiha, M. K., & Chinnu, M. D. (2026). Trans Boundary Crimes and the Jurisdictional Issues and International Cooperation in Dealing with Such Crimes. *Trans Boundary Crimes and the Jurisdictional Issues and International, 2*(04).

Wilson, M., Cross, C., Holt, T., & Powell, A. (2022). Police preparedness to respond to cybercrime in Australia: An analysis of individual and organizational capabilities. *Journal of Criminology*, *55*(4), 468–494. DOI: 10.1177/26338076221123080

Worsley, M. K., Rowe, B. I., & Houston, K. A. (2023). Two Steps Forward, One Step Back: The Legal Response to Sex Trafficking. *Journal of Human Trafficking*, •••, 1–13. DOI: 10.1080/23322705.2023.2289822

Yadav, A., Srivastava, V., & Singh, H. (2026). Enhancing Green Investment through AI and Automation: A Critical Legal Study of Regulatory Frameworks Effectiveness in Tackling Cybersquatting in India. In AI Governance, Law, Policy and Ethics in Green Finance and ESG (pp. 149-166). IGI Global Scientific Publishing. DOI: 10.4018/979-8-2600-1308-3.ch009

Chapter 16

The Use of Blockchain Technology in the Provision of Public Health Service:

A Study on the Estonian Health System

Emre Akcagunduz
http://orcid.org/0000-0003-2829-0794
Trakya University, Turkey

ABSTRACT

Simply explained, blockchain is a distributed system in which all transactions are recorded and documented by the system's users (also known as the blockchain network). Blockchain is a form of data-storing mechanism. It is a system in which the data to be saved is laid out into structures known as "blocks," with each block connected to the next by stamping/sealing. The present study investigates how blockchain technology is being used in the provision of healthcare services in Estonia, what benefits it offers, and how it improves the delivery of public services. The study concluded that blockchain-based medical applications offer considerable time, space, and financial benefits in the delivery of healthcare services in Estonia. This particular situation suggests that blockchain-based medical applications will be adopted in many different countries in the future.

DOI: 10.4018/979-8-3373-9730-6.ch016

INTRODUCTION

In the broadest sense, public administration is the process of developing public policies pertaining to the production of basic goods and services that the public needs (Eryılmaz, 2014). The creation and provision of public services is one of the core responsibilities of public administration. In its broadest definition, public service refers to state-provided services that consider the requirements of the general population and are intended to provide benefits to the public (Çal, 2007). For people to enjoy their lives in peace and happiness, public services are of particular importance. That is due to the wide variety of public services, particularly health and education. In the provision of public services, the public visits the location of the relevant unit and receives the service from public officials. For example, a sick person goes to the hospital for an examination, and someone who needs to pay taxes goes to the tax office. This is how public services are customarily delivered.

Public administration has been directly impacted by the rapid developments in information and communication technologies. This interaction appears as what is known as electronic government (e-government). The system that makes it possible for public services to be delivered online is known as e-government (Akcagündüz, 2013). Particularly since the COVID-19 pandemic, there has been a significant transformation in the way public services are provided. Traditional means of providing public services have had to shift as a result of the COVID-19 pandemic and the lockdown restrictions that went along with it. Since the COVID-19 pandemic, greater emphasis has been placed on enabling residents to access public services from wherever they are, particularly from their homes. Apart from the e-government system, blockchain technology has also started to be implemented to public service delivery.

Data recording, disease diagnosis, remote treatment, medication safety, and supply are all areas in which blockchain technology has been used in the field of healthcare. Benefits of blockchain technology include data recording, which has become increasingly important in managing the needs of a steadily growing global population. Individual health records must be kept since every single individual has a different metabolism as well as health issues. For example, details on a person's blood type, medications, medical histories, genetic susceptibility, and allergies to substances are all significant for the treatment process. There is a serious data storage issue when such are taken into account for every individual. These data are stored in files that are opened in an electronic environment or on paper in the traditional bureaucratic scheme. This leads to a number of issues. For example, the traditional approach of storing medical data in written files results in paper waste, data loss in the event of fire etc. and such other storage issues. On the other hand, digitally stored data within a computer file poses security risks (data theft). For instance, according to a research by Moffit and Stefen (2017), hackers stole the health data of 114 million Americans in 2015. Similarly, Srinivasan stated in his 2016 study that health-related information of 78.8 million customers was stolen from the Anthem insurance company's database. Karadavut's study (2022) reveals that over the past 15 years, malicious hackers have breached and used the health records of more than 200 million people. In his home country, Turkey, 2.5 million people's health data has also been illegally accessed in the same manner. Such examples highlight the importance of storing the health data of the citizens in a secure manner.

Blockchain technology has led to major developments in data protection, preservation, and storage. To begin with, blockchain technology is made up of interconnected structures called "blocks" each of which contains hard-to-crack cryptographic cyphers. For example, Block A contains a cryptographic cypher made up of complex numbers that are difficult to decipher. A blockchain is generated by connecting each block. A modification to one of these blocks necessitates a change to every block before it (Özcan, 2021). Because of this, the risk of data theft with blockchain technology becomes even difficult.

One of the first countries in the world to set up and implement a blockchain-based healthcare system is Estonia, which is the focus of this study. The study examines the impact of blockchain-based healthcare systems on healthcare service delivery in Estonia. Estonia was selected primarily as it has served as a pilot country in the global deployment of blockchain-based healthcare systems.

1. LITERATURE REVIEW

Because blockchain technology is relatively new, research is being carried out to find out where it can be applied. However, in recent years, particularly in tandem with advancements in the financial sector such as Bitcoin, research into the applications of blockchain technology has intensified. According to Aydar and Çetin's (2020) study, blockchain technology is used in healthcare through initiatives including FHIRChain, MedRec, MedChain, Gem Health Network, and MyPCR. According to the report, these programs involve the sharing and security of patient's health-related data. A study on the application of blockchain-based programs including Nebula Genomics, Medicalchain, Medibloc, and Skychain in the healthcare sector was carried out by Kıyak et al. in 2019. A blockchain-based system for collecting and securing people's genome sequences and keeping health record data in the safest and most unchangeable manner is being attempted to be developed in these three projects. According to the study, the programs are now in the planning stage and, once fully operational, will address major issues in the healthcare system. In their 2021 study, Türkdoğan and Kurşun (2021) argue that blockchain technology can be used to address a number of issues in the healthcare industry, including managing the supply chain for medications and medical supplies, storing and protecting personal health records, storing data from clinical trials and using it immediately when necessary integrating blockchain technology into telehealth systems, and enhancing system security. Tahaoğlu et al. (2019) carried out research on the potential applications of blockchain technology. The potential applications of blockchain technology in Turkish healthcare industry were also addressed in this study. According to the study MediLedger, SimplyVitalHealth, Robomed Network, Healthureum, Gem, DokChain, MediBloc, BlockMedx, Patientory, and MedicalChain are among the blockchain-based healthcare systems that are currently under development and these systems are expected to offer significant benefits, particularly with regard to the security and protection of health data. Mızrak and Aslan (2023) suggested a blockchain-based electronic health record system in their study. The proposed solution describes how to store, transfer, and secure health data using a blockchain-based smart contract framework. According to the study by Özdenizci Köse (2021), blockchain technology is used in the healthcare industry for large data protection, sharing, and application. The author identifies four key focus areas for blockchain-based research: health data analysis–clinical research, health insurance, healthcare supply chain management, and medical data management. The author concludes that blockchain technology will soon be widely used in these four fields.

Kuo et al. (2017) discussed the potential applications of blockchain technology in the healthcare and biomedical industries in their study. The benefits and drawbacks associated with using blockchain technology in healthcare and biomedical systems are covered in the contents of the study. According to the study, blockchain-based healthcare system applications have both advantages and disadvantages. Research on the use of Internet of Things technology for healthcare items for remote patient tracking and monitoring was carried out by Xu et al. (2019). According to their study, users' medical data is typically kept in a centralised third party, such as a healthcare facility's database or cloud, because of the limited processing power and storage capacity of IoT devices. This makes the data vulnerable to loss or theft. Xu et al. (2019) suggested the Healthchain system as a solution for such problems. The private key in the Healthchain system ensures that only doctors and their patients can access the system. The viability and security of Healthchain have been proven via experiments. A blockchain-based application known as DPEM was presented by Naresh et al. (2021) for the transfer and security of medical data. The structure of the system is composed of three layers. These layers include a cloud storage architecture, an ECC-based attribute encryption system for managing access control in data sharing, and an elliptic curve-based signature to guarantee anonymity. Through testing, Naresh et al. have proven that DPEM functions in an efficient manner, proving the viability of the system.

A three-layer blockchain system was developed by Zhuang et al. (2020) for storing and transferring medical data in a fast and secure manner. In tests, it took 12 seconds to validate 331,142 simulated data points from 40,000 patients. Furthermore, it took an average of 3.07 seconds to transmit health data to a different site. It was concluded by the study that blockchain-based systems for data transfer and storage may be efficient.

In their work, Mani et al. (2021) presented a model they developed for healthcare data management systems. The Patient-Centric Healthcare Data Management (PCHDM) system is the designated name of the system . The Hyperledger Fabric blockchain serves as the basis for this system. It is intended to protect the privacy and security of medical records. A cloud storage space is part of the system architecture. The integrity of patient records was protected in the system that was developed by using a smart contract-based security system using an algorithm known as "Byzantine fault tolerance." The system has been implemented successfully.

Kumar and Tripathi (2021) and Qathrady et al. (2024) suggested a blockchain-based healthcare data management system, modelling it after the Internet of Things for healthcare objects. All three studies focused on the storage, storage, and transfer of health data. Although the studies emphasize the rapid nature of the Internet of Things structure for medical objects, the security of the data, which utmost issue, is addressed. Blockchain-based systems have also been proposed, utilizing a smart contract system for data security.

Majdoubi et al. (2023) developed an end-to-end encrypted and blockchain-based healthcare data system called SmartMedChain. SmartMedChai is designed on Hyperledger Fabric. SmartMedChai uses the InterPlanetary File System (IPFS) to store encrypted health data, which is a distributed data storage solution that is very flexible and scalable. SmartMedChain employs blockchain-based smart contracts. SmartMedChain has improved the management, security, and transfer of electronic health data over the Internet of Medical Things. The tests performed further proved that SmartMedChain is practical. In 2019, Bautista et al. (2023) developed MediLinker, a blockchain-based healthcare data system, in collaboration with the University of Texas Dell Medical School in Austin, the School of Informatics, the Department of Electrical and Computer Engineering, and the Department of Information Technology Services. MediLinker employs the Hyperledger blockchain network. Data may be saved and exchanged fast and securely using the network's wallets and private keys. The tests confirmed that MediLinker is quite effective and advantageous. Liang et al. (2023) suggested a Rahasak blockchain-based system structure for use in healthcare services in their study. According to the study, the system was established using Aplos smart contracts and Apache Cassandra cloud-based storage systems. The test studies of the prepared model were completed successfully, and the study concluded that this model can be used. MediLinker has been tested and shown to be quite practical and efficient. Liang et al. (2023) put forward a Rahasak blockchain-based structure for healthcare services in their research. According to the study, the system was developed using Aplos smart contracts and Apache Cassandra cloud-based storage systems. Tests of the prepared model were successful, and the study identified specific fields in which it can be applied.

Rao and Naganjaneyulu (2024) concluded that health information data may be safely stored and exchanged using a blockchain-based system. According to the authors, governance principles apply to data protection and transportation, and only stakeholders have access to the data once it has been received. In their study, Malathy and Jaichandran (2024) proposed TDES-EKMC, a blockchain-based system that combines Internet of Things and blockchain technology. The authors suggested a fast and dependable architecture for the Internet of Medical Things (IoMT) that employs the ECMQV-MAC protocol, DC-PC for data storage, and DMBGC for key generation. According to the study, this method allows for the fast and reliable sharing of health-related information.

Sharma and colleagues (Sharma et al., 2024) suggested a system for healthcare services that makes use of elliptic curve cryptography (ECC) within the framework of a digital twin. The authors tried to bring together Internet of Things technology with the digital twin structure and used blockchain technology to address potential system security risks. The model they proposed has achieved a 98% success rate, protecting the confidentiality of patients' health-related data while simultaneously boosting the speed and efficiency of the medical services. In their study, Alkhalifa et al. (2024) noted that although the Internet of Medical Things (IoMT) has been used for patient monitoring, diagnosis, and treatment, there are security wise flaws in this application. Despite the security flaw, IoMT is an exceptionally useful system. It saves time when accessing and uploading patient data in particular. IoMT comes at a relatively moderate cost. Acknowledging these characteristics of IoMT, the authors developed a new system by designing the data security of the system using a blockchain-based structure. The study proposes a model that is secured using IoMT, Privacy-Preserving Federated Learning (PPFL), and Privacy Enhancing Technologies (PETs). Tests revealed that the model's vulnerability had been sorted out, resulting in a solid and reliable structure.

Litvin et al. (2024) referred to health-related data as "big data." The study employed cyb.ai, an artificial intelligence-supported blockchain technology, to collect, store, and share healthcare data. The system was designed to be employed not only locally but also globally. This method will make it easier to get reliable surgical data from anywhere in the world. During the testing phase, the system worked successfully. According to the study, the system will become more established and efficient as more data is entered and uploaded.

The literature review revealed that existing studies on this particular topic fall generally into two main categories. The first category includes studies that review previously completed studies (Systematic Review). In these studies, articles on the subject were grouped and reviewed. The other one are the studies that examine the models established by researchers with engineering backgrounds using any blockchain infrastructure and smart contract technology. A literature review concluded that blockchain-based healthcare systems have yet to be used in a pilot country. Even if there are a lot of projects underway, it is acknowledged that a specific period of time must elapse before these projects may be carried out.

This study, as evidenced by the review of the literature, will be the first to investigate a country that has formally implemented a blockchain-based healthcare system. As a result, this study will make a significant contribution to the literature.

2. RESEARCH METHODOLOGY

The study is generally structured within the framework of qualitative research methods. Qualitative research is defined as "a research process aimed at presenting perceptions and events in a holistic manner through descriptive data, in a natural setting, using qualitative techniques such as observation, interviews, review, and document analysis (including audio and textual materials)" (Yıldırım & Şimşek, 2006, p.39). Qualitative research methods includes various sub-approaches depending on the nature and objective of the study. Some of these methods include document analysis and standard compilation techniques. The data gathered throughout the research process were prepared using the "document analysis" method, which is a subset of qualitative research techniques. According to Kıral (2020, p.173), "document analysis is a systematic approach for examining and evaluating all documents, both printed and electronic." In document analysis, documents relating to the subject are subject to a thorough study to identify data that may be used to achieve the intended objectives. The documents collected through document analysis were synthesised using standard review methods. A traditional evaluation is "a study that synthesises the findings, results, and assessments of two or more published works (such as academic studies and reports) on a specific topic by examining them." (Karaçam, 2013, p.27).

Every phase of the study has been completed through a step-by-step process. A review of the literature was carried out in the first step. Academic databases were searched in order to conduct the literature review. The study made use of two primary academic databases. These are Web of Science and Google Scholar. These two databases were selected for a reason. First of all, the database that has the highest indexing level for Turkish papers is Google Scholar. Almost all articles that Google

Scholar searches come from Turkish databases (e.g. Acar Index and Ebscohost). As a result, Google Scholar was selected as the database and screening source. The Web of Science is another database. This is the database with the best indexing in a foreign language (English) in the world. The research started with a search of the Web of Science database for pertinent studies. We searched the Web of Science database using the terms "blockchain" and "health." 384 research papers were found as a result of the search. We then searched for "blockchain" and "health care" and "blockchain and its use in healthcare." In total, 169 articles were identified in the first group of keywords, and 88 in the second group. Ultimately, using the keywords 'blockchain and healthcare system in Estonia,' no papers or academic studies were located. Articles were reviewed depending on their keywords and abstracts. Following that, a Google Scholar search using the keywords 'blockchain and health' produced 1,830 publications, 'blockchain and its use in healthcare' yielded 1,150 articles, with 'blockchain and healthcare services' 1,640 articles. Following an 8-month review procedure (based on abstracts and keywords), the articles retrieved in both databases were evaluated. Duplicate articles and publications irrelevant to the subject got eliminated at the conclusion of the process. 52 articles that were found to be closely related to the subject were reviewed at the conclusion of the process. There was no thorough research on the application of blockchain technology in Estonian healthcare in any of the said databases.

The findings, outcomes, and evaluations on the studies selected through a traditional review procedure and literature review were analysed. As a result, breakthroughs in blockchain and medical technology were searched. Information about the Estonian government's efforts to provide blockchain-based healthcare services was compiled using the document analysis approach, referencing academic research (books and articles), papers on the subject matter, and official government website pages. The review concluded by making an effort to identify every document pertinent to the topic.

3. USE OF BLOCKCHAIN BASED TECHNOLOGIES IN THE DELIVERY OF HEALTHCARE SERVICES: A CASE STUDY FROM ESTONIA

Estonia is widely regarded as a global model for digital transformation. Estonia's journey towards digital transformation can be better understood by dividing it into clearly defined periods. First and foremost, Estonia declared its independence in 1991 from 50 years of Soviet Socialist Republics Union (USSR) domination. Estonia, which had lagged far behind in terms of technology during the USSR era, put technological development as a top priority soon after independence. In 1994, the initial steps towards digitisation and technical development were made. The Estonian parliament adopted the "Fundamental Principles of Estonian Information Technology Policy" in 1994. At that time, Estonia invested 1% of its Gross Domestic Product (GDP) in the development of information and communication technology, even though it was a recently established state. An important step towards digitisation was taken in 1996 with the commencement of the Tiger Leap Project/Initiative. Facilitating countrywide access to computers and the internet, especially for educational purposes, is aimed through the project. Building the infrastructure for information technology use and providing each student a computer have been the primary objectives of the project. This program has incorporated Estonian schools in the process of digital transformation and enhanced their information technology capabilities. Since its inception in 1996, the project has worked to accomplish its objectives across Estonia by 1999. The process of shifting to a computerised banking system started in 1996. In order to promote digital banking across Estonia, particularly in rural areas, efforts were made to set up the required infrastructure. 97% of Estonian schools had internet access by 1997 (e-estonia.com, 2024a; Hammersley, 2017).

By the year 2000, there was an agreement to conduct cabinet meetings online as a cost-saving measure and to reduce public bureaucracy. As a result of the efforts made, cabinet meetings have started to be held in a digital environment. Significant advantages have resulted from this, especially in terms of time savings. Cabinet sessions, for instance, were shortened from five hours to thirty minutes. This proved that digitisation offers substantial time, space, and financial savings. Cabinet sessions, for example, have been shortened from five hours to thirty minutes. This experience has shown that digitisation offers substantial time, space, and financial savings. Regarding tax payments, another step towards digitisation was made in 2000. Estonia took the initiative to develop a faster and easier way for its citizens to pay their taxes. The introduction of the e-tax system was part of this framework. 98% of citizens may now pay their taxes in as little as three minutes thanks to this system. In addition to increasing tax payments, this has resulted in significant time savings for citizens. The m-Parking application was introduced in 2000 in response to community requests. This app allows users to rapidly pay parking costs using their smartphones. Because it's easy to pay, this has helped avoid traffic jams, particularly in busy city centres. This app has also been used as a model by some other countries. Estonia launched a significant step towards digital transformation in 2001. A system known as X-Road was developed and put into use. In fact, X-Road is a distributed, decentralised exchange of information layer. Integrating the information systems of both public and private sector companies, X-Road is a secure information exchange layer. This platform is used by citizens and organisations in the public and private sectors to access public services. To put it briefly, X-Road is an essential framework that makes it possible for different e-service databases in the public and private sectors to collaborate and connect. Estonia made the transition to a digital identity and digital identity number system in 2002. 98% of the population is covered by this system and has a digital identity and digital identity number. As a result, Estonians can now transact online. Estonia saves 2% of its yearly GDP thanks to digital identity and digital signatures, according to the study. Estonia, with a population of 1.3 million, intends to achieve 10 million digital citizens by 2025, including those from neighbouring countries. This objective is particularly impressive for Estonia, which has a population of 1.3 million people. In 2005, Estonia transitioned to an electronic voting system, which serves as an example for other countries. This system has made voting easier and more convenient for citizens both at home and abroad. The system's success has served as an example for many other countries (e-estonia.com, 2024a; x-road.global, 2025; Martinovic et al., 2017; Sullivan & Burger, 2017; Abualy, 2022).

The year 2007 was the most significant turning point in Estonia's digital transition. In 2007, Estonia was the victim of the world's largest cyberattack. In 2007, Estonians planned to destroy the Bronze Soldier monument in Tallinn, which dates back to World War II and reminds them of the Russian occupation. However, pro-Russian and Russia-supporting groups did not tolerate such a course of action. Following the event, there were events throughout Estonia. As a result of such events, several arrests were made. In tandem with the unfolding of events, Estonia has been exposed to an unprecedented cyberattack in both its own history and internationally. A hacker group based in Moldova was the main claimant of these attacks. However, it has always been rumoured that Russia was behind these attacks. The attack lasted exactly 22 days. Distributed Denial of Service (DDoS) attacks were the most common type of attack observed. Legislative, security, banking, e-government, publishing, and public institution websites were all specifically targeted by the attack. The banking and e-government systems in particular were unavailable for 22 days. This circumstance has occasionally brought life to a halt. For Estonia, this event has been a watershed moment. Estonia first developed and put into effect a cyber-protection plan. The Estonian Defence League Cyber Unit was subsequently established. Due to the concerns about cyber security, Estonia has taken steps to attach importance on blockchain-based digital structures (Koç, 2021; Hansen, 2018; Salma & Munabari, 2023).

By 2008, the Estonian government had initiated several projects, driven primarily by concerns about cyber security, among other considerations. Estonia was able to create a blockchain-based system with the help of partners including the US and the North Atlantic Treaty Organisation (NATO). Thus, Estonian programmers developed the KSI (Keyless Signature Infrastructure) blockchain architecture in 2008. The KSI blockchain system is extremely challenging for changes and provides a blockchain structure based on 100% data security. In 2008, this system was also used to develop

E-health apps. Thus, the essential infrastructure for a blockchain-based healthcare system was established, and data was transferred to a digital environment (e-estonia.com, 2024a; Salma & Munabari, 2023).

3.1. Blockchain- based healthcare services in Estonia: Guardtime and KSI blockchain technology

With the establishment of the Estonian E-Health Foundation (EeHF) in 2005, the digitalisation of Estonia's healthcare system picked up speed. The foundation's primary objectives are to oversee and digitise healthcare regulations, produce educational healthcare pamphlets, and collaborate with the Estonian government to transfer health-related records to a digital environment across the country. The KSI Blockchain system is the most palpable example of Estonia's transition to a blockchain-based healthcare system following the 2007 cyberattacks.

KSI is an e-signature system based on the blockchain. This system was developed through Guardtime. The signature mechanism is verified using the hash tree (Merkle tree) technology. 10^{12} signatures may be recorded every second by the KSI system. KSI operates in this manner: First, the system is logged into using the Know Your Customer (KYC) system. KYC is used by the citizens to register with the system. Numerous criteria, including fingerprints, mobility, and facial recognition, are used for such registration processes. KSI is used to produce a digital signature following system registration. Guardtime developed KSI, a registered digital signature scheme. The signature technique is simply a hash tree/Merkle tree mechanism for ensuring the integrity of digital data. A Merkle tree is primarily a verification system for massive data structures. This technology enables the verification of whether a desired operation is correct. To generate a signature, data is transmitted to Guardtime via the system. Guardtime generates digital signatures. Guardtime gathers hashes of data sent by KSI users every second. These hashes are then combined in a hash tree known as the 'Global Aggregation Tree.' The "Global Root Hash Value-Global Collection Tree" appears at the top of the tree. A signature token that attests to the availability of the data at the moment of receipt and its transmission by a particular user (or over a particular access path) is returned to the user during this time. The "Global Root Hash Value Calendar" is added to the blockchain following the generation of the Global Collection Tree, which also establishes a blockchain architecture in KSI. The "Global Root Hash Value" from each collection tree is added to another Merkle tree, which is essentially what the Calendar Blockchain is. Hash tree combination, signature generation, and verification are handled by four server clusters located in different geographic regions Guardtime provides these servers, resulting in a permissioned KSI blockchain. Because the user's identity must be verified before using the KSI blockchain service, it might be considered to be a private blockchain. Guardtime clearly states this classification. Guardtime specifies that the Calendar Blockchain is made up of another hash tree that links the blocks (Global Root Hash Values) each other. The root of this (meta) hash tree is published on a regular basis, allowing signatures to be independently validated and users to check existing signatures even when Guardtime is no longer available (Reede, 2020).

Figure 1 shows how the KSI blockchain system works. The process can be outlined in the following manner:

1. Healthcare organisations (hospitals and healthcare centres) gather and transmit data in a digital format in the first step,
2. A hash value—a distinct fingerprint made up of encoded characters that represent the document—is appended to the data and validated,
3. Following verification, the data is added to the blockchain as a block.

Figure 1: KSI Blockchain Functionality

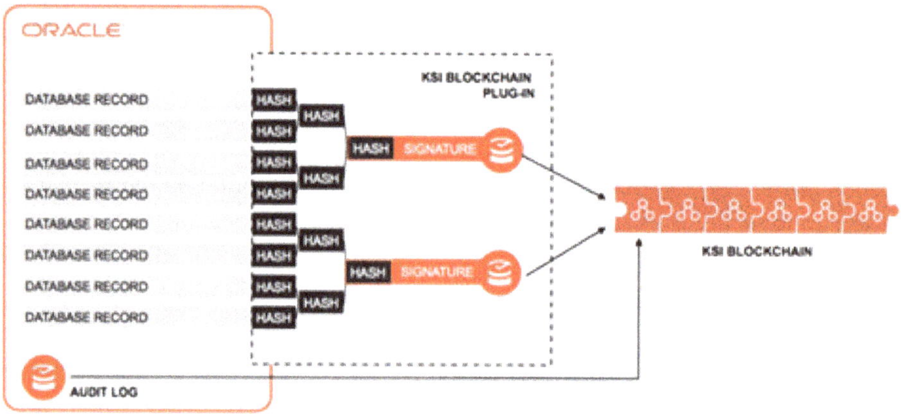

(Source: Semenzin et al., 2022, p. 8)

There are two major advantages to the system shown in Figure 1. Accuracy and data security are indirectly tied to both of these benefits. First, every data record that is entered into the system can be checked to see if it has been modified. Second, the blockchain can be used to confirm if data has been modified (Martinovic et al., 2017). Each new block that is added to the blockchain is connected to the one before it. The SHA256 hashing algorithm is used by the KSI blockchain. Each block in this method has a 32-digit cryptographic hash that is difficult to crack. Each block added to the KSI blockchain after the procedure is completed merges with the other blocks. To generate a password, multiply the number of blocks in the blockchain by

32 (for example, 50,000*32=1,600,000 characters). Breaking this password becomes impossible. This ensures that the system is 100% reliable.

The 1.3 million people in Estonia now receive their healthcare services in a digital setting. 99% of public services are delivered online. The healthcare system in Estonia that uses blockchain technology has over 40 million documents. Treatment summaries, patient referrals, medications, medical diagnoses, reports, and more are included in such records. In addition, a digital gene bank has been generated. The genetic information of more than 200,000 citizens is in this bank. Furthermore, the blockchain-based KSI blockchain architecture now includes this data.

Genome data is vital for gene therapy and for addressing any future health issues for citizens. In order to diagnose and treat the diseases, genomic data is integrated with health service information. Based on each patient's unique genetic typology and profile, doctors may use such data to diagnose and treat particular diseases as needed. This guarantees prompt, efficient, and effective medical interventions. E-prescriptions are used by 99.9% of Estonians. The electronic healthcare system is used to organise and process medical prescriptions. Every hospital and pharmacy in the country has been connected to every other hospital and pharmacy employing this method. As a result, doctors can write prescriptions electronically. Just presenting their ID cards allows patients to receive their medication. In particular, this condition greatly lessens the workload for doctors. Because it reduces paper waste, the system is advantageous to the environment and the economy. The e-prescription system was tested for internationalisation in 2019.

The system was designed in the manner to serve the citizens of different countries as a result of the cooperation with Finland. In January 2019, the first cross-border digital prescription services were introduced in Finland and Estonia, allowing Finnish patients to visit an Estonian pharmacy and get medications prescribed electronically by their Finnish doctors. Since then, the e-prescription system has been extended to Croatian, Czech, Polish, Spanish, Greek, and Portuguese citizens. e-Ambulance is another noteworthy healthcare service in Estonia. The e-health system instantly transmits all of the patient's health-related information, including blood type, allergies, prescriptions, medical history, etc., to the ambulance staff when a citizen with a medical issue calls for one. This makes it possible for the patient to receive the best possible intervention. Telemedicine is another prominent use of Estonia's e-health service. The two types of telemedicine services are synchronous (such as teletherapy, teleconsultation, and remote monitoring) and asynchronous (such as messaging). Additionally, this program offers solutions (such as decision support for the patients, reminders, and notifications) that allow a patient to receive healthcare services without the assistance of a medical practitioner. The Covid-19 pandemic in 2020 led to the temporary implementation of this method. Following positive feedback, the system was developed and now includes e-consultations (electronic consultations between family doctors and specialists), physiotherapy, psychotherapy, remote visits (video visits), speech therapy, occupational therapy, remote speech therapy, and remote occupational therapy (e-estonia.com, 2024b; e-estonia.com, 2025; www.tehik.ee/en, 2025; tervisekassa.ee, 2025; ibanet.org, 2025; Soares et al., 2023).

As evidenced by the aforementioned instances, Estonia is at the forefront of healthcare service digitalisation. International research further confirms this. For instance, in the 2024 Bertelsmann Foundation Digital Health Index, Estonia was ranked first out of 14 EU nations and three OECD member states (brand.estonia.ee, 2025; bertelsmann-stiftung.de, 2025).

4. CONCLUSIONS AND DISCUSSIONS

Estonia leads the way in establishing a model for other countries, as proved by the fact that 99% of its public services are delivered digitally and are cited as models globally. Estonia was the first country to put its cabinet sessions online, which suggests the substantial time savings that would result. Additionally, the consumption of paper and other materials has decreased while tax revenues have increased due to the safe digital payment of taxes.

Similarly, Estonia has successfully improved the overall quality of urban life and citizen satisfaction with m-parking, digital identification, and digital citizenship, bringing it international recognition. Estonia is a country that has surmounted many countries' concerns about digitalisation. The cyberattack that took place in 2007, in particular, set an example not only for Estonia, but for other countries throughout the world. Many countries, including Turkey, are concerned about the digitisation of public services as a result of cyberattacks. However, Estonia managed to overcome these issues through its efforts, which is based on its experiences.

According to a research conducted to support the study, Estonia was the first country in the world to officially put in place blockchain technology in public services. Blockchain technology is exclusively used in specific geographic areas of various countries, according to a review of the literature on the subject. Estonia is the first country to incorporate and make use of blockchain technology in both its technological infrastructure and legal framework.

The study has led to the following results/findings that are relevant to the implementation of blockchain technology in the Estonian healthcare system:

1. Blockchain-based healthcare services have resulted in significant financial savings for Estonia. In the traditional public service delivery approach, the procedures of all type are carried out physically in government offices and documented on paper. However, because Estonia has digitised this process using blockchain,

it has saved money on a variety of products, including paper, stationery, rent, power, office supplies, office furniture, water bills, and many more. Estonia saves approximately 2% of its annual GDP only thanks to digital identity and digital signatures. This clearly indicates how efficient the system is.

2. Estonia has significantly saved time necessary to provide governmental services through digitalisation. In Estonia, public services do not need visits to public offices, unless there is an emergency. Because of this, there is no more time spent on bureaucratic procedures. As a result, people can dedicate more time to themselves.
3. Along with Turkey and other countries, Estonia has clearly showcased that data can be safely used and secured in a digital environment through the implementation of a blockchain-based healthcare system. There are several advantages to offering blockchain-based healthcare services, especially when it comes to data security. The significance of blockchain-based systems has once again been brought to light by the most recent instances of healthcare data theft in the US and Turkey. Blockchain systems achieve the maximum level of security with regard to their cryptographic encryption technique, which is difficult to crack or breach.
4. Estonia has offered its citizens a major advantage in terms of healthcare services by employing a blockchain-based gene bank. Ece and Arslan (2016) noted in their study that there has been considerable progress in DNA research. According to the authors, pharmacogenomic research has made it possible to prescribe genetically tailored medicine. The study also suggests that getting genetic information will make it easier to produce solutions for treatments for complicated diseases that may appear in the future. According to the study, genomic information allows for early diagnosis of the diseases and the therapies to be applicable. The blockchain-based gene bank offers major data storage benefits while also enabling disease diagnosis and treatment. For example, in Turkey, it costs thousands of dollars to store genomic data. This cost might be reduced through blockchain technology. Estonia has already transferred the genetic data of one-fifth of its population to the gene bank. It is projected that this figure will get closer to 50% in the near future.
5. E-ambulance services are also widely used in Estonian healthcare system. Furthermore, this system makes use of blockchain technology. In an emergency, e-ambulance services make it easier to access people's health-related information, ensuring prompt and efficient care. Here, upon request, medical personnel in the ambulance can instantly receive data stored on the KSI blockchain. In this manner, the ambulance doctors can be informed about the patient's blood type, medications, allergies, previous surgeries, etc. This offers the chance for

faster healing by increasing the likelihood of early and precise intervention for patients.

6. By integrating blockchain technology with artificial intelligence, Estonia has developed telemedicine management. Estonia's telemedicine system makes it easier for its citizens to receive medical care from the comfort of their own homes via computers, smartphones, or tablets. The telemedicine infrastructure in Estonia has been integrated into the family medical system. Following this achievement, online services have been introduced in a variety of fields, such as occupational medicine, remote speech therapy, e-consultation, physiotherapy, psychotherapy, remote visits (video visits), and remote professional treatment.

Estonia is a country that prioritises digitalisation in the delivery of public services, as illustrated by the examples listed above. According to the study's findings, Estonia is a country whose blockchain-based healthcare system architecture merits attention and adaptation. According to the author of the said study, it is necessary to examine the systems of countries that have achieved success in this field, especially those that are pioneers in Turkish literature. Many countries have designated experts to Estonia in recent years to research its blockchain-based healthcare system and produce reports that can be implemented back home. Like other countries, Turkey can learn from Estonia's system and apply it to its own.

Conflict of Interest Statement

The author declares that the research was conducted without any commercial or financial relationships that could be construed as a potential conflict of interest.

REFERENCES

Abualy, S. L. (2022). Estonia's gift to the world: The implementation of a blockchain protocol for corporate governance in new york. *Brooklyn Journal of Corporate. Financial & Commercial Law*, *14*(2), 275–303.

Akcagündüz, E. (2013). A different perspective to e-government in turkey: The relation between e-government and savings. *Journal of Doğuş University*, *14*(2), 127–140.

Al Qathrady, M., Saeed, M., Amin, R., Alshehri, M. S., Alshehri, A., & Alqhtan, M. S. (2024). Smart healthcare: A dynamic blockchain-based trust management model using subarray algorithm. *IEEE Access : Practical Innovations, Open Solutions*, *12*, 49449–49463. DOI: 10.1109/ACCESS.2024.3383310

Alkhalifa, A.K., Alanazi, M. H., Mahmood, K., Almukadi, W.S., Qurashi,M.A., Alshehri, A.H., Alanazi, F. & Abdelmoneim, A.M. (2024). Harnessing privacy-preserving federated learning wıth blockchain for secure iomt applıcations in smart healthcare systems. *Fractals Journal*, 1-17. DOI: 10.1142/S0218348X25400201

Aydar, M., & Çetin, S. (2020). Blockchain for health information systems. *European Journal of Science and Technology*, *19*, 533–538. DOI: 10.31590/ejosat.735052

Bautista, J. R., Harrell, D. T., Hanson, L., Oliveira, E., Abdul-Moheeth, M., Meyer, E. T., & Anjum, K. (2023). Medilinker: A blockchain-based decentralized health information management platform for patient-centric healthcare. *Frontiers in Big Data*, *6*(1146023), 1–6. DOI: 10.3389/fdata.2023.1146023 PMID: 37426689

Bertelsmann-stiftung.de. (2025). Smart health systems. https://www.bertelsmann -stiftung.de/en/our-projects/the-digital patient/projektthemen/smarthealthsystems (accessed 02 January 2025).

Brand.estonia.ee. (2025). Healthtech. brand.estonia.ee/sonumid/valdkonnad/ healthtech/#:~:text=1st%20ranking%20in%20The%20Bertelsmann,have%20an %20e%2Dhealth%20record. (accessed 01 January 2025).

Çal, S. (2007). Public service: Attempt for a definition. *Gazi University Law Faculty Journal*, *11*(1-2), 599–655.

E-estonia. (2024a). History of e-estonia development. https://e-estonia.com/story/ (accessed 05 December 2024).

E-estonia. (2024b). History of e-estonia development. https://e-estonia.com/solutions/ e-health/e-health-records (accessed 31 December 2024).

E-estonia. (2025). e-Health: factsheet. https://e-estonia.com/wp-content/uploads/factsheet_e-health.pdf. (accessed 01 January 2025).

Ece, A., & Arslan, E. S. (2016). The importance of personalized medicine and its contribution to next generation dna sequencing technologies. *Türkiye Klinikleri J Med Genet-Special Topics*, *1*(2), 42–45.

Eryılmaz, B. (2014). *Kamu yönetimi: düşünceler, yapilar, fonksiyonlar, politikalar*. Umuttepe Publishing.

Hammersley, B. (2017). Concerned about brexit? Why not become an e-resident of Estonia. https://www.wired.com/story/estonia-e-resident/ (accessed 01 December 2024).

Hansen, R. (2018). Blockchain industry, regulations and policy in estonia. *Asian Research Policy*, *9*(2), 45–55.

ibanet.org. (2025). Telemedicine: a global approach to trends and practices. https://www.ibanet.org/document?id=Healthcare-Telemedicine-Survey-Estonia. (accessed 03 January 2025).

Karaçam, Z. (2013). Systematic review methodology: A guide for preparation of systematic review. *Dokuz Eylül University Faculty of Nursing Electronic Journal*, *6*(1), 26–33.

Karadavut, U. (2022). Blockchain teknolojisi ve uygulamaları. In Ağcakaya, S. (Ed.), *Blockchain teknolojisi ve sağlık* (pp. 129–144). Nobel Press.

Kıral, B. (2020). Document analysis as a qualitative data analysis method. *Siirt Universty Journal of Social Sciences Institute, 8*(15), 170-189.

Kıyak, Y. S., Coşkun, Ö., & Budakoğlu, I. İ. (2019). Blockchain, smart contracts and three implication examples in healthcare. *Hacettepe Journal of Health Administration*, *22*(2), 457–466.

Koç, H. (2021). The new citizenship concept in the digital world: Case of e-citizenship in estonia. *OPUS International Journal of Society Researches*, *17*(35), 2254–2289.

Kumar, R., & Tripathi, R. (2021). Towards design and implementation of security and privacy framework for internet of medical things (iomt) by leveraging blockchain and ipfs technology. *The Journal of Supercomputing*, *77*(8), 7916–7955. DOI: 10.1007/s11227-020-03570-x

Kuo, T. T., Kim, H.-E., & Ohno-Machado, L. (2017). Blockchain distributed ledger technologies for biomedical and health care applications. *Journal of the American Medical Informatics Association : JAMIA*, *14*(6), 1211–1220. DOI: 10.1093/jamia/ocx068 PMID: 29016974

Liang, X., Zhao, J., Chen, Y., Bandara, E., & Shetty, S. (2023). Architectural design of a blockchain-enabled, federated learning platform for algorithmic fairness in predictive health care: Design science study. *Journal of Medical Internet Research*, *25*, e46547. DOI: 10.2196/46547 PMID: 37902833

Litvin, A., Rumovskaya, S., De Simone, B., Kasongo, L., Sartelli, M., Cocclini, F., Ansaloni, L., Moore, E., Biffl, W., & Catena, F. (2024). A new technology for medical and surgical data organisation: The wses-wjes decentralised knowledge graph. *World Journal of Emergency Surgery; WJES*, *19*(37), 1–6. DOI: 10.1186/s13017-024-00563-6 PMID: 39568073

Majdoubi, D. E., Bakkali, H., & Souad, S. (2023). Smartmedchain:a blockchain-based privacy-preserving smart healthcareframework. *Journal of Healthcare Engineering*, *2021*, 1–19. DOI: 10.1155/2021/4145512 PMID: 34777733

Malathy, K., & Jaichandran, R. (2024). Secure healthcare data for block chain networking based on triple des (tdes) protocol and ekmc. *Engineering Research Express*, *6*(4), 1–16. DOI: 10.1088/2631-8695/ad7f28

Martinovic, I., Lucas, K., & Sluganovic, I. (2017). Blockchains for governmental services: design principles, applications, and case studies. *Working Paper, Centre for Technology and Global Affairs*, Oxford Press.

Mızrak, H., & Aslan, S. (2023). Secure blockchain-supported cloud system for patients' electronic health record (ehr) systems. *Fırat University Journal of Engineering Sciences*, *35*(2), 517–526. DOI: 10.35234/fumbd.1289650

Moffit, R., & Steffen, B. (2017). Health care data breaches: a changing landscape. https://mhcc.maryland.gov/mhcc/pages/hit/hit/documents/HIT_DataBreachesBrief_Brf_Rpt_090717.pdf (accessed 08 May 2024).

Naresh, V., R. Sivaranjani & A. Divakar. (2021). Blockchain-based patient centric health care communication system. *International Journal of Communication Systems, 34*(7), e4749. . https://doi.org/.DOI: 10.1002/dac.4749

Özcan, D. (2021). *Blokzincir mimaisi ve merkezi olmayan uygulamalar*. Pusula Publishing.

Özdenizci Köse, B. (2021). Sağlıkta blokzincir. In Bozbuğa, N., & Gülseçen, S. (Eds.), *Tıp bilişimi* (pp. 368–397). İstanbul University Press.

Rao, K. R., & Naganjaneyulu, S. (2024). Designing a block chain based network for the secure exchange of medical data in healthcare systems. *Applied Artificial Intelligence*, *38*(1), 2318164. DOI: 10.1080/08839514.2024.2318164

Reede, M. (2020). *Evaluating the practicality of using blockchain technology in different use cases in the healthcare sector* (Publication No. 4557816) [Bachelor Thesis, Holland-Radboud University]. https://www.cs.ru.nl/bachelors-theses/2020/Mischa_van_Reede___4557816___Evaluating_the_practicality_of_using_blockchain_technology_in_different_use_cases_in_the_healthcare_sector.pdf

Salma, D. A., & Munabari, F. (2023). Blockchain technology: Cyber security strategy in post-2007 cyber-attacks Estonia. *Deviance Jurnal Kriminologi*, *7*(1), 32–45. DOI: 10.36080/djk.2412

Semenzin, S., Rozas, D., & Hassan, S. (2022). Blockchain-based application at a governmental level: Disruption or illusion? the case of Estonia. *Policy and Society*, *41*(3), 386–401. DOI: 10.1093/polsoc/puac014

Sharma, V., Kumar, A., & Sharma, K. (2024). Digital twin: Securing iot networks using integrated ecc with blockchain for healthcare ecosystem. *Knowledge and Information Systems*, *67*(3), 2395–2426. DOI: 10.1007/s10115-024-02273-6

Soares, B., Ferreıra, A., & Mota Veiga, P. (2023). The benefits and challenges of blockchain t-echnology and ehealth implementation in estonia - a literature review. *Applied Medical Informatics*, *45*(4), 118–131.

Srinivasan, S. (2016). Compromises in healthcare privacy due to data breaches. *European Scientific Journal*, *12*(10), 91–98. DOI: 10.19044/esj.2016.v12n10p%p

Sullivan, C., & Burger, E. (2017). E-residency and blockchain. *Computer Law & Security Review*, *33*(4), 470–481. DOI: 10.1016/j.clsr.2017.03.016

Tahaoğlu, M., Özer, Ç., & Parlak, E. (2019). Blockchain technology and possible implementation areas in turkey. [IJEASED]. *International Journal of Eastern Anatolia Science Engineering and Design*, *1*(2), 260–295.

Tehik.ee. 2025. Telemedicine. https://www.tehik.ee/en (accessed 01 January 2025).

Tervisekassa.ee. 2025. Telemedicine. https://www.tervisekassa.ee/en/partner/medicalinstitutions/development-telemedicine (accessed 01 January 2025).

Türkdoğan Görgün, C., & Kurşun, A. (2021). The role and importance of blockchain technology in the health ecosystem. *Hacettepe Health Administration Journal*, *24*(4), 903–920.

Vinodhini, M., Manickam, P., Alotaibi, Y., Alghamdi, S., & Khalaf, O. I. (2021). Hyperledger healthchain: Patient-centric ipfs-based storage of health records. *Electronics (Basel)*, *10*(23), 1–23. DOI: 10.3390/electronics10233003

X-road.global. 2025. https://x-road.global/x-road-technology-overview (accessed 1 January 2025).

Xu, J., Xue, K., Shaohua, L., Tian, H., Hong, J., & Hong, P. (2019). Healthchain: A blockchain-based privacy preserving scheme for large-scale health data. *IEEE Internet of Things Journal*, *6*(5), 8770–8781. DOI: 10.1109/JIOT.2019.2923525

Yıldırım, A., & Şimşek, H. (2006). *Sosyal bilimlerde nitel araştırma yöntemleri*. Seçkin Publishing.

Zhuang, Y., Chen, Y.W., Shae, Z.Y. & Shyu, C.R. (2020). Generalizable layered blockchain architecture for health care applications: development, case studies, and evaluation. *J Med Internet Res*. 27, *22*(7), e19029. Doi: .DOI: 10.2196/19029

Compilation of References

Abdullah, H. O., Maqsood, M., & Nadeem, A. (2025). Digital Evidence in Criminal Proceedings: Legal Standards, Chain of Custody, and Evidentiary Reliability in the Digital Era. *Research Journal for Social Affairs*, *3*(5), 795–805. DOI: 10.71317/RJSA.003.05.0375

Abdulrahman Satam, I., & Szabolcsi, R. (2025). Ethical and Safety Challenges of Implantable Brain-Computer Interface. *Interdisciplinary Description of Complex Systems: INDECS*, *23*(2), 82–94. DOI: 10.7906/indecs.23.2.1

Abid, H. M. R., Aslam, S., Alwan, N., & Khalid, N. (2025). Current readiness on food fraud risk mitigation in developing countries: A review. *Agriculture & Food Security*, *14*(1), 9. DOI: 10.1186/s40066-025-00528-1

Abualy, S. L. (2022). Estonia's gift to the world: The implementation of a blockchain protocol for corporate governance in new york. *Brooklyn Journal of Corporate. Financial & Commercial Law*, *14*(2), 275–303.

Acharya, B. S., Nair, S., & Abdul Salam, A. A. (2026). Quality Analysis and Detection of Adulterants and Contaminations in Milk/Milk Powder by Raman Spectroscopy. *Comprehensive Reviews in Food Science and Food Safety*, *25*(1), e70403. DOI: 10.1111/1541-4337.70403 PMID: 41578976

Adinda, F. A., Rahmawati, E., Suparman, E., Arifin, R., & Ezzerouali, S. (2025). The challenge of admitting electronic evidence in civil procedure law. *Jurnal IUS Kajian Hukum dan Keadilan, 13*(3), 656-680.

Akcagündüz, E. (2013). A different perspective to e-government in turkey: The relation between e-government and savings. *Journal of Doğuş University*, *14*(2), 127–140.

Akhtar, M. S., & Feng, T. (2022). Using blockchain to ensure the integrity of digital forensic evidence in an iot environment. *EAI Endorsed Transactions on Creative Technologies*, *9*(31), e2. DOI: 10.4108/eai.3-6-2022.174089

Akremi, A. (2025). ForensicTwin: Incorporating Digital Forensics Requirements Within a Digital Twin. *Computers*, *14*(4), 115. DOI: 10.3390/computers14040115

Al Husseini, A. A., Alasadi, A. Y., Alsadi, A. M., Hasan, M. H., Jehad, M. T., Hussein, A. M., & Muhamad, M. N. (2025, July). Scalable Blockchain-Based Smart Contract Enforcement Framework for Cross-Border Protection and Verification of Intellectual Property. In *2025 3rd International Conference on Cyber Resilience (ICCR)* (pp. 1-7). IEEE. DOI: 10.1109/ICCR67387.2025.11292063

Al Qathrady, M., Saeed, M., Amin, R., Alshehri, M. S., Alshehri, A., & Alqhtan, M. S. (2024). Smart healthcare: A dynamic blockchain-based trust management model using subarray algorithm. *IEEE Access : Practical Innovations, Open Solutions*, *12*, 49449–49463. DOI: 10.1109/ACCESS.2024.3383310

Alazab, M., Ouda, A., George Bokolo, B., & Liu, Q. (2024a). Artificial Intelligence in Social Media Forensics: A Comprehensive Survey and Analysis. *Electronics 2024, Vol. 13, Page 1671*, *13*(9), 1671. DOI: 10.3390/electronics13091671

Albalwy, F. (2026). Zero-Knowledge-Based Policy Enforcement for Privacy-Preserving Cross-Institutional Health Data Sharing on Blockchain. *Systems*, *14*(4), 385. DOI: 10.3390/systems14040385

Alketbi, S. K. (2024). Emerging technologies in forensic DNA analysis. *Perspectives in Legal and Forensic Sciences, 1*(1).

Alkhalifa, A.K., Alanazi, M. H., Mahmood, K., Almukadi, W.S., Qurashi,M.A., Alshehri, A.H., Alanazi, F. & Abdelmoneim, A.M. (2024). Harnessing privacy-preserving federated learning with blockchain for secure iomt applications in smart healthcare systems. *Fractals Journal*, 1-17. DOI: 10.1142/S0218348X25400201

AlKhanafseh, M., & Surakhi, O. (2024). Evidence preservation in digital forensics: An approach using blockchain and LSTM-based steganography. *Electronics (Basel)*, *13*(18), 3729. DOI: 10.3390/electronics13183729

Al-Mulla, M. S., Hammoud, M., Moussa, A. F., & Barafi, J. (2026). The impact of cybercrimes on the achievement of sustainable development goals: An analytical study. *International Journal of Electronic Security and Digital Forensics*, *18*(2), 240–259. DOI: 10.1504/IJESDF.2026.152245

Alotaibe, D. Z. (2025, April). Blockchain-Based Forensic Investigation Metamodel (BBFIM) for Investigating IoT Cybercrimes. In *2025 4th International Conference on Computing and Information Technology (ICCIT)* (pp. 32-37). IEEE.

Alqarni, A. (2025). A blockchain-based solution for transparent intellectual property rights management: Smart contracts as enablers. *Kybernetes*, *54*(13), 7380–7407. DOI: 10.1108/K-04-2024-1074

ALsheyab, M. S. A.ALsheyab. (2025). Legal analysis of the merits of electronic transferable records: Toward cross-border trade digitalization. *International Journal of Law and Management*, *67*(1), 145–163. DOI: 10.1108/IJLMA-09-2023-0209

Alvarez, O. P., i Vidal, O. V., & Vallespinós, L. D. (2022). Unlocking Blockchain evidence in international arbitration. *Iurgium [previously Spain Arbitration Review], 2022*(43).

Alyas, T., Abbas, Q., Niazi, S., Alqahtany, S. S., Alghamdi, T., Alzahrani, A., Tabassum, N., & Ibrahim, A. M. (2025). Multi blockchain architecture for judicial case management using smart contracts. *Scientific Reports*, *15*(1), 8471. DOI: 10.1038/s41598-025-92842-8 PMID: 40069277

Amerini, I., Barni, M., Battiato, S., Bestagini, P., Boato, G., Bonaventura, T. S., Bruni, V., Caldelli, R., De Natale, F., De Nicola, R., Guarnera, L., Mandelli, S., Marcialis, G. L., Micheletto, M., Montibeller, A., Orru', G., Ortis, A., Perazzo, P., Puglisi, G., … Vitulano, D. (2024). *Deepfake Media Forensics: State of the Art and Challenges Ahead*. 33–48. DOI: 10.1007/978-3-031-85386-9_3

Anand, K. S., & Thakur, D. S. (2025). Challenges and Limitations of AI in Forensic Science: A Critical Review. *International Journal of Research Publication and Reviews*, *6*(6), 5621–5632. DOI: 10.55248/gengpi.6.0125.0672

Angon, O. C. (2024). General Data Protection Regulation, Right to Be Forgotten, Blockchain Technology and Human Rights. *The Age of Human Rights Journal*, (23), e8702–e8702. DOI: 10.17561/tahrj.v23.8702

Apsimet, N., Alimkulov, Y., Konysbay, B., Zhanibekov, A., & Muratova, A. (2026). Challenges of using digital evidence in pretrial investigations of online fraud: Lessons for Kazakhstan from international practice. *IDP. Revista de Internet. Derecho y Política*, (44), 1–17. DOI: 10.7238/idp.v0i44.433072

Arnone, G., & Giacalone, M. (2025). Redefining Dispute Resolution Mechanisms for Digital Assets in the Metaverse: Exploring the Role of Blockchain and Emerging Technologies. *European Journal of Law and Technology*, *16*(2).

Atlam, H. F., Ekuri, N., Azad, M. A., & Lallie, H. S. (2024). Blockchain forensics: A systematic literature review of techniques, applications, challenges, and future directions. *Electronics (Basel)*, *13*(17), 3568. DOI: 10.3390/electronics13173568

Aydar, M., & Çetin, S. (2020). Blockchain for health information systems. *European Journal of Science and Technology*, *19*, 533–538. DOI: 10.31590/ejosat.735052

Azad, T., & Ahmed, S. (2016). Common milk adulteration and their detection techniques. *International Journal of Food Contamination*, *3*(1), 22. DOI: 10.1186/s40550-016-0045-3

Azeem, H. M., Sheer, A., & Umar, M. (2023). Unveiling the power of the right to information: Promoting transparency, accountability, and effective governance. *Al-Kashaf*, *3*(3), 26–39.

Bacon, J., Michels, J. D., Millard, C., & Singh, J. (2018). Blockchain demystified: A technical and legal introduction to distributed and centralized ledgers. *Rich. JL & Tech.*, *25*, 1.

Badkul, S., Kishor, A., Juchnevicius, E., & Madvariya, S. (2025). Blockchain and the Future of Digital Evidence: Opportunities and Challenges for Law Enforcement. *Rethinking the Police for a Better Future: Navigating Policing Challenges with Accountability and Trust*, 287-297.

Bajpai, N., & Panda, V. (2024). INTERNATIONAL JOURNAL OF LEGAL SCIENCE AND INNOVATION Role of Artificial Intelligence in the Detection of Crime & Administration of Justice. *International Journal of Legal Science and Innovation*, *6*. Advance online publication. DOI: 10.10000/IJLSI.111872

Balmiki, V. (2023, October). An evidence collection using blockchain for cybercrime detection. In *2023 4th IEEE Global Conference for Advancement in Technology (GCAT)* (pp. 1-7). IEEE. DOI: 10.1109/GCAT59970.2023.10353259

Barbone, A., Bicocchi, N., Martinelli, M., Morandi, R., & Picone, M. (2026). On-device AI and digital twins: A synergistic approach to intelligent cyber-physical systems. *Future Generation Computer Systems*, *175*, 108068. DOI: 10.1016/j.future.2025.108068

Bashir, H.Dr. Hira Bashir. (2024). DIGITAL FORENSICS: TECHNIQUES FOR INVESTIGATING CYBERCRIMES. *Computer Science Bulletin*, *7*(01), 76–88. DOI: 10.71465/csb130

Bau, J., Bursztein, E., Gupta, D., & Mitchell, J. (2010). State of the art: Automated black-box web application vulnerability testing. *Proceedings - IEEE Symposium on Security and Privacy*, 332–345. DOI: 10.1109/SP.2010.27

Bautista, J. R., Harrell, D. T., Hanson, L., Oliveira, E., Abdul-Moheeth, M., Meyer, E. T., & Anjum, K. (2023). Medilinker: A blockchain-based decentralized health information management platform for patient-centric healthcare. *Frontiers in Big Data*, *6*(1146023), 1–6. DOI: 10.3389/fdata.2023.1146023 PMID: 37426689

Bennet, D., Maria, L., Sanjaya, Y. P. A., & Zahra, A. R. A. (2024). Blockchain technology: Revolutionizing transactions in the digital age. *ADI Journal on Recent Innovation*, *5*(2), 192–199. DOI: 10.34306/ajri.v5i2.1065

Bernards, N., Campbell-Verduyn, M., & Rodima-Taylor, D. (2024). The veil of transparency: Blockchain and sustainability governance in global supply chains. *Environment and Planning C. Politics and Space*, *42*(5), 742–760.

Berrios Moya, J. A., Ayoade, J., & Uddin, M. A. (2025). A zero-knowledge proof-enabled blockchain-based academic record verification system. *Sensors (Basel)*, *25*(11), 3450. DOI: 10.3390/s25113450 PMID: 40968974

Bertelsmann-stiftung.de. (2025). Smart health systems. https://www.bertelsmann-stiftung.de/en/our-projects/the-digital patient/projektthemen/smarthealthsystems (accessed 02 January 2025).

Bhattacharjee, T., Mahapatra, A. S., De, D., & Chowdhury, A. (2025). JudicBlock: Judicial Evidence Preservation Scheme Based on Blockchain Technology. *Blockchains*, *3*(4), 11. DOI: 10.3390/blockchains3040011

Bhatti, N. (2026). The Use of Digital Evidence in Criminal Proceedings. *American Journal of Society and Law*, *5*(1), 10–19. DOI: 10.54536/ajsl.v5i1.7211

Bhushan, T. (2023). The Impact of digital technologies on alternative dispute resolution. *Revista Brasileira de Alternative Dispute Resolution-Brazilian Journal of Alternative Dispute Resolution-RBADR*, *5*(10), 329–352. DOI: 10.52028/rbadr.v5i10.ART16.Ind

Bingyuan, M., & Zhaoxun, C. (2025). Theory of Interest Jurisprudence for the Development of the Notarial System. *Journal of Advanced Research in Social and Behavioural Sciences*, *38*(1), 15–26. DOI: 10.37934/jarsbs.38.1.1526

Brand.estonia.ee. (2025). Healthtech. brand.estonia.ee/sonumid/valdkonnad/healthtech/#:~:text=1st%20ranking%20in%20The%20Bertelsmann,have%20an%20e%2Dhealth%20record. (accessed 01 January 2025).

Buczak, A. L., & Guven, E. (2016). A Survey of Data Mining and Machine Learning Methods for Cyber Security Intrusion Detection. *IEEE Communications Surveys and Tutorials*, *18*(2), 1153–1176. DOI: 10.1109/COMST.2015.2494502

Çal, S. (2007). Public service: Attempt for a definition. *Gazi University Law Faculty Journal*, *11*(1-2), 599–655.

Cami, G., & Karsai, K. (2025). International Cooperation Mechanisms in Criminal Justice: Human Rights Implications and Sovereignty Constraints in Cross-Border Access to Electronic Evidence. *Balkans Legal* [BLESS]. *Economic and Social Studies*, *2*(2), 93–110. DOI: 10.14232/bless.2025.2.93-110

Cao, S., Boyen, X., Deane, F., Miller, T., & Foth, M. (2022). Enabling cross-border trade in the face of regulatory barriers to data flow–the case of the blockchain-based service network. In *Blockchain for Industry 4.0* (pp. 285–303). CRC Press. DOI: 10.1201/9781003282914-15

Casino, F., Pina, C., López-Aguilar, P., Batista, E., Solanas, A., & Patsakis, C. (2022). SoK: Cross-border criminal investigations and digital evidence. *Journal of Cybersecurity*, *8*(1), tyac014. DOI: 10.1093/cybsec/tyac014

Chakraborty, S. (2026). Next-Gen Digital Forensics: Investigating Cybercrime in the Era of AI, Blockchain, and the Dark Web. *The Science of Criminal Investigations*, 286.

Chamim, M., Widodo, K., Riyadi, S., Achyarsyah, P., & Faisal, F. (2025). The role of digital evidence in criminal law enforcement: Challenges of authentication and admissibility in court. *Research Horizon*, *5*(6), 2987–2998. DOI: 10.54518/rh.5.6.2025.950

Chen, J. W. (2022). Dispute resolution in the new digital era-exploring arbitration as a suitable mechanism to resolve disputes over crypto assets. *Contemp. Asia Arb. J.*, *15*, 255.

Chopra, N., & Naqshbandi, M. Q. (2025). The role of blockchain and smart contracts in business law. *Journal of Scientific Research and Technology*, 28-40.

Chougule, H., Dhadiwal, S., Lokhande, M., Naikade, R., & Patil, R. (2022). Digital evidence management system for cybercrime investigation using proxy re-encryption and blockchain. *Procedia Computer Science*, *215*, 71–77. DOI: 10.1016/j.procs.2022.12.008

Corneli, A., Carbonari, A., Spegni, F., Pieroni, T., & Naticchia, B. (2025). On-site safety inspections through marker-less augmented reality and Blockchain notarization of BIM-based processes. *Buildings (Basel, Switzerland)*, *15*(13), 2318. DOI: 10.3390/buildings15132318

Cyber Crime Cases: Issues, Challenges & Solutions Reading Material. (2025). www.jajharkhand.in

Daoud, G. (2023). *The evolving nature of financial crime with the increase of internet capabilities. challenge identification, legal considerations and policy recommendations* (Doctoral dissertation, School of Advanced Study).

Dhabliya, D., Veeraiah, V., Dari, S. S., Kumar, J. R. R., Dhabliya, R., Gupta, A., & Pramanik, S. (2024). An Investigation on the Utilization of Blockchain in the Field of Digital Forensics. In *Revolutionizing the Global Stock Market: Harnessing Blockchain for Enhanced Adaptability* (pp. 1-28). IGI Global Scientific Publishing. DOI: 10.4018/979-8-3693-1758-7.ch001

Díaz-Perez, L. C., Quintanar-Reséndiz, A. L., Vázquez-Álvarez, G., & Vázquez-Medina, R. (2026). A review of cross-border cooperation regulation for digital forensics in LATAM from the soft systems methodology. *Applied Computing and Informatics*, *22*(1-2), 115–128. DOI: 10.1108/ACI-01-2022-0010

Dombrovska, A. (2025). Blockchain Enabled Governance of Intellectual Property: Evidentiary Integrity, Licensing Automation, and Enforcement Design. *Public Administration and Law Review*, (4 (24)), 37–49. DOI: 10.36690/2674-5216-2025-4-37-49

Dunsin, D., Ghanem, M. C., Ouazzane, K., & Vassilev, V. (2024). A comprehensive analysis of the role of artificial intelligence and machine learning in modern digital forensics and incident response. *Forensic Science International Digital Investigation*, *48*, 301675. DOI: 10.1016/j.fsidi.2023.301675

Dylag, M., & Smith, H. (2023). From cryptocurrencies to cryptocourts: Blockchain and the financialization of dispute resolution platforms. *Information Communication and Society*, *26*(2), 372–387. DOI: 10.1080/1369118X.2021.1942958

Ece, A., & Arslan, E. S. (2016). The importance of personalized medicine and its contribution to next generation dna sequencing technologies. *Türkiye Klinikleri J Med Genet-Special Topics*, *1*(2), 42–45.

E-estonia. (2024a). History of e-estonia development. https://e-estonia.com/story/ (accessed 05 December 2024).

E-estonia. (2024b). History of e-estonia development. https://e-estonia.com/solutions/e-health/e-health-records (accessed 31 December 2024).

E-estonia. (2025). e-Health: factsheet. https://e-estonia.com/wp-content/uploads/factsheet_e-health.pdf. (accessed 01 January 2025).

Elijah, J. (2025). *Navigating the Legal Challenges of Cybersecurity and Forensic Evidence in the Digital Era*. Law Nectar.

El-Kady, R. (2025). Unmasking virtual crimes: Investigating and proving evidence in the Metaverse. In *Unveiling Social Dynamics and Community Interaction in the Metaverse* (pp. 389–444). IGI Global Scientific Publishing. DOI: 10.4018/979-8-3693-8628-6.ch018

El-tahlawy, A. S., & Alahmad, W. (2025). Next-Generation Solutions to Combat Food Adulteration: Integrating Advanced Detection Technologies and Risk Mitigation Strategies. In *Advanced Techniques against Food Adulteration* (pp. 123–158). Springer Nature Switzerland. DOI: 10.1007/978-3-031-99454-8_5

Enyiorji, P. (2023). Blockchain-enforced data lineage architectures with formal verification workflows enabling auditable AI decision chains across regulated fintech compliance regimes and supervisory reporting. *International Journal of Science and Research Archive*, *9*(2), 1201–1217. DOI: 10.30574/ijsra.2023.9.2.0559

Eryılmaz, B. (2014). *Kamu yönetimi: düşünceler, yapilar, fonksiyonlar, politikalar.* Umuttepe Publishing.

Eyo-Udo, N. L., Agho, M. O., Onukwulu, E. C., Sule, A. K., Azubuike, C., Nigeria, L., & Nigeria, P. (2024). Advances in blockchain solutions for secure and efficient cross-border payment systems. *International Journal of Research and Innovation in Applied Science*, *9*(12), 536–563.

Fakhouri, H. N., Alsharaiah, M. A., Al Hwaitat, A. K., Alkalaileh, M., & Dweikat, F. F. (2024). Overview of Challenges Faced by Digital Forensic. *2nd International Conference on Cyber Resilience, ICCR 2024*. DOI: 10.1109/ICCR61006.2024.10532850

Farooq, M., Younas, R. M. F., Qureshi, J. N., Haider, A., & Nasim, F. (2025). Cyber security risks in DBMS: Strategies to mitigate data security threats: A systematic review. *Spectrum of engineering sciences*, 268-290.

Fontes, C., Hohma, E., Corrigan, C. C., & Lütge, C. (2022). AI-powered public surveillance systems: Why we (might) need them and how we want them. *Technology in Society*, *71*, 102137. DOI: 10.1016/j.techsoc.2022.102137

Franssen, V. (2024). Cross-border gathering of electronic evidence in the EU: toward more direct cooperation under the e-Evidence Regulation. In *Research Handbook on EU Criminal Law* (pp. 184–211). Edward Elgar Publishing. DOI: 10.4337/9781800886438.00016

Gandhi, K., Sharma, R., Gautam, P. B., & Mann, B. (2020). Safety and regulatory aspects of dairy industry. In *Chemical quality assurance of milk and milk products* (pp. 273–312). Springer Singapore. DOI: 10.1007/978-981-15-4167-4_10

Garrett, B. L., Gutierrez, R., & Scurich, N. (2024). The impact of defense experts on juror perceptions of firearms examination testimony. *Jurimetrics*, *64*(3), 223–248.

Ghanta, S., Pradhan, A. K., Boyapati, P., Biswas, S., & Mohanty, S. P. (2026). Security and Verifiability in Federated Learning: A Zero-Knowledge Reputation-Based Blockchain Framework. *IEEE Transactions on Network Science and Engineering*, *13*, 8005–8022. DOI: 10.1109/TNSE.2026.3676154

Ghasemi, J., & Mahmoudi, N. (2024, October). The application of IoT devices in evidence collection and preservation In legal investigations In the common law legal system of Western countries. In *2024 11th International Symposium on Telecommunications (IST)* (pp. 120-124). IEEE. DOI: 10.1109/IST64061.2024.10843627

Goel, V., Ranjan, R., Baxtiyarovich, R. D., Ibragimovich, S. S., Reymbayevich, S. K., & Zafar, K. (2026, February). Blockchain-Based Evidence Management Systems for Judicial Integrity and Transparency. In *2026 5th International Conference on Innovative Practices in Technology and Management (ICIPTM)* (pp. 1-6). IEEE. DOI: 10.1109/ICIPTM69057.2026.11465195

Grijalva-Salazar, R. V., Caicedo-Mendoza, J. A., Zúñiga-Castillo, A. J., Olivas-Valencia, E., & Fernández-Bedoya, V. H. (2025). Bridging Regulation and Innovation: A Systematic Review of Cryptocurrency Taxation and Fiscal Policy (2020–2025). *Journal of Risk and Financial Management*, *18*(12), 720. DOI: 10.3390/jrfm18120720

Guia, M. J., Mihai, I.-C., & Kordaczuk-Was, M. (2025). Artificial Intelligence Innovations in Law Enforcement Training: CEPOL Strategy 23-27. *Belügyi Szemle*, *73*(9), 1897–1912. DOI: 10.38146/bsz-ajia.2025.v73.i9.pp1897-1912

Hakimi, M., Rahmani, K. R., Ezam, Z., & Shahbazi, H. (2024). Integrating blockchain technology for secure e-government services: Opportunities and challenges. *Journal of Social Science Utilizing Technology*, *2*(3), 317–335.

Hammersley, B. (2017). Concerned about brexit? Why not become an e-resident of Estonia. https://www.wired.com/story/estonia-e-resident/ (accessed 01 December 2024).

Hanif, M., Munir, E. U., Rehan, M. M., Ahmad, S. G., Khan, I., & Setchi, R. (2025). Tiered blockchain framework: A secure, trustworthy, and cost-efficient solution for the digital rights protection. *Blockchain: Research and Applications*, 100308.

Hansen, R. (2018). Blockchain industry, regulations and policy in estonia. *Asian Research Policy*, *9*(2), 45–55.

Haque, E. U., Abbasi, W., Murugesan, S., Anwar, M. S., Khan, F., & Lee, Y. (2023). Cyber forensic investigation infrastructure of Pakistan: An analysis of the cyber threat landscape and readiness. *IEEE Access : Practical Innovations, Open Solutions, 11*, 40049–40063. DOI: 10.1109/ACCESS.2023.3268529

Harris, M. (2023). Blockchain-Based Evidence in Courts: Standards, Reliability, and Admissibility Challenges. *Legal Studies in Digital Age*, *2*(3), 49–63.

Hossain, M. Z. (2026). Emerging trends in forensic accounting: Data analytics, cyber forensic accounting, cryptocurrencies, and blockchain technology for fraud investigation and prevention. *Journal of Artificial Intelligence and Technological Development*, *2*(2), 183–208. DOI: 10.59324/jaitd.2026.2(2).14

Huang, L., Zhao, C., Chen, S., & Zeng, L. (2024). Blockchain: A promising technology for judicial translation services in cases with foreign elements. *Aslib Journal of Information Management*, *76*(5), 713–735. DOI: 10.1108/AJIM-11-2022-0485

ibanet.org. (2025). Telemedicine: a global approach to trends and practices. https://www.ibanet.org/document?id=Healthcare-Telemedicine-Survey-Estonia. (accessed 03 January 2025).

Igonor, O. S., Amin, M. B., & Garg, S. (2025). The application of blockchain technology in the field of digital forensics: A literature review. *Blockchains*, *3*(1), 5. DOI: 10.3390/blockchains3010005

Ikegwu, A. C., Uzuegbu, V. C., & Alo, U. R. (2025). Review of embedded systems and cyber threat intelligence for enhancing data security in mobile health. *J Electron Inf Syst*, *7*(1), 98–120. DOI: 10.30564/jeis.v7i1.10050

Indian Journal of Integrated Research in Law AI-GENERATED EVIDENCE IN INDIAN COURTS: ADMISSIBILITY, RELIABILITY AND THE CHAIN OF CUSTODY CHALLENGE. (n.d.).

Jada, I., & Mayayise, T. O. (2024). The impact of artificial intelligence on organisational cyber security: An outcome of a systematic literature review. *Data and Information Management*, *8*(2), 100063. DOI: 10.1016/j.dim.2023.100063

Jain, H., Jain, K., Paliwal, V., Begmal, C., & Girdhar, P. (2024). Towards Transparent Justice: Promoting Integrity and Efficiency in the Judicial System with Blockchain. *Available at SSRN* 4847643. DOI: 10.2139/ssrn.4847643

Jaradat, M. S., & Rabab'ah, M. M. (2026). FinTech and AI technologies for Enhancing Evidence Verification and Dispute Resolution in Financial Litigation. *International Journal of Advances in Soft Computing and its Applications, 18*(1), 434-452.

Johri, P. (2025). Legal Issues and Models of Ownership for Intellectual Property Materials within Blockchain Systems. *J. Intell. Prot. Stud.*, *9*, 108.

Joseph, J., & Pandey, A. (2026). Cybercrimes in Bharatiya Nyaya Sanhita: A Critical Study on Indian Legal Scenario. In Reshaping Criminology with AI (pp. 155-174). IGI Global Scientific Publishing.

Kadioglu Kumtepe, C. C. (2025). Unpacking the technology of trust: Establishing trust and fairness in online dispute resolution through blockchain and smart contracts. *International Journal of Law and Information Technology*, *33*, eaaf017. DOI: 10.1093/ijlit/eaaf017

Kamal, R., Hemdan, E. E. D., & El-Fishway, N. (2022). Forensics chain for evidence preservation system: An evidence preservation forensics framework for internet of things-based smart city security using blockchain. *Concurrency and Computation*, *34*(21), e7062. DOI: 10.1002/cpe.7062

Kamble, T., Ghuge, M., Jain, R., & Sarbhukan Bodade, V. (2025). Secure data transmission in cloud computing using a cyber-security trust model with multi-risk protection scheme in smart IOT application. *Cluster Computing*, *28*(2), 79. DOI: 10.1007/s10586-024-04847-z

Karaçam, Z. (2013). Systematic review methodology: A guide for preparation of systematic review. *Dokuz Eylül University Faculty of Nursing Electronic Journal*, *6*(1), 26–33.

Karadavut, U. (2022). Blockchain teknolojisi ve uygulamaları. In Ağcakaya, S. (Ed.), *Blockchain teknolojisi ve sağlık* (pp. 129–144). Nobel Press.

Karisma, K., & Moslemzadeh Tehrani, P. (2023). Blockchain: legal and regulatory issues. In *Sustainable Oil and Gas Using Blockchain* (pp. 75–118). Springer International Publishing. DOI: 10.1007/978-3-031-30697-6_4

Kazaure, A. A., Yusoff, M. N., & Jantan, A. (2024). Digital Forensic Investigation on Social Media Platforms: A Survey on Emerging Machine Learning Approaches. [JIStaP]. *Journal of Information Science Theory and Practice*, *12*(1).

Khalid, L., Akhtar, M. U., Khalid, M., & Ahmed, I. (2026). Zero Knowledge Proofs Enabling Ethical AI and Privacy-Preserving Verification in Distributed Systems. In *Ethical AI Applications for Software Engineering and Development* (pp. 123–154). IGI Global Scientific Publishing. DOI: 10.4018/979-8-3373-6038-6.ch005

Khan, M. N. I., & Ahmed, I. (2025). A systematic review of judicial reforms and legal access strategies in the age of cybercrime and digital evidence. *International Journal of Scientific Interdisciplinary Research, 5*(2), 01-29.

Khan, M. U., Zhen, L., Tian, J., Farid, A., Chen, Z., & Liu, H. (2025). From detection to prevention: A cyber-secure AI ecosystem for mitigating milk adulteration and dairy fraud. *Trends in Food Science & Technology*, •••, 105503.

Khanna, A., Jain, S., Burgio, A., Bolshev, V., & Panchenko, V. (2022). Blockchain-enabled supply chain platform for Indian dairy industry: Safety and traceability. *Foods*, *11*(17), 2716. DOI: 10.3390/foods11172716 PMID: 36076901

Khazem, M. M., Al Okagaili, S. M., Jassim, B. M., Hasan, M. S., Ahmed, S. A., Khalaf, I. Z., & Mohammed, A. A. (2025, July). Real-Time Detection of Cybercrime and Digital Forensics Automation Using AI-Based Legal Evidence Collection and Preservation Mechanisms. In *2025 3rd International Conference on Cyber Resilience (ICCR)* (pp. 1-7). IEEE. DOI: 10.1109/ICCR67387.2025.11292443

Khlifi, S., & Zouari, G. (2025). The moderating role of corporate ethics on the relationship between blockchain technology and classification shifting: European evidence. *EuroMed Journal of Business*, •••, 1–30. DOI: 10.1108/EMJB-12-2024-0357

Kıral, B. (2020). Document analysis as a qualitative data analysis method. *Siirt Universty Journal of Social Sciences Institute, 8*(15), 170-189.

Kiressanth, R. RS, K. R., & Santhi, K. (2025, September). Enhancing Digital Forensics: A Cyber Triage Tool for Streamlined and Efficient Investigations. In *2025 IEEE International Conference on Advances in Computing Research On Science Engineering and Technology (ACROSET)* (pp. 1-6). IEEE.

Kisku, U., Singh, A. K., Barman, B., Mohammad, A., Bhakat, C., Pola, A., & Meenia, P. (2025). Blockchain technology for Indian dairy industry: A sustainable food safety model. *Indian Journal of Animal Health*, *64*(1), 27–36. DOI: 10.36062/ijah.2025.06524

Kittappa, T., Snehal, S. M., Amrutha, J., & Mageshwaran, D. R. (2025, November). Emerging Cyber Threats in the Quantum Era: From Neural Hacking to Space. In *Information System Design: Communication Networks and Internet of Things: Proceedings of Ninth International Conference on Information System Design and Intelligent Applications (ISDIA 2025),* Volume 2 (Vol. 2, p. 29). Springer Nature.

Kıyak, Y. S., Coşkun, Ö., & Budakoğlu, I. İ. (2019). Blockchain, smart contracts and three implication examples in healthcare. *Hacettepe Journal of Health Administration*, *22*(2), 457–466.

Koç, H. (2021). The new citizenship concept in the digital world: Case of e-citizenship in estonia. *OPUS International Journal of Society Researches*, *17*(35), 2254–2289.

Kovalchuk, O. Y., Dovhopolyi, Y. I., & Shliakhovchuk, M. V. (2024). Digital Technologies in Justice: Blockchain as an Innovative Way of Dispute Resolution. *JE Eur.*, *L*, 56.

Kreso, I. (2025). Using blockchain technology for preserving digital evidence in digital forensics. *KNOWLEDGE-International Journal*, *68*(3), 331–336.

Krishappa, N., Shivappa, G. G., Zachariah, S., Pattan, K. I., Paria, A., Hiremath, S., & Vaithiyanathan, R. (2025). A Blockchain-Based Framework With Zero-Knowledge Proof Incorporated for Safeguarded Sharing of Genomic Data Through Health Record Systems. *Blockchain in Healthcare Today*, *8*, 10–30953. PMID: 41623334

Krishna, A. Y. V., & Kumar Chaudhary, N. (2026). Enhancing Evidence Integrity and Trust in the Criminal Justice System: A Design and Evaluation of the Blockchain Enabled Evidence Securing and Tracking (BEST) Application. *Journal of the Institution of Electronics and Telecommunication Engineers*, •••, 1–10. DOI: 10.1080/03772063.2026.2617871

Kulkarni, A. V., Mondal, T., & Modi, D. (2025). Enhancing privacy in banking systems: A blockchain-based access management and KYC solution. *Cogent Business & Management*, *12*(1), 2570063. DOI: 10.1080/23311975.2025.2570063

Kumar, D. R., & Singh, P. (2024). The rise of the robo-mediator: AI's transformative role in alternative dispute resolution. *White Black Legal*, *3*(1), 1–11.

Kumar, D., Kumar, S., & Joshi, A. (2023). Assessing the viability of blockchain technology for enhancing court operations. *International Journal of Law and Management*, *65*(5), 425–439. DOI: 10.1108/IJLMA-03-2023-0046

Kumar, D., & Suthar, N. (2025). Assessing the prospects and constraints of blockchain technology for intellectual property management. *The Journal of World Intellectual Property*, *28*(1), 124–140. DOI: 10.1111/jwip.12324

Kumari, S. (2025). Securing Evidence in Digital Forensics Using Blockchain. *Advances in Data Science and Artificial Intelligence: Proceedings of ERCICA 2024,* Volume 1, *1*, 395.

Kumar, R., & Tripathi, R. (2021). Towards design and implementation of security and privacy framework for internet of medical things (iomt) by leveraging blockchain and ipfs technology. *The Journal of Supercomputing*, *77*(8), 7916–7955. DOI: 10.1007/s11227-020-03570-x

Kumar, Y. (2022). AI techniques in blockchain technology for fraud detection and prevention. In *Security engineering for embedded and cyber-physical systems* (pp. 207–224). CRC Press. DOI: 10.1201/9781003278207-14

Kuo, T. T., Kim, H.-E., & Ohno-Machado, L. (2017). Blockchain distributed ledger technologies for biomedical and health care applications. *Journal of the American Medical Informatics Association : JAMIA*, *14*(6), 1211–1220. DOI: 10.1093/jamia/ocx068 PMID: 29016974

Lane, A. M., & Adam, L. (2022). Crime and cryptocurrency in Australian courts. *Monash University Law Review. Monash University. Faculty of Law*, *48*(3), 146–190.

Laukyte, M. (2023). Blockchain and the right to good administration: Adding blocks to or blocking of the globalization of good administration? *Indiana Journal of Global Legal Studies*, *30*(1), 195–225. DOI: 10.2979/gls.2023.a886167

Lesiuk, N. (2023). Ushering in a new era: Assessing the reasonable expectation of privacy vis-a-vis cryptocurrency and blockchain data. *Man. LJ*, *46*, 1.

Liang, X., Zhao, J., Chen, Y., Bandara, E., & Shetty, S. (2023). Architectural design of a blockchain-enabled, federated learning platform for algorithmic fairness in predictive health care: Design science study. *Journal of Medical Internet Research*, *25*, e46547. DOI: 10.2196/46547 PMID: 37902833

Liang, Z. Y., Liu, G. Y., Ren, Y., Yang, M., Jiang, R. W., Luo, Y., & Ma, Y. S. (2025). Trustworthy data space collaborative trust mechanism driven by blockchain: Technology integration, cross-border governance, and standardization path. *Information (Basel)*, *16*(12), 1066. DOI: 10.3390/info16121066

Liao, Y., & Vemuri, V. R. (2002). Use of the K-Nearest Neighbor classifier for intrusion detection. *Computers & Security*, *21*(5), 439–448. DOI: 10.1016/S0167-4048(02)00514-X

Li, H., Oza, D., Yoshida, M., & Noguchi, T. (2026). Privacy-Preserving Emergency Vehicle Authentication Scheme Using Zero-Knowledge Proofs and Blockchain. *IoT*, *7*(2), 35. DOI: 10.3390/iot7020035

Lindeman, J., Luchtman, M., & Van Toor, D. (2024). Admissibility of Evidence in EU Cross-Border Criminal Proceedings: Electronic Evidence, Efficiency and Fair-Trial Rights in the Netherlands. In *Admissibility of Evidence in EU Cross-Border Criminal Proceedings: Electronic Evidence, Efficiency and Fair Trial Rights* (pp. 103-126). Hart Publishing.

Litvin, A., Rumovskaya, S., De Simone, B., Kasongo, L., Sartelli, M., Cocclini, F., Ansaloni, L., Moore, E., Biffl, W., & Catena, F. (2024). A new technology for medical and surgical data organisation: The wses-wjes decentralised knowledge graph. *World Journal of Emergency Surgery; WJES*, *19*(37), 1–6. DOI: 10.1186/s13017-024-00563-6 PMID: 39568073

Maesa, D. D. F., Loporchio, M., & Tietze, F. (2025). Privacy-preserving and automated intellectual property license agreements over heterogeneous blockchain networks. *Blockchain: Research and Applications*, 100288.

Mahajan, R., & Pandit, K. (2024, June). Cryptography and Computational Approaches in Ensuring Data Integrity for Digital Forensic Evidence. In *2024 16th International Conference on Electronics, Computers and Artificial Intelligence (ECAI)* (pp. 1-6). IEEE. DOI: 10.1109/ECAI61503.2024.10607526

Maheshwari, V., & Prasanna, M. (2025). Privacy-preserving authentication for 5G healthcare with HBZKP: Hierarchical blockchain-based zero knowledge proof for secure edge devices. *Ain Shams Engineering Journal*, *16*(8), 103463. DOI: 10.1016/j.asej.2025.103463

Majdoub, I., & Atmani, K. (2025). Privacy paradigm shift: Zero knowledge proofs in criminal e-evidence collection. In *Cybercrime Unveiled: Technologies for Analysing Legal Complexity* (pp. 151–175). Springer Nature Switzerland. DOI: 10.1007/978-3-031-80557-8_7

Majdoubi, D. E., Bakkali, H., & Souad, S. (2023). Smartmedchain:a blockchain-based privacy-preserving smart healthcareframework. *Journal of Healthcare Engineering*, *2021*, 1–19. DOI: 10.1155/2021/4145512 PMID: 34777733

Malaraju, S. K. (2025, August). An Overview of Cybersecurity Risks and Threats in Cloud Computing. In *International Conference on Computing and Communication Networks* (pp. 447-458). Cham: Springer Nature Switzerland.

Malathy, K., & Jaichandran, R. (2024). Secure healthcare data for block chain networking based on triple des (tdes) protocol and ekmc. *Engineering Research Express*, *6*(4), 1–16. DOI: 10.1088/2631-8695/ad7f28

Malik, A., & Sharma, A. K. (2023). Blockchain-based digital chain of custody multimedia evidence preservation framework for internet-of-things. *Journal of Information Security and Applications*, *77*, 103579. DOI: 10.1016/j.jisa.2023.103579

Malik, M., Gahlawat, V. K., Mor, R. S., & Singh, M. K. (2024). Unlocking dairy traceability: Current trends, applications, and future opportunities. *Future Foods : a Dedicated Journal for Sustainability in Food Science*, *10*, 100426. DOI: 10.1016/j.fufo.2024.100426

Malik, M., Mor, R. S., Gahlawat, V. K., & Kumar, V. (2026). Unlocking the potential: Hybrid blockchain and AI-enabled traceability model development and implementation in the dairy industry–proof-of-concept. *Transportation Research Part E, Logistics and Transportation Review*, *205*, 104552. DOI: 10.1016/j.tre.2025.104552

Malve, D., Kumar, R. C. K., Meenal, H., & Hagaldivte, V. (2025). Cybersecurity vulnerabilities and threat mitigation strategies in the Metaverse. In *Defending the Metaverse* (pp. 94–114). CRC Press. DOI: 10.1201/9781003581659-6

Manasi Pritam Zirpe, Shravani Santosh Potdar, & Harshali Rohit Kadaskar. (2024). AI IN DIGITAL FORENSICS. *International Journal of Scientific Research in Modern Science and Technology, 3*(5), 01–06. DOI: 10.59828/ijsrmst.v3i5.208

Martinovic, I., Lucas, K., & Sluganovic, I. (2017). Blockchains for governmental services: design principles, applications, and case studies. *Working Paper, Centre for Technology and Global Affairs*, Oxford Press.

Mbimbi, B., Murray, D., & Wilson, M. (2025). Preserving whistleblower anonymity through zero-knowledge proofs and private blockchain: A secure digital evidence management framework. *Blockchains, 3*(2), 7. DOI: 10.3390/blockchains3020007

Mezzi, E., Mertzani, A., Manis, M. P., Lilova, S., Vadivoulis, N., Gatirdakis, S., . . . Hmede, R. (2025). Who owns the output? bridging law and technology in llms attribution. *arXiv preprint arXiv:2504.01032.*

Miedema, E., Waschull, S., & Emmanouilidis, C. (2026). Towards trustworthy artificial intelligence for decision-making: A lifecycle perspective on knowledge- and data-driven artificial intelligence systems. *Computers in Industry, 174*, 104409. DOI: 10.1016/j.compind.2025.104409

Mishra, R., Arya, P., Narwaria, M., & Kaur, I. (2025, October). Blockchain-Enhanced Chain of Custody for Digital Forensic Evidence Management. In *2025 IEEE International Conference on Blockchain and Distributed Systems Security (ICBDS)* (pp. 1-5). IEEE. DOI: 10.1109/ICBDS67396.2025.11379799

Mızrak, H., & Aslan, S. (2023). Secure blockchain-supported cloud system for patients' electronic health record (ehr) systems. *Fırat University Journal of Engineering Sciences, 35*(2), 517–526. DOI: 10.35234/fumbd.1289650

Moffit, R., & Steffen, B. (2017). Health care data breaches: a changing landscape. https://mhcc.maryland.gov/mhcc/pages/hit/hit/documents/HIT_DataBreachesBrief_Brf_Rpt_090717.pdf (accessed 08 May 2024).

Mohammad, S., Sajid, A., Abbasi, U. S. A., Razzaq, H., Yadav, S., & Khademizadeh, S. (2025). A Review on Analyzing Cloud Computing and Network Cyber Security Threats: Issues and Challenges With Solutions. *Iraqi Journal of Information and Communication Technology, 8*(1), 38–49.

Mummidi, S. S., & Srinivasan, S. (2025, November). Enhancement of Cybersecurity with Blockchain-Based Identity Authentication Systems: Zero-information Evidence Procedures for Secure Access, Biometric Encryption, and Decentralized Trust. In *2025 IEEE 7th International Conference on Computing, Communication and Automation (ICCCA)* (pp. 1-6). IEEE.

Muragijimana, E., Shankar, T. N., Kumar, N., Sah, B., & Padhy, S. (2022, October). Digital crimes in cloud environment and the analysis via blockchain. In *2022 IEEE 3rd Global Conference for Advancement in Technology (GCAT)* (pp. 1-6). IEEE. DOI: 10.1109/GCAT55367.2022.9972221

Murikah, W., Nthenge, J. K., & Musyoka, F. M. (2024). Bias and ethics of AI systems applied in auditing - A systematic review. *Scientific African*, *25*, e02281. DOI: 10.1016/j.sciaf.2024.e02281

Murlidharan, S., Ravulakole, V., Karnati, J., & Malik, H. (2025). Battery management system: Threat modeling, vulnerability analysis, and cybersecurity strategy. *IEEE Access : Practical Innovations, Open Solutions*, *13*, 37198–37220. DOI: 10.1109/ACCESS.2025.3543249

Mustafa, G., Rafiq, W., Jhamat, N., Arshad, Z., & Rana, F. A. (2025). Blockchain-based governance models in e-government: A comprehensive framework for legal, technical, ethical and security considerations. *International Journal of Law and Management*, *67*(1), 37–55. DOI: 10.1108/IJLMA-08-2023-0172

Myeong, G. E., & Ram, K. S. (2025). Blockchain based zero knowledge proof protocol for privacy preserving healthcare data sharing. *Journal of Technology Informatics and Engineering*, *4*(1), 171–189. DOI: 10.51903/jtie.v4i1.296

Nabi, M., Saghir, K., Ullah, F., Hussain, A., & Safeer, A. (2026). Challenges in botanical extract standardization: Adulteration, misidentification, and supply chain variability. In *Botanical extracts* (pp. 180–190). CRC Press. DOI: 10.1201/9781003662785-17

Naresh, V., R. Sivaranjani & A. Divakar. (2021). Blockchain-based patient centric health care communication system. *International Journal of Communication Systems, 34*(7), e4749. . https://doi.org/.DOI: 10.1002/dac.4749

Naseer, M., Gusdevi, H., Rahayudin, R., & Guterres, A. (2026). Blockchain-Based Evidence Legality in Indonesia's Criminal Justice System. *Jurnal Hukum Indonesia*, *5*(1), 40–65. DOI: 10.58344/jhi.v5i1.2351

Nayerifard, T., Amintoosi, H., Ghaemi Bafghi, A., & Dehghantanha, A. (n.d.). *Machine Learning in Digital Forensics: A Systematic Literature Review. (PDF) AI-BASED FORENSIC ANALYSIS OF DIGITAL IMAGES: TECHNIQUES AND APPLICATIONS IN CYBERSECURITY.* (n.d.). Retrieved January 23, 2026, from https://www.researchgate.net/publication/389279515_AI-BASED_FORENSIC_ANALYSIS_OF_DIGITAL_IMAGES_TECHNIQUES_AND_APPLICATIONS_IN_CYBERSECURITY

Nazir, M. A., Hussain, N., Hamid, K., Rasheed, M. D., Akhter, M., Ibrar, M., ... & Zafar, F. (2025). The Silent Guard: ML-Based Zero-Knowledge Proofs in Blockchain Security. *Spectrum of Engineering Sciences*, 1659-1678.

Nazir, R., Laghari, A. A., Dahri, F. H., Shoulin, Y., Alhakeem, Z. M., Hakim, H., & Mughal, Z. A. (2026). A review on machine learning techniques for network security. *Journal of Cyber Security Technology*, *10*(1), 1–45. DOI: 10.1080/23742917.2025.2480730

Ng, M., James, J., & Bull, R. (2024). "What you say in the lab, stays in the lab": A reflexive thematic analysis of current challenges and future directions of digital forensic investigations in the UK. *Forensic Science International Digital Investigation*, *51*, 301839. DOI: 10.1016/j.fsidi.2024.301839

Nguyen, M. D. (2025). Towards a comprehensive land use rights management system: Blockchain and semantics integration with legal compliance in Vietnam. *Artificial Intelligence and Law*, •••, 1–26. DOI: 10.1007/s10506-025-09486-2

Nikesh, M., Bharathi, M., Naaz, S. H., & Srinivas, T. A. S. (2025). IoT's Biggest Headaches: Privacy, Security, and Data Management Challenges. *J. IoT Secur. Smart Technol*, *4*, 1–23.

Noor, A., Raza, A., & Rehman, F. U. (2024). Recent advances in forensic science for evidence collection and preservation: Innovations in sample handling techniques to enhance analytical accuracy and case-specific investigations. *Forensic Insights and Health Sciences Bulletin*, *2*(2), 60–66.

Nukapeyi, S., Bommala, R., Kondreddy, D. S., Amalakanti, C., Ravi, C., & Konuri, T. A. (2024, April). Milk chain with ML & blockchain: Revolutionizing transparency for ensuring milk purity in dairy industry. In 2024 10th International Conference on Communication and Signal Processing (ICCSP) (pp. 970-975). IEEE.

Oghazi, P., Kordestani, A., & Mostaghel, R. (2026). Ecosystem-based framework for organized cybercrime. *The International Entrepreneurship and Management Journal*, *22*(2), 86. DOI: 10.1007/s11365-026-01212-x

Oliveira, N. B. (2023). *The role of international arbitration in resolving cross-border smart contract disputes: opportunities and challenges*. PQDT-Global.

Omotade, A. L. (2025). Neurotechnology and Human-Machine Interfaces: Securing Brain-Computer Interfaces (BCIs) Against Hacking. *World Journal of Advanced Research and Reviews, 27*(01), 2761–2771. DOI: 10.30574/wjarr.2025.27.1.2534

Onyeashie, B. I., Leimich, P., McKeown, S., & Russell, G. (2023, October). An Auditable Framework for Evidence Sharing and Management Using Smart Lockers and Distributed Technologies: Law Enforcement Use Case. In *International Conference on Big Data Technologies and Applications* (pp. 156-167). Cham: Springer Nature Switzerland.

Özcan, D. (2021). *Blokzincir mimaisi ve merkezi olmayan uygulamalar*. Pusula Publishing.

Özdenizci Köse, B. (2021). Sağlıkta blokzincir. In Bozbuğa, N., & Gülseçen, S. (Eds.), *Tıp bilişimi* (pp. 368–397). İstanbul University Press.

Padma, T., Aruna, S., Sujipriya, J., & Zainab, M. (2023). Blockchain based solutions for milk procurement management and adulteration detection. In *ITM Web of Conferences* (Vol. 56, p. 02008). EDP Sciences. DOI: 10.1051/itmconf/20235602008

Padma, U. R., Gnanaprakash, T., Karthik Roshan, R., & Saravanan, G. (2025). Unyielding Integrity & Safeguarding In Digital Forensics Through Blockchain Integration. *African Journal of Biomedical Research*, •••, 28.

Park, Y., & Jeong, D. (2026). A blockchain-based digital evidence management system: Integrating forensic procedures and multi-party authorization. *Information Processing & Management, 63*(5), 104654. DOI: 10.1016/j.ipm.2026.104654

Patil, C. S., Patil, A. P., & Patil, V. B. (2024). Evolution of technologies: A comprehensive analysis of AI, blockchain, and big data analytics. In *AI and Emerging Technologies* (pp. 1–26). CRC Press. DOI: 10.1201/9781003501152-1

Pei, Y. (2025). The Integration of Artificial Intelligence into Smart Policing Systems: Applications and Risk Governance. *Advances in Management and Intelligent Technologies, 1*(4). Advance online publication. DOI: 10.62177/amit.v1i4.486

Perdana, M. R. A., Bhakti, R. T. A., & Maileni, D. A. (2025). Validity of Electronic Signatures in Digital Agreements: An Analysis of the Application of the Intellectual Property Law and the Civil Code in E-Commerce Transactions. *Jurnal Mahkamah: Kajian Ilmu Hukum dan Hukum Islam*, 565-578.

Polu, P. R., Vyas, M., & Ravindra Babu, M. (2026). State-of-the-art analytical technologies for detection of food adulteration: Advances, validation, and future horizons. *Critical Reviews in Analytical Chemistry*, •••, 1–27. DOI: 10.1080/10408347.2026.2625392 PMID: 41686425

Poncibo, C., Gangemi, A., & Ravot, G. S. (2024). Blockchain justice: Exploring decentralising dispute resolution across borders. *JL, Mkt. &. Innovation*, •••, 14.

Poonia, A., Jha, A., Sharma, R., Singh, H. B., Rai, A. K., & Sharma, N. (2017). Detection of adulteration in milk: A review. *International Journal of Dairy Technology*, *70*(1), 23–42. DOI: 10.1111/1471-0307.12274

Popal, M., Ahmad, A., & Arshad, M. (2025). The Significance of Blockchain Technology in Preserving Digital Evidence Integrity in Forensic Investigations. *Journal of Computing & Biomedical Informatics*, *9*(02).

Prasad, V. L. S., Srivastava, V., & Singh, H. (2026). Cyber-Crimes in AI-Enabled Green Platforms: Legal Hurdles in ESG Investing, Prosecution, and Financial Loss Mitigation. In AI Governance, Law, Policy and Ethics in Green Finance and ESG (pp. 265-282). IGI Global Scientific Publishing.

Prasad, N., Diro, A., Warren, M., & Fernando, M. (2025). A survey of cyber threat attribution: Challenges, techniques, and future directions. *Computers & Security*, *157*, 104606. DOI: 10.1016/j.cose.2025.104606

Qasim, M., Rehman, I. U., & Malik, H. (2025). Cross-Border Enforcement of IP Rights in the Digital Era. *Frontiers*, *21*, 49–58.

Raj, Y., & Nagpal, K. (2025). *Cybercrime, Data Breaches & Cybersecurity In India*. www.tijer.org

Rajeev, S., Sharma, K., Dg, I., Ravi, S., Lokku, J., & Adg, I. (n.d.). Editorial Board Chief Patron Editor-in-Chief. *The Indian Police Journal, 72*(1).

Ramya, M., Anuvarshini, B. S., Kanika, G., Lohith, A., & Barath, B. (2025, September). Enhancing Decentralized Identity Management with Zero-Knowledge Proofs for Selective Disclosure. In *2025 6th International Conference on Electronics and Sustainable Communication Systems (ICESC)* (pp. 727-732). IEEE. DOI: 10.1109/ICESC65114.2025.11212333

Rani, D., Gill, N. S., Gulia, P., Yahya, M., Ahanger, T. A., Hassan, M. M., Abdallah, F. B., & Shukla, P. K. (2025). A secure digital evidence preservation system for an iot-enabled smart environment using ipfs, blockchain, and smart contracts. *Peer-to-Peer Networking and Applications*, *18*(2), 5. DOI: 10.1007/s12083-024-01855-z

Rao, K. R., & Naganjaneyulu, S. (2024). Designing a block chain based network for the secure exchange of medical data in healthcare systems. *Applied Artificial Intelligence*, *38*(1), 2318164. DOI: 10.1080/08839514.2024.2318164

Rashid, H., & East, C. M. (2022). Implementing Blockchain for Enhanced Transparency and Efficiency in Cross-Border Logistics. *International Journal of Core Engineering & Management*, *7*(3), 181–192.

Ratul, M. H. A., Mollajafari, S., & Wynn, M. (2024). Managing Digital Evidence in Cybercrime: Efforts Towards a Sustainable Blockchain-Based Solution. *Sustainability (Basel)*, *16*(24), 10885. DOI: 10.3390/su162410885

Reede, M. (2020). *Evaluating the practicality of using blockchain technology in different use cases in the healthcare sector* (Publication No. 4557816) [Bachelor Thesis, Holland-Radboud University]. https://www.cs.ru.nl/bachelors-theses/2020/Mischa_van_Reede___4557816___Evaluating_the_practicality_of_using_blockchain_technology_in_different_use_cases_in_the_healthcare_sector.pdf

Rodrigues, R. (2020). Legal and human rights issues of AI: Gaps, challenges and vulnerabilities. *Journal of Responsible Technology*, *4*, 100005. DOI: 10.1016/j.jrt.2020.100005

Rohilla, P., & Ghoshal, G. (2026). Food adulteration be preservatives, colors etc.—Control strategies. In *Public and Environmental Health* (pp. 483–513). Academic Press. DOI: 10.1016/B978-0-443-43986-5.00001-1

Sachdeva, C., Kaur, P., Gangwar, V. P., & Jasrai, L. (2025). Cross-Border Collaboration in New Digital Era with Blockchain Integration. In *Blockchain in the Tourism Industry: A New Era of Secure and Transparent Travel Solutions* (pp. 235–266). Springer Nature Switzerland. DOI: 10.1007/978-3-031-95341-5_12

Said, G. (2025). Brain-Computer Interface 5.0: Potential threats, computational law and protection of digital rights. *Legal Issues in the digital. The Age (Melbourne, Vic.)*, (2), 134–160.

Sakshi, M., Malik, A., & Sharma, A. K. (2024). A survey on blockchain based IoT forensic evidence preservation: Research trends and current challenges. *Multimedia Tools and Applications*, *83*(14), 42413–42458. DOI: 10.1007/s11042-023-17104-z

Salger, C. (2024). Decentralized dispute resolution: Using blockchain technology and smart contracts in arbitration. *Pepp. Disp. Resol. LJ*, *24*, 65.

Salih, K. M. M., & Ibrahim, N. B. (2023, December). CustodyChainGuardian: Blockchain of Custody Digital Evidence Preservation System. In *2023 IEEE Asia-Pacific Conference on Geoscience, Electronics and Remote Sensing Technology (AGERS)* (pp. 168-175). IEEE. DOI: 10.1109/AGERS61027.2023.10490757

Salma, D. A., & Munabari, F. (2023). Blockchain technology: Cyber security strategy in post-2007 cyber-attacks Estonia. *Deviance Jurnal Kriminologi*, *7*(1), 32–45. DOI: 10.36080/djk.2412

Sanjalawe, Y., Makhadmeh, S., & Alqudah, H. (2024, February). Digital forensics meets blockchain: Enhancing evidence authenticity and traceability. In *2024 2nd International Conference on Cyber Resilience (ICCR)* (pp. 01-06). IEEE.

Santillan-Lima, J. C., Díaz, J. F., Piccirilli, D., Haro-Tufiño, K. A., Urgirles-Rodríguez, B., & Molina-Granja, F. T. (2025, October). Admissibility of digital evidence: integration of technical and legal standards in forensic and judicial contexts. In *International Conference on Advanced Research in Technologies, Information, Innovation and Sustainability* (pp. 252-266). Cham: Springer Nature Switzerland.

Saputra, D. H., & Kusumah, F. (2025). Blockchain Forensics and the Evidentiary Challenges of Crypto-Based Corruption in Developing Countries. *Indonesian Journal of Criminal Law Studies*, *10*(2), 615–658.

Sathe, A., Yadavade, H., Shetty, R., Singh, J., Kashilkar, M., Pangarkar, P., & Deshpande, K. (2024, April). Comprehensive Blockchain-Enabled Web Framework for Evidence Management. In *International Conference on Information and Communication Technology for Intelligent Systems* (pp. 257-268). Singapore: Springer Nature Singapore. DOI: 10.1007/978-981-97-6681-9_23

Semenzin, S., Rozas, D., & Hassan, S. (2022). Blockchain-based application at a governmental level: Disruption or illusion? the case of Estonia. *Policy and Society*, *41*(3), 386–401. DOI: 10.1093/polsoc/puac014

Sezer, B. B., Akleylek, S., & Nuriyev, U. (2025). Pp-pqb: Privacy-preserving in post-quantum blockchain-based systems: A systematization of knowledge. *IEEE Access : Practical Innovations, Open Solutions*.

Shahid, U., Kanwal, S., Bano, M., Inam, S., Abdalla, M. E. M., & Shaikh, Z. A. (2025). Blockchain driven medical image encryption employing chaotic tent map in cloud computing. *Scientific Reports*, *15*(1), 6236. DOI: 10.1038/s41598-025-90502-5 PMID: 39979488

Shami, A. Z. A., Saleem, M., & Ashraf, J. (2025). Cybercrime and Digital Evidence: Investigating the Challenges and Opportunities in Prosecuting Cybercrime and Handling Digital Evidence. *Research Consortium Archive*, *3*(2), 401–411.

Sharma, A., & Kumar, A. (2023). Transforming access to justice in the digital age: The role of e-courts. NUJS Journal of Regulatory Studies, 8(2).

Sharma, R. (2025). The Role of Artificial Intelligence in Digital Forensics: Balancing Efficiency and Privacy. *International Journal of Research Publication and Reviews Journal*, *6*(11), 4482–4486. Www.Ijrpr.Com. DOI: 10.55248/gengpi.06.1125.38159

Sharma, V., Kumar, A., & Sharma, K. (2024). Digital twin: Securing iot networks using integrated ecc with blockchain for healthcare ecosystem. *Knowledge and Information Systems*, *67*(3), 2395–2426. DOI: 10.1007/s10115-024-02273-6

Shmyndruk, O., Ustrytska, N., Serkevych, I., Baltadzhy, P., & Yasin, I. (2025). ICT and modern technologies for training professional mediators in restorative justice and related processes. *Revista Eduweb*, *19*(4), 175–187. DOI: 10.46502/issn.1856-7576/2025.19.04.11

Siddharth, E. (2025). Time-Stamping in Blockchain for Legal Evidence Submission. *Sci. J. Artif. Intell. Blockchain Technol*, *2*(2), 34–42. DOI: 10.63345/sjaibt.v2.i2.205

Silva, S. R. (2025). Blockchain evidence versus the State: RAIMUNDO as a case study. *Oñati Socio-Legal Series*, *15*(4), 1473–1498.

Simanjuntak, E. L., Trinaili, Y., & Said, M. H. M. (2025). The Convergence of Classical Punishment in Money Laundering: Follow the Money Principle Using Blockchain Approach. *Lex Publica*, *12*(1), 264–290. DOI: 10.58829/lp.12.1.2025.298

Singh, B., & Kaunert, C. (2024). Reinventing Artificial Intelligence and Blockchain for Preserving Medical Data. In *Ethical Artificial Intelligence in Power Electronics* (pp. 77–91). CRC Press. DOI: 10.1201/9781032648323-6

Singh, B., Wongmahesak, K., & Chandra, S. (2025). Transforming digital ownership and assessing role of blockchain technology and NFTs in future economy. In *Practical Strategies and Case Studies for Online Marketing 6.0* (pp. 343–368). IGI Global Scientific Publishing. DOI: 10.4018/979-8-3373-2058-8.ch015

Singh, C., Gautam, S. K., Khajuria, H., & Nayak, B. P. (2025). Integrated blockchain-based framework for investigating child sexual exploitation materials (CSEM) in India. *International Journal of Information Technology : an Official Journal of Bharati Vidyapeeth's Institute of Computer Applications and Management*, •••, 1–19. DOI: 10.1007/s41870-025-02852-y

Singh, H., & Naruka, R. (2019). Decriminalisation of adultery in India: Issues and challenges. *Universal Review*, *8*(5), 957–964.

Siqi, C., Rajamanickam, R., Manap, N. A., & Zahir, Z. M. (2024). Application of Blockchain Technology in Cross-Border Telecommunications Network Fraud to Ensure China's Judicial Justice. *Jurnal IUS Kajian Hukum Dan Keadilan*, *12*(3), 472–486. DOI: 10.29303/ius.v12i3.1554

Smith, M., & Tiwari, M. (2024). The implications of national blockchain infrastructure for financial crime. *Journal of Financial Crime*, *31*(2), 236–248. DOI: 10.1108/JFC-01-2023-0006

Soares, B., Ferreıra, A., & Mota Veiga, P. (2023). The benefits and challenges of blockchain t-echnology and ehealth implementation in estonia - a literature review. *Applied Medical Informatics*, *45*(4), 118–131.

Sonawane, A., Lakade, N., Sarkar, S., & Dongre, N. (2024, August). Securing digital evidence in forensic investigation using blockchain. In *2024 4th Asian Conference on Innovation in Technology (ASIANCON)* (pp. 1-7). IEEE. DOI: 10.1109/ASIANCON62057.2024.10837800

Sood, A., Aggarwal, S., & Singh, S. (2024). *ANALYSIS OF DIGITAL FORENSIC PRACTICES IN INDIA*. https://jcsdf.nfsu.ac.in/

Spano, R., Zampella, A., Serino, L., & Campanella, F. (2025). *(Un) accountability of crypto assets exchanges: evidence from a slippery financial field*. Qualitative Research in Financial Markets.

Srinivasan, S. (2016). Compromises in healthcare privacy due to data breaches. *European Scientific Journal*, *12*(10), 91–98. DOI: 10.19044/esj.2016.v12n10p%p

Sule, A. K., Eyo-Udo, N. L., Onukwulu, E. C., Agho, M. O., & Azubuike, C. (2024). Implementing blockchain for secure and efficient cross-border payment systems. *International Journal of Research and Innovation in Applied Science*, *9*(12), 508–535.

Sullivan, C., & Burger, E. (2017). E-residency and blockchain. *Computer Law & Security Review*, *33*(4), 470–481. DOI: 10.1016/j.clsr.2017.03.016

Sun, P. (2025). On a Multidimensional Framework for Cross-Border Cybercrime Asset Recovery in the Digital Era. *China Legal Sci.*, *13*, 136.

Susilowati, C. M. I., & Frans, M. P. (2025). Interpreting power, grooming, and deception in sexual violence cases: a hermeneutic study on legal challenges in Indonesia. *International Journal for the Semiotics of Law-Revue internationale de Sémiotique juridique, 38*(3), 1061-1078.

Szymoniak, S., & Foks, K. (2024). Open Source Intelligence Opportunities and Challenges – A Review. *Advances in Science and Technology Research Journal, 18*(3), 123–139. DOI: 10.12913/22998624/186036

Tahaoğlu, M., Özer, Ç., & Parlak, E. (2019). Blockchain technology and possible implementation areas in turkey. [IJEASED]. *International Journal of Eastern Anatolia Science Engineering and Design, 1*(2), 260–295.

Tang, Z. (2023). Smart Courts in Cross-Border Litigation. *Rabels Zeitschrift für ausländisches und internationales Privatrecht/The Rabel Journal of Comparative and International Private Law*, (H. 1), 118-143.

Tehik.ee. 2025. Telemedicine. https://www.tehik.ee/en (accessed 01 January 2025).

Tervisekassa.ee. 2025. Telemedicine. https://www.tervisekassa.ee/en/partner/medicalinstitutions/development-telemedicine (accessed 01 January 2025).

Toprak, S. (2009). The new face of terrorism in Turkey: Actor unknown political murders. *Journal of Forensic Sciences, 54*(6), 1388–1392. DOI: 10.1111/j.1556-4029.2009.01154.x PMID: 19737338

Tripathy, S. S.Sudhanshu Sekhar Tripathy. (2025). A comprehensive survey of cybercrimes in India over the last decade. *International Journal of Science and Research Archive, 13*(1), 2360–2374. DOI: 10.30574/ijsra.2024.13.1.1919

Trivedi, M., Singh, H., & Intaratat, K. (2026). *Role of artificial intelligence in water and energy efficiency for food sustainability. AI and machine learning for clean water and sustainability: Liquid gold.* Cambridge Scholars Publishing Inc.

Türkdoğan Görgün, C., & Kurşun, A. (2021). The role and importance of blockchain technology in the health ecosystem. *Hacettepe Health Administration Journal, 24*(4), 903–920.

Vaghela, R., Gowda, V. D., Taj, M., Arudra, A., & Chopra, M. (2024). Digital evidence collection and preservation in computer network forensics. In *Handbook of Research on Innovative Approaches to Information Technology in Library and Information Science* (pp. 42–62). IGI Global Scientific Publishing. DOI: 10.4018/979-8-3693-0807-3.ch003

Vajpayee, K., Parekh, P. B., Dash, H. R., & Shukla, R. K. (2025). Food forensics: Fundamentals and technical advancements. In *Advances in forensic science: Emerging technologies and techniques* (pp. 37–84). Springer Nature Singapore. DOI: 10.1007/978-981-96-8971-2_3

Varsha, A., Kumar, N. A., Bichanga, S. N., & Chakraborty, P. (2025). Future Direction in Digital Forensics and Cyber Security. *Emerging Threats and Countermeasures in Cybersecurity*, 467-493.

Verma, S. (2024). Digital Forensics: Using Blockchain in Cryptocurrency Investigations. In *Fintech, and Blockchains Trends in The Financial Sector* (pp. 84-96). Bentham Science Publishers.

Verma, S., Kumar, A., Pandey, S., & Negi, P. (2023, July). Blockchain and Cloud Computing used in Preservation of Crime Scene Evidences. In *2023 2nd International Conference on Edge Computing and Applications (ICECAA)* (pp. 7-11). IEEE. DOI: 10.1109/ICECAA58104.2023.10212110

Vinodhini, M., Manickam, P., Alotaibi, Y., Alghamdi, S., & Khalaf, O. I. (2021). Hyperledger healthchain: Patient-centric ipfs-based storage of health records. *Electronics (Basel)*, *10*(23), 1–23. DOI: 10.3390/electronics10233003

Vismiha, M. K., & Chinnu, M. D. (2026). Trans Boundary Crimes and the Jurisdictional Issues and International Cooperation in Dealing with Such Crimes. *Trans Boundary Crimes and the Jurisdictional Issues and International, 2*(04).

Wagner, S. M., Fink, A. A., Ehrnsperger, J. F., & Düpree, P. (2025). Supporting Intellectual Property Protection: Blockchain Technology as a Catalyst for Open Innovation. *California Management Review*, *67*(3), 164–185. DOI: 10.1177/00081256251320366

Walters, R. (2025). Smart contracts and international commercial arbitration. In *Routledge Handbook on Transnational Commercial Law* (pp. 390–414). Routledge. DOI: 10.4324/9781003394822-25

Wan, J. (2025, November). Research on the Application and Risk Control of Cloud Computing in Accounting from the Perspective of Network Security. In *2025 IEEE 11th International Conference on Edge Computing and Scalable Cloud (EdgeCom)* (pp. 183-188). IEEE. DOI: 10.1109/EdgeCom66327.2025.00037

Wang, Y., Zhou, Y., Yang, D., & Guo, H. (2025, May). Innovative Pathways for Blockchain-Enabled Intellectual Property Pledge Financing: A Case Study of the "Zhiyirong" Platform. In *International Conference on Blockchain and Trustworthy Systems* (pp. 404-417). Singapore: Springer Nature Singapore.

Wang, S., Li, Y., & Khaskheli, M. B. (2024). Innovation helps with sustainable business, law, and digital technologies: Economic development and dispute resolution. *Sustainability (Basel)*, *16*(10), 3910. DOI: 10.3390/su16103910

Wang, Y., Xu, K., Wan, Q., Huang, Y., & Guan, Q. (2026). OChain: A blockchain oracle system for dynamic plagiarism detection of software copyrights. *Computer Networks, 281*, 112175. DOI: 10.1016/j.comnet.2026.112175

Widya, G. M., & Santoso, B. (2025). Notary's Authority in Making Deeds of Agreement to Protect Trade Secrets. *Widya Pranata Hukum: Jurnal Kajian dan Penelitian Hukum, 7*(1), 18-36.

Wilson, M., Cross, C., Holt, T., & Powell, A. (2022). Police preparedness to respond to cybercrime in Australia: An analysis of individual and organizational capabilities. *Journal of Criminology, 55*(4), 468–494. DOI: 10.1177/26338076221123080

Worsley, M. K., Rowe, B. I., & Houston, K. A. (2023). Two Steps Forward, One Step Back: The Legal Response to Sex Trafficking. *Journal of Human Trafficking*, •••, 1–13. DOI: 10.1080/23322705.2023.2289822

Wu, S. (2024). The Legal Problems of Blockchain Technology in Cross-border E-Commerce. *J. Econ. Law, 1*(4), 20–28. DOI: 10.62517/jel.202414403

Xiao, S., Qin, X., Tian, Y., & Dang, Z. (2025). Blockchain-Based Framework for Secure Sharing of Cross-Border Trade Data. *Computers, Materials & Continua, 83*(2), 2351–2373. DOI: 10.32604/cmc.2025.062324

X-road.global. 2025. https://x-road.global/x-road-technology-overview (accessed 1 January 2025).

Xu, J., Xue, K., Shaohua, L., Tian, H., Hong, J., & Hong, P. (2019). Healthchain: A blockchain-based privacy preserving scheme for large-scale health data. *IEEE Internet of Things Journal, 6*(5), 8770–8781. DOI: 10.1109/JIOT.2019.2923525

Yadav, A., Srivastava, V., & Singh, H. (2026). Enhancing Green Investment Through AI and Automation: A Critical Legal Study of Regulatory Frameworks Effectiveness in Tackling Cybersquatting in India. In AI Governance, Law, Policy and Ethics in Green Finance and ESG (pp. 149-166). IGI Global Scientific Publishing. DOI: 10.4018/979-8-2600-1308-3.ch009

Yadav, R. T. (n.d.). AI-Driven Digital Forensics. *International Journal of Scientific Research & Engineering Trends, 10*, 2395–2566.

Yadav, S., & Singh, R. R. (2026). Decentralized Dispute Resolution in International Trade with Blockchain and Smart Contracts. *Journal of Legal Affairs and Dispute Resolution in Engineering and Construction, 18*(2), 04526006. DOI: 10.1061/JLADAH.LADR-1470

Yeoh, P. (2017). Regulatory issues in blockchain technology. *Journal of Financial Regulation and Compliance*, *25*(2), 196–208. DOI: 10.1108/JFRC-08-2016-0068

Yıldırım, A., & Şimşek, H. (2006). *Sosyal bilimlerde nitel araştırma yöntemleri*. Seçkin Publishing.

Yin, Z., Wang, Z., Xu, W., Zhuang, J., Mozumder, P., Smith, A., & Zhang, W. (2025). *Digital Forensics in the Age of Large Language Models*. https://arxiv.org/pdf/2504.02963v1

Zamil, M. Z. H., & Khan, T. M. (2025). AI-Driven Digital Evidence Triage in Digital Forensics: A Comprehensive Review. *ISDFS 2025 - 13th International Symposium on Digital Forensics and Security*. DOI: 10.1109/ISDFS65363.2025.11011908

Zeb, S., & Lodhi, S. K. (2025). AI and cybersecurity in smart manufacturing: Protecting industrial systems. *American Journal of Artificial Intelligence and Computing*, *1*(1), 1–23.

Zhang, H., & Gong, X. (2024). The research on an electronic evidence forensic system for cross-border cybercrime. *The International Journal of Evidence & Proof*, *28*(1), 21–44. DOI: 10.1177/13657127231187059

Zhang, T. (2025, November). A Neuro-Symbolic and Blockchain-Enhanced Multi-Agent Framework for Fair and Consistent Cross-Regulatory Audit Intelligence. In *Proceedings of the 2025 International Conference on Digital Society and Intelligent Computing* (pp. 254-261). DOI: 10.1145/3788910.3788948

Zhao, Y., & Chen, H. (2024). Enhancing access to digital justice: Digital governance of dispute resolution and dispute prevention in online commercial activities. *Journal of International Dispute Settlement*, *15*(2), 273–304. DOI: 10.1093/jnlids/idae001

Zhuang, Y., Chen, Y.W., Shae, Z.Y. & Shyu, C.R. (2020). Generalizable layered blockchain architecture for health care applications: development, case studies, and evaluation. *J Med Internet Res*. 27, *22*(7), e19029. Doi: .DOI: 10.2196/19029

Zhuk, A. (2025). Beyond the blockchain hype: Addressing legal and regulatory challenges. *SN Social Sciences*, *5*(2), 11. DOI: 10.1007/s43545-024-01044-y

Zou, L., & Chen, D. (2024). Using Blockchain Evidence in China's Digital Copyright Legislation to Enhance the Sustainability of Legal Systems. *Systems*, *12*(9), 356. DOI: 10.3390/systems12090356

About the Contributors

Dorottya Edina Kozma Ph.D. is a certified economist (Associate Professor) with a professional background spanning academia and the private sector. Her expertise in sustainable development, environmental accounting and practical experience in company management aligns with her active involvement in various projects and events. Her primary research areas include sustainable development goals, circular economy, climate change and environmental control management and ESG. She has participated in projects focused on environmental accounting, ESG, climate change. Additionally, she is highly engaged in professional and educational activities, including curriculum developments, ESG e-learning course.

Swarnima Gorani working as a Assistant Professor, Sharda School of Law, Sharda University Greater Noida, India. She is a distinguished Company Secretary and Legal Scholar specialising in both Criminal and Corporate Law. With more than 2 years of industry experience and a robust academic foundation, Ms Gorani holds a dual degree in Commerce and Law, a postgraduate degree in Law with a concentration in Criminal Law, and a degree in Company Secretaryship. She has participated in and presented her research at numerous international conferences and faculty development programs. Her contributions include multiple book chapters and journal publications, and she has presented her research at numerous international conferences. Additionally, she is an active reviewer for Scopus-indexed journals and books. Notably, Ms Gorani has achieved significant accolades, including an All India Rank of 13 in the Company Secretary examination and a Gold Medal for her performance in her Law degree.

Otilia Manta is a PhD Supervisor at the School of Advanced Studies of the Romanian Academy (SCOSAAR) and Professor at the Romanian-American University, where she teaches International Financial Relations, FinTech, and Entrepreneurship. She holds a PhD in Economics (Finance) and is a Scientific Researcher at the Romanian Academy. She is an expert in investment projects, capacity building, and sustainable development at both local and global levels, with over 25 years of experience in financial and banking consultancy, EU-funded project management, and multidisciplinary scientific research. As an Evaluation Expert, Rapporteur, and Vice-Chair for EU-funded projects, she has contributed to the successful implementation of numerous programmes and projects financed by the European Commission. In addition, she has been involved as an expert and rapporteur within other international financial institutions. Prof. Manta is the author and editor of over 80 books and book chapters and has published more than 500 scientific papers and articles in national and international journals. She is the founder and publisher of two magazines and more than 20 international scientific journals and has served as a reviewer for over 500 ISI-indexed scientific papers. Her academic work focuses on digital finance, FinTech, responsible financial innovation, and the development of innovative financial instruments for complex and sustainable systems. Her research bridges theory and practice, addressing major societal and economic challenges through financial innovation. Her scientific excellence has been recognized through numerous international awards and distinctions, including gold medals awarded at prestigious international scientific and innovation competitions. She has also served on the boards and advisory councils of internationally renowned academic and scientific institutions, contributing to strategic development, academic evaluation, and the promotion of high standards in ethics, integrity, and educational excellence.

***

Emre Akcagunduz received his BSc and MSc in Public Administration from Trakya University in 2009 and in 2012 respectively. He completed his PhD in the Faculty of Social Sciences at Istanbul University in 2019 and currently employed as an Associate Professor in the Faculty of Economics and Administrative Sciences at Trakya University. His areas of interest are Public Administration, e-government, ethics, local governments, municipalities,blockchain,leadership, provincial administrations and administration theories.

Saurabh Chandra is an accomplished legal scholar. With a robust academic foundation, he earned his Bachelor of Arts and Bachelor of Laws (B.A. LL.B.) from the prestigious Aligarh Muslim University (A.M.U.). He further specialized in Business Laws, completing his Master of Laws (LL.M.) at the renowned National Law School of India University (NLSIU), Bangalore. Dr. Chandra's academic journey culminated in a Doctorate in Law (Ph.D.) from the esteemed National Law University (NLU) Delhi. With almost two decades of teaching experience, he has numerous publications to his credit. His expertise is complemented by a robust portfolio of scholarly publications. Dr. Chandra brings a wealth of experience in Academic Administration, having successfully held various key administrative positions.

Kiranbhai Ramabhai Dodiya is an experienced Cyber Forensic Expert and Assistant Professor specializing in cyber security and digital forensics. He has taught at prestigious institutions and is currently pursuing a PhD in Biochemistry and Forensic Science. With a strong background in ethical hacking and malware analysis, Kiranbhai is passionate about educating students and contributing to the field of cyber forensics. His expertise includes malware forensic, computer forensics, and data recovery software. Kiranbhai's commitment to professional growth is evident through his participation in workshops, seminars, and research publications. He is dedicated to shaping the next generation of professionals in the field and combatting cybercrimes.

Om Prakash Kannaujia is a dedicated legal academician, researcher, and educator with significant contributions in the field of legal education and constitutional studies. With more than eight years of teaching experience, he has earned recognition for his academic commitment, research aptitude, and student-oriented approach in legal education. Born on 10 July 1983, Dr. Kannaujia completed his early education in Uttar Pradesh and pursued higher studies in law with determination and academic dedication. He obtained his Bachelor of Laws degree from Banaras Hindu University with specialization in Contract Law, Family Law, and Law of Torts. He later completed his LL.M. in Constitutional Law and Jurisprudence from Babasaheb Bhimrao Ambedkar University in 2014. He qualified the prestigious UGC-NET examination in Law in December 2015 and was awarded a Ph.D. in Law by University of Allahabad in May 2022. Dr. Kannaujia has served as Assistant Professor in the Department of Law at Teerthanker Mahaveer University from July 2014 to August 2019, where he contributed actively to teaching, academic mentoring, and institutional development. He also served as Assistant Professor (Guest Faculty) at Allahabad Degree College, a constituent college of the University of Allahabad. His teaching interests include constitutional law, jurisprudence, human rights, and socio-legal studies. An active researcher and conference participant, Dr. Kannaujia has presented papers in various national and international seminars on contemporary socio-legal issues including right to education, environmental protection, food security, human rights, unemployment, and women empowerment. His presentations reflect a strong concern for social justice, constitutional values, and public welfare. Dr. Kannaujia has also published several research articles in reputed academic journals. His publications focus primarily on food security, right to food, judicial responses, and public policy in India. His scholarly works include articles such as "Analysis of Food Security in India with Reference to the National Food Security Act, 2013," "Right to Food and Judicial Response in India," and "Challenges and Prospects of Food Security Policies in India." These contributions demonstrate his deep understanding of constitutional governance and welfare legislation. In addition to academics, Dr. Kannaujia completed professional legal training through internship experience at Ganesh Law Chambers, Prayagraj, where he gained practical exposure in legal drafting, rejoinders, counter affidavits, and case analysis. Known for his sincerity, discipline, and academic excellence, Dr. Om Prakash Kannaujia continues to contribute meaningfully to legal scholarship and higher education. His dedication to teaching, research, and socio-legal awareness reflects his commitment toward strengthening legal education and promoting constitutional values in contemporary society.

Bhagirath Gohil, Dysp is an accomplished officer of the Gujarat Police, serving as Deputy Superintendent of Police(Dysp) in Gujarat, India. With extensive experience in law enforcement and cybercrime investigation, he has contributed significantly to strengthening digital crime detection and public safety mechanisms. His professional expertise includes cybercrime enforcement, financial fraud investigation, intelligence coordination, and technology-enabled policing. Mr. Gohil has actively supported the integration of digital forensic methodologies and advanced investigative tools within policing practices. He remains committed to enhancing institutional capacity, promoting ethical policing standards, and advancing technology-driven approaches to modern law enforcement challenges in India.

Bhrigu Raj Mourya is a distinguished academician, legal researcher, author, and administrator presently serving as Associate Professor at MATS University. With more than fifteen years of teaching experience in legal education, he has contributed significantly to academic excellence, research advancement, and institutional development in the field of law. Born in Village Toro Mafi, Bikapur, District Ayodhya, Uttar Pradesh, Dr. Mourya pursued his higher education with dedication and academic distinction. He completed his Bachelor of Laws from Dr. Ram Manohar Lohia Avadh University and earned his Master of Laws degree from Chaudhary Charan Singh University. He qualified the prestigious UGC-NET examination in 2012 and later completed his Ph.D. with a specialized research study titled "The Role of DNA Profiling Evidence on Criminal Justice System in India: An Analytical Study." Dr. Mourya has an impressive record of scholarly publications. He has published numerous research papers in UGC Care-listed and Scopus-indexed journals on diverse themes including criminal jurisprudence, constitutional law, intellectual property rights, cyber terrorism, environmental law, artificial intelligence, and forensic science. His academic writings demonstrate a strong interdisciplinary approach, especially in understanding the relationship between law, technology, and society. In addition to research articles, he has authored and edited several books and book chapters. His notable contributions include works on child labour, domestic violence, DNA profiling in criminal justice, freedom of speech, and the role of artificial intelligence in legal education and practice. These publications reflect his commitment to addressing contemporary legal challenges through academic scholarship. Throughout his academic career, Dr. Mourya has served in reputed institutions including Raffles University, Teerthanker Mahaveer University, Modern College of Law, and Dewan Law College. Along with teaching, he has actively undertaken important academic and administrative responsibilities such as IQAC Head, NAAC Coordinator, Member of Executive Council, Research Committee Chairman, and Moot Court Convenor. Dr. Mourya has also participated in numerous national and international seminars, workshops, faculty development programmes, and conferences, reflecting his dedication toward continuous learning and professional growth. His academic vision focuses on quality legal education, research innovation, student mentorship, and the integration of technology with legal studies. Through his scholarly achievements and institutional contributions, Dr. Bhrigu Raj Mourya continues to inspire students and researchers while contributing meaningfully to the advancement of legal academia in India.

Govind Singh Rajpal is an eminent legal scholar and researcher. He post-graduated from the University of Bikaner with a Master of Laws (Mercantile Law) and a Postgraduate Diploma in Criminal Law. He then earned his Ph.D. from the University of Bikaner in 2011. For the past 16 years, he has been involved in academic administration and research. He is currently employed as a Professor at School of Law, MIT-ADT University, Pune. He supervises a number of Ph.D. research scholars, and 4 of them have already been awarded doctorates. He has more than 28 research papers published in national and international journals of repute. He has published a book on "Judicial Activism: A Step Towards Holistic Adjudication" and 4 Chapters in books, he has presented 18 Research papers National and International Conferences. Participated in orientation programme and attended various FDP.

Vijay Srivastava is an Associate Professor of Law at Amity University Madhya Pradesh, India, with over seventeen years of teaching experience and industry exposure . He holds a Ph.D. in Law and specializing in International Commercial Arbitration, Alternative Dispute Resolution, Company Law, Taxation, IPR, and Contract Law A trained Mediator and Conciliator, he has supervised doctoral research, published widely in Scopus-indexed and peer-reviewed journals, and actively contributes as a conference convener, keynote speaker, and moot court judge with a strong commitment to global legal scholarship and academic excellence.

Index

A

AI-Driven Digital Forensics 37, 50, 62, 67

B

Blockchain 1, 2, 3, 4, 5, 6, 7, 8, 9, 10, 11, 12, 13, 15, 16, 17, 19, 20, 21, 22, 24, 25, 31, 32, 33, 34, 35, 52, 69, 70, 71, 72, 73, 74, 75, 76, 77, 78, 79, 80, 81, 82, 84, 85, 87, 88, 89, 90, 91, 92, 93, 97, 100, 101, 102, 103, 104, 105, 107, 108, 109, 110, 111, 112, 113, 114, 115, 116, 117, 118, 119, 120, 121, 122, 123, 124, 125, 126, 127, 128, 129, 130, 131, 132, 133, 134, 137, 139, 140, 141, 142, 143, 144, 145, 146, 147, 148, 149, 150, 151, 153, 154, 155, 156, 157, 158, 159, 160, 161, 162, 163, 165, 166, 167, 168, 169, 170, 171, 172, 173, 174, 176, 177, 178, 179, 180, 181, 182, 183, 184, 186, 187, 189, 190, 191, 192, 195, 196, 197, 198, 199, 200, 201, 202, 203, 204, 205, 206, 207, 209, 210, 211, 213, 214, 215, 216, 217, 218, 219, 220, 221, 222, 223, 225, 226, 227, 228, 229, 230, 231, 232, 233, 234, 235, 236, 237, 238, 239, 240, 243, 244, 245, 246, 247, 248, 249, 250, 251, 252, 253, 254, 255, 256, 257, 258, 259, 261, 262, 263, 264, 265, 266, 267, 268, 269, 270, 271, 272, 273, 274, 275, 277, 278, 279, 280, 281, 282, 283, 284, 286, 287, 288, 289, 290, 291, 292, 293, 294, 295, 296, 297
Blockchain Evidence 4, 12, 13, 81, 102, 103, 111, 114, 117, 119, 120, 125, 129, 133, 147, 150, 154, 165, 191, 203, 207, 243, 244, 246, 247, 248, 249, 250, 251, 252, 254, 255, 256, 257, 261, 262, 263, 264, 267, 268, 269, 271, 272, 273
Blockchain Intervention 19, 31, 33
Blockchain Notarization 178, 179, 180, 210, 211, 214, 222
Blockchain Security 126, 131, 187
Blockchain Technology 2, 3, 5, 6, 8, 10, 11, 12, 13, 15, 16, 17, 19, 21, 33, 34, 52, 69, 73, 74, 78, 84, 85, 87, 89, 90, 91, 92, 100, 104, 107, 108, 110, 114, 119, 121, 122, 124, 128, 134, 139, 140, 144, 146, 153, 154, 155, 156, 157, 159, 162, 165, 167, 169, 171, 173, 176, 179, 190, 195, 199, 205, 210, 213, 214, 215, 221, 222, 223, 225, 226, 228, 230, 232, 233, 237, 239, 240, 243, 244, 245, 247, 249, 250, 251, 252, 254, 256, 257, 258, 259, 261, 262, 263, 264, 268, 270, 274, 277, 278, 279, 280, 282, 284, 287, 289, 290, 291, 292, 296

C

Chain of Custody 1, 3, 4, 8, 9, 15, 19, 20, 21, 25, 27, 29, 30, 32, 46, 59, 65, 71, 73, 74, 76, 87, 89, 90, 92, 94, 95, 97, 98, 100, 107, 110, 111, 114, 116, 123, 124, 128, 132, 140, 146, 150, 155, 156, 158, 164, 165, 167, 169, 171, 189, 190, 192, 193, 194, 195, 196, 198, 202, 205, 211, 232, 244, 245, 246, 248, 249, 252, 253, 256, 261, 263, 265, 268, 270, 272
Cloud Storage Risks 123, 131
Confidential Evidence 173, 175, 176, 179, 180, 181, 182, 183
Contractual Disputes 175, 209, 210, 211, 212, 221
Criminal Investigations 69, 71, 78, 84, 87, 91, 93, 94, 102, 107, 114, 117, 120, 123, 124, 128, 134, 155, 156, 158, 159, 162, 165, 171, 244, 252
Cross-Border Evidence Sharing 107, 110, 112, 251
Cybercrime Evidence 69, 71, 87, 90, 101, 102, 127, 158, 160, 162, 169
Cybercrime Investigation 47, 50, 63, 84, 92

Cybercrime Prosecutions 243, 246
Cyber Fraud 1, 2, 3, 4, 5, 6, 7, 8, 9, 10, 11, 12, 192
Cybersecurity 15, 54, 66, 67, 120, 127, 136, 137, 187

D

Dairy Traceability 34, 35
Digital Evidence 2, 4, 8, 9, 10, 15, 16, 26, 27, 29, 40, 47, 52, 53, 63, 68, 71, 72, 73, 75, 81, 84, 85, 87, 89, 90, 91, 92, 93, 94, 95, 97, 98, 99, 100, 101, 102, 103, 105, 107, 108, 109, 112, 114, 117, 118, 119, 120, 121, 123, 124, 126, 135, 155, 157, 159, 162, 163, 164, 165, 170, 171, 172, 186, 190, 191, 193, 194, 195, 196, 199, 201, 203, 205, 206, 226, 243, 244, 245, 246, 247, 250, 252, 257, 258, 259, 261, 262, 264, 267, 268
Digital Forensics 9, 15, 37, 39, 40, 41, 42, 43, 49, 50, 53, 54, 55, 56, 57, 58, 59, 60, 61, 62, 63, 65, 66, 67, 68, 69, 70, 71, 72, 74, 76, 77, 81, 82, 84, 85, 87, 88, 89, 91, 92, 93, 94, 97, 99, 100, 101, 102, 104, 120, 124, 129, 131, 137, 155, 156, 158, 159, 160, 162, 163, 165, 167, 168, 171, 189, 190, 191, 192, 193, 195, 196, 199, 200, 201, 203, 205, 206, 243, 245, 251, 252, 256, 257, 258, 264, 271, 274
Digital Governance 38, 241
Digitalization 120
Digital Rights Management 216

E

Evidence Admissibility 90, 97, 99, 134, 182, 193, 195, 246, 249
Evidence Integrity 16, 75, 78, 85, 90, 93, 97, 134, 146, 158, 165, 171, 193, 239, 259, 266
Evidences 75, 198, 206
Evidentiary Frameworks 19, 24, 53

F

Food Forensics 25, 36

H

Healthcare 91, 186, 187, 277, 278, 279, 280, 281, 282, 283, 284, 287, 288, 289, 290, 291, 292, 293, 294, 295, 296

I

Immutable Records 162
Intellectual Property Protection 223

J

Judicial Recognition 235

L

Legal Evidence 1, 2, 4, 8, 10, 139, 141, 146, 150, 171, 189, 192, 201, 203, 204, 259
Legal Evidence Preservation 1, 4, 8, 189, 192

M

Milk Adulteration 19, 20, 24, 25, 26, 28, 29, 31, 34
Mutual Legal Assistance 78, 107, 112, 118, 164, 263, 269

P

Predictive Forensic Intelligence 49
Privacy-Preserving Notarization 184
Public Administration 144, 222, 278
Public Services 147, 277, 278, 285, 289, 290, 291, 292

R

Reliability 2, 9, 13, 15, 25, 26, 56, 59, 65, 77, 89, 90, 91, 93, 94, 95, 99, 100, 101, 129, 132, 150, 157, 158, 164, 165, 167, 189, 190, 191, 192, 193,

194, 195, 200, 201, 204, 243, 244, 245, 247, 249, 250, 251, 264, 268, 269, 270, 272, 274
Right to Information 139, 140, 143, 144, 146, 153

S

Smart Contracts 3, 4, 7, 12, 20, 21, 32, 70, 74, 75, 76, 78, 80, 82, 85, 89, 93, 101, 107, 110, 111, 112, 113, 114, 117, 118, 123, 124, 126, 127, 128, 129, 141, 145, 146, 149, 151, 153, 156, 157, 160, 166, 168, 169, 172, 173, 178, 179, 180, 181, 182, 183, 190, 192, 196, 198, 199, 200, 203, 205, 209, 210, 211, 214, 215, 216, 218, 219, 220, 221, 222, 223, 225, 226, 227, 228, 229, 230, 231, 232, 233, 234, 235, 236, 238, 240, 246, 251, 253, 263, 265, 270, 281, 282, 294
Smart Contract Vulnerabilities 117, 217
Social Engineering 38, 123, 124, 125, 126, 127, 128, 130, 133, 254

T

Technology 2, 3, 5, 6, 7, 8, 10, 11, 12, 13, 15, 16, 17, 19, 21, 24, 28, 31, 32, 33, 34, 35, 40, 52, 53, 54, 55, 56, 58, 59, 60, 63, 65, 67, 68, 69, 70, 73, 74, 77, 78, 81, 84, 85, 87, 88, 89, 90, 91, 92, 94, 97, 100, 103, 104, 105, 107, 108, 110, 111, 114, 116, 117, 118, 119, 121, 122, 124, 126, 128, 134, 136, 137, 139, 140, 142, 143, 144, 146, 147, 150, 153, 154, 155, 156, 157, 158, 159, 161, 162, 165, 167, 169, 170, 171, 173, 174, 175, 176, 179, 182, 187, 190, 192, 195, 199, 203, 205, 206, 210, 213, 214, 215, 217, 220, 221, 222, 223, 225, 226, 228, 229, 230, 232, 233, 235, 236, 237, 238, 239, 240, 243, 244, 245, 246, 247, 248, 249, 250, 251, 252, 254, 256, 257, 258, 259, 261, 262, 263, 264, 266, 267, 268, 270, 271, 273, 274, 275, 277, 278, 279, 280, 281, 282, 283, 284, 285, 287, 289, 290, 291, 292, 293, 294, 295, 296, 297
Transnational Cybercrime 53, 108, 109, 110, 118, 244

U

Unauthorized Access 12, 72, 123, 124, 128, 194, 198

Z

Zero-Knowledge Proofs 10, 90, 92, 101, 102, 110, 125, 141, 146, 151, 167, 169, 173, 174, 176, 177, 179, 181, 182, 186, 187, 201, 202, 203, 214, 221, 236, 237, 254, 256, 257, 264, 265, 267, 272

www.ingramcontent.com/pod-product-compliance
Lightning Source LLC
LaVergne TN
LVHW080901300926
849162LV00003B/506